The Middle East

Quest for an American Policy

Edited by Willard A. Beling

State University of New York Press Albany 1973

The Middle East: Quest for an American Policy
First Edition
Published by State University of New York Press
99 Washington Avenue, Albany, New York 12210

Printed in the United States of America

Library of Congress Cataloging in Publication Data
The Middle East.

Revised and updated papers from a conference entitled "The Middle East in the 1970s," held Apr. 8–10, 1970 at the 47th session of the Institute of World Affairs, sponsored by the University of Southern California.

Includes bibliographical references.

1. Jewish–Arab relations. 2. United States—Foreign relations—Near East. 3. Near East—Foreign relations—United States. 4. Near East—Politics. I. Beling, Willard A., ed. II. Institute of World Affairs, Los Angeles University of International Relations. III. Los Angeles. University of Southern California.

DS119.7.M472 1973 327.73'056 73-4281
ISBN 0-87395-228-6
ISBN 0-87395-229-4 (microfiche)

Contents

Preface

In many respects, the present volume represents a sizeable departure from traditional works on Middle Eastern international relations. Most such works, be they edited collections or books by one or more authors, tend to offer partial explanations using only traditional methodological approaches. Furthermore, they tend to suffer from what might be called factor monism, i.e., the tendency to explain, describe, or predict international relations phenomena only in terms of one or a few variables (e.g., Islam, a charismatic leader, Arab nationalism, etc.) or one or more levels of analysis (societal, idiosyncratic, and so on).[1]

In the present instance, however, a conscious attempt was made to incorporate studies employing different methodological approaches on all political systems or subsystems affecting international relations in and with the Middle East. The overall result is a broad synthesis which helps both the student of the area and the interested layman see the "picture" whole, while alerting them of its complexity. Finally, it should be stressed that an impartial, academic approach has been emphasized in the selection of the studies presented here—a much desired objective in an area which has produced so much passionate literature.

In part 1, the Middle East itself is considered alone as an entity, as a subordinate system of the international political system. The chapters in this section focus on the actors of the area and interactions within the subsystem itself, i.e., between single nations of the subsystem. They also examine the chain reaction to these interactions among the actors outside the Middle East subsystem.

Introducing part 1, Malcolm Kerr examines in chapter 1 the psychopolitical problems of national imagery held by Arabs and Israelis—perceptions of themselves, their adversaries, and of the Arab-Israeli conflict itself. Within the framework of his presentation, the intractable Arab-Israeli conflict becomes infinitely more understandable. In chapter 2, Willard A. Beling reinforces Professor Kerr's observations and conclusions in a study of the political ecology of the Middle East. George Lenczowski and Don Peretz then deal strong body blows in chapters 3 and 4, respectively, to so-called

1. See J. D. Singer, "The Level-of-Analysis Problem in International Relations," in *The International System: Theoretical Essays*, ed. Klaus Knorr and Sidney Verba (Princeton: Princeton University Press, 1961), pp. 77–92.

Arab unity and Israeli unity. Michael Hudson's contribution in chapter 5 is a logical sequel to Professor Peretz' chapter, in that the latter discusses the Arabs *within* Israel as one of several divisive elements generating internal opposition, while Professor Hudson treats for the most part the Palestinian resistance movement *outside* Israel. In chapter 6, Roger Harrell treats linkages between internal and external political behavior in the Middle East. Does internal instability, for example, spill over a nation's borders in the form of external conflict? Finally in chapter 7 of part 1, Charles McClelland and Anne Gilbar measure and evaluate the interactions of the Middle Eastern states among themselves and with other states.

A most important aspect of the present volume is the fact that, for the first time, a variety of methodological approaches—ranging from quantitative content and interaction analyses to traditional/historical analyses—were employed to examine the international relations problems of a particular world region. While the first five chapters of the first section are so-called traditional analyses, for example, the last two are quantitative. The scholarly representatives of these sometimes "contending approaches" frequently find themselves "vibrating on different frequencies," [2] but the net product of their being brought together in one volume is a fruitful beginning of much needed mutual communication. A comparison of the findings arrived at by differing methodological approaches must certainly work to the benefit of social sciences.

In part 2, the chapters focus on interactions between major actors of the international political system and the Middle East subsystem. Philip Dadant and Ciro Zoppo, strategists of the RAND Corporation, treat in chapters 8 and 9, respectively, Great Power rivalry and interactions in the Middle East which, because of its geographical location, natural resources, and low level of indigenous power, has been subjected to repeated manipulation, colonization, and superpower intrigue. Both authors address themselves to the rapidly changing Soviet and American strategic positions in the Middle East, which is in obvious flux. Finally in chapter 10 of this section, Samir Anabtawi examines the role of the Third World in the Middle East. Adopting a "neutralist" position between East and West, Afro-Asian states have hoped that as a bloc they could play a major role in international politics. Both Arabs and Israelis have sought, therefore, to woo the Third World to their respective sides of the conflict.

2. See Klaus Knorr and James Rosenau, eds., *Contending Approaches to International Relations* (Princeton: Princeton University Press, 1969).

Measuring the Third World's response, the author then evaluates it within the framework of the international political system.

Part 3 concerns itself with the process of foreign policy formation, in this case, American policy for the Middle East. Perhaps no other area of American foreign policy has focused on itself as much domestic interest and attempts at influence as the Middle East. To this end in chapter 11, William Quandt examines interest group behavior such as that of oil companies, Zionists, and others. Will the Middle East be viewed as vital to United States interests in the 1970s, he asks, as it has been earlier? If not, what does this portend for the area, for Israel? George Kent then treats in chapter 12 the role of Congress in forming American policy for the Middle East. Are there parallels between American involvement in Indochina and the Middle East? Specifically, has Congress asserted itself to guide or constrain the President's hand in the Middle East, something which it obviously failed to do in Indochina? In chapter 13, Charles Wagner examines the climate of elite newspaper opinion vis-à-vis American policy in the Middle East. What role in American policy formation, if any, have these "opinion leaders" sought to play? His is a quantitative content analysis of selected elite American newspapers. Concluding part 3, John Orr considers in chapter 14 the Arab-Israeli conflict within a theological framework. Among other things, he asks *why* the Christian Church has looked at the Middle East crisis differently from the Vietnamese conflict, on which Christian critics have been both aggressive and articulate. Professor Orr's treatment provides a fresh countervailing moral balance to the preceding chapters which are cast, quite naturally, in a framework of pragmatic political realism.

The chapters in the present volume emphasize a variety of analytic levels. Malcolm Kerr, for example, suggests that individual Arab and Israeli *perceptions* of one another lie at the root of their intractably hostile relationships; at the other end of the spectrum, Charles McClelland and Anne Gilbar work with data relating only to the *actions* one state takes toward another. In between these two extremes are to be found studies at the national and societal levels of analysis; e.g., studies on military capabilities, social attributes which predict international behavior, and so on.

In conclusion, while no claim to complete objectivity can ever be made for a work on the Middle East, it should be apparent to the scholars that relatively open-minded analysts have offered balanced and linguistically neutral commentaries, while marshalling empirical data to support controversial positions.

Acknowledgments

This volume grew out of the Forty-seventh Session of the Institute of World Affairs, sponsored by the University of Southern California in cooperation with the colleges and universities of the Pacific area. The oldest continuing institute of its kind in the United States, the Institute of World Affairs was founded in 1924 under the leadership of the late Chancellor Rufus B. von KleinSmid. Some of the highest ranking American and foreign scholars and statesmen have participated in its sessions.

Entitled "The Middle East in the 1970s," the conference was convened at the von KleinSmid Center of International and Public Affairs, the University of Southern California. Organized and directed by Willard A. Beling, the conference provided the forum for the presentation of papers and for subsequent discussions and commentaries, which the authors could use in preparing the final drafts which have become the chapters of this volume. The authors have in the meantime further revised and updated their contributions specifically for this publication.

Convened on 8–10 April 1970, the conference could not have taken place without the support of the Institute of World Affairs and the sponsorship of the University of Southern California. The Middle East/North African Program at the University of Southern California provided the direction and logistical support.

In addition to the authors of the chapters of this volume, the following scholars (with titles and affiliations as of the time of the conference) played an active part in the conference, some as panel chairmen or discussants, and others in various other important roles: Ross N. Berkes, Director of the School of Politics and International Relations, University of Southern California; Louis Cantori, Assistant Professor of Political Science, University of California, Los Angeles; Ward E. Y. Elliott, Assistant Professor of Political Science, Claremont Men's College; Norman Fertig, Associate Dean, Letters, Arts, and Sciences, University of Southern California; John Glaser, Assistant Professor of International Relations, University of Southern California; Paul E. Hadley, Dean of University College and Summer Session, University of Southern California; Gerry A. Hale, Assistant Professor of Geography, University of California, Los Angeles; Brice Harris, Associate Professor of History, Occidental

College; Shah Wali Khan, Assistant Professor of Political Science, California State Polytechnic College, Pomona.

Fred Krinsky, Chairman of the Political Science Department, University of Southern California; Charles Mayo, Dean of the Graduate School, University of Southern California; Aurelius Morgner, Professor of Economics, University of Southern California; A. E. Keir Nash, Assistant Professor of Political Science, University of California, Santa Barbara; Margarite Nash, Lecturer in Political Science, University of California, Santa Barbara; Charles Powell, Associate Professor of International Relations, University of Southern California; Henry Reining, Jr., Dean of the von KleinSmid Center of International and Public Affairs, University of Southern California; Morton Schwartz, Assistant Professor of Political Science, Randolph Siverson, Assistant Professor of Political Science, and Arthur C. Turner, Professor of Political Science—all three from the University of California, Riverside.

Finally, grateful mention is made of the yeoman service which the following contributed to the success of the conference: Catherine Teel, Administrative Assistant; Ron Lewis, Jon Parssinen, and Ron Sherwin, Staff Assistants.

List of Contributors

Samir N. Anabtawi	Associate Professor of Political Science, Vanderbilt University. He has contributed a number of articles on the Middle East to scholarly journals. Professor Anabtawi is a specialist on interactions between the Third World and the Middle East.
Willard A. Beling	Professor of International Relations, Coordinator, Middle East/North African Program; Director, International Public Administration Program; and Director, Overseas Programs in the Middle East and North Africa, University of Southern California. Former editor of the *Maghreb Digest,* his recent publications include *Pan-Arabism and Labor; Modernization and African Labor;* (editor and contributor) *The Role of Labor in African Nation-Building;* and (co-editor and contributor) *Developing Nations: Quest for a Model.*
Philip M. Dadant	Chief of the Tactical Operations Group, System Sciences Department, the RAND Corporation. Concerned for a long time with systems analysis and strategy, he most recently led a study of military potentials in the Middle East. While most of his publications are classified in-house documents, some are available to the public from the RAND Corporation.
Anne Gilbar	Research Assistant for two years on the World Event/Interaction Survey with Professor Charles McClelland, University of Southern California.

Brought up in Israel and New York, she received her education at the Sorbonne, the State University of New York at Stony Brook, and the University of Southern California, where she earned a masters degree in International Relations.

Roger H. Harrell — Assistant Professor of Political Science, San Fernando Valley State College.

Michael C. Hudson — Director, Center for Middle Eastern Studies, School for Advanced International Studies, Johns Hopkins University. A recognized authority on the Palestinian Arab resistance movement—on which he has, among other subjects, published a number of important studies—he is the author of *The Precarious Republic: Political Modernization in Lebanon.*

George Kent — Associate Professor of Political Science, and Research Associate, Dimensionality of Nations Project, University of Hawaii. Concerned professionally with the Middle East, Professor Kent has published a number of articles on the area.

Malcolm H. Kerr — Professor and Chairman of the Department of Political Science, University of California, Los Angeles. Born and reared in the Middle East, he has committed himself professionally in the meantime to the study of the politics of the area. In addition to important articles on the Middle East in scholarly journals, he has published the following monographs: *Lebanon in the Last Years of Feudalism, 1840–1868; Islamic Reform;* and *The Arab Cold War, 1958–1967.*

George Lenczowski

Professor of Political Science, University of California, Berkeley; and Director, Middle East Research Project, American Enterprise Institute for Public Policy Research. He is the author of numerous articles on the Middle East and international affairs as well as the following major works: *Russia and West Iran; The Middle East in World Affairs; Oil and State in the Middle East;* (editor and co-author) *United States' Interests in the Middle East;* and (editor) The *Political Awakening in the Middle East.*

Charles A. McClelland

Professor of International Relations, University of Southern California; former Dean of Instruction, San Francisco State College; former Director, Center for Research on Conflict Resoultion, University of Michigan; and former editor of *Background,* journal of the International Studies Association. Introducing the system approach to the study of international politics in 1955, he has since then been engaged in research on international behavior. The author of many publications on international politics, his relatively recent *Theory and the International System* has been well received in the academic community.

John B. Orr

Director of the School of Religion, University of Southern California. His chapter in this volume picks up an early interest in Middle Eastern affairs: he had spent a year in the area on a research grant investigating aspects of the issue which he treats in this volume. His most recent

	publications are: (co-author) *The Radical Suburb;* and (co-author) *Moral Alternatives.*
Don Peretz	Professor of Political Science; and Director of the Southwest Asia-North Africa Program, State University of New York at Binghamton. Professionally associated with the Middle East for a number of years, he has published a rich library on the politics of the Middle East. Some of his most respected larger studies are the following: *Israel and the Palestine Arabs; The Middle East Today;* (co-author) *The Middle East;* and *Middle East Today;* (co-author) *The Middle East Reader.*
William B. Quandt	Formerly with the RAND Corporation, and subsequently an International Fellow of the Council on Foreign Relations. Equally at home in both the Maghreb (North Africa) and the Levant, he has published important works on the politics of the entire Middle East. He is the author of *Revolution and Political Leadership: Algeria 1954–68.*
Charles H. Wagner	Teaching Assistant, International Relations, University of Southern California.
Ciro Zoppo	Associate Professor of Political Science; Executive Director, Arms Control and Foreign Policy Seminar; former Associate Director of Arms Control Research Program, University of California, Los Angeles; and Consultant to the RAND Corporation. A specialist on international politics and military strategy, he has published a number of works in these areas.

Part I

The Middle East: Subsystemic Interactions

CHAPTER 1

The Arabs and Israelis: Perceptual Dimensions to their Dilemma

MALCOLM H. KERR

The decision-makers who determine the policies and actions of nations do not respond to reality, whatever that may mean, as much as they do to their images of the situation. This chapter concerns itself with both Arab and Israeli images—of themselves, their adversaries, and the conflict itself. Their respective perceptions of themselves and their adversaries, Malcolm Kerr points out, now practically preclude settlement of the conflict.

The author sees no light at the end of the tunnel unless both Arabs and Israelis abandon the psychologically comforting but destructive images that they hold of themselves and their adversaries.

Is there any prospect that the Arabs and Israelis will abandon their respective images, or will they continue to reinforce them?

This chapter will examine some of the predominant views of Arabs and Israelis toward their adversaries and themselves and toward the character of the conflict. It will not attempt to analyze their actual behavior, still less the merits of their arguments, but only to survey some of the psychological and ideological background from which each side proceeds. Nonetheless, this is a rather audacious undertaking. There are few major political problems, if any, currently raging in the world which rest to such a degree on the psychological insecurities and fantasies of the protagonists. Alongside the historians and political scientists who have traditionally studied the Arab-Israeli problem, it seems that we especially are in need of the contribution of a social psychologist. I am not that man, but in his absence I shall plunge in anyway and attempt to outline some of the areas in which his task might lie.

If only the Arabs, or the Israelis—depending on one's perspective—would be reasonable! But in this situation, what is reasonable to one observer is the rankest prejudice to another. In general, it is striking how considerably Arab and Israeli attitudes (and, I should add, those of many American Jews, who must be recognized as participants in the conflict) tend to parallel each other. This may seem surprising in view of the great differences between the contemporary culture, material advancement, political fortunes, and historical circumstances of Israeli and Arab society. Yet the similarities of attitude follow implicitly from the character of the conflict itself, in which mutually exclusive claims are laid to a common territory, so that by definition one side's salvation is the other's diaspora. In addition, it may be signicant that while all nationalisms are in a sense political religions, Jewish and Arab nationalism have both arisen in an especially direct way out of their respective religious traditions and are perhaps as much unbroken extensions as surrogates of religious sentiment. This may help account for the special measure of self-righteousness by which both sides distinguish themselves.

In the following pages, I shall briefly discuss five areas of mirrored Arab and Israeli viewpoints. These are: (*1*) a sense of one's own special historic destiny in the face of challenge by the adversary; (*2*) a caricaturized image of the adversary; (*3*) a belief in the necessity of awaiting or forcing a fundamental transformation in the adversary's character and outlook; (*4*) the accretion of vested political and psychological interest in the continuation of the conflict; and (*5*) the prominence of a religious mentality and of quasi-religious symbolism coloring political attitudes.

Obviously the parallels in these areas are far from precise, and it is not my contention that in each case Arab and Israeli attitudes are neatly balanced or that they always assume similar forms. But the resemblances are there nonetheless, and in some instances it appears that a mechanism of reciprocity is at work. For those whose interest in the Arab-Israeli problem arises from partisan attachment to one or the other side, it may be healthy to reflect on how much the forces of light and darkness have in common. To others with a more detached interest in analyzing the nature of the conflict or in considering questions of American policy toward it, I hope to suggest that the difficulties may be even more considerable than they have imagined, since they are deeply rooted not only in the protagonists' conflicting interests and strategies but also in their mentalities.

The Sense of Destiny

Both Arabs and Israelis over the past twenty-five years (and both Arab nationalists and Jewish nationalists for a generation and more preceding the creation of Israel) have exhibited a common tendency to view themselves in a very special historical light. We might consider this as part of the phenomenon of nationalism that has swept Europe and North America over the past century and which is now sweeping the Third World with special intensity. But in the case of the two conflicting nationalisms in the Middle East, a sense of one's own destiny has tended to be a particularly self-preoccupied conviction in which people see themselves as playing divinely ordained roles in human history. Both in the Arab and the Jewish case there is a good deal of religious background and revivalism involved in the process, but there is also something assertively secular in them, involving a sharp break with the past.

Let us look first at the Arab side. Many of the major reformist intellectuals and politicians in the Eastern Arab world of the past century who have preached nationalism, reform, renaissance, and revolution, whether in religious terms or in secular terms, have spoken both of the notion of reviving the special genius of the past of the Arabs, cast heavily in an Islamic framework, and also of the unique secular mission of the Arab nation in the future. It is sometimes imagined that revolutionary movements are of very recent vintage in Arab countries, introduced by Nasser or the Baath party. But the political and intellectual history of the Arab world since 1800 provides a good many antecedents. One can point to a century-long tradition of Arab publicists, reformers, and intellectuals who have wrestled with the problem of trying to reconcile past tradition with the need for future liberation, modernization, and secularization of their society. A long procession of such figures as Jamal ad-Din al-Afghani, Mustafa Kamil, Muhammad Abduh, Abdullah Nadim, Abdul Rahman al-Kawakibi, Ahmad Lutfi al-Sayyid, and Hassan al-Banna and the Muslim Brethren, all substantially preceded Gamal Abdul Nasser and his military reformers in combining these two strands of thought: radical innovation on the one hand, revival of a classical civilization on the other. Particularly the religious spokesmen among them, such as Afghani, Abduh, and the Muslim Brethren, have focused to a large extent on the notion of revitalizing the special virtues and genius of the early age of Islam. But all of them also have gone beyond this to try to assert the relevance of this classical tradition to the present and the future in a manner that breaks sharply with the more recent past of the last several centuries, during which internal decay and external aggression allegedly corrupted the classic virtues of society.

In this process of revolutionary revitalization we have also a mixture of secularism and modernized spirituality in which some have championed the ascendancy of religion over secularism or vice versa, while others have spoken in terms of some kind of amalgamation of the religious message and the secular one. Arab nationalism has been marked by the historic consciousness of Arabs of their own peculiar character as the progenitors of Islam, as the people among whom Islam first arose and in whose language the Koran was revealed and propagated. Thus today, while Arabism and Islam are not seen as coterminous, nonetheless it is possible for Arabs to see themselves as having a special predestined role as the core or "substance" of Islam (*maddat al-Islam*), and to see the purity of Islamic virtues which had developed among the Arabs as having been corrupted in more recent centuries by Turks, Persians, and other latecoming adherents. But it is possible also for Arabs to see religion as a degenerate force of backwardness, or blind tradition and superstition, which the modern age must overcome and which it is the task of revolutionaries to help modern society overcome and thus to go on to something revolutionarily new. The extremes can touch in this case: those who preach the most militant kind of return to the most ancient and romantic past point in Islamic history—the earliest generation of Islam during and just after the lifetime of the Prophet—have a great deal in common with those who today preach the most revolutionary break with religious traditions. Both are turning their backs on many centuries of social and cultural tradition, and those who preach a return to an early historical model always define it in allegorical terms that are not logically so very different from the kind of utopia that the militant secularists are preaching.

Of course, the modern history of Arab nationalism has also been shaped to a significant extent by Christians. One can mention the early Arab nationalists of Christian Lebanon in the latter half of the nineteenth century; the Syrian National party of Antoun Saadeh, a Greek Orthodox Lebanese, which was particularly strong in the 1940s and 1950s; Michel Aflaq, the founder of the Baath party in Syria, also a Greek Orthodox; and many other figures, intense Arab nationalists or, in Saadeh's case, Syrian nationalists, but also intense secularists for whom it would have been absurd as Christians to preach an Islamic message. But the secular utopias that these Christians offered as substitutes for an explicitly Islamic one were equally based, implicitly, on historical myth and allegory. They all preached messages to the effect that the Arab (or Syrian) nation had its own classical genius that had been captured in more recent centuries and which must now somehow be revived, and that the nation must rediscover itself and build a new ideal community based on its ancient virtues. It seems to me that this is virtually an Islamic notion, only at one remove, in the hands of these Christians. They were, after all, products of a society that was predominantly Muslim, and they addressed overwhelmingly Muslim clienteles.

Whether or not the leaders of Arab nationalism have been religiously oriented, therefore, and whether they have been Muslim or Christian, they have tended to spread a notion of a special destiny of the Arabs. They have called for a reassertion of will, for the breaking of chains, for the identity of the self, for a rediscovery of the directions and purposes of society. This, as in other nationalisms, has been an intensely self-centered concern. It is militant, self-consuming, and parochial, and it is set against a notion of the obstructionism, ill-will, and conspiracy of outside enemies and detractors who must somehow be overcome.

If one is to give society a major overhaul, the presence of foreign enemies looms as a great obstacle. In the Middle East, presumed enemies are everywhere to be seen, and not altogether without reason. There has now been well over a century of an inordinate foreign presence and influence over the local and international affairs of the area, dating from the earliest manifestations of Ottoman military weakness and economic decay. In the twentieth century there has been the shattering experience of European colonial rule, and since 1948 there has been the still more shattering experience of the establishment of Israel in the very midst of Arab society—a new foreign state populated predominantly by people immigrating into Palestine from Europe in the first instance, then from within Arab society itself. Israel has presented a fundamental challenge or even an insult to Arab society. Israel is dedicated to its own goals but also dedicated in the eyes of many Arabs to obstructing the march of Arab progress; to conserving European and American interests; to using those interests for its own sake; to attempting to keep the Arabs divided, weak, and backwards; and particularly to fastening on those elements within Arab culture and society that the revolution is particularly dedicated to struggling against: the tradition-bound mentality, the subservience of the masses, and the lack of understanding of the components of modern progress. Consequently Arab social, political, cultural, and economic ills tend to be seen by nationalist revolutionaries as the implicit allies of the Zionists, who in turn are seen as the implicit allies of the western colonialists.

All of this offends the hopes of Arabs for a self-directed, forward-looking, unified revolutionary movement, and stimulates their apprehension that rather than achieving self-direction, they may fall prey to the directions imposed upon them by other people. There is a sensitivity to tutelage, to advice from the outside, to appeals for moderation in the name of international interests, to the demand that Arabs should accommodate themselves somehow to the interests of outsiders either for the sake of the world or for their own sake.

Now let us look at the Israeli side of this picture. Its contours are quite different in many of the specific details but rather similar in the general direction in which they point.

We should begin, as in the case of Arab nationalism, with the consideration of the revolutionary character of the Zionist movement. Zionism is, in fact, one of the most awesomely successful revolutionary movements on record, and it has succeeded in working a wholesale reversal of historical fortunes for Jews. This reversal has not happened simply by chance but has been the result of extraordinary revolutionary leadership and commitment. Israel would not have become what it is today, it would not have succeeded in establishing itself, in bringing forth a population from the scattered corners of the world, in transforming Palestine from a sleepy and backward Ottoman province into a thriving, technologically advanced, culturally sophisticated, militarily powerful society, nor would Jews have emerged from ghetto life to become highly successful farmers and soldiers, were it not for a revolutionary commitment of the very strongest sort.

The impressive accomplishments of Israel are commonly recognized, but the notion of her leaders as revolutionaries is a little harder to accept easily. We look at some of the outward personal qualities of a number of Zionist and Israeli leaders of the past two generations, and we find people who in many ways appear to be rather conventional: Chaim Weizmann, the reflective academic, the man of moderation and diplomacy; Abba Eban, the urbane scholar; Golda Meir, the former school-teacher and grandmother in her kitchen. It is difficult to picture these people as genuine revolutionaries. On the contrary, they seem to convey an image of Israel as a rather conventional middle-class society dedicated to quiet and peaceful pursuits to whom war, upheaval, and violence have come as an unsolicited result of the hostility of its neighbors.

Perhaps we should look more closely at the reality of this picture and consider the proposition that Weizmann, Mrs. Meir, and Eban, along with others such as Moshe Dayan and David Ben-Gurion, really ought to be classified as revolutionaries of the most determined and single-minded variety, and perhaps much more genuinely so than a good many flamboyant Arab colonels and publicists. They have been dedicated to the transformation of Jewish existence, and the transformation of the land of Palestine, by means that no one would have thought possible prior to its happening. They did so both by galvanizing the support of Jewish communities all over the world and by conducting a long and unremitting struggle against enormous odds—the established interests of the British Empire, the systematic murder program of Hitler, the inertial force of assimilation of Jews into national communities around the world, and, of course, the hostility of the Arab world.

Having said this much, we need hardly dwell on the point that Jewish nationalism is dedicated to the notion of the special future destiny as well as past history of the Jewish people. There is a long religious tradition to substantiate this idea, but beyond it there is the very message of Zionism: that Jews should emerge from their diaspora, that they should transform the conditions of their existence, that they should be farmers and builders as well as merchants and scholars, and even that national identity rather than Judaic religious belief and practice is most central to Jewish character.

In any case, the momentum gained from the success thus far in achieving these ideals in the face of tragedy and continuing adversity has left the Zionist movement and its leaders conditioned to the notion that struggle against murderous enemies is an inherent and permanent aspect of their cause, and that it is precisely within the context of that struggle that the new Jewish national character is being forged and the New Jerusalem being built. Yet at the same time, the material strain on resources imposed by military budgets is so considerable that a countervailing idea is also inevitably much in their minds: that Israel's fulfillment of her destiny is being held back, as well as being stimulated, by the continuing Arab opposition.

The Image of the Adversary

As a general rule there has been little serious interest on the part of members of one side in the reality, character, and problems of existence of the other. This might be characterized as a problem of mutual nonrecognition. Nonrecognition does not primarily refer to the lack of political and diplomatic recognition but of moral and psychological recognition. The political problem of diplomatic recognition is familiar to everyone, the Arabs having consistently challenged the legitimacy of a Jewish state, or even of a Jewish national community in Palestine, ever since the Balfour Declaration of 1917.

Diplomatic nonrecognition on the Arabs' part reflects a much deeper problem, however. Not only the propriety, but the reality of Jewish life in Israel with its policies, concerns, problems, and achievements has not presented itself to the minds of Arabs except in caricature. Arabs have readily picked up from Western (sometimes Jewish) sources challenges to the idea of Jewish nationhood, on the ground that assimilation is the only proper answer to Jewish dilemmas. "Judaism is a religion like any other"; and "Jews cannot have a double loyalty both to the nation of their citizenship and to Israel."

During the period of the British mandate, large numbers of Arabs were in daily contact with Jews in Palestine and thereby gained some sense of the social, economic, and personal realities of the Jewish community. Arabs outside Palestine had little of this exposure, and from 1948 to 1967 the only Arabs who had it were Israel's own Arab citizens, who lived in complete isolation from their fellow Arabs. During this latter period there appears to have been an increasing tendency for both Palestinians and non–Palestinian Arabs to see the Israeli in allegorical terms, as an artificial creature, an extension of societies other than the Israeli one, manipulated by a cadre of conspiratorial leaders. Thus while it has been understood that Jews immigrating to Israel learn Hebrew and that Sabras speak it as a native language, nonetheless the Israeli population was still seen as an unassimilated cultural composite, and it was not recognized that a distinctive national Israeli culture had taken root. Likewise, while it was generally understood that the Israeli economy had made considerable progress, Israel's well-known dependence on large-scale outside assistance encouraged the Arabs to deny that within Israel there was any real wellspring of initiative, construction and desire to create a means of independent livelihood based on something other than parasitism.

More particularly, Israeli political objectives have been consistently seen by the Arabs as simple and unlimited, summed up in the term "expansionism." Every Israeli retaliatory raid, to say nothing of every Israeli-Arab war, has strengthened the Arab belief in a permanent Israeli conspiracy to expand her borders at Arab expense. Given the presumed aim of expansion, whether from the Nile to the Euphrates or on a more modest basis, the easy conclusion has been that "the only thing the Israelis understand is force" or that the only alternative means of bringing them to reason is to wait for the day when their foreign patrons, particularly in the United States, will tire of artificially propping them up with financial and political support. Meanwhile, the fear of Israeli expansion is tied to the fear of unlimited, continuing immigration into Israel. The potential availability of fifteen million other Jews in the world as future citizens in Arab apprehensions transforms the nation of three million immigrants into a considerably larger one. Here, the Arabs have seemingly taken at face value the aspirations of the most militant Zionists who declare their hopes of promoting continued immigration. At the same time, the Arab belief is widespread that very few Jews in the world, now or in the past, have really wanted to live in Israel, and that the present population is there only as a result of unscrupulous appeals, so that in the absence of the machinations of the Zionist leadership the Palestinian problem never would have arisen or persisted.

The general result of all this on the Arab side is a profound lack of curiosity among Arabs about the real character of the adversary. While outside observers can readily see that the Israeli reality is exceedingly complex on all fronts—political, social, cultural, and psychological—the Arab presumption of that reality tends to be highly simplistic. There have been dismayingly few Arab intellectuals or political leaders who have displayed serious interest in Israeli affairs, even remotely approaching, say, the interest of analysts in Western countries in the affairs of the Soviet Union or Communist China. Until the June War in 1967, there was little debate about the proper solution of the problem beyond the consideration of alternative utopian slogans on the disposition of Palestine once the Arab victory was achieved. Since 1967 such things have begun, although it has remained very difficult for Arabs to speculate out loud about the desirability of settling for anything like the pre-1967 status quo, even though a number of governments have made diplomatic commitments to it.

Certainly Arabs are no more inherently incapable of thinking about politics in rational terms than all the other people in the world, and on a private basis consideration of the problems assumes a much more serious and realistic form than it does in public. But what is it that prevents this private capacity from finding a public expression? There does indeed seem to be a general psychological problem relating not only to recent political circumstances in the Arab world but to elements in the traditional culture as well, in which a pluralist and relativist notion of social morality offends established values, and in which it is inherently difficult to extend recognition to undesirable propositions and phenomena.

We now turn to the Israeli side of the picture of mutual nonrecognition. It is perhaps more difficult for many to agree that there is a problem of Israeli nonrecognition of Arabs, since Israel's public position ever since her establishment has been one of willingness to conclude a formal peace with the Arab states. However, even on the diplomatic level the reality is not so simplistic; and more importantly, we are concerned here not with diplomacy but with psychology.

Whatever the Israeli readiness to enter into normal interstate relations with Lebanon, Syria, Jordan, and Egypt—if at least they should accept Israeli terms of settlement—there has been no such official attitude toward the Palestinians. This was a natural outgrowth of the experience of the mandate period, in which the rightfulness of the presence of Jewish immigrants in Palestine was under continual challenge by Palestinian leaders. However, it also extended to the period beyond the 1948 war, in which the claims of the uprooted Palestinian population to a right of occupancy was not accepted by the Israeli government. Ironically, the legitimacy of the Jordanian presence on the West Bank was not accepted either, and we are left with an open question of whether in official Israeli eyes any entity other than Israel herself held valid claim to any of the territory of the former British mandate.[1]

Do the Palestinians exist as a people? This is a counterpart to another question which must be raised for Arabs: Do Jews exist as a people? In both cases the official answer has been negative. Since 1967 a lively debate has emerged within Israel about the future of the Palestinian people. That debate, however, has not reached the official level, and it remains the Israeli government's official view (as stated on several occasions by Prime Minister Meir) that Palestin-

1. This question is highlighted in the case of Jerusalem. After the June War the Israeli view was promptly advanced that Jordanian presence in that city had been illegitimately based on conquest in 1948, but with the implication that Israel's own presence in her side of the city had not been marred by any such lack of title. Thus the Arab section of Jerusalem, not being legitimately Jordanian, could only fall by default to Israel sovereignty.

ians can only be recognized as Arab individuals who happened to live in the area designated as a British mandate before 1948; consequently their future destiny lies not as an entity of their own but as individual members assimilated into surrounding Arab states. Politically this stems of course from practical considerations. If the Palestinians constitute a nation, it is necessary to deal directly with them rather than to seek to solve the problem by establishing relations with neighboring Arab states. Furthermore, recognition of Palestinian rights would place a considerable restriction on Israeli options regarding the future of the West Bank and the Gaza Strip.

Psychologically speaking, however, the problem runs much deeper. The Palestinians were referred to in the Balfour Declaration of 1917 as "the existing non-Jewish communities in Palestine," despite the fact that at that time they constituted approximately 90 percent of the total population. The whole movement of Jewish immigration into the country in the face of constant Arab objections could only be justified in the minds of the Zionists themselves if the social and national reality of Arab Palestine were minimized. This may have been relatively easy toward the beginning, as there was no historic entity of Palestine to give shape to local Arab political aspirations; and indeed, politically conscious Arabs in Palestine identified at that time with a Syrian nationalist movement centered in Damascus. But as time passed, and as the conflict within Palestine sharpened in the 1920s, thirties, and forties, a Palestinian nationalism did emerge and the denial of its reality became increasingly difficult. On the other hand, as the moment of Israel's creation approached in 1948, that denial became all the more essential, and it has remained important at some psychological levels ever since. For Israelis, to acknowledge the national character and rights of the Palestinians means potentially calling into question some of the rights that they have prescriptively acquired for themselves since 1948, particularly in terms of the denial of the entitlement of repatriation of Palestinian refugees. It is easier consequently to see the Palestinians as an unfortunate, nonpolitical mass of people, manipulated by their own leaders, who fled in 1948 for unnecessary reasons and who are more logically destined for assimilation into neighboring states than for repatriation to their former homes.

In this light, it is perhaps not so surprising that according to a poll reported in the Israeli press early in 1971, 38 percent of Israeli respondents thought that neither a Palestinian people nor a Palestinian entity existed; 33 percent thought they did, and the rest did not know. In another pool about the same time, 29.9 percent considered the Palestinians as a group possessing a political identity of their own, while 55.5 percent did not.[2]

As for the view of the rest of the Arab world, we must recognize that here there is an Israeli counterpart to the simple-minded Arab assumption that Israelis understand nothing but force. Arab objectives tend to be seen by Israelis as also unlimited, and here the key word is not "expansionism" but "extermination." The "horde of barbarians" signified by fifteen million Jewish supporters and potential immigrants to some Arab minds is easily matched by 100 million Arab "barbarians" in the minds of Israelis: an enormous numerical majority likely to lay waste to all that has been accomplished in Israel over the past generations, once the moment of opportunity arrives for them.

In this respect we witness an Israeli transposition of European conditions to the Middle East, supported by at least outward plausibility. Anti-Semitism and extermination were stark realities in Europe and had much to do, of course, with the rise of modern Zionism and the creation of the Israeli state. Given the unremitting Arab hostility, and given the rise in recent decades of anti-Jewish feeling within Arab countries, the current realities fit neatly into past Jewish historical memory. What reason is there for Israelis, on the emotional level at least, to see any difference between a threat to their individual and collective existence posed by the Arabs from that posed in previous generations by Nazis and other Europeans? Indeed it would be surprising if there were not a considerable fixation of these notions in many Israeli minds. We should add, however, that they have much more basis in the minds of European Jews in Israel than of Jews from Iraq, Yemen, Egypt, or North Africa. Some of the latter indeed suffered hardships in times just prior to their immigration to Israel but they have nothing like the scorching historical memories of the Ashkenazim.

Again as in the case of the Arabs, as a result of all of this we find among the Israelis a self-centered lack of curiosity about the realities of life on the other side: of Arab policies, concerns, problems, and achievements. Again we find that while outsiders can readily recognize the complexity of these Arab realities, the Israeli perception of them tends to be simplistic.

However, this problem is a bit less stark on the Israeli side than on the Arab one. There are significant numbers of Israelis, including many intellectuals and some politicians, for whom an interest in

2. *Davar*, 6 January 1971; *Maariv*, 26 March 1971. Cited by Amnon Kapeliouk in *Le Monde Diplomatique*, June 1971, p. 3.

Arab affairs is serious and genuine and for whom the sensationalism and irresponsible speculation that stamps the minds of the masses and the ideologues are destructive and distasteful. It is important to recognize the voices of men in past and present Israeli society such as Judah Magnes, Simha Flapan, Jacob Talmon, Shimon Shamir, and others, who have earnestly sought to create within Israel a sense of intercultural community with the hostile Arab environment and to empathize with the Palestinians. It is significant also to note the presence in Israeli universities of distinguished students of Arab history and culture who among them have produced some of the outstanding scholarly literature of recent years on Arab affairs.

Nonetheless, the problem of lack of curiosity about the enemy's realities remains an Israeli problem as well as an Arab one. And it does have a history of long standing. In the early history of Zionism slogans were common such as, "A people without a land for a land without a people," or "Palestine should become as Jewish as England is English." It seems more than symbolically significant that many Zionists of the older generation, such as David Ben-Gurion, Golda Meir, and Levi Eshkol could play out their lifetime careers in Palestine and Israel without learning Arabic.

The problem is vastly compounded by the involved attitude of Jewish communities outside Israel, particularly in the United States, where distance makes it possible to entertain the luxury of thinking of the Middle East solely in terms of Israeli problems and interests. For them, Israel's national success thus far has made it possible to put off asking the question: "What is the nature of the people surrounding Israel with whom she must deal if peace is to be established?" It may be that there is a parallel here: that Israelis have a greater sense of the reality of the Arabs than do Jewish outsiders, just as there is a greater sense among Palestinians of the reality of Israel, than there is among non-Palestinian Arabs.

A word should be added about the character of the present debate within Israel about the future of the Palestinians. The debate is real and important, but it is limited in scope as well as in clientele. The fundamental topic appears to be whether to and how to enable the Palestinians to achieve a national existence of their own, centered on West Bank territory. It has stopped short of anything beyond this, and it may be said that the debate is a luxury which only the victors can readily afford, since it aims at creating conditions of peace which would leave the Israeli state and society itself completely intact within already existing frontiers and without making any particular sacrifices. The notion of even a token return of Palestinian refugees to their former homes in Israel is not part of this debate; and if there is any real awareness among Israelis participating in this discussion of the depth of the Palestinian psychological commitment to the idea of return, that awareness has not become visible.

The Hard Line

Both Arabs and Israelis possess their maximalist and minimalist advocates, or, to turn a phrase, their hawks and their doves. Within each side there has always been an uncertain balance between arguments in favor of forcing the issues with the enemy, and in favor of sidestepping them. Each side has recurrently had to face the same difficult questions: to whose benefit would an extended period of accommodation, or de facto coexistence, redound? Is the other side more to be feared in conditions of direct confrontation, with hostilities uncontrolled, or within conditions of coexistence in which one's own concessions might be taken advantage of?

Here in the debate between "hawks" and "doves" we are mainly concerned with the rational calculation of strategy rather than with emotions, although of course the emotions loom very large in the background. In what follows we shall dwell primarily on the Arab side, because it seems to be the more complex and less widely understood.

While incapable of mounting any effective action against Israel, the Arabs have been decisively hampered by their own uncertainty on strategic fundamentals. They have been unable since the beginning of the conflict to decide on their long-range objectives and have therefore failed to develop adequate operational principles consistent with their capabilities.

In the absence of a policy based on calculations, the Arabs have tended to fall back on the conviction that the Zionist movement constituted an elementary aggression at their expense and was therefore completely unacceptable.

Of course, many Arabs are acutely conscious that their own confidence in the legitimacy of their grievances against Israel is no sufficient basis for an effective policy, and that they cannot do without some form of cost-benefit strategy that takes into account power realities. Many would claim, in fact, that the traditional Arab position of refusing to discuss solutions with Israel has been realistic. They would argue that as long as the preponderance of power is on

Israel's side it is imperative to avoid open warfare with her, but that it is equally important to preserve the integrity of their own case, and to avoid granting her permanent concessions, pending the time when their own superiority in numbers and resources will shift the balance. Hence the present need is to conduct a holding operation by preventing Israel's integration into the Middle Eastern society of nations, while limiting the damage that she can do to them. This phase may last a long time, during which the Arabs run admitted risks of vulnerability to Israeli retribution, but the argument is that Arab society can absorb these risks—even when they eventuate in such disasters as that of 1967. Meanwhile, this admittedly puts the Arabs in the contradictory position of holding Israel to her international responsibilities while seeking to remain relatively free of their own, but they are hardly alone in the history of nations in attempting to derive some benefit from such a double standard.

The difficulty with this analysis is not that it is irrational or unrealistic in itself, but that it is incomplete as the basis for a consistent policy as long as the ultimate objective is left indeterminate. If the objective has some identifiable limit, it becomes easier to exercise the restraint and marshal the international support that can restrict the damage incurred from Israel in the interim. Without such a limit, the objective tends to be thought of by the public, and perhaps by some policy makers as well, in utopian terms, with the result that in moments of crisis (such as May 1967) it is sentiment rather than reasoned strategy that rises to the surface.

The objective has not been defined partly because the competing Arab states and political movements have been unable to agree on it: to do so would require that their leaders enjoy a more uniform outlook on the world in general, and more confidence in their relations with their publics and with each other than has been the case. Particularly, they would have to be freed of the temptation to practice one-upmanship against each other. Partly also, however, they have not defined their objective because the practical pressure on them to do so has never been overwhelming. Each government could always reasonably hope to sidestep the next crisis by adroit improvisation; war with Israel was always a risk, but never inevitable, as long as the Arabs themselves did not intend to begin one. The argument mentioned earlier—that the costs of military defeats could be absorbed anyway—strikes us as a rationalization for the Arab incapacity to avoid the risk.

As an astute Anglo-Arab commentator forcefully pointed out shortly after the June War, the Arabs have been unable to decide whether their policy should aim at destroying the Israeli state or only at the limited objective of containing it.[3] Not only the rhetoric but also the concrete policies have fluctuated between these two ideas under varying circumstances. If Israel's very existence as an independent state is unacceptable, then it is necessary to prepare either to defeat her decisively in battle or to force her eventual disintegration from within by continuing military intimidation, diplomatic isolation, and economic blockade. On the other hand, if the object is to limit Israel's size and power and to extract a major accommodation from her on the Arab refugee question, then some internationally recognizable basis for defining Israel's rights and obligations as a state becomes necessary, and the Arab states must make plain not only what they demand of Israel, but what they are prepared to concede to her.

On the other side of the coin, Israel is held by the Arab side to be obligated by a number of international agreements and principles: the United Nations General Assembly's partition resolution of 1947; other assembly resolutions calling for the right of repatriation for Arab refugees; the 1949 armistice agreements; the inadmissibility of territorial acquisitions by conquest; etc. The belief is common that Israel has always sought territorial expansion, and the fact that she has expanded from previously drawn borders (in 1948 and 1967) is felt to be conclusive evidence of such intent, just as the occurrence of Israeli punitive raids on neighboring territory is believed to be evidence of her inherently aggressive nature, and of the assertion that despite what her leaders say, they do not really want peace. On many occasions prior to 1967 Arab authorities such as President Nasser stated to Westerners that peace would be possible if Israel would accept the United Nations resolutions, that the Egyptian blockade of the Suez Canal to Israeli shipping was a response to Israel's exclusion of the refugees, and that the record would show that it was Israel who failed to respect the armistice agreements. All these arguments, in purporting to hold Israel to her international agreements and obligations, logically implied an Arab willingness to respect Israel's rights that were the counterpart of those obligations: in the case of the armistice agreements, military security on Israel's side of the line; in the case of the United Nations resolutions, sovereign existence within the partition boundaries.

The response of the Egyptian and Jordanian governments to the 22 November 1967 Security Council resolution was in line with this

3. Cecil Hourani, "The Moment of Truth," *Encounter* 29, no. 11 (November 1967): 3–14.

approach of limited objectives: in response to Israeli withdrawal, they were ready to renounce claims of belligerency and respect Israel's sovereign rights within recognized frontiers. In February 1971 they went a significant step further: in response to questions put by Dr. Gunnar Jarring, both Arab governments declared their readiness in principle to conclude a formal peace agreement with Israel, in exchange for the recovery of their territories. Meanwhile the Jordanian government cracked down on the Palestinian resistance movement and virtually eliminated it as a military and political force within the country. Several other Arab governments condemned these actions, however, and even the Egyptians were careful to keep their lines open politically to the Palestinian organizations. And while the Sadat regime sought to persuade the outside world of the sincerity of its commitment to a lasting settlement with Israel, it found it inexpedient to press this message on Arab opinion, thus leaving room for an impression that the Israeli evacuation might be only a prospective stepping-stone to a renewal of the original conflict.

Thus the Arab effort to contain Israel and to defend themselves against her military superiority has been seriously undermined by the counterpart effort to keep in doubt the principle of Israel's independent existence. As long as the very question of existence was kept open, there was little room for any serious elaboration of the means by which the international community could be expected to underwrite the containment effort. All that could be secured was a very general, and in practice undependable, commitment from the three Western powers to uphold the territorial integrity of both sides—undependable because Israel's disrespect for Arab security could always be attributed to the Arabs' disrespect for hers. In consequence, Britain and France readily discarded their commitment in 1956 at Suez, and the United States did so (if in more passive fashion) during and after the war of 1967. As long as Israel's right to exist was in question, it would be natural for many outside onlookers to conclude that in fact it was the only question. The more modest, but practically speaking more substantial question from the standpoint of Arab interests—what kind of Israel should the Arabs accept, and on what terms—went unexamined, because the Arabs failed to raise it convincingly.

The most coherent single reason for the Arab failure to define their position clearly lies with their own internal divisions. A decision to moderate their objectives in Palestine and define them in some meaningful and practical form which the Israelis and other interested states can recognize and respond to would require considerably more consensus, collective responsibility, and mutual restraint than the inter-Arab scene has afforded in the past two decades. We have seen in the United States how difficult it was for twenty years for politicians to carry on intelligent public discussion of the much less sensitive question of relations with Communist China. Arab politicians face a much more difficult problem.

Each Arab regime has been so internally insecure and, in the atmosphere provided by the pan-Arab idea, so exposed to criticism by its neighbors that its leaders have tended to shrink from taking unorthodox positions on the ritually symbolic question of Palestine and Israel. It is a problem that has offered innumerable opportunities to embarrass one's rival should he seem to take an independent position, for the established official position of intransigence neatly symbolizes several important virtues: honor, protection of one's kinsmen, and courage and steadfastness in the face of adversity. Israel presents the collectivity of Arab states with a problem much too difficult for them to cope with in their present condition of political weakness.

There is a long record of competition among rival Arab states to use the Israeli issue against each other and for their own individual advantages, beginning with their uncoordinated and disastrous intervention in Palestine in May 1948. There is also a long record of competitive efforts to promote rival organizations and movements among the Palestinians.

That Arab states used the cause of Palestine against each other but were unable to agree what else to do with it was symptomatic of the serious problems they each faced in establishing orderly progress and authority within their own societies. The situation was made possible in the first place, however, because Palestinian Arabs themselves had always lacked effective organization and leadership of their own. Until 1948 they were victims of factionalism among their own prominent families (the Nashashibis and the Husseinis) and of their failure to respond to the limited opportunity that the British mandate gave them to establish their own communal institutions in a manner analogous to that of the Jews. Just as the Palestinian community found itself dependent on the outside Arab states in 1948 for military support that the latter were incapable of providing, it also had to depend on them then and afterward for political and diplomatic leadership with no better result. And despite their inability to render assistance, the Arab states did succeed in preventing the Palestinians from developing institutions of their own, by means of their insistence on sponsoring and exploiting Palestinian organizations for their own competitive purposes.

Thus the Palestinians' interests remained in the hands of non–Palestinian Arab regimes whose interests were bound to be somewhat different. For the governments of the Arab states, it was practical to coexist with Israel as a hated neighbor, as long as she was confined to her own territory; for the Palestinians, Israel's national existence entailed the denial of theirs. The no-war, no-peace policy of the Arab states was a de facto compromise between their own practical interests and those of the Palestinians. It was an expensive compromise, for it pulled them into a conflict from which they could not withdraw once they were involved, and which could only damage their own prosperity, security, international diplomacy, and domestic political stability; but until 1967 the price they paid was not prohibitive, and the Palestinians were not in a position to force them into making heavier commitments.

It was in reaction against this situation which had built up for twenty years that the Palestinian resistance movement dramatically emerged after the June War and declared its insistence on keeping the struggle with Israel open—on escalating it, in fact, and stimulating additional clashes between Israel and Egypt and Jordan so as to forestall a settlement between them. In so doing, it posed an implicit challenge to the authority and the established state interests of both the Cairo and Amman regimes, especially the latter. But for some of the same reasons that the Arab states had previously found it difficult to turn their backs on the unattainable goal of destroying the Israeli state, so Egypt and Jordan could not now readily disavow the Palestinian resistance groups across the cease-fire lines, and the retaliations of the Israeli armed forces sufficed to inhibit concessions from either side.

We shall now turn more briefly for a look at the Israeli "hard line." Within Israel the debate runs among groups ranging from those who insist on Peace with a capital *P* but who are unwilling to make more than the barest concessions for the sake of it, down to those who would concede a great deal for even an accommodation with the Arabs falling short of a formal peace treaty. The proponents of the toughest policy are impressed with the need to retain initiative in Israeli hands and the worthlessness of Arab pledges of moderation; those with the softest line are concerned with what they see as the long-term isolation and exposure of Israel if she remains unyielding to Arab claims and international pressures.

In one way or another the debate has gone on in shifting contexts since the early days of the British mandate. During the mandate period Zionists of hard-line and soft-line persuasion debated such questions as whether eventual Jewish statehood was essential in Palestine or whether some form of binational state shared with the Arab majority was a sufficient objective. If statehood were to be achieved how much territory must the state encompass? Was some form of partition acceptable? Was it advisable to pursue Zionist objectives primarily by negotiation with the British government, or with Arab groups? Or were such negotiations fatally entangling, and was it essential for the Jews to employ their own direct methods, including those of terrorism?

In 1947–48, with the advent of the UN partition plan and the war the nature of the question shifted. Given the Arabs' rejection of the plan for Jewish independence, how were they to be dwelt with? Was it best simply to secure those territories allotted to the new Jewish state and attempt once and for all to reconcile the Arab population to this prospect? Or, given the Arabs' hostility, was it desirable to encourage their exodus and enlarge Israel's territory? Once Arab refugees had fled, was it advisable to accept the return of any significant number of them? And once the frontiers had been expanded beyond those assigned in the partition plan, as a result of the war, how flexible should the new Jewish state be on those frontiers?

Following the 1948 war and throughout the armistice period up to 1967 the major issue was whether to accept the modus vivendi of the armistice system, as a form of de facto coexistence in the hope that in the long run Arab hostility would abate somewhat and a normal existence for Israel would evolve, or whether Israel should force the issue by military means and make the armistice system unbearable for the Arabs, so as to press them into the acceptance of permanent peace.

The question of the viability of the armistice was a highly complicated one. Challenges to that system arose not only from the Arab side in the form of illegal border crossings, sabotage, and the refusal of Arab governments to build permanent peace treaties out of the armistice agreement, but also in the form of Israeli actions which undermined the armistice. Accepting the viability of the system would not simply have meant allowing Arab violations of it to go unpunished, but more particularly to avoid stimulating such violations from the Israeli side by escalated counter violations; by progressive Israeli encroachment on the status of demilitarized zones on the frontiers; by proclaiming the disputed city of Jerusalem as Israel's capital; by developing the port of Eilat, occupied in the last days of the war in 1949, and subsequently using its development as a basis for pressing the issue of navigation through the Strait of Tiran; and by making an issue of Israeli passage through the Suez Canal at critical junctures in a manner calculated to upset periods of relative tranquility on the Israeli-Egyptian armistice line.

The question of the viability of the armistice also entailed the larger question of what evolution might occur among the Arabs through the process of their own social and political development. Under the aegis of the armistice system, with hostility suspended but still existent, was time on Israel's side? Could she afford the rise of serious progress and leadership among her Arab neighbors? Or was it necessary for her to bring matters to the stage of armed confrontations before decisive events within Arab society occurred? The militant answer to this latter question was given by Prime Minister Ben-Gurion in 1957, in a speech to the Knesset shortly after the Israeli government's reluctant acquiescence to United States and United Nations demands that she withdraw from the last remnants of territory occupied in the Sinai war:

> This campaign diminished the stature of the Egyptian dictator and I do not want you or the entire people to underestimate the importance of this fact. As one of those persons who receive their salaries for looking after our security . . . I always feared that a personality might rise such as arose among the Arab rulers in the seventh century or like him [Kemal Ataturk] who arose in Turkey after its defeat in the first World War. He raised their spirits, changed their character, and turned them into a fighting nation. There was and still is a danger that Nasser is this man.[4]

After the 1967 war the internal debate in Israel turned to a different order of questions. How much advantage should Israel take of her hitherto unsuspected but now dramatically proven strength? Once the victory was achieved, what to do with it? Should it be used as the starting point of a magnanimous gesture by which Israel might hope to convince the other side of her modest intentions? To this the clearly given answer was no, as Israeli opinion was virtually unanimous in asserting that the victory should at least be used for serious bargaining purposes, if not for simple territorial expansion.

4. Quoted in Kennett Love, *Suez: The Twice-fought War* (New York, McGraw-Hill Co., 1969), p. 676.

Alternatively, however, the victory might have been employed as a device simply to secure the legitimation of the status quo ante: that is to say, after June 1967 it appeared that Egypt and Jordan, at least, would have been indeed willing, at long last, to renounce their former irredentism against Israel once and for all, if only they could secure the complete return of their territory. Again, however, this alternative was not adopted. A third alternative, which in fact was followed, was to use the victory for maximizing Israel's military predominance, thus confronting the Arabs with the toughest possible choice: either to continue the struggle on highly unfavorable terms, or to accept a full peace with Israel on terms that would provide her with military advantages for the future.

The latter alternative got the upper hand, just as the more militant alternatives had tended to get the upper hand on previous occasions from 1917 onward. Repeatedly over the years, the "hawks" had their way and in fact dragged many of the "doves" along with them. In the time of the British mandate the path of negotiation and compromise with the British government was ultimately rejected, and successfully so; in 1948 and 1949 the maximum was made of Israel's victory over the Arabs including the exclusion of the Arab refugees and the insistence on maximum territory boundaries. In the period of the armistice between the wars, the policy of major reprisals, encroachment on demilitarized zones, etc., was largely followed, apart from exceptions during certain periods. And now, in the aftermath of June 1967, again the hard line has been followed.

Why is this? Generally it appears that the hard line consistently emerges in Israel as the most plausible one both in the minds of national leaders (whom we have referred to earlier in the paper as revolutionaries) and among the security-minded masses. It is plausible because both these groups tend by instinct to read the worst into the intentions and character of the Arab adversary and to read the most into the opportunities that they see presented by circumstances offering them. Seizing on such opportunities (the annexation of East Jerusalem and the retention of other occupied territories, for example) obviously increases the intransigence of the Arabs, but to this dominant voices in Israel can readily retort that the Arabs are intransigent in any case on the things that matter, i.e., those having to do with recognition of Israel's basic right to exist as a Jewish state, so that it is better to offer the Arabs the hardest possible reality and force them to capitulate to it. Should it be argued that the Arabs cannot make such a capitulation—that peace in the foreseeable future is too much to demand of them—again there is a retort: very well, peace with the Arabs cannot now be made, but no peace is worthwhile anyway unless it involves a genuine transformation of Arab attitudes entailing a willingness to accept a strong and well-established Israel. If this involves a long wait, so be it; the dilemma will lie with the Arabs and not with Israel.

Oddly enough this intransigent line is one that appeals to both the most militant revolutionary attitudes in Israel—those of the Ben-Gurionists, Herut members, and others—and to many persons with a nonideological attachment to normalcy, who sense no need to run risks by making dangerous concessions to the Arabs and who prefer to take comfort from Israel's present military superiority. There is no urgency; time remains on Israel's side for some period yet, and painful choices are therefore to be avoided.

Vested Interests in the Continuation of the Conflict

Social psychologists have often told us that conflicts between groups may have their constructive psychological uses, and that they may be helpful in establishing the internal working order of social processes on both sides. To some extent it seems clear that we have such a case in the Middle East. Indeed, Arabs and Israelis commonly accuse each other of deliberately stimulating the conflict for their own internal purposes, and in this each side speaks a measure of truth.

This is a complex and risky field in which to venture, and the following remarks are offered only as tentative suggestions. I would at least maintain, however, that there is a considerable field for research in this area, both among Arabs and Israelis.

Perhaps the starting point for analyzing the functions of the conflict within Arab society is to paraphrase Lord Acton in reverse: "Weakness tends to corrupt, and absolute weakness corrupts absolutely." The Arabs have dealt with the Zionist movement, and subsequently the state of Israel, for over a half a century from a position of glaring weakness. They have failed systematically in Palestine since the time of the Balfour Declaration, and meanwhile they have faced enormous problems within their own societies in the uncertain process of modernization and development. They have been faced throughout their modern history by the anxiety-breeding presence of superior Western military, technological, and cultural power. Amid continuing signs of weakness and inadequacy on their part, the natural result has been for frustration to harden intransigent attitudes among the Arabs and in some respects to push elements of reality further and further into the background. Weakness has posed an emotional block to a balanced perspective.

This is not strictly a psychological problem, however, but also a political one, inasmuch as from the most rational point of view intransigence may at times be the most successful weapon available to the weak; and as already mentioned, it has always been plausible for Arab political strategists to argue that it was important not to bargain away material parts of their cause during a temporary period in which Arab bargaining power was low.

Alongside the overall background of weakness of the Arab position, a number of stock charges are commonly put forward to explain the Arab attitude. The common expression is that "if Israel did not exist the Arabs would have to invent her." This allegation subsumes a number of detailed considerations. Hatred of Israel is said to be the only thing that rival Arab states and factions are able to agree upon. We need to enter some reservation about this, since in terms of practical politics it is not accurate that Arabs have agreed on what to do about Israel. It might be more to the point to suggest that over the years the problem of what to do about Israel, coupled with the practical inability to do very much at all, has provided each Arab faction with a stick to beat the others with. It has thus stimulated rather than prevented conflict within the Arab world.

Another explanation is that Israel is a wedge or a barrier, physically speaking, to Arab unity and that to overcome this barrier, Arabs seeking unity have a vested interest in waging the struggle against her and pressing it even to the point of Israel's physical removal. Again serious reservations are in order: it may be very much doubted whether the physical barrier which Israel poses, for example, to land transportation between Egypt and the Fertile Crescent countries, has really been of much significance in explaining the failures of the Pan-Arab movement of the past twenty-two years.

Most importantly, however, those who say that the Arabs would have to invent Israel if she did not exist are pointing to psychological factors and particularly to the notion that the struggle with Israel enables the Arab states to avoid their own internal failures by distracting public attention from them. We should recall that the Arab-Israeli problem itself contributes to those failures not only by foisting the social and political burden of Palestinian refugee populations on a number of Arab governments, but also by undermining the reputation of each Arab regime and adding an enormous strain to national budgets in the form of military expenditures.

Nonetheless, despite the crudity of the general allegation that Israel is necessary for the Arabs there are some kernels of truth within it. For example, it has become a stock means of establishing elementary legitimacy for Arab politicians and public speakers to voice their extreme hostility toward Israel in a ritualistic manner, and this has had certain tangible effects. In addition to sticking in the mind of the Arab public and reinforcing its predisposition to pursue a militant line, the ritual has drugged the mind of the Arab public and deterred it from plunging into serious debate about Israel in which grave disagreements could well emerge to the surface. As long as it is physically possible for Arab states to see the conflict continue—as long as they can afford not to acquiesce in a definitive solution to it—it will be politic for them to avoid acrimonious internal debates over the problem. In this connection it is important not to delude ourselves into supposing that the point is now or has ever been close at hand at which the Arab states could no longer afford the continuation of the struggle, costly as it may be. The result, in any case, is not so much that the very existence of the conflict is a boon to the internal peace of Arab society—quite the contrary—but that given its existence, the path of least resistance within the Arab world is to avoid taking positive steps to settle it.

Turning to Israel, again we find a complex picture in trying to relate psychological and political components of the conflict. Just as on the Arab side we must be careful not to accept uncritically the proposition that the conflict is completely functional, so also on the Israeli side we must be careful not to imagine casually that "the only thing that Israel wants is peace" and that continuation of the struggle is completely useless and destructive from an Israeli point of view. On balance it would appear to me in fact that the continuation of the struggle is at least as functional for Israeli psychological and political purposes as it is for Arab ones, although it assumes different forms in each case.

Again, as we said of the Arabs, weakness corrupts. But here again we are not speaking of a continuing present weakness, but of lingering psychological memories of past helplessness through the ages, culminating in the Holocaust. Nor, unlike the Arab case, are we referring to any current element of frustration or ineptitude on the Israeli side.

Zionism arose in part as a reaction within Jewish society against the historic situation in which the task of the weak was to accommodate himself as best he could to a society of hostile and stronger neighbors, in which he made compromises and adjusted himself in tentative and insecure fashion to the best of his ability. The tradition of the ghetto and the overpowering symbol of the Holocaust have meant for Israel that one protects himself and builds his future only by his own efforts, and, for some Israelis, that power emerges from the barrel of a gun. It has meant a systematic distrust of intermediaries and outside patrons such as the British mandate or the United Nations, and it has also meant a distrust of any reliance on half-promises or even full promises emanating from the Arab side.

It is this kind of self-reliant and suspicious psychology on which Israel was built, a psychology which stemmed from circumstances of bitter struggle and memories of danger. Struggle and danger have meant the continuation of special determination, ruthless and forceful leadership, and social cohesion that have made Israel what she is today. Throughout the mandate period the Jewish community in Palestine was in a way a garrison society; Israel was born in 1948 as very much of a garrison state, and she has thrived as one since that time. The psychological benefits of the presence of continuing dangers on the frontiers may seem dubious to many people in the final balance of things, but thus far they have played a major part in Israel's success, and those concerned with Israel's future welfare cannot dismiss them lightly. What would become of the Zionist commitment and of patriotic enthusiasm within Israel, and within Jewish communities outside, should Israel one day become a secure, peaceful, obscure, humdrum Middle Eastern state like any other? At the very least it would mean the end of the revolutionary character of Israel's leadership, and it would surely open the door to much more intense internal conflict between rival factions than has been allowed to surface heretofore.

This applies not only to Israelis but perhaps even more importantly to the level of support and enthusiasm of foreign Jewish communities, particularly in the United States. Before the 1956 and 1967 wars, attitudes toward Israel among Jewish communities abroad, while certainly positive in general, were marked by a certain degree of uneasiness and criticism about hardline elements of Israel's position toward the Arabs. The actual eruption of hostilities, however, while underlining Israel's generally exposed position, seems to have had the effect of stifling such misgivings and stimulating enthusiasm. The reaction of the American Jewish community to the June War is a case in point, in which the deliverance of Israel from an apparent threat of extermination gave rise to a vast emotional and financial outpouring.

Thus, in a sense it may be that if the Arabs did not exist it would be necessary for Israel to invent them. At least, this proposition seems as plausible a one as the reverse.

Religious Overtones of the Conflict

Under this heading what I emphatically do not have in mind is the false notion, widespread among ill-informed people, that the Arab-Israeli conflict is a contemporary extension of some age-old religious antagonism between Muslims and Jews. Instead I refer simply to aspects of the current mentality of each side, in which the conflict lends itself to symbolism of a quasi-religious kind, either directly in the context of the religious traditions of Islam and Judaism or in a more general context that we can recognize as having a religious quality.

Both Judaism and Islam offer their adherents a religious view of history, entailing a strong traditional concept of the workings of a divine hand in human affairs. This is evident from the texts both of the Old Testament and the Koran. More particularly, the concept stems from the historical mythology of the early Judaic and Islamic communities, which were politically organized as nations of believers invoking special divine protection and in pursuit of a special divinely promised destiny of earthly as well as spiritual salvation. Both, furthermore, were in prolonged periods of armed conflict with nonbelievers, in which their successes were directly attributed, according to their tradition, to divine favor.

More than this, it has been part of the tradition of each religion to portray God as putting his chosen community of the faithful to the test, and submitting them to failure, hardship, and suffering prior to the bestowal of ultimate salvation, once it was merited by their steadfastness. This has been a much more explicit and prominent Jewish tradition than a Muslim one, yet the Muslims' traditional view of their own history does give great weight to the idea that the worldly success of the community depends upon its religious piety, that the destruction of Baghdad by the Mongols (like the destruction of the Jewish Temple by the Romans) was a form of visitation of divine wrath, and that Muslims are destined to rule themselves and not to fall subject to the rule of others provided they prove themselves spiritually worthy.

From today's perspective, it might be said that in the religious imagery of the Israeli side, the time of Jewish suffering has passed and the rise of the Israeli state is an assurance of its nonrecurrence, while from the standpoint of the Palestinians and other Arabs, the time of suffering is now. It is possible for Arabs to compare their present plight to such past episodes as the Crusades, but what might strike an outsider as even more significant is the parallel between the symbolic reference points of today's Palestinians and those of the traditions of the Jews. The refugee camps of eastern Jordan, Lebanon, and the Gaza Strip are the Sinai-like wilderness, awaiting the appearance of an Abraham or a Moses to lead his people into the Promised Land, now inhabited by an insolent and godless population of barbarians. At the same time, since 1948 we have witnessed a considerable tendency among some Arabs to imagine that a mere blast of the trumpet by their equivalent of Joshua would suffice to cause Israeli walls to come tumbling down.

Meanwhile, as the Arab diaspora continues, a vision has grown of Palestine as a land of milk, honey, and orange groves, stolen from its rightful owners by the unbelievers. Refugee children are taught catechism-like assertions of their Palestinian origin and pledges of their determination to return, as if to say: "Lest I forget thee, O Jerusalem (or Jaffa, Haifa, or Ramle)"; and the incantation of political declarations on Palestine by both private individuals and public figures resembles the recital of ritual oaths and prayers. The Arabs now solemnly celebrate their own ritual Days of Atonement on 2 November (the anniversary of the Balfour Declaration), 15 May (Israeli independence), and 5 June (the outbreak of the Six-Day War).

Last but not least, there is the vision of the millenium, in the form of the decisive Arab victory and the Return from the diaspora to a "secular democratic Palestine" (surely a religious vision, despite the reference to secularism). The oft-repeated willingness of Arabs to wait 100 years or more, until the return is enacted by their grandchildren's grandchildren and the easy assumption that their determination will not flag during the interim bear the mark of religious conviction rather than political judgment.

The religious symbols on the Jewish side of the conflict are more explicit, and the transition from Biblical faith to the modern political struggle is more direct. For Zionists it is easy to see the twentieth century reenactment of Biblical history: the migration into Palestine after prolonged wanderings in the diaspora; to some, the quasi-prophetic mystique of David Ben-Gurion; the battle with the Canaanites, and the miraculous tumbling of Jericho's walls. Traditional prayers and Biblical passages are full of references to the people of Israel, to Jerusalem, and so on. It seems at first remarkable, although on closer examination it is really not at all surprising, how "religious" the convictions of nonreligious Israelis and other Jews can be about the sanctity of their cause, their moral title to possession of the land, the centrality of the city of Jerusalem and the Wailing Wall to the national purpose of Israeli life, the significance of maintaining Israel as a Jewish rather than multireligious society, and overall, the sense of historic destiny surrounding Israel's place in the world.

The seeming reenactment of Biblical history and other religious overtones in Israel's situation are sharpened by the unremitting hostility of the Arab enemy, for this hostility provides the conflict with an atmosphere of Armageddon-like totality and finality, of fateful portentousness, of moral challenge and involvement that might not otherwise have been present. And in turn, the religious atmosphere can only encourage in Israelis and their sympathizers a sense of the specially ordained righteousness of their cause, of being charged with a sacred mission to see the conflict through to its successful end steadfastly and determinedly refusing to yield to the temptations of half-solutions by means of compromise and modus vivendi.

Conclusions

It is fashionable in some circles, after describing the tragedies and complexities of the Arab-Israeli conflict to public audiences, to profess to see light at the end of the tunnel. I see none. What I have tried to suggest is that the hard-line political strategies predominantly pursued by both sides over the past two generations have been continuously reinforced by the accretion of psychologically comforting but politically destructive self-justifications and distorted perceptions of the adversary, culminating in a spirit in each camp of rigid self-righteousness. The prospects for settlement would be dim enough were God thought to be a partisan of either protagonist; but alas, he has emerged as the ally of both. It seems clear that if both Israel and the surrounding Arab society are capable of sustaining the conflict indefinitely into the future, it is not because it will really profit them, but because the material price they pay is easier to sustain than the abandonment of their respective myths.

CHAPTER 2

Arabism: An Ecological Variable in the Politics of the Middle East

WILLARD A. BELING

Distributed geographically, people are as much geographic objects—either individually or in groups—as mountains and rivers. Relationships between different human groupings within a geographic habitat, therefore, are valid ecological relationships, as real as those between humans and nonhuman objects of the environment. This is political ecology.

Identifying the Arab world first as an environed entity surrounded by nonhuman and human objects, Willard A. Beling then defines Arabism as its most important entity-attribute. It affects relationships between the Arabs and all environing peoples, both non-Arab and non-Islamic. The author also treats certain countervailing characteristics—i.e., environing conditions—of the environing peoples. Some of these almost guarantee hostile interrelationships between the environed Arab world and its milieu, e.g., between the Arabs and Israelis.

Are these characteristics fixed? Does the ecological framework suggest a deterministic pattern? Given the characteristics of the environed entity and its milieu, for example, what are the prospects for Arab-Israeli peace?

The term ecology derives etymologically from a Greek word meaning the study of the house and, by extension, the study of the environment in which something lives. All definitions are concerned with three elements that form an integral ecological framework which will collapse if any single element is removed: environment, environed organism(s), and interrelationships. This is the ecological triad.

Departing from a tendency of general ecologists to envisage the environment in nonhuman terms—that is, limited to the physical environment—political ecologists use the term environment more broadly to embrace both nonhuman and social phenomena. They frequently substitute, therefore, milieu for environment, because it conveys social implications more clearly. Living people emerge as both the environed organism(s)—treated individually or collectively—and as part of the milieu (or environment). Relationships between different human groupings within a geographic habitat, therefore, are valid ecological interrelationships, as real as those between humans and their nonhuman environment.[1]

The Environed Organism

Selection of any geographical region and, within it, particular human groupings to focus on, of course, is an arbitrary matter. One could select any number of communities in the Middle East. There, for example, both the Arab world and Israel lend themselves to the role of environed organisms. For purposes of this study, however, the Arab world has been selected for this role. It has been involved over a very long period of history with its non-Arab milieu, thus providing a variety of political interactions from which to draw observations, plus a period long enough to test these observations. Of equal significance, the Arab world can also be identified as a distinct political community within the international political system.[2]

1. The author has found particularly helpful the various studies of Harold and Margaret Sprout, e.g., *An Ecological Paradigm for the Study of International Politics,* Woodrow Wilson School of Public and International Affairs Center of International Studies Research Monograph no. 30 (Princeton: Princeton University Press, 1968); *The Ecological Perspective on Human Affairs, with Special Reference to International Politics* (Princeton: Princeton University Press, 1965); *Toward a Politics of the Planet Earth* (New York: Van Nostrand Reinhold Co., 1971); and their many articles. See also Bruce M. Russett, *International Regions and the International System: A Study in Political Ecology* (Chicago: Rand McNally & Co., 1967).

2. Relative to this last point, when Bruce M. Russett embarked on his study of international political regions, he noted that he had no a priori judgments as to the number of regions, what they are, or where they should be found. (Russett, *International Regions,* delineated international regions on the basis of the following five criteria: relative cultural homogeneity, similar political attitudes and UN voting patterns, sharing membership in international organizations, trade relations, and geographical contiguity.) Indeed, his first question was "what is a region?" He acknowledged that the notion of a region may well be valid, but he correctly observed that a region varies according to the definitions given to it, as Roderic H. Davison illustrated so well in his article, "Where is the Middle East?" *Foreign Affairs* 38, no. 4 [July 1960]: 665–75.) Using an entirely inductive method, Russett suggested that his groupings would probably

Although frowned upon theologically in classical Islam, Arabs were an elite grouping in the early days of Islam. They subsided subsequently and completely disappeared as the elites within the Islamic community, but then reemerged in the late nineteenth century totally a la mode as Arab nationalists pitted against Ottoman Turks. Arabism won international legitimacy during the Arab Revolt of World War I, and also during World War II, when Arab nationalism again served British interests in the Middle East.

In the meantime, Arabism has come to predominate as a nationalist phenomenon, distinct from Pan-Islamism and in many ways opposed to it. That Arabism is a higher form of Islamic elitism (and Pan-Arabism an elite form of Pan-Islamism) may be overstating the case. Nevertheless, Arabism as a distinct nationalist phenomenon within Islam and, of course, within the Middle East is a reality.[3] Indeed, Arabism marks the region as indelibly as its geographic characteristics. This is the *Arab* World! It is the thesis of this chapter that as an ecological variable (political rather than physical, to be sure), Arabism plays a very important role in the politics of the Middle East.

be equivalent to a geographer's *regional types* rather than the regions of the regionalists. But significantly, the Middle East emerged as a distinct region in his quantitative study, as it also had in Leonard Binder's earlier, but quite different, traditional study. ("The Middle East as a Subordinate International System," in idem, *The Ideological Revolution in the Middle East* [New York: John Wiley & Sons, Inc., 1964], pp. 254–78, which had appeared earlier in *World Politics* 10, no. 3 [April 1958]: 408–29.) Both Russett and Binder also found an *Arab* cluster within the Middle East, although the latter concerned himself primarily with the larger Middle East itself. He used the existence of a *religious alternative to nationalism* as the major criterion for delimiting the Middle East as an international political subsystem. Accordingly, his Middle East embraced everything from North Africa to Afghanistan and Pakistan. But one can refine further the Middle Eastern subsystemic phenomenon; there is an Arab cluster which derives from both Binder's and Russett's criteria. For Arabism is also a distinct religio-nationalist phenomenon. (Islam is inalienably associated with Arabism, for example. Being Arab means being Muslim, according to Morroe Berger, *The Arab World Today* [New York: Doubleday, 1962], pp. 335–36. See also in this regard, Michel Aflaq, *Fi Sabil al-Ba'ath* [In the cause of the Ba'ath] [Beirut, 1963], pp. 50–60.) Binder hints at the Arab clustering—his thrust, of course, was regional—but Russett's quantitative analysis clearly identifies an Arab clustering within the Middle East.

3. See Adel Daher, *Current Trends in Arab Intellectual Thought*, RM-5979-FF (The RAND Corp., 1969), p. 5, who notes the ideological conflict between the two nationalist ideologies (i.e., between Pan-Arabism and Pan-Islamism) and the attempts of Arab intellectuals to rationalize Pan-Arabism over against Pan-Islamism.

Arab-milieu Interrelationships

In ecological terms, Arabism is a clear-cut case of an entity-attribute, in fact, the most important political entity-attribute of the Arab world. It affects relationships between Arabs and all environing peoples, both non-Arab and non-Islamic.

To illustrate the term within a general ecological framework, one can point to the failure of tropical fruit trees to grow in northern climes. But while one could say that the failure stems from the fruit trees' intolerance of the cold, an entity-attribute, another could argue that it is the climate which is at fault, an environing condition.[4] Both are involved, in fact, just as both entity-attributes and environing conditions are involved in the interrelationships between the Arab world and its milieu.

1. ARABISM: ENTITY-ATTRIBUTE

Sometimes dismissed as mere Arab xenophobia, Arab intolerance of Israel or the West is more than this. It is also more than just the nationalism that is common to all nations which seek to win their sovereignty, or to maintain it, after it has been won. In the Arab world, the struggle to rid the Middle East of alien forces derives from the peculiar nature of Arab nationalism.

a) Non-Islamic Intrusions

Being in large measure Islamic, Arabism is naturally intolerant of non-Islamic intrusions in the Arab world. In the Islamic Community of the past, this had been articulated theologically for community implementation (e.g., in the *jihad*). In the contemporary "secular" Arab world, on the other hand, it has been implicit rather than explicit. Articulation is, in essence, unnecessary; it would be redundant. For intolerance of non-Islamic intrusions is as much an accepted fact within the Arab nation as it was in the earlier theological *al-Ummah al-Islamiyyah* ("Islamic community"). The latter has provided, as is well known, inspiration as well as etymology to the *al-Ummah al-Arabiyyah* ("Arab nation").

Arabism is an all-pervasive political entity-attribute; it exists throughout the Arab world. For some Arab states, it has meant

4. See Sprout and Sprout, *An Ecological Paradigm* for an enlargement of this figurative parallelism.

THE ENVIRONED ARAB WORLD

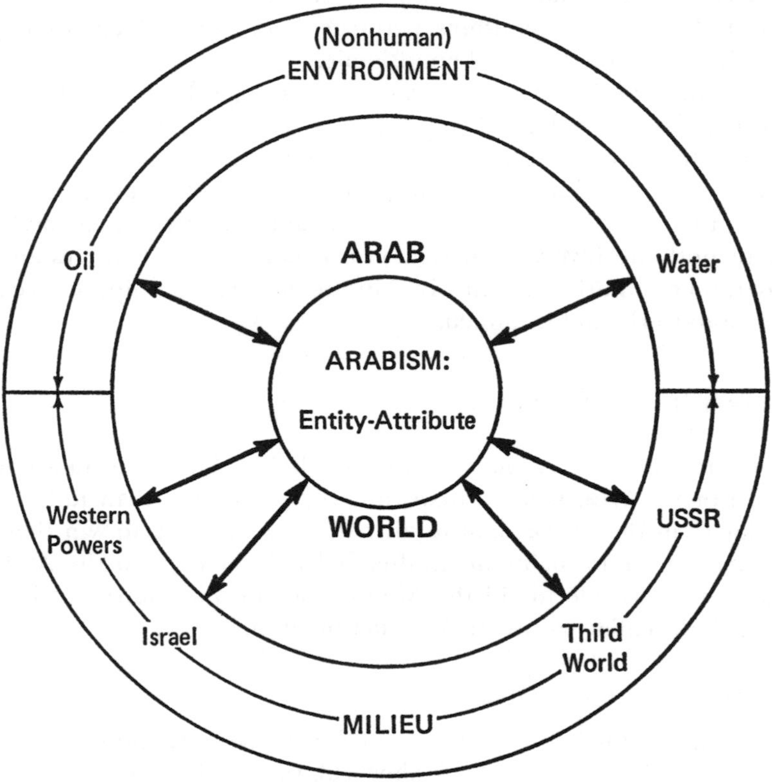

commitments against intrusions wherever they occur in the Arab world, as reflected in Nasser's oft-repeated analogy: "If there is a hole in the bottom of the boat [i.e., a threat to Arabism anywhere in the Arab world]. . . ." For others, such as Morocco, Jordan, Saudi Arabia, or Tunisia, it has not meant the same conspicuous commitment that Syria, Egypt, Libya, or Algeria have made. Nevertheless, these so-called conservative Arab states subscribe to the same Arabism, albeit in a more reserved fashion. All have opposed non-Islamic intrusions in the area, most obviously those from the West that had dominated the area for years.

b) Non-Arab Intrusions

Arabism is by its very nature also xenophobic toward all non-Arab intrusions, be they Muslim or otherwise. Observers tend sometimes to forget, for example, that Arab nationalism's original spark derived from the struggle against the Muslim Turks, rather than from anti-Westernism. While the present Turkish-Arab antipathies grew out of Ataturk's policy of turning one's back on the former Ottoman provinces in the Arab world and Islam, the Turkish annexation of Alexandretta, designs (real and imagined) on territory in the Fertile Crescent, and Turkey's NATO alliance, they also derive in some measure from Arab memories of the relatively recent Ottoman hegemony in the Arab world. Turkey now falls, therefore, almost completely within the European, instead of the Middle Eastern, clustering.[5] In the subsystemic Arab-Israeli conflict, moreover, Turkey has maintained relations with the Israelis.

Arabism as an entity-attribute also helps explain Arab-Iranian dissonance in international affairs, particularly relative to Israel and the West. When the Arabs refused to sell Israel crude oil, for example, Iran supplied them with it. Similarly, Iran associated itself with the Western defense system which the Arabs had rejected. Arab Muslims (Sunnis) regard Persians as second-class Muslims, of course, because they are Shi'ite Muslims. Moreover, they are non-Arabs. The North African Berbers and other non-Arab communities had been Arabized, for the most part, as well as Islamized. Thus, they became

5. See Binder, *Ideological Revolution* and Russett, *International Regions*. Further to apparent Arab elitism vis-à-vis non-Arab Turks or other Muslims, see Abd al-Rahman al-Bazzaz, "Islam and Arab Nationalism," in Sylvia G. Haim, *Arab Nationalism: An Anthology* (Berkeley and Los Angeles: University of California Press, 1962), pp. 172–88. He notes regarding the Turks, for example, that "the Moslem Arabs were . . . in spite of external appearances, his [the Muslim Turk's] real colonizers, mentally, spiritually, and culturally" (p. 185).

Arabs *musta'ribah* ("Arabs"). The Persians, on the other hand, had rejected Arabization. Indeed, they have an intense pride in their own rich historical and cultural pre-Islamic past; e.g., the lavish 2,500th anniversary celebration in 1971 of the reign of Cyrus the Great. In more recent years, Persians have also been turning from Islamic, and thus Arabic, given names to classical Iranian names. This again distinguishes them from the Arab world. For the Arab world focuses logically on Islamic rather than pre-Islamic beginnings, since these represent the *al-jahiliyyah* ("time of ignorance"), particularly for the Arabs as Arabs. Limited physically to Arabia, Arabs per se were indeed comparatively few in numbers and without any history to speak of prior to Islam. In essence, the emergence of the Arabs not merely as Muslims but as Arabs coincided with the coming of the Prophet Muhammad. An Arab himself, he brought them into their own. Deriving from these apolitical beginnings, religio-political Arabism has developed occasionally at the expense of good relations with non-Arabic Islamic states like Iran and Turkey.

2. ISRAELI ENVIRONING CONDITION

The religio-nationalist phenomenon, of course, also prevails in Israel where it triggers crises from time to time, with concomitant responses in international Jewry.[6] Obvious cases in point are the who-is-a-Jew incidents.[7] But these are only the overt symptoms of a much larger problem that concerns not only citizenship for immigrating Jews (the Law of the Return), but also the class of citizenship one is entitled to in Israel. Non-Jews, for example, do not enjoy first-class Israeli citizenship. Without the fuss or world-press coverage that accompanies the first, the Israelis have used a time-honored process to deal with this second problem.

To cope with the personal legal status of its non-Jewish citizens

6. See Binder, *Ideological Revolution,* who posits the religio-nationalist phenomenon for the entire Middle East. It should be pointed out, of course, that some observers hold another point of view. Dudley Kirk, for example, in Hans W. Weigert et al., eds., *Principles of Political Geography* (New York: Appleton-Century-Crofts, Inc., 1957), pp. 405–39, insists that Israeli nationalism is almost indistinguishable from secular nationalism in Western Europe and that Arab-Israeli conflict is almost exclusively a political, national, and cultural, rather than religiously sponsored, phenomenon—a reading which is inadequate in the author's opinion.

7. See the *Los Angeles Times,* 25 January and 17–19 June 1970 and 27 September 1971 regarding who-is-a-Jew crises in Israel.

who do not fall under the religious (rabbinic) law of the state. Israel applies in modified form a *millet* system which they inherited from the British. In earlier times, the Muslims had devised the millet system to cope with non-Muslims, particularly Jews and Christians, within the Islamic community. It is somewhat ironical, therefore, that Israel now applies a similar system to its own Muslim and Christian minorities. It is also anachronistic, of course, since the millet system has essentially disappeared elsewhere in the Middle East.

The point to be made, of course, does not concern the validity or morality of the Israeli millet system. Rather, it illustrates the nature of the state. Related ecologically to the environed Arab world, Israeli religio-nationalism is an environing condition that is equally as intolerant as Arabism, the entity-attribute of the Arab world. Together, of course, they practically guarantee hostile interrelationships at the international level between Arabs and Israelis. Indeed, peace in the Middle East between Arabs and Jews is remote, if not impossible, when considered within this framework alone.

3. THIRD WORLD ENVIRONING CONDITION

Interrelationships between the Arab world and the Third World can also be analyzed within this same ecological framework. While attempting to woo the Third World to its side in its struggle against Israel, for example, the Arab world frequently finds that Arabism unhinges its best conceived efforts. A clear case in point occurred at the Pan-African Cultural Congress which Arab Algeria sponsored in July 1969. Irrepressible Arabism asserted itself over against négritude, an environing condition of the African milieu, and an open conflict between Arabism and négritude undid much of what the Arabs hoped to achieve at the congress.[8]

4. ARAB ENTITY-ATTRIBUTE VIS-À-VIS THE SOVIET UNION

Most popular political treatments of the Middle East place it within a cold war framework, particularly as the Soviets enhance their position in the Middle East at the expense of the West. Israel and the Arabs are then cast as the good guys and bad guys, respectively: in essence, Israel represents the United States, while the Arabs rep-

8. Cf. *Le Monde Diplomatique* 16, no. 185 (October 1969).

resent the Soviets. But the ecological framework provides still another perspective. As an entity-attribute, for example, Arabism practically precludes fraternal interrelationships with the non-Islamic non-Arab milieu, be it Israeli, Western, or Soviet. Even while using Soviet weapons and support in its attempt to rid the Middle East of Israel, therefore, the Arab world is unlikely to embrace either the Soviet Union or its ideology.

Arab antipathy toward Soviet intrusions in the Middle East has not been articulated, of course, to the same degree as it has been vis-à-vis the Western Powers and Israel. But then the Soviet role in the area has also been somewhat dissimilar. The Russians have never occupied any Middle Eastern area, for example, even though they might want to (e.g., their abortive attempt to take over Persian Azerbaijan in 1945). Moreover, the Soviets have been actively aiding the Arabs against Israel. Yet, while the Arab world appreciates Soviet assistance in its subsystemic struggle, Arabism is very strongly opposed to the penetration of Soviets and Soviet ideology in the Middle East.

The grip that Arabism holds even on revolutionary Arabs confuses the Soviets and, in fact, the Left in general. The achievement of Algerian independence in 1962, for example, was due, at least in part, to moral and material support from the Left. In turn, the Left expected a positive response from the Algerians. But their revolutionary Algerian colleagues endorsed "old fashioned" Arabic instead of French as the national language of independent "revolutionary" Algeria, and "regressive" Arabism as Algerian national policy—all leaving the French Left, among others, aghast.[9] Amar Ouzegane, former General Secretary of the Algerian Communist party, was an excellent example of this phenomenon. Published during this period, his *Le Meilleur Combat* was intended to be a defense of socialism, but turned out instead to be a pure and simple apology for Arabism over against Marxism.[10]

Another case in point of Arab-Soviet ideological conflict occurred in 1957 when Syria appeared to be on the verge of slipping into

9. See *l'Express*, 1962. In this regard, see also Damien Helie, "L'Autogestion industrielle en Algérie," *Autogestion*, Cahier no. 9–10 (September–December 1969): 37–57, who, while pleased that Algeria had adopted a socialist format, notes: "Up to the present, Algerian socialism is much more colored by the specific [i.e., Arabo-Islamism] than by Marxism."

10. Ouzegane, *Le Meilleur Combat* (Paris: René Julliard, 1962). It had been written originally, quite significantly for the Algeria of that period, in Arabic. See the author's review of the book in the *Maghreb Digest* 4, no. 1 (January 1966): 53.

orbit as a Soviet satellite. At the behest of the Syrians, Egypt bailed Syria out by creating the United Arab Republic. More recently, a bloody anti-Communist putsch took place in the Sudan in 1971, after the Sudanese Left, apparently with tacit Soviet approval and support, had seized power. In 1972, President Sadat reduced the Soviet presence in Egypt to a mere shadow of its former self. Ideological considerations, among others, were an important input in the Egyptian decision-making process.

In the meantime, of course, most of the Arab states had long since outlawed their local Communist parties. From all available evidence, therefore, the Soviets appear as frustrated as the Western powers had been in the area.

Restructuring Ecological Imbalances

Unappreciated by many observers, the Arab world has really been phenomenally successful over a relatively short span of time in restructuring the disadvantageous interrelationships which it faced at the turn of the century.

1. WESTERN INTRUSIONS

Non-Islamic/non-Arab intrusions have in large measure been eliminated from the Middle East. Turkish hegemony of the Arab world passed away in World War I, and the subsequent Western occupations were lifted from large areas of the Middle East during and after World War II. Only vestiges of the former colonial empires still remain in the Middle East. Pitting in the meantime the major actors of the international system against one another, the Arab world has successfully resisted most subsequent attempts at occupation (or reoccupation) of the Middle East. Whether or not it should be considered in the same framework, the United States has nevertheless also relinquished almost all of the bases it had established in the Middle East during the height of Soviet-American tensions.

Western economic intrusions in the area have also been reduced considerably since the days of the Ottoman Empire. Capitulations to foreigners, which became the rule during the Ottoman Empire, continued in effect for some time in various Middle Eastern states even after its demise. In the meantime, however, Western-owned operations have been gradually Arabized. Egypt took a major step in this direction when it nationalized the Suez Canal Company and, in the wake of the Anglo-French attack in November 1956, most of the foreign-owned companies and banks. Syria and Iraq have been equally effective in eliminating foreign-owned operations. While the Arabs had not nationalized on a significant scale foreign-owned oil operations, they had taken over the domestic marketing of petroleum products in a number of states. In a less dramatic, but equally effective move, they Arabized large areas of the manning patterns of foreign-owned oil operations. Up until the 1970s Arab nationalists had hesitated to move impetuously, or alone, to nationalize foreign-owned oil interests in the Middle East, since the very real problems implicit in Iran's failure to nationalize its oil operations in the early 1950s were still valid. In the meantime, the trend toward nationalization is building in the Arab world; e.g., Iraq nationalized the Iraq Petroleum Company (IPC) outright in 1972, while the other Persian Gulf states were negotiating for a share of the foreign-owned oil companies operating within their boundaries.

Achieving independence later than most in 1962, Algeria has nevertheless been more effective in Arabizing its economy than almost any other Arab state. The colons had themselves opted to vacate their agricultural domains and quit Algeria on the eve of Algerian independence, as did most of the French entrepreneurs in the Algerian economy. Algerians merely took over what they left behind. When they then negotiated their oil concession agreement with the French in 1965, the Algerians took advantage of the past experiences, and talents, of their Arab colleagues. Planning ahead in the meantime at an even more sophisticated level, the Algerian government next employed an American consulting firm to help nationalize the domestic marketing of petroleum products, a domain dominated by foreign-owned companies (among them American companies). Continuing its drive toward Algerianization of the oil industry, they then nationalized in 1971 51 percent of the French oil operations that remained.

Elsewhere in the Maghreb, Libya has also won significant gains from the foreign-owned oil operations, yet nationalizing only one company's operations (British Petroleum) so far. Although Tunisia has reversed major areas of its economic policies since the ouster of Ahmed Ben Salah as head of planning in the fall of 1969, nationalization and rigorous Destourian Socialism had already eliminated most foreigners from the Tunisian economy. Of all the Arab states, Morocco retains the largest colony of foreigners in the local economy.

2. THE ARAB-ISRAELI IMBALANCE

Arab success vis-à-vis Israel, however, is an entirely different matter. Their own contributions to the fact apart, the Arabs had seen the non-Arab Turks driven from the area during World War I, and their non-Islamic/non-Arab successors in the process of leaving the Middle East during, and following, World War II. From the Arab point of view, therefore, the creation of the state of Israel in 1948 was particularly ironical. It portended involvement with a new—at least to them—"intruder" in the Arab world, the non-Islamic/non-Arab Israelis, plus the possible return of the Western powers in the wake of the Israeli intrusion.

Failing on their own in 1948 to eliminate Israel, the Arabs went to the only armorer available to them in the international political system, the Soviet Union. This act catapulted the Middle East into the cold war framework. Added to another very important input, viz., from the American domestic political system, it assured Israel of American military, financial, and moral support. In the meantime, the Arabs have suffered two more military defeats at the hands of Israel, which has indeed enlarged its area at the expense of the Arabs. While quite successful against the Western powers, therefore, Arab efforts to restructure the disadvantageous interrelationships with Israel have so far obviously failed.

The Potential for Change in the Environed Organism

While one speaks of "natural balance" in general ecology, this concept does not apply in human ecology because of the human factor. Man's potential, indeed, his propensity to change the environment, of course, was the spark that ignited popular interest in general ecology in the 1960s. Needless to say, his ingenuity carries over into man-milieu interrelationships, where flux rather than the status quo is the norm.

Various means to measure the potential of a given nation exist. Many analyses begin, for example, with an inventory of a nation's resources. A more feasible approach, perhaps, is to evaluate the limitations on achievements vis-à-vis the Arab-milieu interrelationships.[11]

11. For this approach the author is indebted to Sprout and Sprout, *An Ecological Paradigm*, p. 35 and following.

1. TECHNOLOGICAL LIMITATIONS

In terms of technological limitations, of course, the Arab world itself is currently unable to restructure disadvantageous interrelationships in its favor. Technological limitations in the military are a case in point. France's decision after the Six-Day War to supply Libya with a large number of jet fighters was not really meaningful, for example, since Libyan pilots were unavailable, and will not be available for a long time in the future, to fly the sophisticated aircraft. Nasser candidly admitted that Egypt lacked trained personnel to operate the military hardware which the Soviet Union had lavished upon it since 1955. This was obvious, of course, in the confrontations of 1956 and 1967. Maneuvering within this reality, the White House justified its refusal on several occasions to provide the additional jet aircraft that Israel insistently demanded to restore the arms "balance" in the Middle East.

But this sort of limitation is not absolute. Tools can be acquired, as both Arabs and Israelis have so clearly demonstrated, and skills can be developed in both environed and environing human organisms. Although the Arabs acquired military hardware more quickly and in greater abundance than the Israelis, they have been slower in achieving the skills to use the matériel effectively. To cope with the technological imbalance, Egypt moved in two different directions: (*1*) it avoided jet combat with the Israelis, even dispersing its jet aircraft around the Middle East out of range of Israeli bombers, until it too could train a corps of skilled pilots. The Israelis sought to provoke the Egyptians into premature air combat, in turn, in order to eliminate Egyptian pilots before they reached skill levels that matched those of the Israelis; (*2*) Egypt imported skills to offset Israeli technical superiority. Soviet pilots, for example, substituted in certain situations—some still unclear to outside observers—for unskilled Egyptian pilots, thus injecting a new variable into the equation.

2. PERCEPTUAL LIMITATIONS

Perceptual limitations are also very important. The lack of Arab opportunity to perceive limiting factors which, if perceived, could be avoided and, in equal part perhaps, Arab failure to perceive the perceivable as such have both contributed to disadvantageous interrelationships. Ecologically, the former is an environing condition, unperceivable, while the latter is an entity-attribute inherent in the environed organism.[12]

Concealment, of course, will always limit perception. This is an environing condition within the environment/milieu. The ability to perceive the perceivable, on the other hand, is an entity-attribute which can be developed within the environed organism. The Arabs, for example, have sharpened their perception since 1948. Prior to the 1948 Arab-Israeli war, Arabs in general had blamed the Western Powers for Zionist successes. But following the 1948 defeat, they began to see that they themselves were the cause of their failure. Musa 'Alami and other nationalists urged,[13] therefore, and Arab politicians embarked upon, one reform after another—frequently undone, to be sure, in one military coup after another—to the end that Arabs would be able to stand up to the Israelis as their equals.

In the wake of the 1967 war, they finally recognized that neither the West nor the Arabs were the real cause of their failures. Instead, the Israelis were the cause and, even worse, there was little prospect that the Arabs would either catch up or defeat them in a head-on confrontation. Within this framework, Cecil Hourani's analysis shortly after the Arab defeat in 1967 is significant. Since the Arabs cannot catch up with the Israelis, it implies, relax and let the area catch up with them until they too become orientals like the Arabs! [14]

3. INADEQUATE RESOURCES

Finally, limitations deriving from inadequate resources are the most obvious. But while resources represent at any given moment absolute limitations, they are subject over time—sometimes relatively short periods—to transformation and change, particularly under the impact of dynamic human ingenuity. This, of course, sets man apart from all other environed entities. Kuwait, Saudi Arabia, Libya—all are excellent cases in point in the Arab world. Unimportant in the relatively recent past, they have in the meantime become important actors in the Middle Eastern subsystem through the exploitation of petroleum reserves.

12. Ibid.

13. See Musa 'Alami, *'Ibrat Falastin* [The lesson of Palestine] (Beirut, 1949).

14. Hourani, "The Moment of Truth," *Encounter* 29, no. 11 (November 1967): 3–14.

Change and Transformation in the Milieu

Two points on which general ecologists focus are the rates of natural and technological change, whether in military technology, population, or some other area. For when growth continues unabated, it reacts with some aspect of the ecological framework with important implications. Applying a much broader brush than will be used here, for example, Professor Russett suggests that the prospects for continued growth—both natural (e.g., population) and technological (e.g., military)—are so real that he anticipates a period of instability, at least, and perhaps violent change in the international system within the relatively near future.[15] Implicitly, of course, his conclusions also relate to the Middle East.

1. UNABATED TECHNOLOGICAL CHANGE AMONG THE MAJOR POWERS

The rate of technological change in the Soviet Union, particularly in the military, has had an important bearing on the Middle East. The Soviet advance from no nuclear capability at the end of World War II, to some capability in the 1950s, to parity with the United States in the late 1960s, to superiority in the early 1970s has been nothing short of phenomenal. Soviet advances in conventional military capabilities and deployment have paralleled nuclear development—all being reflected in strategic advances in the Middle East at the expense of the West.

a) Changes in Major Power Relations in the Middle East

The United States has been withdrawing gradually from its commitments overseas. Under pressure from other demands on its ultimately limited resources, the United States has not opted for the headlong retreat that some would like to see. Nevertheless, American withdrawal from involvements overseas is an obvious and continuing phenomenon that has an important bearing on the Middle East. The American withdrawal from the Middle East is more than matched by the growing Soviet military capability in the area. The American Sixth Fleet, for example, is no longer unchallenged in the Mediterranean. Further to the point, nuclear brinkmanship is far more dangerous today, and thus less likely to be employed in the

15. Bruce M. Russett, "The Ecology of Future International Relations," *International Studies Quarterly* 11, no. 1 (March 1967): 12–31.

Middle East, than it was say during the Cuban crisis in 1961, or during the 1967 Six-Day War, when President Johnson got on the hot line to the Kremlin to warn the Soviet Union against direct involvement in that conflict. Since 1967, large Soviet deployments of conventional military, air, and naval capabilities have taken place in the Middle East, while the American deployments have at best remained at the same level, if not in fact declined (e.g., the loss of Wheelus Air Base in Libya). In any case, the Soviet Union has greatly improved its military position in the Middle East vis-à-vis the United States.

The French and British withdrawals from the Arab world that precipitated, at least in part, direct American involvement in the area—i.e., to fill the so-called "vacuum" they had left in the area—are now in their last stages. The British withdrawal from "East of Suez" in 1971 terminated Britain's colonial involvement in the area. Now, just as the Americans succeeded Britain and France in the Middle East with a different style, the Soviet Union promises to replace the Americans in the area, but again with a different style. For while still intruded upon, the Arab world is now intruded upon at its own invitation. The Soviets are there to serve the subsystemic interests of the Arabs—unlike the Americans who were concerned with the larger systemic problems. American bases, for example, stood aloof from the area's conflicts; they were constructed for a Soviet, rather than Middle Eastern, confrontation. The Soviet military presence in the Middle East, on the other hand, is subsystemic in its orientation; e.g., Soviet missiles in Egypt are not targeted against the United States, but against Israel. That the Soviets also serve their own interests in the larger international system, however, is acceptable to the Arabs—but only in that order. If Arab interests were not first served, the Soviet presence would be as intolerable as the American presence had been.

b) Client-State Relationships in the Middle East

Historically, the Middle East subsystem has not been the master of its own fate: the major actors of the international system strongly influence the area. Like Egypt and several other Arab nations, therefore, Israel has opted for a client-state relationship outside the Middle East subsystem. Indeed, Israel now depends both militarily and economically upon the United States for its paramountcy within the Middle East subsystem, if not for its very existence. But the influence of Israel's patron nation (viz., the United States) is declining in the Middle East while that of the Arabs' patron nation (i.e., the Soviet Union) is rising. In addition to the client-state relationship, of course, Israel has additional backup in international Jewry, particularly in the West. It is estimated, for example, that the World Zionist movement has funneled five billion dollars into Israel since 1948. Roughly one billion dollars has come from the United States alone, or its citizens, since the Six-Day War.

Nevertheless, all is not rosy in Israel. Israel's trade deficit is reportedly in the area of one billion dollars annually. Inflation is an endemic problem, with devaluation of the Israeli pound a concomitant factor. The high costs of the military machine that it needs to defend itself, and Jewish immigration, which Israel encourages with special bonuses, have become public issues. They used to be discussed only within the government. International Jewry could help in the past to offset a large part of the deficits in the Israeli economy; they have become too large in recent years. In essence, Israel desperately needs outside aid, particularly aid from the American government, to achieve its national policy goals. But whether even the same rate of American aid will continue is a moot point, particularly as the American presence, not to mention its interest, declines in the area. If not, Israel will be forced to make serious adjustments in its national policy goals. For like Egypt, Israel has allocated its national resources very thinly on several fronts.

2. UNABATED GROWTH IN MILITARY TECHNOLOGY AND ARSENALS IN THE AREA

Unabated growth in military technology and arsenals in the Middle East has resulted in continuous Arab-Israeli conflict and hot wars. It promises more hot wars, perhaps even involving the major powers. But the unabated growth in technology could also mean the *immediate* resolution of the conflict situation: Israel apparently possesses nuclear military capabilities which it would quite certainly use, if it had to. Nevertheless, it would have to be more than localized nuclear war. For this would probably be no more effective than conventional warfare in resolving the Arab-Israeli conflict. World opinion would probably condemn, and then undo, Israeli use of nuclear weaponry, even on a local scale. The Arab states do not yet have nuclear capabilities, and appear a long way from achieving them. In any case, the unabated growth in military technology and conventional arsenals means continued efforts, through force, to correct imbalances that the Arab world feels exist between it and its milieu (e.g., Israel), and vice versa.

3. UNABATED POPULATION GROWTH

The relative sizes of Arab and Jewish populations have always been a serious concern, first to the early Zionists who sought in vain through Jewish immigration to build up a Jewish majority in Palestine, and later to Israel which has sought a larger population base to meet the threat implicit in the disproportionately Goliath-like Arab populations that surround it. But since 1967, the greatly disproportionate sizes of Israeli and Arab populations are only one part of the population problem. The new factor is the *higher growth rate* of the Arab population within Israel itself. For deriving from the conquests of the Six-Day War, the proportion of Palestinian Arabs to Jews within Israel's new boundaries rose to a level that, if their higher growth rate continues, Palestinian Arabs will outnumber Jews in Israel itself within a few decades, all other factors remaining constant.

Within this context, the campaign for the release of Soviet Jews to migrate to Israel is perhaps as much ecologically inspired as it is humanitarian: they are the last large group of Jews who might voluntarily migrate to Israel. The other large concentrations of Jews in Western Europe and the United States have not, for the most part, shown any inclination to migrate to Israel, although the rate picked up after the Six-Day War in 1967. In any event, Jewish immigration is basic to the survival of the Jewish character, if not the state itself, of Israel.

The environed Arab entity has reacted to the Jewish "intrusion" in the Middle East much as it had reacted to the Christian crusades. While they fought both intrusions, they failed to halt the occupations in the Middle East. Disproportionate populations were, however, one of several factors that led ultimately to the undoing of the Christian crusader states, as they also threaten Jewish Israel. The parallel cannot be forced, of course, since Israelis cannot *return* to their own states as the crusaders ultimately did to theirs.

4. UNABATED RESOURCE CONSUMPTION IN THE MILIEU

While treating the human milieu for the most part, the author is also interested in the nonhuman environment, particularly imbalances of natural resources in the Arab world and its milieu. Unabated growth in consumption of the limited resources, of course, exacerbates the conflict that already exists between the Arab world and its milieu. Water, short almost everywhere in the Middle East, and oil are two good cases in point.

a) Water Resources

Israel retained the Golan Heights following the Six-Day War in 1967 in the name of military security. But its decision to remain there derived also undoubtedly from hydrological considerations. For Israel had secured in this occupied area control over the headwaters of the Banyas River which Syria had threatened from time to time to divert away from Israel. The Banyas River is a tributary of the Jordan River.

Within this same hydrological need, suggestions have been made now and then since the Six-Day War that the Litani River, which unlike the Banyas River lies entirely outside Israel,[16] would make an ideal "natural" border between Lebanon and Israel. Palestinian guerrilla raids from south Lebanon have precipitated the suggestions following the Six-Day War. But Zionist/Israeli proposals to incorporate the Litani River into Israel's water resources had been made on many occasions, both considerably before the state of Israel was established and since 1948.[17]

Unabated Israeli industrial and population growth carries serious implications vis-à-vis the surrounding Arab states. If all the Soviet Jews migrated to Israel, for example, its population would immediately double itself, generating new pressures on Israel to enlarge its relatively limited water resources. Unless a concomitant technological breakthrough were achieved in the desalinization of sea water,

16. The Banyas, Hasbani, and the Yarmouk rivers rise in Arab states, but are tributaries of the Jordan River. The water of these rivers belongs, therefore, by international law to both Arabs and Israelis. Lying entirely within Lebanon, on the other hand, the Litani River belongs solely to Lebanon.

17. See, for example, "The Zionist Organization's Memorandum to the Supreme Council of the [Paris] Peace Conference, 3 February 1919," in J. C. Hurewitz, *Diplomacy in the Near and Middle East: A Documentary Record 1914–1956* (Princeton: D. Van Nostrand Co., Inc., 1956), 2:45 and following. In February 1954, Israel issued its so-called Cotton Plan—named after hydrologist-consultant John C. Cotton—which incorporated the Litani River in the development of the Jordan River watershed. For a treatment of this and other proposals, see Don Peretz, "Development of the Jordan Valley Waters," *Middle East Journal* 9, no. 4 (Autumn 1955): 397–412; and Georgiana G. Stevens, *Jordan River Partition* (Palo Alto: Stanford University Press, 1965).

in fact, Israel's increased demands for water might only be satisfied at the expense of its Arab neighbors; viz., from the Litani and Hasbani rivers in Lebanon, and the Yarmouk River between Jordan and Syria. These are the most obvious and available sources of water to meet Israel's growing demands.

b) Petroleum Resources

Unabated growth in the consumption of petroleum, and/or the concomitant depletion of petroleum reserves, will have an important bearing on interrelationships between the Arab world (which holds more than 75 percent of the world's proven oil reserves) and its milieu, which is far less abundantly endowed. The major source of energy in West Europe, for example, is now petroleum which, in turn, comes for the most part from the Arab world. For Europe as a whole has no significantly productive gas or oil fields of its own to replace Middle Eastern sources. The Rumanian oil fields, for example, apart from being located in East Europe, have been in decline for some years. As for the gas and oil discoveries in the North Sea, apparently they will not be able even to take care of the growth alone in consumption in Europe during the present decade.

Israel's critical lack of oil production was, of course, resolved in 1967 when it occupied Sinai which not only had established producing fields, but also newly discovered reserves. While not stated publicly as such, this as much as any other consideration influenced Israel to continue its occupation of Sinai. The Arab states had, of course, refused to sell oil to Israel. While Iran sold Israel oil, it had to pass through hostile waters, viz., the Red Sea and the Gulf of Aqaba. These considerations, therefore, weighed heavily against any decision to return Sinai to Egypt.

Petroleum production in the Middle East, which was roughly doubled between 1960 and 1970, promises to be more than doubled again in the next decade. Most of the production in the past had gone to the West European market, where consumption had risen phenomenally since World War II. But the demand for petroleum in the Soviet Union and its satellite states is apparently rising at a similarly rapid rate, but with a potential for growth that is even higher than in the West, that is, if consumer consumption is allowed to develop in East Europe. Soviet petroleum reserves had appeared adequate; the Soviets exported oil to the West. In the meantime, however, the Soviet Union had apparently concluded that its reserves were less adequate than they had once appeared to be. In any case, the Soviet Union in the late 1960s broke into the magic circle of Western, or pro-Western, oil operations in the Middle East, e.g., in Iran and Iraq, albeit using again a different style than the concession agreements that the Westerners had employed. The Soviet role in the Arab-Israeli conflict enhances their entrée throughout the Arab world, which until recently had been the chasse gardée of Western oil companies.

The Europeans had earlier equated Middle Eastern oil with their national interests. Britain publicly stated in the 1950s, for example, that it would go to war if its sources of oil in the Persian Gulf were threatened; in fact, it moved troops into Kuwait when Iraq threatened in 1959 to incorporate Kuwait into Iraq. But colonial troops no longer exist for this purpose, nor would they be adequate anymore to the task if they did. This explains, at least in part, the reorientation since 1967 of French and British policies vis-à-vis the Middle East. Decried as Gaullist anti-Semitism, for example, pro-Arabism became a fact in French policy after the Six-Day War in 1967. France switched from being armorer of Israel to armorer of the Arabs, particularly those with oil. Britain also revised its posture regarding the Arab-Israeli conflict, becoming less favorably inclined toward Israel.

In the late 1960s, pressures in the United States also began to build to remove, or at least relieve, import restrictions on foreign oil, essentially Middle Eastern oil. The Presidential Task Force on Oil Imports, for example, indicated that imports of Middle Eastern oil should be tripled.[18] Since 1971, "cheap" Middle Eastern oil no longer exists. But this has not obviated the other reason for importing Middle Eastern oil, viz., the rapid depletion of American oil reserves in the face of unabated growth in consumption. According to some estimates, petroleum reserves in the United States would hardly be adequate for another fifteen years at present consumption levels; enormous new reserves must be discovered. Contrary to the premature publicity the Alaskan discovery had been given, for example, some experts believe that it could provide at best only a two-year supply for the United States—i.e., if, over the objections of the environmentalists, it becomes possible to exploit the Alaskan reserves! Indeed, environmentalists will probably hasten the elimination, or reduction, of import controls on Middle Eastern oil.[19]

18. See *U.S. News and World Report,* 12 January 1970.

19. For background on Middle East and world oil developments, see *BP Statistical Review of the World Oil Industry—1968* (London: The British Petroleum Co., Ltd., 1969); Michael Tanzer, *The Political Economy of Inter-*

While substitutes exist for petroleum-derived energy in the form of coal, gas, hydroelectricity, atomic power, and so on, there is no indication that they will replace petroleum, or that alternative petroleum-producing areas will replace the Middle East in the foreseeable future. A new-found national interest in Arab oil may well vie, therefore, in the near future with American moral commitments to Israel. Moral commitments, of course, rank somewhat lower on the spectrum of national interests than security interests, whatever that may embrace. The sudden American switch vis-à-vis Nationalist China is one of the more recent cases in point.

In essence, the pendulum is apparently still swinging in favor of the environed Arab entity. While it is not an irresistible thrust, Arabization has grown steadily and strongly since World War I. It may well continue into the foreseeable future at the expense, ultimately, of Israel.

Conclusion

Arabism has been the major factor in the politics of the Middle East since the late nineteenth century: first vis-à-vis the Turks, then the French and British, followed by the Americans, and now Israelis. Entity-attributes are not immutably fixed—nor, for that matter, are environing conditions—particularly in human ecology, thus providing some hope for a peaceful resolution of the Middle Eastern conflict situation. Nevertheless, dramatic changes are unlikely in either the Arab entity-attribute or the Israeli environing condition in the foreseeable future.

Deploring or moralizing about the nature of the Arab world will not change it any more than they would change the physical entity-attributes of environed organisms, such as tropical fruit trees. Rather, nations must deal with the Arab world as it is. Committed to the defense of Israel, on the one hand, the United States has followed essentially a moral line. It hopes against hope that the Arab World will ultimately relent and accept Israel's presence in the Middle East. Dealing with the political realities of the area pragmatically, on the other hand—to the point of turning its back quite often on the local Communist parties—the Soviet Union has achieved significant advantages in the Middle East at the expense of

national Oil and the Underdeveloped Countries (Boston: Beacon Press, 1969); *Middle East Economic Survey; Petroleum Press Service;* and *World Petroleum.*

the Western Powers. But that Arabism will suddenly become nonoperative in Arab-Soviet interrelationships is also a complete misunderstanding of the situation.

The key to both American- and Soviet-Arab interrelationships at present, therefore, is obvious, viz., a correct attitude toward Israel. Withdrawal of its support of Israel will, for example, improve American-Arab interrelationships. But that this withdrawal of American support will also improve Arab-Israeli interrelationships does not follow. This is, of course, the dilemma of Washington's policy makers. Nor, ironically, will Soviet-Arab interrelationships necessarily deteriorate if the United States withdraws its support of Israel, since this is only one side of the coin—and another input into the dilemma of Washington's policy makers! For so long as Israel exists, the Arabs will object to it as an alien intrusion and welcome outside support to eliminate the Israeli intrusion.

As nation-statehood develops and blooms in the Middle East, one might expect it to replace Arabism. In essence, Egyptian, Syrian, and other forms of local nation-state nationalism will replace Arabism. Admittedly, it may well undo attempts at institutionalized Pan-Arab regional unification. But this is only one manifestation of Arabism, which exists as an entity-attribute of the Arab world whether or not institutionalized Pan-Arab unity exists.

The Palestinians are a good case in point of the relationship between burgeoning nationhood and Arabism. Like the earlier Algerians, they also had some difficulty in self-identification as a nation. Only through their experiences in refugee camps outside Palestine have they finally evolved into full-fledged "Palestinian" nationalists rather than merely Arab nationalists. But this reinforces, rather than eliminates, "Arab" involvement in the conflict with Israel. The Arab world logically continues, therefore, to use "Arab" instead of "Palestinian," even when referring to the guerrillas who are for the most part Palestinians. Western news media also use "Arab" instead of "Palestinian," to the apparent disservice of the Palestinians as such, albeit in unwitting recognition of an important political reality of the Middle East, Arabism.

Identified as an ecological phenomenon, Arabism becomes then as real as pigmentation or some other physical entity-attribute of a people. Frequently mislabeled anti-Semitism, Arabism would be what it is even if there were no Jews. This is the nature of the Arab world—and the dilemma it poses for American policy makers, not to mention all proponents of Arab-Israeli peace!

CHAPTER 3

The Arab Cold War

GEORGE LENCZOWSKI

One of the myths of the Arab-Israeli conflict concerns Arab unity. Actually, the Arabs are far from being united; indeed, serious internecine struggle has characterized relations within the Arab world.

The author of this chapter traces the origins and implications of the Arab cold war that characterized the period between 1957 and 1967. What has happened in the meantime? Has the division between the conservative and revolutionary Arab camps, or the polycentrism within the latter, been resolved in the face of a much stronger Israel that emerged from the 1967 war?

The radicalization process in the Arab world is a major concern to the West, particularly the United States. If the radicalization process wins out over the conservative camp, what implications does this development hold for the international political system, e.g., vis-à-vis Soviet-American relations?

Inter-Arab politics of the last half a century have revolved around the four main themes of identity, freedom, unity, and ideology. Each gave rise to controversy and divisions; moreover, all were interrelated and present all the time through the era under review. However, each of these themes figured as a dominant concern at a given time. Thus it is possible to distinguish four periods corresponding to the emphasis on each of the four themes in the development of Arab nationalism.

Main Themes of Inter-Arab Politics

FIRST PERIOD: FOCUS ON ARAB IDENTITY

In the early stages of modern Arab politics, the first concern was that of differentiating between the national and the Islamic consciousness. Long debates and exhortations of the turn-of-the-century era of Arab Awakening set the stage for the decisions of World War I. This soul-searching found its most dramatic expression in the Arab Revolt against the Ottoman Empire. The Revolt provided a turning point in the development of Arab nationalism: Arab national identity asserted its preponderance over Islamic solidarity; Muslim Arabs in alliance with the Christian British fought Muslim Turks allied with the Christian Germans.

SECOND PERIOD: FOCUS ON LIBERATION

Once the Turkish rule was overthrown, substantial parts of the Arab world found themselves under the foreign dominance of their erstwhile British and French allies. Disappointed and resentful, Arab patriots concentrated their efforts on emancipation from this tutelage. For roughly a quarter of the century (1920–45) the struggle for independence overshadowed other concerns. It cemented the ties of nationalism between Arab Christians and Arab Muslims. Although usually fought on a local scale, i.e., separately in Iraq, Egypt, Syria, and Lebanon, the struggle for independence brought about a good measure of spiritual unity and emotional solidarity. In terms of the ultimate objective, i.e., full freedom from foreign control, this appeared as the least controversial of the issues. However, it was not free from controversies related to the kind of relationship to be established with the former imperial powers after liberation or during the twilight period of transition from dependence to full sovereignty. In Iraq, the debate revolved around the wisdom and need of collaborating with the British as against a radical severance of all ties. In Lebanon it revived the old question of whether this heterogeneous state should look toward the Christian West for protection against submergence in the Muslim "sea" around it. In Egypt it posed the problem of whether its highly stratified social structure with the attendant inequalities would or would not be perpetuated if close ties of alliance with Britain were maintained.

THIRD PERIOD: FOCUS ON UNITY

Attainment of independence by most Arab states by the mid-1940s brought to the fore a concern repeatedly voiced in the past but never given priority. It was the concern for unity. Chronologically, the movement may be said to fall into two sub-periods: the first focusing on the Arab League and the second revolving around various other unity schemes and their implementation.

At first glance, it might appear logical that once they achieved independence, the Arabs would be free to attend, unhampered by restrictions, to the problem of political unification and that liberation from foreign rule should precede the focus on the structure of the Arab polity. However, to the extent to which the struggle for liberation was fought on a local scale—thus resulting in the creation of several independent entities—it caused the development of a built-in obstacle to the achievement of unity inasmuch as ideal unity would demand the abolition of the newly won sovereignty of each of the component parts.

Unity interpreted as a deep spiritual bond and as political solidarity became, from the outset, accepted by virtually all segments of Arab public opinion. But the consensus never went much beyond this minimum. The Arab League, created in 1945, conformed to it because the League was, in concept and practice, no more than an association of sovereign powers, each entitled to veto any attempt to impose the will of others upon itself. But to the more ambitious exponents of Pan-Arabism, the loose structure of the League was clearly insufficient. They envisaged and strove for a higher degree of integration, the highest type of which would be a unitary Arab state stretching from the Persian Gulf to the Atlantic. Between these two extremes a number of intermediate schemes were advanced both in theory and in practice. Regional schemes limited to the Fertile Crescent were proposed by leaders in the Hashimite monarchies (King Abdullah of Jordan and General Nuri al-Said of Iraq) as well as by the Syrian Social Nationalist party. Wider schemes of federal unification were submitted by Fadhil Jamali of Iraq and Nadhim al-Qudsi of Syria. And a higher type of unity was preached simultaneously by President Nasser of Egypt and the Syrian-based Baath party. The culmination of these latter efforts could be seen in the creation of the United Arab Republic in 1958 which, by merging Egypt and Syria into a unitary state, seemed to provide a nucleus for all-embracing Arab political structure. Rather rapidly it was followed by two federative agreements, one between Iraq and Jordan (the so-called Arab Federation) and the other between the United Arab Republic and the Kingdom of Yemen.

But the very nature of these agreements indicated that the concept of unity was neither universally accepted nor uniformly interpreted by its exponents. Tribal, local, and dynastic rivalries stood in the way of its unquestioned acceptance and implementation. The

Hashimite unity proposals were resisted by the suspicious House of Saud while any prospect for the strengthening of Baghdad evoked an almost automatic resistance from Cairo. On the other hand, any extension of Egyptian influence into Syria filled with fear Syria's smaller neighbors such as Lebanon and Jordan. In most general terms, the issue could almost always be narrowed down to the struggle between unity and localism or—to use a current Arab phrase—between nationalism (conceived as Pan-Arab loyalty) and regionalism (conceived as loyalty to one's own state). In the modern Arab political vocabulary regionalism has acquired a negative connotation: for an Iraqi to have primary loyalty to Iraq is wrong: his loyalty should be to the Arab nation as a whole.

Attempts to implement the various unity agreements were short-lived and invariably ended in failure. The Iraqi-Jordanian federation was brought abruptly to an end by the revolution in Baghdad in July 1958. The United Arab Republic–Yemen federation broke up in 1961. And the United Arab Republic itself suffered a blow when Syria seceded in 1961 to leave Egypt with the mere name of the dissolved unitarian structure.

FOURTH PERIOD: FOCUS ON IDEOLOGY

In the decade of the 1960s ideological issues emerged as the primary concern of inter-Arab politics. This could be ascribed to two major causes: (*a*) the emergence of a number of new governments born of revolution, and (*b*) the failure of the unity schemes tried in the late 1950s. The new governments sought legitimacy by attempting to formulate ideological justifications for their existence, while the disappointed Pan-Arab leaders, particularly those in Cairo and Damascus, tried to discover the reasons for failure of unity experiments and prescribe appropriate remedies.

By the early 1960s, non-Communist Arab radicals developed an ideological framework within which minor differences were tolerated. This framework was based on a broad agreement as to the evils of the past and present; these were identified as Zionism, imperialism, and domestic reaction in the form of feudalism, monopoly capitalism, and tribalism. Considerable latitude was allowed with regard to the religious question in a modern state. Broad remedies included: in foreign policy, non-alignment and neutralism; in Arab politics, commitment to Arab unity; in domestic politics, abolition of the multiparty system and promotion of social equality, accompanied by mobilization of the masses; and in the field of economics, a dominant role to be played by the state, with a subordinate role assigned to the private sector. Broadly known as Arab Socialism, this ideology developed its Egyptian, Syrian, Iraqi, and other variants with a gradation of claims as to the "scientific" nature of the principles in question. The strongest common denominator was the revolutionaries' hatred of their conservative predecessors, their glorification of the state power at the expense of individual freedom, and their distrust of the political and economic power of the West.

The radicals diagnosed the collapse of unity experiments as being due to the difference of socioeconomic systems of the states that attempted to unite or federate. Thus Syria seceded from the union because her structure was essentially bourgeois while Egypt had already undergone a revolution. Attempts to unite such disparate entities were doomed to failure. What was needed was the occurrence of a revolution in a country prior to unification. Implicit in this theory was the need to propagate revolution and assist it wherever it took place. For a Pan-Arab nationalist, revolution thus ceased to be a mere matter of domestic concern: it acquired a Pan-Arab dimension and gave him the moral right to interfere in the politics of countries other than his own.

Thus the dichotomy between the conservative and revolutionary regimes was bound to come into the open: the revolutionaries simply did not believe in peaceful coexistence insofar as inter-Arab politics were concerned. By the early 1960s, the Arab world developed a certain statistical symmetry in this respect. The conservative camp numbered five states (Saudi Arabia, Kuwait, Jordan, Libya, Morocco—all monarchies); so did the radical camp (United Arab Republic, Syria, Iraq, Algeria, Republic of Yemen); while three remaining Arab states could be described as a loosely noncommitted "third force" (Lebanon, Tunisia, Sudan).

The Arab Cold War, 1957–67

It was this overlapping of the focus on unity with the focus on revolution that produced the phenomenon known as the Arab cold war in the decade following the Suez crisis. The war was essentially psychological in nature; the weapons used were political, propagandistic, and economic, with a liberal addition of undercover measures. In the latter sector, the Egyptians were especially active, using their military attachés, professional secret service agents, and local volunteers. Pamphlets and instructions were distributed, occasional kidnappings were performed, and firearms were smuggled. At one time or another Egyptian military attachés were caught red-handed in Jordan, Libya, Saudi Arabia, Iraq, and Lebanon. To the harrassed nonrevolutionary regimes the Egyptian political power appeared like an octopus whose tentacles were reaching far and wide. Such activities gained in intensity in 1958–59, following the Syro-Egyptian merger and the revolution in Iraq. To many Arab moderates it seemed that the old order was crumbling and that the Nasser-type radicals were about to assume control in the entire area in a broad sweep of revolution and subversion.

The two countries that put up the strongest resistance to the march of the revolution were Jordan and Saudi Arabia. King Hussein's book, *Uneasy Lies the Head,* bears an eloquent first-hand testimony to the trials and tribulations that he and his followers had to undergo to assure survival in the face of provocations, threats, and attempts at assassination. On two occasions, in 1957 and 1958, he had to quell attempts at a coup. In both cases the United States and Britain declared their interest in Jordan's survival and resorted to limited military demonstrations to back up their words. As for King Saud, early in 1957 he perceived the error of his earlier alliance with Nasser—an alliance directed against the pro-Western moderate elements of Syria and Iraq—and threw his weight and money to combat the revolutionary tendencies emanating from Egypt. Relations between Riyadh and Cairo deteriorated to such an extent that the United Arab Republic government claimed to have discovered a plot, financed by Saud, to assassinate Nasser. However, Saud's awakening came somewhat belatedly. His previous policy of aiding Nasser in Syria and Iraq had in the meantime undermined the position of pro-Western moderates in both countries to such an extent that they were unable to stem the revolutionary tide despite Saud's turnabout.

The cold war occasionally degenerated into a hot one. This was, first, the case of Lebanon in 1958. Initially a civil war, the major stake of which was the presidency of the republic, it soon was transformed into a conflict involving foreign powers. The newly created United Arab Republic engaged in substantial armed intervention to assure the victory of the rebel coalition; the likely goal of it was to convert Lebanon into an Egyptian satellite. Judging such a development incompatible with its interests in the area, the United States landed troops on Lebanese shores in July 1958. The outcome was the creation of a compromise coalition government; however, America's main aim, that of preventing the satellization of Lebanon, was accomplished.

The second "hot" case was that of the conflict in Yemen. Following the overthrow of the monarchy in September 1962, the revolutionaries soon found themselves embroiled into a civil war with those tribesmen who remained loyal to the king. Although here (as earlier in Iraq) the coup had been performed by native forces without the active aid of Egypt, the case was too tempting in terms of the newly forged theories of Arab revolution and unity to forego the opportunity of intervention. Thus within a few weeks, Egyptian troops were brought to Yemen to sustain the republican regime; their numbers grew to attain a figure estimated at about 80,000. The royalists, on the other hand, sought and obtained Saudi assistance in arms, money, and supplies. Thus reinforced through outside aid, both Yemeni camps fought a fierce and protracted war that did not abate until the withdrawal of Egyptian troops in 1967 in the wake of the Arab-Israeli conflict. The Yemen war could be likened to the Spanish civil war of the mid-1930s. It was a war both military and ideological and it involved foreign powers because of their interest in spreading or preventing the revolution. One of its by-products was a series of direct military clashes between the United Arab Republic and Saudi Arabia which took the one-sided form of Egyptian aerial bombings of certain Saudi localities. Clearly threatened and fearful lest this be a prelude to an all-out invasion-plus-revolution, the Saudi government sought and obtained from the United States public pledges of support for its integrity and independence. Demonstrative flights of United States warplanes over the Saudi skies served as a symbol of reassurance to Riyadh and a warning to Cairo.

But while thus the chasm between the conservative and the radical camps in the Arab world was assuming brutally wide proportions, the radical camp itself suffered strains and stresses of considerable magnitude. The first major fissure in what previously seemed like a monolithic front appeared in 1958–59 when Dictator Kassem's Iraq chose not to affiliate with the United Arab Republic and instead to follow a path of full independence. Kassem's slogan of an "Eternal Iraqi Republic" coupled with his suggestive title of the "Sole Leader" clearly challenged the concepts of Pan-Arab unity under Cairo's aegis. As a result, Egyptian-Iraqi relations deteriorated to an all-time low, which exceeded in the bitterness of mutual acrimony even the reciprocal hostility of the Hashimite era.

Similarly, hopes for a drastic reversal of attitudes after Kassem's overthrow by the Baath party in 1963 did not materialize. By the spring of that year not only Iraq but also Syria was ruled by the Baath, a party dedicated to Arab unity. It was natural, therefore, that both regimes should seek understanding with Nasser. Yet the tripartite negotiations in April and in the subsequent months ended in failure and recrimination, and the elaborate unity documents signed in Cairo remained a dead letter. Minutes of the Cairo negotiations reveal lively debates between Nasser and the Baathists on such subjects as federalism, ideology, exclusivity of one-party organization, and the division of constitutional authority. Behind these phrases, however, was a deep mutual distrust and a jealous hold on power which neither side wanted to abdicate or diminish.

The era of the Aref brothers in Iraq (1963–68) brought a noticeable improvement in Iraqi-Egyptian relations. Agreements providing for a gradual achievement of unity—via the creation of a Joint Political Command and an ideological "equalization"—were concluded in 1964 and 1965. Yet these agreements remained largely a dead letter while Iraq persisted in its separate ways and independent status. At the most, it was possible to speak of a degree of spiritual dependence of the Aref brothers on Cairo. This dependence never reached truly political or military dimensions.

The Baath party being an all-Arab organization with open or clandestine branches in many Arab countries, it might be expected that its assumption of power in two or more countries would bring them together into unity or close cooperation. Again, the reality went counter to the theory in this case. By 1968 Syria and Iraq were for the second time ruled by the Baath. But in the meantime the party suffered inner splits which generated hostility bordering on hatred between its Iraqi and Syrian organizations. Even the need for military cooperation on the so-called Eastern Front following the Arab-Israeli war did not prevent Syria from restricting the movements of, and harassing, the Iraqi commander of the joint Eastern Front troops.

This review of dissensions in the radical camp would be deficient without mentioning Algeria. While broadly following the policies of neutralism, socialism, and "national liberation," and thus being in harmony with the attitudes of other revolutionary states, the Algerian regime maintained strong individuality and self-reliant strength which precluded its merger with Egypt or any other Arab state on a voluntary basis.

To conclude: the Arab world was not only divided into conservative and revolutionary camps; the revolutionary camp was clearly polycentric. Polycentrism itself could be as damaging to Arab unity as the basic conservative-radical division and in some cases it overshadowed the latter. In both types of division the vested interest in power of the established governments appeared to be the overriding consideration.

Arab Summitry of the 1960s

Of three Arab evils—Zionism, imperialism, and reaction—the first appeared somewhat subdued when the cold war was turning hot between the radicals and the conservatives. Zionism and Israel were never absent as a problem, but certainly in the early 1960s they did not claim priority in public attention and official policies of the Arab countries.

Israel's insistence, however, on the diversion of the Jordan waters to its own use precipitated a crisis which modified the cold war and brought about attempts at putting an end to it. Arab response to Israeli challenge took the form of a series of summit meetings: the first held in Cairo in January 1964, to be followed by the second in Alexandria (September 1964), and the third in Casablanca (September 1965). Initially called to cope with the problem of the Jordan waters, these meetings soon transcended their early scope. The Jordan waters problem was attended to at the first meeting in Cairo, at which it was decided that (*a*) the Arabs would not fight a war with Israel over this issue; (*b*) they would counter the Israeli action by diverting the headwaters of the Jordan River and its tributaries, most of which were located in the sovereign Arab territories; (*c*) they would set up an appropriate technical organization, financed by collectively pledged contributions, to accomplish this latter objective.

More important were the unintended by-products of the summit meetings. Of these, three deserve special mention. First, it was decided to create the Palestine Liberation Organization (PLO) with a military arm, the Palestine Liberation Army (PLA), and to assign a special budget to both. Secondly, at the Alexandria meeting, a serious attempt was made to end the war in Yemen and bring about reconciliation between President Nasser and King Faisal of Saudi Arabia. In fact, an appropriate agreement was concluded, to be followed by further conferences of the interested parties. And thirdly, participants of the Casablanca meeting signed an Arab Solidarity Pact, the purpose of which was to put an end to the political and propaganda warfare among member-states of the Arab community.

In terms of inter-Arab relations, the balance sheet of the summit meetings seemed to point to net gains of the conservative camp. True enough, the conservatives who were never too sanguine on the Palestine issue had to conform to the more militant patterns set by the radicals, but this militancy seemed more verbal than actual; and the renunciation of war with Israel at the first (Cairo) meeting constituted a reassurance against recklessness. On the other hand, reconciliation between the two camps born out of the need for anti-Israel solidarity was bound to benefit the conservatives because, in practice, it would require the more dynamic and aggressive radical camp to desist from further attacks and subversion against the monarchies. In other words, the summitry-engendered peace between the two camps was expected to be based on the existing status quo and would thus give the harassed conservative regimes a period of respite.

It is precisely for this reason that the Syrian Baathists, being the most militant and radical among the Arab Left, viewed the summitry with a critical eye and accepted invitations to attend with considerable reluctance. Prior to the summit meetings, their favorite target was Saudi Arabia, with Jordan, Kuwait, and Libya as alternating seconds. The Arab Solidarity Pact obligated them to stop their barrages against these regimes. If properly implemented, it would make Radio Damascus programs dull and possibly throw out of work some professional propagandists who specialized in baiting the Saudis and their conservative brethren.

Under the circumstances, no major surprise was registered when the Syrians were the first to breach the Solidarity Pact. The enforced politeness toward their adversaries was clearly not to their taste. Furthermore, radicalism thrives on movement and aggression; it cannot remain stationary. Within a few weeks after Casablanca, Syrian media began complaining about the advantage the "reactionaries" drew from the pact to entrench their position and throttle the "progressive" movement. Before long, Saudi media began retorting to these criticisms. Within a few months, the Solidarity Pact was a dead letter. Suspicions once aroused were not easy to calm. This relapse into the cold war condition found its reflection in the failure to effect the Yemeni settlement in spite of a succession of bilateral and multiparty meetings held through 1964, 1965, and 1966.

Saudi disenchantment with the failure of the radicals to keep their promises led King Faisal to adopt a counter-strategy in the form of launching an appeal for Islamic solidarity. As ruler of the Prophet's native land and guardian of Islam's holy places, Faisal not only felt a special responsibility to assure the solidarity of all Muslims but also looked upon Islam as a desirable counterweight to excessive nationalist-based Arab radicalism. He made the first moves in this direction during his state visit to Teheran in December 1965, during which he issued, jointly with the Shah, a statement calling for Islamic cooperation. His radical adversaries immediately launched an attack, accusing him of virtual treason to the Arab cause through his close association with the Shah and of using the Islamic appeal as a reactionary stratagem to distract the attention of the masses from the issues of progress and revolution. Despite his denials, he was attacked for his alleged desire to form an Islamic Pact, with all the ugly connotations that any pact other than a purely inter-Arab one had meanwhile acquired in the Arab political vocabulary. Such a pact, his detractors claimed, would only be a window-dressing for the reentry of imperialist, hence even possibly Zionist, influence in the area.

It thus became evident that the Arab summitry of the mid-1960s did not erase the basic conservative-radical dichotomy. Nor did it abolish the Arab revolutionary polycentrism. Its most important by-product was to revive the issue of Palestine which had been semidormant between 1956 and 1964. But, in spite of the creation of the Palestine Liberation Organization, the revived Palestine issue had only outwardly a harmonizing effect upon Arab politics. In reality, it created a new and difficult situation for President Nasser who, as the leading champion of Arab nationalism, was increasingly expected to match words with deeds with regard to Palestine. Before long, he began experiencing strong pressures from Syria, whose Baathist rulers (engaged in intermittent border warfare around Lake Tiberias) felt no scruples in pointing to the UN Emergency Force (UNEF) in Sinai as a shield protecting Nasser from a showdown with Israel. The implication was that Egypt was selfishly hiding behind this shield and that it did not perform its Arab duty. The Damascus chorus was soon joined by Jordan and Saudi Arabia: it was probably the only time that the propagandists of these three countries spoke with the same voice against the same target. Nasser's desperate reaction was to remove the UNEF from Egypt and to announce the blockade of the Strait of Tiran. Thus it may be said that, to a considerable extent, the Arab-Israeli war of June 1967 was the result of both the Arab cold war and Arab polycentrism.

Impact of the June War on Inter-Arab Relations

Considering that, prior to the June War, the conservative camp was on the defensive, the defeat of two revolutionary states at the hands of Israel, namely the United Arab Republic and Syria, gave the conservatives a temporary respite. However, as a matter of general impact, the cause of Arab revolution was strengthened inasmuch as the June War generated greater dissatisfaction with the existing conditions, as well as a demand for more radical restructuring of Arab society and improvement of its performance in the domestic and foreign sectors.

Because of the demands of Arab solidarity and military coordination in the face of Israeli challenge, the Arab cold war became muted. Similarly, the lines dividing the conservative from the revolutionary camps became somewhat blurred. The muting of the cold war found its expression in the revival of the summitry: two postwar summit meetings were held—in Khartoum (September 1967) and Rabat (December 1969). In terms of inter-Arab relations, the Khartoum meeting was ambivalent: it produced a degree of interdependence between the conservative and revolutionary states by providing for subsidies to be paid by Saudi Arabia, Kuwait, and Libya to the war-torn Egypt and Jordan. The subsidies were, on the one hand, an expression of charity and solidarity; on the other, they could be regarded as blackmail and protection money. The meeting at Khartoum gave also the opportunity to put an end to the Egyptian and Saudi intervention in Yemen. However, it did not effect a settlement of a lingering civil war between the two native factions.

The blurring of the lines between the two camps occurred as a result of Jordan's closer alignment with the United Arab Republic. This turn in their mutual relations could be attributed to their heavy military involvement in the Israeli conflict and to the similar magnitude of their territorial losses to the enemy.

Preoccupied with Israel's military preponderance and restrained in its revolutionary impetus by a new financial relationship with the monarchies, Egypt ceased to be the most dynamic member in the radical camp. The old militancy of Cairo gave place to a new militancy of Syria, South Yemen, and partly Iraq. In contrast to the

United Arab Republic, Syria and Iraq refused to accept the UN resolution of 22 November 1967, regarding the settlement of the Arab-Israeli conflict. Syria, moreover, reverted promptly to her pre-1967 position in boycotting the summit meetings as useless and beneficial to reactionary regimes. Persisting in slogans of the war of national liberation via the mobilization of Arab masses, she was militantly critical of any government or group disagreeing with her and tended to draw closer to the Communist world, i.e., to both Russia and Mao's China.

As for South Yemen, this newly created republic displayed marked indifference to the pledges of inter-Arab peace made at Casablanca and Khartoum. Ruled by bold and rather desperate men, it soon became a center of radical revolutionism in the Arabian Peninsula. It developed into a base for the revolutionary movement of "liberation" in the Muscat Oman and the Persian Gulf; and in 1969 it clashed militarily with Saudi Arabia over certain disputed borderlands.

Identification with the West of the conservative regimes rendered their position increasingly difficult; it encouraged various dissenting elements to strike blows at the established structures. The year 1969 witnessed a revolution in Sudan (May) and in Libya (September) as well as two abortive attempts at subversion in Saudi Arabia (June and August). As a result, the conservative camp suffered a numerical reduction from five to four (Saudi Arabia, Kuwait, Jordan, Morocco) while the third force, due to Sudan's defection, shrank to two (Lebanon and Tunisia). The addition of Libya, Sudan, and the newly created People's Republic of South Yemen to the radical camp increased its strength from the original five to eight (United Arab Republic, Syria, Iraq, Algeria, Yemen, South Yemen, Sudan, Libya). These adverse developments induced Saudi Arabia to adopt greater vigilance vis-à-vis the revolutionary threat by pursuing two simultaneous lines of policy: (*a*) resistance to further increases of subsidy to the United Arab Republic; (*b*) revival of the Islamic solidarity slogan as an ideological counter-strategy against the increasing Pan-Arab militancy. The Islamic appeal received an accidental boost as a result of the Al-Aqsa Mosque fire in Jerusalem under Israeli occupation. The gathering of Islamic states (Arab and non-Arab) in Rabat in September 1969 gave such proponents of Islamic solidarity as Saudi Arabia, Iran, and Morocco an opportunity to expand their influence. Because of the symbolic and emotional dimensions of the Jerusalem issue, even the former opponents of Islamic alignments (such as Egypt) felt obliged to attend the Rabat meeting. King Faisal's next step was to convene the second Islamic conference in Jeddah in March 1970. Although boycotted by Syria and Iraq, the conference was attended by an impressive number (twenty-two) of Muslim states. To give it a more lasting significance and assert her own leadership, Saudi Arabia secured the decision to establish a permanent secretariat to be located in Jeddah. The United Arab Republic delegation which opposed the motion found itself outvoted by an overwhelming majority.

While thus at least one conservative state was scoring a diplomatic success, the radical camp displayed a tendency to institutionalize its separateness through a variety of devices. These could be enumerated as follows:

1. Syria stepped up her propaganda calling for separate summit meetings which would be restricted to "progressive states" only
2. the United Arab Republic, Libya, and Sudan concluded an agreement for cooperation in late December 1969, thus signalling the formation of Egypt-centered revolutionary alliance in the northeast Arab Africa; this gave rise to speculations about the pooling of Egypt's skills with Sudan's manpower and Libya's oil resources as a new dimension of strength
3. a conference of five "confrontation states" took place in Cairo in February 1970. It was attended by four radical states: the United Arab Republic, Syria, Iraq, and Sudan, and one non-radical, Jordan. "Confrontation" referred to the special military position of the participants in relation to Israel. The inclusion of Sudan looked like a courtesy gesture to the new revolutionary regime inasmuch as its exposure to direct warfare with Israel was virtually nonexistent. There were indications that a similar gesture was contemplated toward Libya, but because Libya's freshly concluded arms deal with the French (purchase of 100 Mirage aircraft) was subject to her nonbelligerent status, it was decided not to jeopardize the deal by her attendance
4. in mid-March 1970, an ideological conference gathered in Khartoum. It grouped not only delegates from the radical states but also leaders of the radical movements in nonrevolutionary states, for example Kamal Jumblat, head of Lebanon's Progressive Socialist party. Although lacking an official imprint, the conference could be viewed as another expression of solidarity of the radical groups in the Arab East
5. on 17 April 1971 The United Arab Republic, Libya, and Syria

formed the Federation of Arab Republics (Sudan, an initial candidate for membership decided to postpone its adherence because of domestic difficulties); as a result of this act, Egypt reverted to its historical name, with the official designation "Egyptian Arab Republic"

6. on 2 August 1972 Egypt and Libya signed the Benghazi Declaration pledging to establish within a year a single unitary state which would obliterate the constitutional separateness of the two countries

The June War spurred the growth of the Palestinian revolutionary movement in the form of various *fedayeen* organizations. Its official political instrument, formally recognized by all Arab states, is the PLO, created three years before the June War. The military side is represented currently by some fifteen fedayeen groups, in addition to the official PLA. The Palestine liberation movement is a weighty element in the Arab radicalization process because of (*a*) its use of violence, (*b*) its program calling for the rejection of the November 1967 UN resolution and the abolition of the racially based Jewish State of Israel, and (*c*) its challenge to the established Arab governments, both revolutionary (United Arab Republic, which had accepted the UN resolution) and nonrevolutionary (Jordan and Lebanon). An element of radicalism could also be noticed in the Marxist ideology—with strong Leninist and Maoist undertones—espoused by some fedayeen groups, especially the Popular Front for Liberation of Palestine (PFLP) of George Habash and the Palestine Democratic Front (PDF) of Nayef Hawatmeh. Even though the largest of the guerrilla groups, the Fatah, refused to identify itself with any ideology, the general impact of the movement was highly unsettling to the established order. The fedayeen had at one time or another profoundly shaken the existing official structures in Jordan and Lebanon: in Jordan to the point of achieving a virtual duality of power; in Lebanon by creating chaotic conditions in certain parts of the country, seizing power in refugee camps, and engaging in armed clashes with the government security forces.

The Palestine resistance movement suffered a serious reverse when, in his quest to regain full authority in Jordan, King Hussein fought and defeated the fedayeen in September 1970. Similarly, the advent to power of Anwar al-Sadat in Egypt and Hafez al-Assad in Syria in the fall of 1970 had an adverse effect on fedayeen influence. On the one hand, Sadat's commitment to a "political" settlement of the Arab-Israeli conflict contradicted the fedayeen program; on the other, Assad, jealous as he was of his newly won power, preferred to supervise and restrain the fedayeen in Syria rather than allow them complete freedom of action.

In spite of these setbacks, the Palestine resistance movement carried enough weight to generate a number of moves in inter-Arab politics. Thus, in response to the violent confrontation in Jordan, the sixth summit conference, which convened in late September 1970, produced the so-called Cairo Agreement between the nine attending state delegations and the PLO. It set forth the conditions for coexistence between the Jordanian government and the fedayeen and provided for a Tunisian-chaired Arab team to supervise their implementation. Subsequent disagreements between Jordan and the PLO led to joint—though futile—mediation efforts by Saudi Arabia and Egypt. Moreover, solidarity with the fedayeen (whether genuine or pretended) led such diverse governments as those of Kuwait and Libya to suspend the Khartoum-stipulated subsidies to Jordan.

A similar solidarity consideration—with an eye to the domestic militant factions—prompted the two mutually antagonistic regimes of Iraq and Syria to take identical measures of closing their borders and air spaces to traffic with Jordan in a display of punitive policy toward King Hussein. Assassination of Jordan's Premier, Wasfi al-Tal—chief architect of the 1970 antifedayeen drive—by the extremist PFLP in a Cairo hotel late in 1971 marked another step in the bitter struggle between Jordan and the guerrillas.

Thus, despite its military defeat in Jordan and the dubious effectiveness of its warfare against Israel, the Palestine resistance movement continued to exert a degree of influence upon the policies of established Arab governments. The main thrust of this influence was to combat and discredit any emerging tendency toward moderation and compromise in the Arab-Israeli conflict.

Conclusion: Pattern for the 1970s

The June War–generated inter-Arab solidarity expressed itself only in a limited way in the political, economic, and military sectors; it has not erased the basic dichotomy between the revolutionary and non revolutionary states; this dichotomy, occasionally approaching the cold war proportions, has continued to manifest itself in a variety of ways and is likely to persist through the 1970s as long as there exist different sociopolitical systems in the Arab world. Similarly, the existing revolutionary polycentrism has not disappeared and is likely to persist in spite of the tendencies to achieve greater solidarity among the "progressive" regimes. The June War has, furthermore, added a new dimension to the inter-Arab struggles, that of the Palestine revolutionary movement which appeals to the Arab masses over the heads of the established governments regardless of their hue. The choice for these governments is to (*a*) sponsor a dependent guerrilla organization (this was done in Syria and Iraq); (*b*) reach accommodation with the existing independent fedayeen organizations (this involves reduction of sovereignty, sometimes drastic); (*c*) restrict the fedayeen and thus induce armed conflict (examples of this have occurred in Jordan and Lebanon). Whatever the choice, the fedayeen remain a force which adds a new complication to the already established pattern of the Arab cold war.

Last but not least, inter-Arab struggles have had an impact on the Arab states' relations with the outside world. Under the conditions of the Arab cold war, the West—particularly the United States—has invariably stood closer to the conservative camp not because it favored monarchies and traditionalism per se but because of serious differences with the revolutionary camp. These differences could be narrowed down to three principal ones: (*a*) the radical camp's proclivity to interpret neutralism in a pro-Soviet sense; (*b*) the radicals' method of striving for Arab unity through intervention, subversion, and threats to integrity of other Arab states; and (*c*) the politically motivated economic measures taken by the radical states, measures not quite compatible with Western notions of economic freedom and sanctity of contracts. Despite these differences, the bridges between the West and the radical camp have generally been maintained in the decade of the cold war, 1957–67. The United States has scrupulously abstained from intervention in strictly domestic occurrences such as the revolutions in Iraq, Yemen, Sudan, and Libya, even though in some cases governments friendly to Washington were overthrown. American intervention occurred only in a situation where there was an obvious outside interference in the domestic process, namely during the Lebanese crisis of 1958. Generally, Washington's tendency was to come to terms with the governments born of revolution, recognize them early, maintain normal relations, and even extend economic and technical assistance if solicited. Republican Yemen, even while the civil war was raging, could serve as a good example of such a policy.

The radicalization process, accelerated and intensified by the Arab-Israeli crisis, has been relevant in this respect because, in addition to the domestic, it has also had its external dimension. The latter is expressed by the increasingly pro-Soviet orientation of the older and newer revolutionary states in the area; to the extent to which the revolutionary camp has increased its numerical size, Soviet influence in the area has also followed an upward trend. The expulsion of Soviet military advisers from Egypt in July 1972 has brought about a complication in the relations between Moscow and the leading Arab revolutionary state; it has not caused a complete break because Cairo's dependence on Soviet arms and broader politico-economic assistance had become too pronounced to afford such a rupture; moreover, whatever losses the Soviet Union suffered in Egypt were compensated by the simultaneous strengthening of her ties with Syria and Iraq in the political, military, and economic sectors.

Somewhat in contrast to the classical period of the Arab cold war (1957–67), the current radicalization process is primarily related to the American stance toward the Arab-Israeli conflict. The more the United States is identified in Arab eyes with unconditional support of Israel, the stronger the process of radicalization is likely to be. In its external manifestations this process will signify a growth of hostility to the United States and the corresponding forging of closer links with the Soviet Bloc and the Communist camp in general. The inherent causal relationship of the two phenomena can be neither denied nor exorcised away.

CHAPTER 4

Israeli Diversity: The Problems Of Internal Opposition

DON PERETZ

Prior to the 1967 Six-Day War, Israel could always count upon national unity against the external Arab threat. But Israel is no longer the monolithic state that many think it is. Indeed, it never was. The ethnic, cultural, and ideological mix within the state practically guaranteed, in fact, serious strains on Israeli nation-statehood.

The Arabs within Israel itself represent, of course, the most obvious problem area. Not all are Israeli citizens, e.g., the large number of Arabs who remained within the areas that Israel occupied during the Six-Day War. But many of them are Israeli citizens; they had chosen to remain rather than flee when Israel was established in 1948. Prior to the 1967 war, they had posed no security threat to the state. Now, however, many Arabs within Israel pose, at best, internal loyal opposition and, at worst, insurrection against Jewish rule.

But the problem of internal opposition also derives from within the Jewish Israeli community. The culturally disparate Sephardim (Oriental Jews) and Ashkenazim (Western Jews) are cases in point. The former resent allegations of inferiority and concomitant discrimination from the latter, who predominate in government and other elite posts. The dove-hawk controversy vis-à-vis the surrounding Arab states is another of the divisive issues within Israel. There are others. What do these factors portend for Israel? After overpowering the Arabs, for example, will Israel disintegrate through disunity? Or will it become, as some observers have suggested, an oriental country like its Arab neighbors?

Following liberation wars, the so-called developing or emerging nations have frequently suffered attrition, rather than growth, in their pursuit of constructive national tasks. Israel, on the other hand, seems to have become stronger in a variety of ways after each of its wars with the Arab states. Transitory as its growing power in the Middle East may be in the long run, for the immediate future its security position against the Arab states, if not against the Palestinians, seems to have been greatly enhanced. Not only in a military sense, but in terms of economic growth (despite current fiscal and monetary problems), in terms of developing internal cohesion among its diverse ethnic Jewish groups and disparate political parties; and in its relations with world Jewry, Israel has so far prospered from victory.

At the time of its establishment in 1948 the small Jewish community of some 650,000 people, called the Yishuv, although constituting only about a third of Palestine's population, was a distinctive national entity, stronger in most respects than the Arab two-thirds majority. More than half the population was born in Europe, over a third was native born, and 8.8 percent came from other Middle Eastern countries. Even though it was an ethnically and politically heterogeneous community, the economic, educational, cultural, social, and paramilitary organization of the Yishuv endowed it with a national élan and communal integrity that was the source of its strength against the outside world. The Yishuv was among the most egalitarian societies then existing, with relatively small wage and income differentials, little social conflict, and almost no intracommunal racial tension.

Political differences reflected in a Western European spectrum ranging from Communist and Left Socialist to middle bourgeois nationalist, had no violent manifestations and was expressed in a self-contained electoral system with an unusually high level of popular participation. Such internal opposition as existed on the eve of statehood in 1948, for example, among Jewish Communists or in the zealously orthodox Aguda Israel group, was minor and most of it was dissipated with the outbreak of the first Arab-Israeli war. As a result of the 1948 war Jewish public sentiment within the Yishuv and abroad was galvanized in support of the fledgling state. Aguda Israel, which had opposed establishment of the state, joined the new government. Mapam, a party which prior to 1948 advocated binationalism, also rallied in support of the new Jewish Israel. Influential Jewish organizations abroad such as the American Jewish Committee and the Jewish Board of Deputies in England, which only a few years earlier had called themselves non-Zionist, also became protagonists of Israel. Israel experienced the trauma of birth in the 1948 war, but it also experienced as a direct result of the Arab threat, a national revival touching Jewish communities throughout the world and resolving for those who led the new state serious potential dilemmas of internal and external opposition.

During the next twenty years, Israel was transformed despite the apparent fixity of its political-economic-social establishment. Still largely European born, with the exception of the country's young military commanders most of whom were Sabras,[1] the aging leadership reflected the era when the Jewish state was on the way. Most cabinet ministers, members of parliament, high government and party officials, leaders in fields of commerce, industry, education, publishing, and cultural life represented the ethnic groups and social classes that had led the prestate Zionist movement to establishment of Israel. Yet by 1967 those born in Europe and America were only 29.7 percent of the population. Sabras, largely a youth population in 1948, were now 42.8 perecnt. Other Asian and African-born Jews who were 27.5 percent of the population, now constituted with their offspring over half of the country's inhabitants.

The Oriental Majority and the European Establishment

The mass immigration of Jews from Asian and African countries, usually called Oriental or Sephardi in contrast to Western Jews mostly of European or Ashkenazi origin, changed not only the demography, but the socioeconomic structure of the Yishuv. While still a relatively egalitarian society, inequality had also become a reality in Israel. This was evident in growing disparities in income distribution, in increased social welfare cases, in the education gap between Oriental and European Jews, and in differences in professional attainment between the two groups. Statistics published in the mid-1960s by the Council of the Sephardi Community of Jerusalem showed that 2 of the 16 cabinet members, 16 of 120 Knesset members, and 88 out of 1,213 senior civil servants were Oriental Jews. Sixty percent of all children entering primary school, but only 25 percent of secondary school children and a mere 8 percent of university students were Orientals. About half the Oriental wage-earners were nonskilled. Their families, one and a half times the size of European families, had twice as many children under four-

1. "Sabra" is the Hebrew word for cactus; it is applied colloquially to native-born Jewish Palestinians and Israelis. Like the cactus, they are supposedly prickly on the outside and sweet on the inside. The term has come to mean a particularly European type.

teen-years-old. Nearly a quarter of the Orientals lived four or more to a room.[2]

These disparities seemed to have relatively little political impact nor did they engender any significant internal opposition until 1971. According to an anthropologist who has dealt extensively with the Israeli scene, Dr. Alex Weingrod, "The most explosive case of communal antagonism took place in 1959, when rioting broke out in several cities. The demonstrators were mainly North Africans: the street mobs—those who smashed store windows in Haifa and Beersheba—were verbally protesting against police brutality and their own bleak residential conditions. But mainly they were disappointed and frustrated by their low position, and angry and resentful against the society that neither sympathized with nor understood them." [3] Aside from the 1959 riots there were no incidents of mass violence by Orientals against the establishment until the emergence of a protest group calling themselves "Black Panthers" in 1971. A mass demonstration by the Panthers in Jerusalem in May 1971, which erupted into five hours of violent confrontation with the Israeli police, dramatically drew attention to the plight of Oriental Jews. Although the "Black Panthers" were believed to represent no more than a few hundred of the youths from the 15 to 20 percent among the Israeli population "below the poverty line," their organization and activities prompted an immediate response. Even American Jewish supporters of Israel were stirred by the gap between the growing affluent middle class Israelis and the 100,000 families living in poverty, 90 percent of whom were Oriental Jews.

Political manifestations of this discontent have been minimal, far less than in other (including Western) societies where ethnic

2. Council of the Sephardi Community of Jerusalem, *Danger Jewish Racialism!* (November 1964?). According to the *Jerusalem Post Weekly*, 24 November 1969 (hereafter cited *JPW*) more than half, or 68, of the members elected to the Seventh Knesset were born in Eastern Europe, including 35 born in Poland and 14 in Russia. Twenty-eight were Sabras, including the seven Arab members (New Communists, two; Mapai Arabs, four; Alignment-Mapam, one); and fifteen were Jews from various Arab countries. A study of fifty-five Israeli cabinet members from 1948 to 1969 by Richard Dekmajian showed the following countries of origin: Syria, one; Yemen, one; Palestine, eight; South Africa, one (Eban); Rumania, two; Austria, one; Canada, two; Germany, six; Lithuania, one; Russia (Soviet Union and Ukraine), twelve; Poland (present frontiers), fifteen; unknown, five.

3. Alex Weingrod, *Israel Group Relations in a New Society* (London: Praeger, 1965), p. 41.

differences are frequently accompanied by large socioeconomic gaps. Only in the First Knesset (1949–51) were Jewish members chosen by ethnic parties; one Yemenite and four Sephardim were elected. While later attempts to organize Jewish ethnic parties have been attempted, they have failed to elect a single Knesset member. In the election during October 1969, the only party with an ethnic appeal, Young Israel, received just over 2,000 votes or a mere .15 percent of the ballots. Except at the local level, such lists have failed during the last decade to win even one percent of the votes, thus producing no direct parliamentary representation.

The problem of ethnic political representation has not been overlooked by the political parties. Nearly every cabinet has had one or two Sephardim members, in the Ministry of Posts, Police, or in both. The various major parties have usually designated a Sephardi parliamentary representation. Consciousness of the problem has been more evident in local than in national politics where several municipal campaigns have been influenced by the ethnic factor.

In the euphoria of victory after the Six-Day War in June 1967, many Israelis commented favorably on Oriental battle performance leading to the conventional wisdom that a fundamental change had taken place. "On the one hand the Orientals, who had felt cut off from the main stream of Israeli society, now feel that they are a part of that society; on the other the veteran Europeans, who used to have premonitions about the efficiency of the Orientals and their ability to stand the test of a modern society, now show signs of having revised their attitude for the better." [4]

Surveys taken after the war indicated that the fundamental change was more illusory than real. One survey taken by the Ministry of Labor showed that 85 percent of the seventeen-year-old Israeli-born youths of European parentage had three or more years of secondary school. Only 27 percent of seventeen-year-old Sabras of Oriental parentage reached the same educational level.[5] While there was improvement in the educational attainments of Oriental born Jewish youths between 1961 and 1968, the social gap persisted. This was perhaps reflected in the endogamy index indicating that intermarriage between Oriental and Western Jews was still relatively low. Between 1960 and 1967 government statistics showed that Western grooms with Oriental brides decreased from 9.5 to 7.1 percent and Oriental grooms with European brides rose from 5 to 8.4 percent

4. *Israel's Oriental Problem* 3, no. 5 (March 1968): 1.
5. Ibid.

of all marriages, or an increase in intermarriage from 14.5 to 15.5 percent.[6]

Attempts by Arab propagandists, including the various Palestinian nationalist organizations, to make political capital of differences between Oriental and Western Jews in Israel by encouraging the former to rise as an internal opposition have been fruitless. Appeals to the "suppressed" Oriental Jews through broadcasts from the surrounding nations are treated more with levity than any semblance of seriousness. Despite a substantial undercurrent of prejudicial attitudes held by European Jews toward the Orientals, the latter have often tended to adopt these attitudes themselves rather than to seek retribution through subversive activities or anything approaching pro-Arab attitudes.[7] A survey by Hebrew University sociologists indicated that there is a "tendency of Orientals to be more hostile or reserved towards Arabs than Europeans are . . . it might have been hypothesized that they might have served as mediators. This is clearly not the case, however. The explanation supplied by many Oriental respondents refers to negative experiences during their previous life under Arab domination." Furthermore, "Orientals aspire to close the gap between themselves and the Europeans in order to gain their full share in prestige, power, and wealth in Israeli society. In other words, the Europeans serve as their reference group. Consequently, the Arabs are a negative reference group. . . . What the Orientals most reject in the Arabs are the Arab elements which they still possess. By expressing hostility towards the Arabs, an Oriental consciously (or unconsciously) attempts to rid himself of those 'inferior' elements in his own identity." According to this survey, social distance and hostility toward Arabs increased even more after the June 1967 war, a conclusion reached even before the outbreak of commando and terrorist attacks on civilian centers.[8]

It was precisely this tendency toward Europeocentrism that caused concern among many intellectuals of Oriental origin. Expressed congently by Nissim Rejwan, an Israeli born in Iraq, criticism centered on "The declared goal of 'remoulding' the Oriental [which]

6. Israel Government Central Bureau of Statistics, *Statistical Abstract of Israel 1969*, no. 20 (n.p.): 68 (Israel Government Central Bureau of Statistics hereafter cited CBS).

7. Yochanan Peres, "Ethnic Attitudes Among Jews and Arabs in Israel," draft of paper based on survey conducted in Israel during 1967 and published in Michael Curtis (ed.), *People and Politics in the Middle East* (New Brunswick: Transaction Books, 1971).

8. Ibid.

was pursued with a vigor and a self-assurance that in retrospect seem truly staggering. Moreover, side by side with the cleansing and the purifying, and as a perfectly logical outcome of the great fear of which 'every Jew' was seized lest the low-grade culture of the Orientals gain a foothold in Israeli society . . . precautions were taken. Using a variety of threadbare excuses and rationalizations, the dominant group practiced a systematic policy of exclusion and incapacitation, a policy which did not leave unaffected even the country's institutions of higher learning." Citing various Israeli authorities including former prime minister Ben-Gurion, Rejwan points out that the European establishment maintained the goal of "lifting the Orientals up to our own Western level." Charges by a spokesman of the Sephardi Community Council in Jerusalem that the establishment was pursuing a policy of "cultural genocide" raised many hackles, but, according to Rejwan, "The whole question, of course, is in reality one of sheer semantics." [9]

A prevailing attitude is that expressed by Ben-Gurion to Eric Rouleau, of the Paris daily *Le Monde:* "We do not want Israelis to become Arabs. We are duty bound to fight against the spirit of the Levant, which corrupted individuals and societies, and preserve the authentic Jewish values as they crystalized in the Diaspora." [10]

"Our suspicion," Rejwan comments, "is that the authentic Jewish values which Mr. Ben-Gurion is so eager to preserve have just about nothing to do with Jewish values and Jewish culture as, say, a Yemenite, Moroccan, Persian, or Iraqi Jew would understand the term." [11]

Rejwan, and a few other Jews of Oriental origin, most of them from Iraq which prior to the mass Jewish exodus in 1950 had a highly developed and culturally sophisticated Jewish communal elite, maintain that Israel's establishment is seeking to absorb Oriental Jews into their own Eastern European culture based "on the assumption that there exists in Israel a fairly well-defined 'native' culture to which these immigrants have to adapt and into which they can and have to be fused." Many of these Oriental intellectuals doubt the existence of such a distinctive culture capable of absorbing Asian and African Jews who have deep-rooted cultures of their own. Rather, they make a plea for democratic pluralism in which

9. Nissim Rejwan, "The Two Israels: A Study in Europocentrism," *Judaism* 16, no. 1 (Winter 1967): 97–108.

10. *Le Monde,* 9 March 1966. Quoted in Rejwan, "The Two Israels," pp. 97–108.

11. Rejwan, "The Two Israels," pp. 97–108.

various groups coexist maintaining their own distinctive cultures. Although not opposed to integration, Rejwan believes that it must not be one-sided "in the sense that members of the weaker groups are integrated *into* rather than *with* the dominant group." Acceptance by the more powerful Western Jewish community of democratic pluralism "must obtain in Israel *before* the stage can be set for genuine integration. It is a pity, and not a little surprising, that some Israelis should feel somewhat bewildered about the prospect of a pluralist society. In the circumstances, such development offers the only alternative to Levantinization—or something far worse," Rejwan concludes.[12]

While the contrast between an Oriental Jewish majority and the Europeocentered Israel establishment has not yet produced any startling problems of internal opposition, due in large measure to the far greater threat of Arab invasion, there may come a time when the Arab threat has disappeared or greatly declined. Then views such as those of Rejwan could become the basis for political division. As the number of university-educated Oriental Jews increases, and as they ascend to higher economic and social positions, blockage at the top of the ladder could in the future arouse frustrations that would become politically significant.

Israeli Arabs

Not until after the Six-Day War was the Arab minority in Israel, which reached more than 400,000 by 1969, considered a serious potential internal opposition. Prior to the war there were surprisingly few instances of Israeli-Arab opposition to the Jewish state. Among Israeli Jews, attitudes toward the country's Arab citizens were ambivalent. On the one hand, conventional wisdom denied the existence of discrimination against Arabs generally, or against Israeli Arabs in particular. "The Jews don't hate the Arabs, but want only peace with them," has been a commonly heard theme among Jewish Israelis in their discussion of Arab-Jewish relations. On the other hand, still another theme has been, "since we live in the area, we know how to deal with the Arabs."

After a recent visit to the area, Drew Middleton of the *New York Times* observed that "the Israelis believe they understand the Arabs better than anyone else, but they also display a blatant superiority

12. Ibid.

towards the Arabs."[13] Another sympathetic observer, Stephen S. Rosenfeld, writing in the *Washington Post* of Israeli attitudes, reported that the Israeli police act on the view that "Arabs are like burning straw—they flare up quickly and cool down quickly. . . . The Israeli has a split image of the Arab: at once the murderer of Jews and the villager sleeping on the ground as his wives labor nearby."[14]

Before partition of Palestine by the United Nations in 1947, Zionist leaders realized that there would be a substantial Arab population in the Jewish State, but had no clearly defined plans for dealing with the problem. There was, for example, no published draft constitution indicating the proposed legal relationships between Jews and a presumedly large Arab minority in the envisaged Jewish state. Zionist conceptions of the future of Palestine ranged from that of Chaim Weizmann in which the country would become "as Jewish as England is English," to that of Dr. Judah Magnes who vainly sought a binationalist approach with political and numerical parity between Jews and Arabs.

Problems of internal Arab opposition to Israel during its first two decades were largely resolved by Arab defeat and flight of the overwhelming majority of Arabs from Israel-held territory, leaving within the new state 156,000 non-Jews (mostly Arabs) or 17.9 percent of its initial 872,678 inhabitants. With the large influx of Jewish immigration during this early period, the percentage of Arabs in Israel soon declined to between 10 and 12 percent, despite one of the highest birthrates in the world (44 per thousand in 1962) and a low deathrate, comparable to that usually found in developed countries.[15]

Between 1948 and 1967 Israeli Arabs were not considered a major potential source of internal opposition or danger. This is not to say that there were no security precautions. Indeed, a major complaint of Israeli Arabs was the complex of special regulations, inherited by Israel from the British mandatory government and imposed upon the country's minority. These measures, initially quite restrictive, were gradually relaxed, until on the eve of the June War they directly affected relatively few Israeli Arabs.

During the first days of statehood, Israeli security authorities were given extraordinary powers to control movements of Arab citizens,

13. *New York Times,* 8 March 1970 (hereafter cited *NYT*).

14. *Washington Post,* 8 March 1970.

15. CBS, *Moslems, Christians and Druzes in Israel. Populations and Housing Census 1961* (Jerusalem, 1964).

impose curfews, requisition property, make arrests without warrants, enact military regulations free of civil restraints, and to banish or exile from their residences those Arabs who security authorities considered dangerous. During the 1950s and 1960s, pressures rose among various political parties represented in the Knesset to abolish or greatly modify the authority of the army to unilaterally take such measures. By 1950 the nightly curfews that had been imposed on Arabs immediately after the first Arab-Israeli war were lifted. Gradually it became easier for Arabs to obtain permits to leave their villages. Movement within security zones where most Arabs lived was facilitated until permits were issued by the military government on an almost open basis.[16]

With each passing year, the Ministry of Defense found it increasingly difficult to obtain the necessary parliamentary renewal of its extraordinary security authority, until in 1966 military government was abolished completely. The remnants of security controls in Arab-inhabited areas were then turned over to the police and applied generally to lists of several hundred persons believed to be politically dangerous. While the average Israeli Arab was now little affected by the remaining security restrictions, those who were considered militant political activists, or even potential militants, were kept under vigilant police surveillance.

A major source of discontent among Israeli Arabs was the requisition of 40 to 60 percent of their agricultural land for purposes of "vital development, settlement or security." Critics, both Jewish and Arab, of the requisition measures charged that they severely hindered development of the agricultural sector of the minority community, causing serious economic dislocation and decline in living standards of many farmers. Government spokesmen maintained that the measures helped to consolidate and thereby improve productivity of Israeli Arabs' land cultivation. Much of the land, they charged, had been expropriated from large absentee landholders and had been worked by sharecroppers. Above all, there was the security rationale justifying requisitions of large Arab-owned tracts along the borders with Jordan, Lebanon, and in the sparsely settled Galilee region of northern Israel.[17]

16. See the extensive discussion of the Arab minority in Don Peretz, *Israel and the Palestine Arabs* (Washington, D.C.: Middle East Institute, 1958); Ernest Stock, *From Conflict to Understanding* (N.Y.: The American Jewish Committee, 1968); Sabri Jiryis, *The Arabs in Israel* (Beirut: Institute for Palestine Studies, 1968). See also the extensive discussion of land problems in the issue on the Arabs and Israel in *New Outlook* 5, no. 3 (March–April 1962).

17. *New Outlook* 5, no. 3 (March–April 1962).

Regardless of the strength or weakness of justifications for the land requisitions, there can be little doubt that they had a profound effect on the socioeconomic structure of the Israeli Arab minority. They substantially altered land-holding patterns with a decline in large estates and a relative increase in the number of small holders. Whereas under the mandate 75 to 80 percent of Palestine's Arab population had derived its livelihood from agriculture, the proportion declined in Israel to 40 percent, although there was no major decline in rural residence. As a result of diminishing agricultural employment, larger numbers of villagers worked in Jewish urban areas, bringing back to their rural homes new views of the world, different consumption patterns, and new ways of life.[18]

Numerous cases involving both security measures and land requisitions were brought to the Israel courts by Arab citizens, but since the courts, unlike those in the United States, are guided in the final analysis not by a written constitution (which Israel does not yet possess), but by laws enacted by parliament, complainants had little defense against the security arguments pressed by the government and backed by parliamentary legislation. There were, however, numerous instances in which the courts warned against arbitrary and high-handed actions taken by the security authorities, although the courts were unable to countermand such actions.[19]

Israel's policies vis-à-vis its Arab minority should be viewed in the context of the country's general security position. Since its establishment in 1948, Israel had been at war with all its Arab neighbors, fighting not only three full-scale wars, but continual border action, either in retaliation for Arab incursions, or as a means of exerting pressure on the surrounding states to make peace. Throughout this period of conflict, nearly all Arab citizens of Israel have had close family ties with Palestinian refugees in the countries that have considered themselves at war with the Jewish state. In many cases, Israeli Arab families are remnants of *hamulas* (extended families) which fled from the cities, towns, and villages of the country. Inevitably, the sentiments and sympathies of Israel's Arab minority are closely linked with those of refugees across the unfriendly borders. The situation has caused deep-rooted psychological problems for the Israeli Arab. An ambiguous situation has been created in which, according to a survey taken by Israeli sociologists, "a feeling of uncertainty and marginality is . . . one of the 'leitmotifs' in the identity of the Israeli Arab, or in the phrasing of one of our re-

18. *New Outlook,* p. 43.
19. Peretz, *Israel and the Palestine Arabs,* chap. 9.

spondents: 'I sometimes think that we are neither real Arabs nor real Israelis because in the Arab countries they call us *traitors* and in Israel—*spies*." [20]

The official Israel image of the Arab position in Israel conveys a situation of well being and prosperity despite the "necessary inconveniences" to which the minority must unfortunately be subjected because of the war. The government, for instance, maintains that the income of Israeli Arabs is four times that of "other Arabs in the Middle East," that through extensive government financing of irrigation, land reclamation, agricultural mechanization and modernization, health improvement, and village reconstruction, the Israeli Arab has ascended to a standard superior to that prevailing elsewhere in the Arab world.[21]

Appropriate for purposes of comparison are the stages of development of Israeli Jews, Israeli Arabs, and West Bank Arabs. According to the government, occupational structure of Israel's non-Jewish population (nearly all Arab) in 1966 resembled more closely the structure of the West Bank than of Israel's Jewish population. Nearly 40 percent of Israel's Arabs were employed in agriculture, forestry, and fishing compared to 50 percent on the West Bank, and just over 10 percent of the Israeli Jewish population. In other employment categories, a comparison of the 1961 Jordan census with the Israeli non-Jewish population employed in 1966 indicated little difference. The two major disparities were in construction—19.6 percent of the Israeli non-Jews versus 10.9 percent of Jordanians—and in the "unspecified" occupation category in which 19.3 percent of male Jordanians were listed.[22]

Per capita national product in the West Bank during 1966 was about $280 compared to Israel's 1967 per capita product of approximately $1,500. While no precise figures were available on per capita non-Jewish or Israeli Arab income, a survey by the Central Bureau of Statistics showed that in 1968 the average yearly income of the urban employee family, with 1.5 wage earners and 5.8 family was I£ 6,994, or per capita income of about $335, less than half

20. S. N. Eisenstadt and Yochanan Peres, "Some Problems of Educating a National Minority (A Study of Israeli Education for Arabs)," U.S. Department of Health, Education, and Welfare, Division of Higher Education, Project No. OE-6-21-013, p. 14.

21. Israel Government, *Facts about Israel 1969* (Jerusalem, 1969), pp. 62–66.

22. State of Israel, Prime Minister's Office, Economic Planning Authority, *Economic Survey of the West Bank (Summary)* (Jerusalem, 1967); CBS, *Statistical Abstract of Israel, 1967*, no. 18 (Jerusalem, 1967).

that of the average Israeli, and much closer to the West Bank Jordanian income of 1966.[23]

A survey of facilities indicated that a higher percent of Arab households in Israel possessed various types of equipment than were owned in the West Bank. For example, 63.6 percent of the non-Jewish homes in Israel had kitchens whereas ownership in the West Bank was 45.5 percent, compared to 88.2 percent in Israel as a whole. On the other hand, fewer Israeli Arab homes—34.1 percent—had inside toilets than in Jordan, which had a figure of 40.5 percent compared to 89.0 percent for Israel as a whole. The greatest differences were in rural areas where 41.5 percent of Israel Arabs, compared to a mere 4.1 percent of West Bank inhabitants, had running water. Electricity was available for 25.4 percent of rural Israeli Arabs, but for only 6.7 percent of West Bank Arabs.[24]

The implication of these figures is that the Arab community in Israel retained a distinctive character evident in its towns and villages, resembling more those of Palestine Arabs living in Jordan than Israeli Jewish towns and villages. While there were many changes in the lives of Israeli Arabs during the past twenty years, they were still closer in socioeconomic position to West Bank Jordanian Arabs than to Israeli Jews.

Against the background of the continuing war, socioeconomic differences between Israeli Jews and Arabs reinforced still another aspect of difference. The aims and ideals of Israel, its leadership, officials, organizations, symbols of loyalty, and its very raison d'etre have been ethnically Jewish. The speeches of national leaders in the parliament and in political meetings at home and abroad constantly emphasize that Israel is a *Jewish* state, one of whose essential purposes is to ingather the "exiles" (Jews now living in the diaspora). The cultural mainstream of the state is Hebrew-Jewish. Many of its main contributors have come from the thousand-year-old Jewish tradition of Eastern Europe. Most of them spent little if any of their lives in the Middle East environment, and their cultural heritage holds little attraction for the Arab community.

According to the Israeli government, "before and during the Six-Day War, the overwhelming majority of Israel's Arabs openly

23. Comparisons based on per capita national product cited in *Economic Survey of the West Bank*, and *Facts about Israel 1969;* Israeli-Arab income figures obtained directly from CBS.

24. CBS, *Housing Conditions, Household Equipment, Welfare Assistance and Farming in the Administered Areas*, Census of the Population 1967, no. 2 (Jerusalem, 1968); *Statistical Abstract of Israel, 1967*.

identified themselves with the defense of her liberty and sovereignty. They volunteered to help the war effort as blood-donors, by replacing farm-laborers called up to fight and in other ways." [25] However, this apparent confidence in the Arab minority was not revealed in the allocation of responsible government positions or in the country's political, economic, or social establishment. While some 2,500 Arab citizens were said to be employed in the Civil Service, a perusal of recent editions of the Israel *Government Year-Book* listing several hundred top officials reveals fewer than a dozen Arab names. To date, there have been no Arab cabinet members and only two subcabinet members. Not only are Arab names missing from such obvious ministries as Defense and Foreign Affairs, but the Directors and Assistant Directors for Christian, Muslim, and Druze affairs in the Ministry of Religious Affairs are Israeli Jews.

While Muslim and Christian Arabs are not subject to compulsory military service, Druzes are now conscripted and achieve officer rank. There are Arab police officials of all faiths, although most of them serve in areas of the country populated by their coreligionists under direction of Jewish superiors.

Prior to 1967 there was no extensive Arab internal opposition in Israel. Such opposition as existed in parliament against Israeli policies was expressed largely by the Communist party, at least two of whose parliamentary representatives were Arab. The left socialist Mapam party usually had an Arab member in its Knesset delegation, and between two and five Arabs were elected on regional lists sponsored by the Mapai party. In the overwhelming majority of cases, Arab members of the non-Communist delegations voted with their respective parties, Mapam or Mapai, even on issues of concern to Arabs, such as security or land expropriations; on rare occasions they were permitted to abstain or vote contrary to the party majority. Throughout this twenty-year-period, the Arab vote was high and Mapai candidates received the largest number of ballots.[26] Critics maintained that Mapai secured its position in the Arab community through designating, as its selected candidates, Arabs with extensive family connections who maintained the *hamula* network, and through Mapai control of military government which could influence employment opportunities, permission for students to receive or not receive permits to leave their home areas, and by

25. *Facts about Israel 1969, 1967.*

26. For a distribution of Arab votes in Knesset elections see Appendix A at the end of this chapter.

control of other matters vitally concerning Arab inhabitants of the military zones. On many occasions, the most severe critics of the military administration and the government's Arab policies were Jewish members of the loyal opposition. Long before its termination, military government was opposed by a spectrum of political parties ranging from the Communists and Mapam on the Left to the Liberal party and Herut on the right.[27]

Such opposition as existed openly was usually expressed through the Communist party which tended to compete with Mapam for second place among the country's Arab voters. Various attempts to organize an effective non-Communist opposition failed because of the inability of its potential members to effectively cooperate, and because of interference from military government authorities. One attempt to organize an Arab political movement, *El Ard* ("The Land"—named after the group's newspaper), was banned by the Ministry of Interior when it attempted to register as a political party for the 1965 elections. The group was charged with being an antistate organization on the grounds that it had sent a letter to the United Nations containing serious accusations against the Israeli government with respect to the Arab minority. When the group appealed to the Supreme Court for recognition, it was rejected on the grounds that it did not recognize the state within which it chose to operate and that it opposed the existing free regime. The court cited as evidence failure by *El Ard* to use the term "Israel," and its objective of solving the Palestine problem by considering the country an indivisible unit, according to the wishes of the Arab people. Its establishment was therefore considered inappropriate within Israeli democracy. Shortly after the court's decision supporting the ban on recognition of *El Ard* as a political party, three of its leaders were arrested on the charge that captured infiltrators had been seized with orders to contact the organization. In November 1964, the group was outlawed as an illegal association by the Ministry of Defense under the British 1945 emergency regulations.

While Israeli Arab internal opposition has been far from effective in galvanizing any mass following, a nationalist sentiment did emerge among high school and university-educated youth and was often expressed in literary themes. *El Ard* was one aborted attempt to channel "intellectual" opposition into publication. The founders of *El Ard* originally attempted to publish an Arabic language weekly

27. Peretz, *Israel and the Palestine Arabs*, chap. 6, for a discussion of military government.

newspaper, but after thirteen issues were printed the government closed it down and began prosecution of six of the staff on charges that the group constituted a threat to the state. The group later reformed as the *El Ard* publishing company. After lengthy court procedures, the Supreme Court authorized its registration as a company, but it failed in efforts to again obtain permission to publish an Arabic weekly.

Much of the poetry written by Israeli Arabs after 1948 reflected latent nationalist opposition based on attachment to the land, hence selection of the name *El Ard* by the above-mentioned oppositionists. This poetry frequently uses agricultural symbols, applying to them a national connotation. "Love for a girl, for the village, and the homeland are perceived by the Israeli-Arab poet as a single indivisible emotion. The 1948 war is described in this literature as the shattering of a rural idyll (conceived in romantic and nostalgic images) and a severance from a familiar and beloved landscape. Those who remained behind must watch over the inheritance for those who were scattered.

"In this way the Israeli Arabs who did not take refuge with the majority of their brethren in Arab countries found a legitimation of their minority status in a Jewish country." [28]

Such poetry which is widely read and extremely popular among the young Israeli Arab intelligentsia tends to describe the Arabs of the country living in misery and helplessness. Other themes are rebellion against the older generation believed to have betrayed their fellow countrymen, opposition to restrictions of the military government and security authorities, protest against economic and social conditions, strong attachment to Arabism, and identity with Afro-Asian nationalism.

Latent feelings of Arab nationalism emerged politically elsewhere in 1965 when the Israel Communist party split into two factions, the New Communists who were mostly, but not all Arabs, and the parent Israel Communist party, most of whom were Jewish. The split was caused by differences between Jewish and Arab Communists over the Middle East policies of the Soviet Union, Israel, and the Arab states. The parent group, smaller in number than their new offspring, while critical of Israeli policy, also criticized the Soviet Union and the Arab states for their militancy and consistent hostility to Israel. The New Communists, the larger of the two fac-

28. Yochanan Peres and Nira Yuval-Davis, "Some Observations on the National Identity of the Israeli Arab," *Human Relations* 22, no. 3 (n.d.): 221–22.

tions, backed Soviet Middle East down the line. After the June War, the New Communists demanded Israel's total and immediate withdrawal from all occupied areas, whereas the largely Jewish faction maintained that the war has been necessary for Israel's survival and that there should be no withdrawal without peace.

Among Israeli Arabs, nationalist feeling was intensified after the war and expressed in more militant attitudes and greatly increased Israeli Arab participation in overt actions against the Jewish state. According to Israeli sociologists, there was a startling increase in the number of Israeli Arab school children who thought that it would be necessary to wage still another war against Israel despite defeat in the previous three.[29] Many fewer Arabs felt at ease in Israel according to the survey. Latent opposition to Israel was revealed in the survey which asked: "How, in your view, did the war influence the attitude of the Arabs to the State of Israel?"

TABLE 1

Percentage of Influence of the War on the Arab Attitude to Israel

	ROSE	REMAINED THE SAME	FELL	N
Respect	43	17	40	299
Fear	52	34	13	282
Hatred	73	23	4	291

TABLE 2

Classification of self-definition (Israeli, Arab) Percentage before and after the June war

	ISRAELI		ARAB	
	1966	1967	1966	1967
First grade	49%	18%	18%	20%
Second grade	19%	25%	18%	29%
Third grade	16%	8%	41%	20%
Fourth grade	12%	11%	14%	15%
Fifth grade	14%	36%	18%	25%
N	166	184	144	143

29. Ibid., pp. 228–29.

The extent to which an underground Israeli opposition was developing with sympathetic ties to the Arab commando movement was revealed in the increased frequency of Israeli Arab arrests for participation in terrorist activities. By the end of 1969, 100 Israeli Arabs had been arrested as suspected saboteurs, a number larger than the total charged with subversion during the decade prior to the June War.

The growing tension between Israeli Arabs and Jews and the decline of amicable relations was indicated in the appeal to the Knesset by Mapam's Arab member, Abdel Aziz Zaubi who pointed out, "We are citizens of the State of Israel and members of the Arab nation. We are torn in a war raging between our State and our People. . . . The only solution is Peace." In condemning Arab terrorism Zaubi emphasised that "we also have built this state . . . we have paved its roads, ploughed its fields and watered its orange-groves. . . . Don't let the labor of twenty years go down the drain. . . ." [30]

A warning to Israeli Arabs against the dangers of internal opposition was issued in December 1969 by the prime minister's adviser on Arab affairs, Shumel Toledano: "According to our appraisal, a contest is now in progress in Arab population centers between nationalist Arabs and positive sentiments. . . . From now on, the Government and various public bodies will do their utmost to support these positive elements, while, on the other hand, we shall fight to the bitter end against all nationalist factors." He emphasised that the government would not tolerate nationalists on any local government board or committee. "We shall work to bring about a situation where an Arab nationalist is ostracised in his own village," Toledano warned.[31]

Hawks versus Doves

Other issues occasionally surfaced in Israeli politics after 1967, but matters related to national security, defense, and the occupied territories have dominated the scene. On occasion labor disputes, the increasingly precarious economy, and the dispute over "who is a Jew" have come to the fore, but none of these issues intruded into

30. *Jewish Observer and Middle East Review* 18, no. 52 (26 December 1968): 11 (hereafter cited JOMER).

31. Ibid., p. 12.

the debates that dominated the parliamentary election of October 1969, its immediate political prelude, or aftermath. Both before and after the election, politics ran from hawkish to dovish rather than along the conventional left to right political axis. Security made rather strange bedfellows, bringing together in a wall-to-wall coalition government such diverse views as those of Mapam Marxists, Herut nationalists, and orthodox Mizrachi rabbis. After Golda Meir accepted the U.S. proposals for a renewal of the cease fire along the Suez Canal in 1970, Herut left the coalition government and again joined the opposition.

In terms of Israeli politics hawks favored no political or military concessions to the Arab states and no commitment to withdraw from any areas occupied during June 1967. Doves advocated anything less than the territorial status quo, although only a tiny minority supported return to the pre-June 1967 armistice frontiers. During the 1969 elections opposing ends of the axis were represented by small factions which failed to win as much as one seat in the Knesset.

At one end of the axis was the newly formed Peace List, whose Hebrew symbol (*Nun-Samech-ness*) means "miracle" in English. The list was headed by a group of university professors, journalists, politicians, and intellectuals who advocated return of occupied terroritories, after a peace settlement. One Peace List leader was Natan Yellin-Mor, former commander of the Stern group and its representative in the First Knesset from 1949 to 1951. The Peace List, the Jewish faction of the divided Israel Communist party and a small group of Mapam members who broke with their party when it joined the new Labor Alignment,[32] had considered a coalition with the Haolam Hazeh or New Force party headed by the colorful Uri Avneri.[33] This attempt to form a United Peace Front was aborted

32. The Alignment for the Unity of Israel's Workers was formed in 1965 from Mapai and Achdut Ha'avoda-Poalei Zion (unity of labor-workers of Zion). Both groups were labor parties established originally in the 1920s which split, reformed, split, and reformed. Later Rafi (the Israel labor list founded in 1965 after a split from Mapai) also joined the Alignment which re-fused into one party, the new Israel Labor party. In 1969, Mapam, the left-wing United Workers party, formed from several other labor groups, joined the new Labor party for purposes of creating a single electoral list. Mapam had a less binding tie than the other three founding groups, hence the list appeared during the elections as the Alignment rather than the Labor party.

33. Haolam Hazeh (this world) or the New Force party was named after the sensational weekly magazine published by the party leader, Uri Avneri. He has emphasized neutralism in foreign policy, separation of state and religion, greater

when the various factions found it impossible to work together, more because of personality than substantial ideological differences. Final election returns doubled Avneri's Knesset representation from one to two seats, and gave one seat to the Israel Communist party led by the veteran Zionist leader, Dr. Moshe Sneh.[34]

The Land of Israel List at the other end of the axis was also led by a former Sternist leader, Dr. Israel Elded, who demanded that any peace settlement be based on existing cease-fire lines. He urged the government to encourage emigration of Arab inhabitants from the occupied territories. The Land of Israel List claimed a respectable following among a number of former leading political leaders, writers, intellectuals, and retired military men, but it failed to win a single seat.

Prior to the election there was little practical difference among the major parties—with the singular exception of the Arab New Communists—on matters of security and foreign policy, although there was extended discussion about the future of the occupied territories. Only the Arab Communists demanded immediate and total evacuation, whereas differences among other parties were over how much territory, rather than when to evacuate.

Mapam developed a peace program calling for withdrawal of Israeli forces "to safe and agreed-upon boundaries," after "a stable peace is assured by a contractual agreement . . . between us, Egypt, Jordan, and Syria." The agreed upon "safety-borders" would have to include "united Jerusalem under our sovereignty, in which a measure of self-government will be assured to the Arab minority and self rule of the Moslems and the other religions of the places holy to them . . . the Gaza Strip will be incorporated into Israel on the assumption that Jordan will be given free access to the sea, and with Jordan's participation in the solution of the problem of the refugees concentrated in that strip . . . our security border will include the Golan Heights . . . evacuation of Judea and Shomron (the West Bank) with agreed-upon security-border-corrections . . . demilitarization of the territories evacuated by us on the West Bank and Sinai . . . a commitment to liquidate all terrorist activity by the neighboring states, with the signing of the

cooperation between Jews and Arabs. Its following has included many youths and a larger number of Arabs than the traditional Zionist parties.

34. Dr. Moshe Sneh, leader of Maki (Israel Communist party) and its single elected member to the Seventh Knesset was formerly a member of Mapam, the General Zionists, and leader of the Haganah (Jewish defense force) in its underground days during the mandate. He died in 1972. Avneri's party with two seats split after 1969.

peace agreement . . . an agreed-upon solution with the neighboring states on the refugee problem, and our part in that solution, including our agreement to absorb a number of refugees within our borders . . . guarantee of free navigation in the Suez Canal and the Tiran Straits, as well as assuring an Israel presence in some form at Sharm-el-Sheikh." The party urged immediate adoption of a "liberal policy in the territories, expressed in open bridges, and in cooperation between the economies of the West Bank and that of Israel . . . [including] upgrading of the self-government in territories, to a higher level within the given framework of military rule and the objective must of security . . . [also striving] for a solution of the problem of the refugees who are under our rule, by instituting a daring program of productiveness in industry, trades, agriculture, hired labor and individual farming, and by transforming refugee camps into normal settlements." [35]

Mapam leaders criticized Defense Minister Moshe Dayan and his followers for being adventurers and expansionists. While they still considered the United States an imperialist nation, opposing its intervention in Viet Nam, in contrast to Golda Meir and a number of her followers who supported the American war effort, the leftists also had become increasingly critical of the Soviet Union, especially after their sons fought against Russian tanks and planes in Sinai and the Golan Heights.

Within the wall-to-wall coalition formed in May 1967 on the eve of the Six-Day War, there was diverse opinion about military occupation policies in the territories. Mapam was suspicious of the Defense Minister and his supporters, fearing that their apparent no-evacuation policies would close options for peace negotiations. Among labor leaders there was fear that permission granted to between twenty and thirty thousand workers from the occupied areas to find employment in labor-scarce Israel would eventually undercut the Jewish labor force. By 1973 this number was between 50 and 60,000. Although Arabs from the occupied territory received legal wage rates and were hired through the Histadrut labor exchange, there had already developed a black market in cheap Arab labor, raising the spectre of "Levantanization," a threat that even former prime minister Ben-Gurion warned against in his advocacy of total evacuation from all territories, except Jerusalem and the Golan Heights in return for peace.

With some 1.5 million (by 1973) Arabs (nearly half the total

35. Opening statement of Meir Yaari, member of Knesset at the Israel foreign policy debate of Mapam's political committee, mimeographed statement (n.d.).

number of Palestinian Arabs) now under Israeli jurisdiction, many Zionist leaders feared for the future of Israel's Jewish character. Should Israel continue to hold on to the occupied areas, especially the West Bank, East Jerusalem, and Gaza, within a generation or less the present Jewish majority would be swamped because of the extraordinarily high birth rate among Palestine Arabs, one of the highest in the world. Mapam leaders, who at one time had advocated binationalism (when Palestine's Jewish population was a third or less of the total) now regarded the concept as anachronistic and no longer politically "realistic." Furthermore disparities between the Westernized and technologically advanced Yishuv, and the less economically developed Palestine Arabs made precarious close association of the two communities in a single political state. Such a fusion would, they believed, inevitably create a group of second-class citizens within Israel.

Leaders of Herut,[36] Defense Minister Dayan, and others in the Labor Alignment either openly advocated retention of territories, or were ambiguous about their plans for the future. They emphasized that the June War created new realities and established "new facts." Integral to this spectrum of views was Dayan's assertion that Israel was in the West Bank "of rights and not on sufferance, to visit, live and to settle . . . we must be able to maintain military bases there . . . we must, of course, be able to prevent the entry of any Arab army into the West bank." If inhabitants of the West Bank accept our conditions, said Dayan, "it seems to me of lesser importance whether the West Bank chooses to be part of Jordan with some autonomy, whether it prefers to be independent, or simply to be part of Jordan . . . I am quite sure that we, for our part, must decide what is essential for us to make our stand on it." Arabs would not be forced to become Israelis, according to the Defense Minister, but in his view should be permitted to retain Jordanian citizenship while living in Israeli-controlled enclaves. Even in Jerusalem which "is part of Israel," the 70,000 Arabs should not be obliged to become Israelis.[37]

Despite divergent viewpoints within the government, its policies have moved increasingly toward establishment of "new facts." This has meant not only incorporation of East Jerusalem within Israel,

36. Herut was formed from the pre-state Irgun Zvai Leumi (national military organization) by Begin in 1948; it joined with the Liberal bloc (formed in 1961 from General Zionists and progressives), to form Gahal as the main opposition party in 1965.

37. *JPW,* 27 October 1969.

staking out the Golan Heights as a necessary security acquisition, construction of expanded road networks and military bases in all occupied areas, use of oil and other mineral resources in Sinai, but, by 1970, also establishing 21 Jewish settlements in the regions acquired during June 1967.[38] By 1973 this number had doubled. Of these, 11 had already been established in the Golan Heights by various political groups, including Mapam. Plans called for a total of 20 such settlements within the 250,000 acres of the Golan area to accommodate 4,000 families. None of the various political groups other than the New Communists advocate authorizing return of the more than 100,000 former Syrian residents of Golan. The approximately 7,000 Druzes who remained have made their peace with Israel and are treated, as are the Israeli Druzes, like a favored and protected minority. Although their language is Arabic, Israeli policy separates them as a group apart from the Arab community. During 1972, however, several prominent Druzes living in the Golan Heights were arrested and charged with espionage for Syria.

During 1969 three Jewish settlements were established in the Jordan Valley by the Orthodox Mizrachi and Labor parties with plans for a string of five similar settlements in the Jordan Valley depression, an arid strip which was depopulated by exodus of Arab refugees during and after the last war. These settlements would fit within the scheme of Yigal Allon, Israel's Minister of Labor and Deputy Prime Minister, to create a ring of Jewish settlements around most Arab-inhabited parts of the West Bank, with Jenin, Nablus, and Ramallah as their center and Hebron as a southern extension. Two Mizrachi moshaves were reestablished near Hebron on the strategic site of the former Etzion Bloc whose Jewish settlers were driven out in 1948. Allon's master plan calls for establishment of a Jewish suburb in Hebron whose former Jewish community was expelled or massacred in the 1929 disturbances and riots.

Three new kibbutzim had been set up in the southern end of the Gaza strip and in northern Sinai by 1970, with two more planned. Thus the network of new settlements joined by villages established before June 1969 along the Israeli side of the armistice lines would surround the Gaza area with Jewish settlements.

Establishment of "new facts" has also included government encouragement of Israeli business and commercial operations in the occupied areas. Jewish investors have been apprised of benefits to be realized from cheaper prices for raw materials, lower interest rates on loans, government sureties in regard to security and tax

38. *JOMER* 18, no. 40 (3 October 1965): 14–15; *NYT* 18 March 1970.

relief, all under the law to encourage investment in Israel. Special subsidies are offered nonresidents who enter partnerships with inhabitants of the occupied areas. Defense Minister Dayan commented on long-term economic policy in the occupied areas: "Does any of us imagine that one can establish local enterprises there which will not be tied to the Israeli economy, when in fact one is speaking about Jewish capitalists, Israeli enterprises that will establish offshoots in the territories . . . can Israel, or Israelis, or Jews, invest in the territories without tying their enterprises there with the Israeli economy, with workers from Israel, with Israeli ownership?" [39]

While these "new facts" raise apprehension among Israeli doves, official policy within Prime Minister Golda Meir's new government remains, "everything is negotiable." The fear among doves is that the more extensive the enlarging network of "new facts" becomes, the more likely that they will become political realities as did the "facts" which extended Israel's borders from those of the 1947 partition plan to the 1949 armistice frontiers. As the dangers of changing reality become more pressing, the greater the tendency for the small opposition to speak up.

To date this opposition is small in number, weak in political influence, and heckled on occasion by the jingo press. *New York Times* editor James Reston commented after a visit to Israel in February 1970 that "the Israelis have not only closed ranks on the war, but seem to have closed their minds about new ways of getting out of it. The Israeli government is not challenged seriously by the political opposition, by the press, by the universities, or even by the religious leaders. Spiro Agnew would love it in Jerusalem: the spirit of my country right or wrong." [40] Since the terrorist massacres in Munich at the 1972 Olympic Games and those at Lod airport in Israel, this atmosphere has become even more restrictive.

The results of the election in October 1969 indicated a shift in public support to the center and right of center which advocated more hawkish than dovish policies, it was toward deeper entrenchment of the status quo rather than toward modification of the existing territorial, political, and security situations. This was evident in the increase of four seats received by Gahal, led by the Herut leader and former Irgun Zvai Leumi commander, Menachem Begin,

39. *Ma'ariv,* 17 April 1969; *Haaretz,* 11 November and 9 and 16 December 1968.

40. *NYT,* 13 February 1970.

who advocates retention of all occupied territories and firmer retaliation against hostile Arab acts.

The effectiveness of the former Mapam opposition was vitiated by incorporation of the party within the Labor Alignment, running on the same list with the Israel Labor party, and sharing responsibility within Golda Meir's wall-to-wall coalition. Mapam's peace plan and its critique within the cabinet of schemes to settle the West Bank can hardly be called effective opposition. Its opposition is certainly no more effective than Foreign Minister Abba Eban's proposed moratorium on massive reprisals to stop escalation of violence. Despite internal cabinet discussion, both the expansion of Jewish settlement and the escalation of reprisals continued.

Perhaps more effective in the long run will be discussion stimulated by controversy over the Palestine entity. It was initiated by growing evidences of Palestine Arab nationalism after the June War, and focused on Israeli policy toward the West Bank inhabitants. Should they be recognized as an independent national entity, an autonomous nation under Israeli controls, or be returned to Jordan. Resolution of this question will of course be settled as part of the larger dilemma concerning the occupied territories.

Golda Meir on several occasions questioned the validity of the Palestinian concept, stating that she could not understand what special rights the Arabs of former mandatory Palestine had to call themselves "Palestinians." "Aren't we Palestinians too, by the same measure," she asked. Noting that when she had come to the country in 1921 Palestine included Jordan with its borders extending to Iraq, she exclaimed "this is the Palestine to which I came! What, then, is the 'Palestine entity' and who speaks in its name?" [41] Another cabinet Minister, Israel Galili said "we do not regard the Palestine Arab as an ethnic category, as a distinct national community in this country." [42]

The most influential opposition to these views was expressed by Arie L. Eliav, new Secretary General of the Israel Labor party who has made no secret of his views supporting creation of a Palestinian Arab state on the West Bank and perhaps in Gaza. "The Arab-Palestinian nation," he pointed out, "emerged as a twin to the Jewish nation. . . . The Palestinian Nation is identifiable as a national entity by a national consciousness, by continuous territory where most of the Palestinians live, by a history of several decades replete

41. *JOMER* 19, no. 11 (13 March 1970): 7–8.
42. *Jewish Liberation Journal* 1, no. 5 (November–December 1969): 4.

with battles and wars, and a diaspora which maintains a link with the Palestinian homeland. At the same time it is conscious of a common national catastrophe, sacrifice, suffering, heroes. It has dreams and the start of a national literature and poetry.

"Our relations with the Palestinian Arabs constitute the most important element of our relations with the Arab world as a whole, and the two are inseparably linked. Herein lies the key to the solution of the overall problem," Eliav maintained. He too offered a peace plan involving surrender of the territories in exchange for treaties containing security guarantees. Eliav even urged accommodation on Jerusalem. "We must find a solution together with the religious bodies involved. . . . What was hateful to us for generations let us not do to others. We must come to an arrangement with the Moslem and Arab world." The Labor party official also advocated Israeli contribution to the refuge problem along lines similar to those recommended by Mapam. "A policy of this kind on Israel's part—in regard to the Palestinian Arabs, the territories, borders, Jerusalem, and the refugees—is consistent with the true aims of Zionism and of Israel." [43]

Within Israel views such as these that question many aspects of the government security policies are discussed in the press by university professors, intellectuals, businessmen, and within the Mapam party. Estimates of their strength have ranged from "small numbers" to "very large, covering a broad spectrum." [44] There is general agreement that "when it comes to security, the doves, not less than the hawks, oppose unilateral withdrawal without a peace settlement or a peace settlement without guarantees.

"The doves are against a policy of 'faits accomplis'—establishment of Jewish civilian settlements in the occupied areas—but they approve of military installations necessary in a war and to be dispensed with in peace. They do not oppose changes of frontiers if required purely for security needs. But they fight annexationist tendencies or ideologies.

"Even those ready to give Al Fatah the credit of a genuine 'resistance movement' would rise in arms against any attempt to destroy the Jewish state."

43. Arie L. Eliav, "We Shall Never Deny the Palestinians Their Right to Self-Determination . . . ," *The New Middle East* 2, no. 8 (March 1970): 8–9.

44. For "small numbers" see James Feron, *NYT*, 15 March 1970; for "very large," see *New Outlook* editor Simha Flapan in *NYT*, 15 March 1970.

Preoccupation with the debates on security, occupied territories, and Israel-Arab relations has tended to push to the background issues of no less vital importance which could also determine Israel's fate. Derived from ever escalating security costs are matters of national economic survival. Prices of sophisticated equipment, such as jet airplanes purchased in the United States, have greatly increased defense expenditures since 1967 so that about one-fourth of the GNP is eaten up by military supply. According to the Minister of Finance and Commerce, "We should be a nation of 15 million inhabitants to handle a defence burden like that, not 2.5 million." [45] The result has been an outflow of foreign currency reserves at such a rapid rate that it threatens to exhaust the reserves within a relatively short period of time.

To prevent disaster, leading Hebrew University economists demanded that the government take the politically unpalatable measure of still another devaluation of the Israeli pound which, in fact, took place in the fall of 1971 and again in 1973. Another group of senior bank economists maintained that there was no point in devaluing unless the move was accompanied by strict economic planning and controls. Without such measures, they felt that the devaluation would fail as it had in the past. Both bankers and professors agree that without drastic steps the economy will quickly drift into dangerous waters with potentially graver results for the country.

Measures recommended by the economists would mean even sharper curtailment of war on poverty, which would affect the the Oriental Jewish community more than the Europeans, thus tending to widen the gap between the two groups. Politically, this could also be dangerous.

Economic controls would affect organized labor most immediately. Despite close connections between the dominant Labor party and the Histadrut,[46] the establishment has been meeting greater and greater difficulty in coping with labor unrest which has expressed itself in wildcat strikes. Cartoons and caustic comments in some of

45. JWP, 18 August 1869.

46. The Histadrut or General Federation of Israeli Workers, is Israel's powerful trade union body established in 1920. It not only dominates the labor field, but it controls most public health insurance services, it owns and operates newspapers and publishing companies, and it controls through its various economic subsidiary organizations a larger share of the national economy than any single private group or combination.

the press have wondered if this internal opposition is not more serious and damaging to the country than the relatively ineffectual Arab guerrilla activity.

Still another type of loyal opposition is that which has raged around the question, "who is a Jew?" a few independent-minded Israelis have insisted on placing rights of conscience over national rights. They maintain that questions of religious or group identification are matters for personal, rather than government determination. As a result of a complicated Supreme Court decision supporting the individual who brought the case before it, another controversy was stirred, forcing the government to adopt legislation redefining Jewish identity for purposes of obtaining citizenship.[47] The issue even threatened relationships with Jewish communities abroad, especially the Conservative and Reform Jewish communities in the United States. While the disagreement led to serious dispute between the American Reform and the Israeli rabbinate controlled by the Orthodox, relations were smoothed out with the government. Spokesmen for the Reform movement agreed not to press for equal rights in Israel at the moment, because they "understand the difficulties and problems and . . . do not wish to add to the burdens and problems the people and Government face today." [48]

Appendix A

Percentage Distribution of Arab Votes in Knesset Elections

Party Stand on Military Government	Party List	First Election	Third Election	Fifth Election
Consistently against	Communist	24%	16%	22%
	Mapam	11%	7%	12%
Sometimes for, and Sometimes against	Liberals	2%	2%	1%
	Achdut Avoda		2%	5%
	Herut			2%
Consistently for	Mapai and Mapai Arabs	40%	65%	49%
	Religious		2%	4%

47. Extensive discussion of this problem can be found in *JOMER, JPW, NYT,* and other publications during February and March 1970 and subsequently.

48. *NYT,* 5 March 1970.

CHAPTER 5

The Palestinian Resistance Movement Since 1967

MICHAEL HUDSON

The Palestinian guerrillas go under many names. Representatives of both extremes, Israelis identify them as terrorists and murderers, while Arabs hold them up as national heroes. Obviously, it depends upon one's sympathies.

The Palestinians never really posed a serious threat to Israel's vital security, even during their heyday. Nevertheless, they brought considerable political and psychological pressure to bear on Israel from 1968 through 1970. Thereupon, Jordan (with United States help) practically eliminated guerrilla activities from Jordan; many observers wrote them off as an effective political force. But they survived the disastrous setbacks.

Does this mean, therefore, that Palestinian guerrilla activities will return to the same level in the Middle East? Will fedayeen-*inspired turmoil recur in the area, bringing new suffering and peril for Israel—all sowing the seeds of new frustration and economic regression for the Arabs, further decimation of the Palestinians, destruction of American interests, and continued risk of superpower confrontation?*

The author of this chapter presents a broad picture of the Palestinian national resistance movement, tracing its devlopment, structure, ideology, and effectiveness.

This chapter attempts to describe the reemergence of a Palestinian Arab national movement *al-Muqawama al-Filistiniyya* (the Palestinian resistance) during the years following the June War, in 1967. Perspectives and concepts from comparative politics are employed to

The support of the Johns Hopkins School of Advanced International Studies, the Brooklyn College Political Research Center, the Yale World Data Analysis Program, and the American Philosophical Society is gratefully acknowledged. The impressions and judgments are based in part upon interviews conducted during the period 1968–70.

facilitate description and evaluation. An effort is made to assess the violence capabilities, structural development, and ideological trends of the movement in the light of general theoretical considerations, and also in the context of the politics of the Arab world.

From the spring of 1968 through the fall of 1970, the guerrillas developed the capacity to carry out serious protracted violence against Israel. The guerrilla organizations themselves became more elaborate structurally and began to develop important political functions of a nation-building character. The movement was becoming more radical ideologically, a development which reinforced its overall cohesion although serious elite rivalries persisted. These developments increased the influence of the movement over Arab governments, but they also increased its threat potential, thus complicating the relationship. As far as the superpowers were concerned, the Palestinians injected an element of instability in the local political-military situation and a consequent additional risk of great-power confrontation. Thus, when Jordan and the United States moved to eliminate guerrilla activities from Jordan, the Palestinians found they had no effective outside supporters.

The Palestinian guerrillas never constituted more than a minor threat to Israel's vital security. They were irregulars, fighting a hit-and-run war of harassment, the only type of military activities possible for the Arabs whose regular armies remained vastly inferior to the Israeli army. Even during the period of most intense guerrilla activity, the Israelis maintained that the impact was of only marginal significance.[1] While public reporting of casualities may have been understated, Israel still maintained basic public security without a large standing commitment of troops. Casualty ratios remained in Israel's favor, although the margin of superiority was disputed.[2]

Even before Jordan's crackdown on the guerrillas, the Jordan River cease-fire line had been sealed off to a degree by means of electronic fences and surveillance. Guerrilla sources claimed that the efficacy of these measures was exaggerated.[3] On other fronts too,

1. See Y. Harkabi, "Fedayeen Action and Arab Strategy," *Adelphi Papers, Number 53* (London: The Institute for Strategic Studies, December 1968), p. 34.

2. See Hisham Sharabi, "Palestine Guerrillas: Their Credibility and Effectiveness," *Supplementary Papers* (Washington, D.C.: Georgetown University Center for Strategic and International Studies, 1970), pp. 10–12, 46–47. After studying Israeli and Palestinian casualty figures, Sharabi suggests that "the ratio of Israeli monthly fatalities must be considered close to, if not exceeding, those of the Palestinians" (p. 11).

3. Sharabi, "Palestine Guerrillas," pp. 17–19.

the situation was annoying but not alarming. The Golan Heights of Syria remained the quietest sector, and the Israelis continued to build permanent settlements there. South of the Dead Sea there were periodic engagements, the most serious ones occurring in the vicinity of the potash works and the secret Dimona nuclear installation. Eilat experienced a handful of incidents, two of them involving sabotage by Arab frogmen, but the port remained fully active. At the other end of the country, the border with Lebanon became increasingly active. In terms of military threat, however, Israel's generals continued to regard the western front with Egypt a far greater menace than the eastern front with Syria, Jordan, Iraq, and the guerrillas; and their behavior showed it. Israel's main line of defense, its generals said, was in the skies over Egypt.[4]

In contrast, the eastern front presented no similar vital threat: the conventional Arab forces there were numerically inferior to a mobilized Israeli defense force. They lacked even the pretence of air cover and adequate air defense, and their overall coordination and leadership remained feeble. As for the guerrillas, in their prime they constituted *in toto* a force of less than 50,000 men, of whom a much smaller number were actually front-line fighters, lightly armed.[5] Furthermore, the Israelis could count on these guerrillas being hindered in greater or lesser degree by the host countries, Lebanon, Syria, and Jordan.

Nevertheless, the Palestinians were able to apply important political and psychological pressure on Israel from 1968 through 1970. Numerous border incursions and a rash of terrorist acts against Israeli or "pro-Israeli" installation in Europe occurred. An insurrectionary condition prevailed in Gaza while sporadic guerrilla actions took place on the West Bank. Linkages developed between the Palestinians who had been incorporated in the Israel created in 1948 and those who were caught in the areas Israel occupied in 1967.

4. The concern in Israel in March 1970 over the American decision to postpone supplying additional Phantom jet fighters derived from this consideration and from reports that the Soviet Union was strengthening Egyptian air defenses. See for example James Feron, "Israeli Jets Seek to Foil SAM-3s," *The New York Times,* 25 March 1970, and Francis Ofner, "Missiles for Arabs Grate Israel," *The Christian Science Monitor,* 24 March 1970, the latter reporting statements by Defense Minister Moshe Dayan and Foreign Minister Abba Eban.

5. Sharabi, "Palestine Guerrillas," p. 21.

Political Development

The political emergence of the Palestinian resistance after 1967 was an event of revolutionary importance in the Arab world, according to numerous observers including Israelis and Americans.[6] It developed a degree of leadership, organization, and mass support quite superior to earlier efforts during the British Palestine mandate and to those of other political movements in the Arab world. It developed a modest violence capability against Israel which the Israelis found politically intolerable. More significant, however, was the challenge it posed to the authority of all the Arab regimes in the confrontation zone with Israel, a challenge that was to precipitate a grievous setback in 1971.

It is not difficult in retrospect to explain the rise of Palestinian activism. There existed in the Arab states, and especially in the Palestinian Arab community, conditions more favorable to revolution than ever before. The Palestinian Arabs, their traditional society disrupted and their misery self-evident, were particularly mobilizable. If one could chart a relative deprivation curve for the Palestinians, it might well have corresponded to the hypothesis of Tocqueville and his modern interpreters: a steady rise in well-being, especially in education, among the dispersed Palestinians after their eviction from Palestine in 1948, and with it a growing awareness of the injustice suffered. The disaster of 1967, suddenly lowering the level of well-being and renewing the injustice, served to precipitate a climate receptive to new leadership.[7]

No less important was the behavior of Israel. It now occupied, in addition to all of Palestine, significant portions of Syria, Jordan, and Egypt. This condition made it impossible for Arab leaders to put the question of Israel "on the back burner," as President Nasser did between the wars of 1956 and 1967.[8] A political culture inherently

6. See for example, Don Peretz, "Arab Palestine: Phoenix or Phantom," *Foreign Affairs* 48, no. 2 (January 1970): 322–33; C. L. Sulzberger, *The New York Times* 17 and 19 October 1969, 13 and 22 February 1970; and the statements of Arie Eliav, Secretary General of the Israeli Labor Party, *The Economist*, 24 January 1970, p. 31.

7. James C. Davies, following Tocqueville and Crane Brinton, presents such a thesis in "Toward a Theory of Revolution," *American Sociological Review* 27, no. 1 (February 1962): 5–19. See also Chalmers Johnson, *Revolutionary Change* (Boston: Little, Brown, and Co., 1966), chaps. 4 and 5.

8. Kennett Love, *Suez: The Twice-Fought War* (New York: McGraw-Hill, 1969), pp. 83–84, 679–85.

fragmented because of primordial culture divisions, external divisive forces, and uneven modernization,[9] had been subjected to a new Israeli intrusion. The success of Israel's aggresssive stance was continually reaffirmed by new victories. To many Arabs nonviolent alternatives appeared ever more naive.

By 1970 the biggest, richest, and most structurally complex guerrilla group was Fatah, the Palestine Liberation Movement. Founded in the aftermath of the Suez War, Fatah numbered but a handful of members when it began its first armed incursions into Israel in 1965. Following the 1967 war it began to enlarge its activities, and after the battle at Karamah in March 1968, it burgeoned with popular support. By March 1970 Fatah had established itself in Jordan as "a state within a state," with an army, hospitals, social security system, and tax collectors." [10] A second important group, also established before the 1967 war, was the Palestine Liberation Organization (PLO). Originally an instrument of the Arab states, the PLO, directed by Ahmad Shukairy, was far from a revolutionary fighting organization. Nevertheless, it was quite successful politically and administratively in laying the groundwork for the renewed Palestinian political identity. Shukairy exploited the diplomatic status bestowed upon the PLO by the Arab summit conference of 1964, and he began to reorganize the dispersed Palestinian elite by convening the first Palestine National Council in Jerusalem in 1964.

The Council, consisting of some 115 representatives of important segments of Palestinian society and its major associations, was selected by the PLO executive committee annually, and functioned as a kind of constituent assembly of the Palestine diaspora. The PLO also began to develop a Palestine Liberation Army (PLA), mainly in Gaza, before the June War. After the June War, the PLO leadership was discredited but its apparatus remained to function as the executive "umbrella" for the movement as a whole. Fatah gradually gained control of the Palestine National Congress and the PLO Executive Committee. The old PLA asserted its independence of the

9. For theoretical treatments of these factors in new nations, see K. W. Deutsch, "Social Mobilization and Political Development," *American Political Science Review* 55, no. 3 (September 1961): 493–514; Clifford Geertz, "The Integration Revolution: Primordial Sentiments and Civil Politics in the New States," in id. (ed), *Old Societies and New States* (New York: Free Press, 1963), pp. 105–57; and Manfred Halpern, *The Politics of Social Change in the Middle East and North Africa* (Princeton: Princeton University Press, 1963).

10. Sharabi, "Palestine Guerrillas," p. 28.

PLO and began reconstituting itself, and a new guerrilla-style military unit called the Popular Forces emerged. Syria, and later Iraq, sponsored their own Palestinian guerrilla forces, Saʿiqa and the Arab Liberation Front (ALF), respectively; and the Kingdom of Jordan sought without much success to develop guerrilla groups as a counter-weight to the independence Palestinian organizations.

There was also a trio of Palestine guerrilla groups whose orientation was generally Marxist-Leninist-Maoist. These were the offshoots, The Democratic Popular Front (DPFLP), and the Popular Front (General Command). While numerically and financially weak compared to the other groups, these organizations were disproportionately influential because of the widespread appeal of their radical ideology. The PFLP and the DPFLP in particular, placed heavy stress on political indoctrination, setting an example which Fatah increasingly emulated; and they sought to present the Palestinians' problem in the context of Western imperialism.[11] Most important, the spectacular terror and sabotage operations of the PFLP strengthened the coherence and morale of the Palestinian movement generally.

During the first year or so following the June War a large number of commando groups appeared. An important step in coordinating guerrilla activity was taken early in 1969 with Fatah's winning control of the PLO structure and with the establishment of the Palestine Armed Struggle Command (PASC) in Amman. The PASC too was dominated by Fatah and included all the major groups with the exception of the Popular Front. The latter group, led by George Habash, refused to join for fear that the largely nonrevolutionary leadership of Fatah jeopardized the cause. A year later, in February 1970, following another abortive attempt by the government of Jordan to restrict guerrilla activity, a new "umbrella" organization was announced, called the Unified Command for the Palestinian Movement (UC), and it included Habash's Popular Front. Some Palestinian observers now began to speak of the formation of a Palestine National Front. During its first two years of major activity, significant progress had been made toward consolidation among the guerrilla organizations. But in light of the persistent and growing tensions between the resistance and the governments of Jordan and Lebanon, not to mention Israel, this progress was recognized to be insufficient. In June 1970 a new executive coordinat-

11. Gerard Chaliand, "The Palestinian Resistance Movement (in early 1969)," English translation of an article in *Le Monde Diplomatique,* March 1969 (Beirut: Fifth of June Society, 1969), pp. 20–30.

ing body appeared, the Central Committee of the PLO, embodying the old PLO Executive Committee and additional representatives from all the commando groups; and shortly thereafter a General Secretariat of the Central Committee was established. This new apparatus may have helped the guerrillas to hold their own as long as they did during the Jordanian army onslaught of September 1970, but it was clearly unable to supply enough coherence to prevent the inexorable, near-fatal erosion of resistance capabilities that followed it. Even as the Eighth Palestine National Council was meeting in Cairo in July 1971, to carry out yet another executive reform, the Jordan army was preparing to liquidate the final guerrilla enclaves in North Jordan. While much coordination had been achieved and the proliferation of smaller groups eliminated, the leadership had been unable to agree on a common policy toward the Arab states; Fatah and the "moderates" courted regimes like Saudi Arabia and Jordan while the radical organizations, especially the PFLP and a new group called Black September, attacked them.

Structure of the Palestinian Resistance Elite

If one could observe the Palestinian resistance elite from the perspective of a general model of elite structure, one might be better able to interpret the nation-building capabilities of the movement. A useful typology for structural comparison proposed by Louis J. Cantori [12] reformulates the distinction made by Michels and others between mass and elite parties to inquire whether parties are "penetrative" or "nonpenetrative," the former type displaying articulated party organization at all levels and areas of society. It also distinguishes between parties with traditional elites and modern elites at the middle and lower levels of societies, and parties with only a national-level elite. Parties with penetrative organization are more likely to generate and utilize "grassroots" support than those without it. Parties with modern elites at the national, middle, and lowest levels of society are more powerful agents of rational change than parties with a three-tiered traditional or only a national elite. Most potent, theoretically, are parties with both penetrative organization and a three-tiered modern elite.

12. Louis J. Cantori, "Islam, Political Legitimacy and the Istiqlal Party of Morocco" (Paper delivered at the African Studies Association, Montreal, Can., October 1969), pp. 3–5. His formulation draws upon the works of Michels, Duverger, Hodgkin, and Zolberg, among others.

There are two problems in trying to analyze the Palestinian resistance in terms of this paradigm. One is that there is no Palestinian nation with the attributes of territory and sovereignty. The Palestinians are distributed now mainly among four sovereign jurisdictions—Israel, Jordan, Syria, and Lebanon. The second problem is that there is a dearth of information on the elite and organizational characteristics of the Palestinians.

Until the 1970–71 reverses in Jordan, Palestinian guerrilla organizations appeared to exist not only at the "national" level but also at the middle and lower levels of Palestinian society. One of the political advantages for the guerrillas was that there were no longer any powerful parties at the national level; indeed, the national elite itself had been greatly attenuated by the experience of the diaspora. To a large extent the guerrilla groups did not simply penetrate a national elite but actually reconstituted it. Fatah had a network of political and military branches that appeared to engage all sectors of the Palestinian community: refugees, villagers and peasants, urban proletariat outside camps, middle-class professionals and business people, and the very well-to-do commercial elite. This was the case not just around Amman, but wherever there were Palestinians: throughout Jordan, in Syria, Lebanon, and even among Palestine émigré communities in Europe and the Americas. The extent of elite development in these sectors varied a good deal. Early in 1970 Fatah, through its military wing Asifa, seemed particularly strong in the lower-class camp and noncamp population of Jordan and Syria, and, through its domination of the PLO, among the old "upper-class" national elite. The radical organizations—the PFLP and the DPFLP—seemed to be well organized in the camps, especially in Gaza and Lebanon, and within the professional and intellectual sectors generally. Jordan's liquidation of guerrilla and militia forces in late 1970 and 1971 was accompanied by massive security operations and purges of Palestinians in the cities and camps; these unquestionably uprooted or neutralized much of the resistance infrastructure.

The distribution of resistance cadres in the Palestinian communities under Israeli rule seemed confined mainly to Gaza. On the West Bank the Israelis made occasional efforts to cultivate the traditional notables, such as Shaykh Muhammad al-Jaabari of Hebron, as a barrier to resistance penetration. But there was enough guerrilla organization in the intermediate and lower strata to discourage significant collaboration by the notables. Much the same situation applied to the Palestinian Arab community of Israel itself:

here, it appeared at times that there were guerrilla or guerrilla-inspired groups among the urban middle-class professionals and in some villages.

There is little doubt that the resistance elites were modern rather than traditional in orientation. From all accounts, they were largely Western-educated, both through refugee schools and institutions of higher learning in the Arab world and in the West. There was a high proportion of professionals—school teachers, engineers, and doctors—in influential positions in the movement. Doctrinal and strategic statements, as well as commentaries on current affairs that emanated from the movement were analytic, means-end oriented, as well as rhetorical and expressive. Although the soundness of strategic doctrine has been questioned,[13] its authors would not seem to have held traditionalist world views.[14]

But while one could assert that the resistance elite was free of the parochial-primordial traditionalist perspectives of most earlier "national" leaders, one could not go further to claim that its orientation to modernity was sufficient to produce an integrated set of political attitudes and priorities. For example, undertones of sectarian tension were noticeable occasionally at the middle levels; and after the defeats in Jordan a prominent element in the radical critique directed at Fatah was that it had fallen increasingly under the influence of former Muslim Brethren. After the defeats in Jordan, another theme in the radical critique gained more public attention—the charge that the PLO-Fatah leadership was too much a part of the old, regressive, and declining liberal-bourgeois elite to lead the Palestinian revolution. And within the radical camp itself the doctrinal issue over the role of the petit-bourgeois class indicated that there was disagreement about which segments of Palestinian society could produce a properly modern revolutionary movement.

To what extent did these new elites penetrate the different levels of Palestinian society? The evidence from interviews indicates that the resistance movement specifically sought to do so; how well they succeeded is harder to say. The various groups differed in their emphasis on such a policy, with the radical popular Front and Democratic Front making the strongest effort.[15] Fatah, the largest but least "political" of the groups, began its activities in 1965 without

13. Harkabi, "Fedayeen Action and Arab Strategy," pp. 34–35.

14. See for example, Fatah's analyses of its crises with the Lebanese and Jordanian governments, *Fateh* 1, no. 4 (10 November 1969) and 2, no. 4 (15 February 1970) respectively.

15. Chaliand, "The Palestinian Resistance Movement," pp. 23, 28–30.

the resources to activate the community: its "foco" strategy aimed at creating a climate for such penetration through initiating violence against the enemy. But after the battle at Karamah in March 1968, Fatah sought increasingly to articulate its organization at all levels. At the "national" level there was a proliferation of informational and propaganda activities. Notable among these was the Fatah radio, broadcasting from Cairo, which, in addition to disseminating guerrilla communiques, presented educational programs on Palestinian history and culture. Fatah also undertook nation-building activities at the intermediate and lower levels through medical, educational, and welfare programs, mainly in Jordan, for guerrillas and their families. Refugee camps provided a favorable environment for penetration, so that groups with even limited resources like the PFLP and DPFLP made considerable progress. The resistance as a whole tried to move toward the Chinese and Vietmanese model of popular mobilization and away from organizational models hitherto known in the Arab world.

Comparison with Other Movements

Some insight into the potentialities and limitations of the Palestinian resistance may be gained by comparing it to other radical reform or nation-building movements. Among such organizations in the Arab world one might include parties such as Wafd, the Destourian Socialist Party, the Syrian Social Nationalist Party (PPS), and the Baath; and movements such as the Arab Nationalist Movement, the Muslim Brethren, and the Algerian National Liberation Front (FLN). What might one expect to learn from such comparisons? On the theoretical level, according to some scholars, political parties are instruments of national political development.[16] If the Palestinian movement has attained the viability of a healthy nationalist party, its long-term significance may be greater than its initial performance indicates. Or alternatively, does the guerrilla movement exhibit the defects that contributed to the failings of several of these groups?

Compared with the organization of the Viet Cong, the Palestinian resistance, even when at its strongest in early 1970, was inferior

16. Samuel P. Huntington, *Political Order in Changing Societies* (New Haven: Yale University Press, 1968), chap. 7.

both in terms of elites and penetrativeness,[17] but it compared quite favorably with parties and movements in the Arab world.

It is instructive, first of all, to compare the guerrilla movement with Palestinian organizations before 1948. It would appear that until around 1933 there were no parties organizationally distinct from alliances of the religious, landed, and commercial notables in Palestinian Arab politics.[18] Those notables were mainly cosmopolitan and Western-oriented, but not politically modern either in outlook or organization. But as the pressures of Jewish immigration created more tension, more elaborate parties did appear, such as the Istiqlal and several regional, middle-class parties. Clans long influential in political affairs, notably the Husseinis and the Nashashibis, began to organize more formally. The Husseinis sponsored the *Hizb al-ʿarabi al Filastini* (Arab Palestine party) and the Nashashibis sponsored the *Hizb al-Difaʿ al-Watani* (National Defense party); both, however, retained their religious and feudal bases of support. Hajj Amin al-Husseini, the Grand Mufti, exploited the influence of the Supreme Muslim Council to dominate the national movement and the smaller bourgeois parties that had arisen. Hajj Amin and his Arab Palestine Party controlled the Arab Higher Committee, a coalition of six parties, that tried to coordinate the rebellion of 1936–39.[19] There is little evidence that these Palestinian organizations, either singly or together, had well-developed elites at the intermediate or lower levels, although, given the small size of Palestine and the extensiveness of the main families, there was probably some representation. As to the degree of organizational penetration or articulation, they do not seem to have possessed it to any significant degree. While the rebellion itself was widespread, involving hundreds of fatalities and tying down a large British occupation force, it appears to have been a spontaneous and uncoordinated peasant uprising. The post-1967 Palestinian resistance, despite all its structural weaknesses, would seem to represent a con-

17. Douglas Pike, *Viet Cong* (Cambridge: The MIT Press, 1966), chaps. 6 and 12.

18. John Marlowe, *The Seat of Pilate* (London: Cresset, 1959), p. 130 and following.

19. Naji ʿAlloush, *al-Muqawama al-ʿArabiyya fi Filastin 1917–1948* (Beirut: Palestine Liberation Organization Research Center, 1967), pp. 63–100; Marlowe, *The Seat of Pilate*, chap. 9; Christopher Sykes, *Crossroads to Israel* (London: Collins, 1965), pp. 175–87; and Hisham Sharabi, *Palestine and Israel: The Lethal Dilemma* (New York: Pegasus, 1969), pp. 184–91.

siderable advance over the earlier groupings in terms of the modernity and diffusion of its elites and its organizational articulation.

A list of the most structurally developed parties or movements elsewhere in the Arab world in the contemporary period would probably include the following: the Moroccan Istiqlal, the Algerian FLN, the Tunisian Neo-Destour, the Egyptian Wafd and Muslim Brethren, the Syrian Social Nationalist Party (PPS), the Arab Nationalist Movement (ANM), and the Baath. The first four were movements of independence from colonial rule. The last four, with the qualified exception of the Muslim Brethren, were revolutionary postindependence, transnational movements, none of which has been conspicuously successful in achieving its goal. They all employed, and justified, violence as a means to their ends. The Palestinian resistance emerged both as a revolutionary independence movement and a movement with transnational implications. If all these parties were operating in roughly similar political environments and facing similar problems, we might suppose that the Palestinian resistance would have had to match the best of them in terms of structural development even to approach its own goal, much less fulfill them; such a degree of development would be a necessary though hardly sufficient condition of success.

Table 1 based on Cantori's categories, summarizes our comparisons.

TABLE 1
Summary of Comparisons of Resistance Groups
ORGANIZATION

Elite	*Penetrative*	*Nonpenetrative*
Modern	Palestinian Resistance FLN (Algerian) Neo-Destour (Tunisian)	Baath PPS (Syrian)
Traditional	Istiqlal (Moroccan) MB (Muslim Brethren)	Wafd (Egyptian)
None (below the national level)		ANM (Arab Nationalist Movement)

Relative to other major Arab protest movements, we classify the Palestinian resistance in which we include the PLO, the Palestine

National Council, and the main guerrilla organizations) along with the FLN and Neo-Destour as possessing modern elites at the national, immediate, and local levels, and highly articulated (penetrative) organization. Parties with at least two features of advanced structural development include the Istiqlal and Muslim Brethren, with a penetrative (though traditional) elite at the subnational levels, and the Baath and PPS, with a modern (though nonpenetrative) elite at the subnational levels. A party scoring at the "advanced" level on only one structural dimension is the Wafd, which is judged to have had elites (though traditional and nonpenetrative) at the subnational levels. None of the parties under consideration would seem to fall easily into the category of "penetrative but with only a national elite," although a case could be made for locating the Baath, the Syrian neo-Baath, the PPS, or the ANM there. The Arab Nationalist Movement would seem to be the least-developed structurally of the group, having apparently only a national elite in the major cities of the Arab east. Modern though it is, we do not find evidence that it has penetrated Arab society structurally. On the other hand, the ANM has been known to be able to cause mass disturbances in several Arab countries (Lebanon, Syria, Iraq, South Yemen), and it maintained clandestine networks in Jordan and Gaza.

Cohesion in the FLN undoubtedly declined after independence, but at its height its effectiveness was unparalleled in the modern Arab world, despite its internal divisions. The Neo-Destour, according to some observers,[20] began to ossify in the late 1960s, but it still remained the most successful postindependence party in the Arab world. The Istiqlal, though suffering from the freeze on party politics in Morocco since 1965, developed a traditional base at the intermediate and local levels.[21] The elites of the Muslim Brethren, although characterized by traditional perspectives and fundamentalist religious values, were structurally well articulated, with the primary subnational units being the branch and family.[22] If one considers the Baath as a pan-Arab party, with specific country commands, and within those regions local party elites in various cities and districts, then the party would seem to have possessed elites

20. See for example Stuart Schaar, "A New Look at Tunisia," *Mid East* 10, no. 1 (February 1970): 45.

21. See Cantori, "Islam, Political Legitimacy and the Istiqlal Party of Morocco," pp. 6–12; the solidity is expected to vary, however, within the country.

22. Richard P. Mitchell, *The Society of the Muslim Brothers* (London: Oxford University Press, 1969), chap. 6 and pp. 195–200.

below the national level.[23] Despite this degree of articulation, the Baath's integration and influence in its various constituencies seems always to have been limited. If one considers the Baath, particularly since the emergence of the Syrian neo-Baath in February 1966, as a collection of separate parties, then the diffusion of elites is less clear although the lack of penetration would seem to have remained constant. The Syrian Social Nationalist party presents a structural form similar to the Baath: at its height it possessed elites beyond the "national" level but had not mobilized a popular following.[24] While the Wafd maintained an infrastructure throughout Egypt, its subnational activities seem to have limited it to promoting special interests except during election periods, and thus its penetration of Egyptian society was only sporadic.[25]

Of the two North African parties it most closely resembled, the situation of the Algerian FLN was closest to that of the Palestinians: both were struggling to displace an intruded, well-entrenched, technologically superior political community. Granted that important dissimilarities also existed—notably the existence in Israel of a completely mobilized population well over twice the size of the French population of Algeria, functioning in a smaller, more defensible and controllable territory—it still may be desirable to pursue the comparison. A detailed analysis in terms of performance is beyond the scope of this paper; it is possible, however, to comment on the first years of each revolution. According to Gallagher, the FLN had grown from a few hundred men in the autumn of 1954–55 to a trained army of 60,000 equipped with automatic weapons in the spring of 1958.[26] The Palestinians, as indicated above, might have trained 30,000 to 50,000 men between 1965 and 1970.[27] While Sharabi cautions that not all trainees necessarily become regular combatants, it is not clear that Gallagher's figure refers only to combatants; and one may conclude that the rates of development are similar.

23. Kamel S. Abu Jaber, *The Arab Ba'th Socialist Party* (Syracuse: Syracuse University Press, 1966), pp. 139–46; Avraham Ben-Tzer, "The Neo-Ba'th Party of Syria," *Journal of Contemporary History* 3, no. 3 (1968): 161–82.

24. Michael W. Suleiman, *Political Parties in Lebanon* (Ithaca: Cornell University Press, 1967), pp. 100–103.

25. Anouar Abdel-Malek, *Egypt: Military Society* (New York: Vintage Press, 1968), p. 60; and Jean and Simonne Lacouture, *Egypt in Transition* (London: Methuen, 1958), pp. 240–44.

26. Charles F. Gallagher, *The United States and North Africa* (Cambridge: Harvard University Press, 1963), p. 106.

27. Sharabi, "Palestine Guerrillas," p. 21.

The trends in number of military operations also afford a means of comparison. If we juxtapose operations reported by Fatah with armed attack events in Algeria, coded at the Yale World Data Analysis Program from the *New York Times Index,* we discover that during the first two years of the respective uprisings Algerian armed attacks clearly exceeded Palestinian. In the third, fourth, and fifth years (1957–59), Algerian violence declined seriously but it rose again in 1961 and 1962, culminating in the Evian accords. Palestinian operations increased sharply during their third, fourth, and fifth years (1967–69), but then went into a similar though sharper decline in 1970–71 because of the Jordan problem.

A conservative interpretation would suggest that the Palestinians were not markedly inferior to the Algerians at comparable stages of their respective insurgencies. One might therefore infer that the Palestinian resistance, like the Algerian, could survive a period of military suppression, other things being equal. Of course, other things were not exactly equal: the Palestinians faced more formidable foes than did the Algerians. Gallagher notes that 60,000 FLN guerrillas were holding down half a million French troops four years after the insurgency began. But it seemed clear that neither the guerrillas nor the Arab armies together were holding down more than 70,000 mobilized Israeli soldiers [28] at any given moment in the post-1967 crisis period, although 200,000 more Israelis could be mobilized on very short notice. Furthermore, the Palestinians had to face more formidable opposition in their "sanctuaries" than did the Algerians; and it was this Arab-state opposition, not the Israelis, that led to the setback of 1971.

If our classifications are accurate, it would seem that the Palestinian resistance had some structural advantages over several of the most significant Arab parties and movements, and that it bore structural resemblance to two of the most successful of these groups: the Algerian FLN and the Tunisian Neo-Destour. The eastern Arab world had not produced a political movement as well-developed as the Palestinian resistance was until 1971. Needless to add, this unusual degree of structural development alone could not support a prediction of "success" for the Palestinians. All the organizations to which it may have been structurally superior failed to a large extent to achieve their aims in the fragmented political culture of the Arab East. Furthermore, the Palestinian guerrillas were not

28. Drew Middleton, "Israelis vs. Arabs . . . ," *The New York Times* 24 March 1970, p. 14.

competing simply with other parties or movements, but with established states—not only Israel, but also Jordan, Lebanon, Syria, and Iraq, and indirectly with the great powers.

Ideological Conflict: Conventional vs. Radical Perspectives

The Palestinian resistance movement after 1967 was a nationalist uprising, not a social revolution. The dominant theme was recovery of the land and the reestablishment of a distinctively Palestinian community on it. But the radical elements in the movement sought to implant an ideology that would transcend local, parochial, or liberal-bourgeois nationalism. The radical guerrillas tried to introduce modernity and democratic socialism in their attempt to avoid the errors of the past. Modernity meant a rational and programmatic strategy of liberation. Democratic socialism meant a redistribution of power, wealth, and opportunity toward the disadvantaged classes, both Arab and Jewish. The rhetoric, values, and strategic doctrine of the Third World Left became increasingly evident, not only in the PFLP and DPFLP but also in Fatah itself and among younger Palestinian intellectuals generally.

The core of Palestinian resistance ideology was the return of all Palestinian Arabs outside Palestine to live in a secular, democratic state of Palestine with all of the present inhabitants, irrespective of their religion or cultural background, provided that these people consent to live peaceably in the new state.[29] It is true that this doctrine was never articulated fully or authoritatively for the movement as a whole. But those who seize upon the sloganistic character of Palestinian ideological goals to support accusations of irrationality or bad faith misunderstand the function of ideology, which, as Clifford Geertz puts it, is "to render otherwise incomprehensible social situations meaningful, [and] to so construe them as to make it possible to act purposefully within them. . . ." [30]

The resistance movement used this formula to win wide support from the Palestinian and other Arab communities. It was simple

29. In January 1970 Palestinian leaders publicly urged the amendment of the section of the Palestine National Covenant that included in the liberated state of Palestine only those Jews who had lived in Palestine before 1948, to include all Jews living there now as equal partners in a non-Zionist state. *Fateh* 2, no. 2 (19 January 1970): 10. See also *The Economist*, 7 March 1970, p. 30.

30. Clifford Geertz, "Ideology as a Culture System," in David Apter (ed.), *Ideology and Discontent* (New York: Free Press, 1964), p. 64.

and yet ambiguous enough to attract diverse and conflicting elements. As interpreted by the Fatah and PLO leadership, it differed little from the traditionalist and liberal-bourgeois Palestinian and Arab nationalist appeals of the mandate era. But to others, notably in the PFLP and the DPFLP, it symbolized a radical populist ideological perspective whose most salient attributes were secularism, participation, and social justice in the context of the national liberation revolution.[31] During the 1960s, younger Arab intellectuals generally, not just Palestinians, were increasingly drawn to them as were the new elites of many developing countries. Secularism meant a political society free from the influence of traditional religious authorities—non-sectarian, not multisectarian. The reconstituted Palestine must be a society in which the adherents of all religions have equal civil status. Democratic participation meant a politics of popular representation and accountability, not of bourgeois parliamentary oligarchy or military clique. The opportunity for participation must be made available to hitherto excluded elements of society, such as the peasantry, the urban poor, and women. Social justice meant a redistribution of goods and opportunities in order to redress the historical social inequalities.

Thus, in terms of substantive ideology there was widespread agreement within the resistance elite over the fundamental goal of a secular, democratic Palestine but there was also conflict over how such a society should be governed and its resources allocated. On this question, the radical Marxist vision of the PFLP and DPFLP challenged the comparatively liberal-pragmatic orientation of Fatah and the PLO.

In terms of instrumental doctrine, one could discern a similar pattern of agreement and disagreement within the resistance elite. The resistance as a whole became committed to the principle of a struggle of popular liberation as the means to creating a secular democratic Palestine. This commitment was sealed when Fatah became the acknowledged voice of the Palestinian revolution after the battle of Karamah in March 1968, and it marked a distinct break

31. So that the differences between the radicals will not be overstressed, it is worth noting the lengthy statement by Fatah in January 1970. While deferring any explicit statement on the political-social-economic organization of liberated Palestine, it emphasized that a "democratic and progressive Palestine . . . rejects by elimination a theocratic, a feudalist, an aristocratic, an authoritarian or a racist-chauvinistic form of government. . . ." It would provide equal opportunities in work, worship, education, political decision-making, cultural and aristic expression. *Fateh* 2, no. 2 (19 January 1970), p. 10.

with Palestinian elite thinking of the previous two decades. To a lesser degree it seemed also to differ from the relatively parochial and anomic violence doctrine of leadership in the 1936–39 uprising. There was basic agreement between Fatah and the radical groups on the necessity for violence, but there was conflict over related questions such as indoctrination, activism, and—most seriously—relations with Arab states.

It was in the adoption of violence as its strategic centerpiece that the resistance showed itself most radical and unified. The pragmatic leadership of Fatah accepted just as willingly as the radicals in the Popular and Democratic Fronts the Maoist dictum that power grows out of the barrel of a gun. The Third-World concept of peoples' liberation war, formerly only marginal in the political thought of the Arab East, was the keystone of the guerrillas' program. The guerrillas read Mao, Giap, and Guevara, not necessarily out of agreement with their social goals, but for their practical expertise. For Fatah in particular, radical social and military analysis was instrumental for attaining ends not altogether radical in themselves. Palestinian intellectuals found Frantz Fanon's analysis of the psychologically liberating effects of violence relevant to their situation; and guerrilla training applied Fanon's insights. And as Palestinians looked back on that period in the brief history of the guerrilla movement when they were strong, they could find confirmation for Mao's dictum.

The radical groups placed a higher priority on indoctrination and activism than did Fatah and the other organizations. Indoctrination and education must be carried out systematically among the Palestinians, the other Arabs, and the Israelis. The Palestinians must be politicized—imbued with a "new mentality" that abjures self-pity and despair, so that they can participate in the common struggle. The other Arab masses must be persuaded to pressure their reluctant elites to support the Palestinian people's war. And the Israeli population—particularly the disadvantaged Arab Palestinians and Arab Jews—must be offered a preferable alternative to its present life in the Zionist state. Activism stressed the development of individual and community capabilities, as opposed to the attitude of fatalism prevalent in the traditional sectors of Palestinian and Arab society. Among the activist traits which the guerrillas attempted to instill in themselves and in their children were the modern—indeed Western—virtues of achievement, self-reliance, and leadership initiative. The guerrilla image that dramatically won the support of the Arab people was that of an individual who has taken his future into his own hands, who sacrifices personal advantages, who works as part of a team for a noble purpose.

The radicalization of Palestinian ideology, both in its substantive and instrumental aspects, was particularly dramatic within the liberal, American-educated professional elite, previously classifiable as "moderate" or "pro-Western." [32] In searching for an explanation, two factors seem to be important. One of course is the trauma of the 1967 war and the intransigence in postwar Israeli behavior. This behavior unquestionably forced many Palestinians into advocating radical countermeasures. The other factor was the realization by many younger Palestinians than nonradical politics failed to achieve national and social goals. The experience of the Palestinian community during the mandate was to them sufficient evidence that the traditional elite had lacked vision, was naive in terms of tactics, and thus was inadequate to the challenge of Zionism and British colonial power.

The liberal-democratic model also had failed in the Arab world. While independence was due in no small measure to the activities of the nationalist upper bourgeoisie, the postindependence parliamentary regimes in the Fertile Crescent and Egypt had been crippled because of their narrow base, their corruption, and ultimately their instability. By the time of the June War, Lebanon was perhaps the only surviving liberal-democratic regime, and it was by no means free of the general defects of parliamentary systems in the Arab world. Parliamentary governments had given way increasingly to military regimes.

The modernizing military represented an alternative to liberal democracy. The ideals of pluralism, political freedom, and electoral competition, to be realized through a process of bargaining and compromise, gave way to an emphasis upon reform, rectitude, and development through rational hierarchical—military—decision-making. The regime of the Free Officers in Egypt was by far the most successful example of this military-reformist model, but in other countries such as Syria and Iraq it was disappointing, even in terms of basic stability. While these regimes had proclaimed support for the Palestine cause, even the best of them had been impotent to resist, much less destroy, Israeli injustice. Even apart from the Israel question many radicalized Palestinians and other Arabs came to

32. See Adel Daher, *Current Trends in Arab Intellectual Thought,* Resources for the Future, Research Paper RM-5979-FF (Santa Monica, Calif.: The RAND Corp., December 1969), pp. 13–27.

feel that the military reformists hardly represented an ideal political order: their socialist revolution was more rhetorical than actual, their regimes more dictatorial than participatory. Radical populism, with its strategy of total political mobilization, thus had considerable appeal even beyond the Palestine conflict.

Ideology in developing nations often serves an integrating function, and this basically would seem to have been the case with the nascent Palestinian political community, notwithstanding the radical-conventional conflict. The resistance as a whole found that a radical perspective rendered the Palestinian situation (in Geertz's terms) comprehensible and facilitated purposeful action. Ideological commitment also functioned to insulate the committed from alternative courses based on fundamentally different assumptions. In the Palestinian case, this tendency, one suspects, reinforced the linkages between elites and masses and reduced somewhat the divisive effects of primordial factionalism.

It would be incorrect, however, to state that a single radical ideology became implanted throughout the Palestinian political community; as we have observed, the ideological revolution met formidable opposition in the mainstream of the movement. The deepest divisions arose between those who favored a complete socialist revolution in liberated Palestine and who saw Western imperialism generally rather than Zionism specifically as the enemy to be confronted, and those whose idea of the future Palestine was less explicitly revolutionary, who wished to direct their violence strictly against Zionist institutions, and who were willing to enter into compromising alliances with nonradical, even reactionary elements in the Arab world for support. Within the community as a whole, it would seem that the younger generation and especially its better-educated elements identified itself with the first position, while the older generation was closer to the second. The militancy of some in the latter group was tempered with fatigue and an unwillingness to accept the imperialism theory; and among some there was still hope for a diplomatic solution and compromise, even though it would fall short of stated goals.

This ideological divergence was reflected in the different guerrilla groups. PLO leadership, both before and after the war, tended toward the "moderate" position: perhaps the age, the American or British education, and the successful business and professional status of many of these men and women account for it. The Fatah leadership too seemed to hold a less doctrinaire view, and a less elaborate conceptual framework for comprehending the Palestinian situation, in the immediate postwar period. The most authentic and significant of the radical groups was the PFLP. It insisted that the liberation of Palestine was organically linked to the complete liberation of the entire Arab world and stressed the class aspects of the struggle. "The World Zionist Movement and Israel exist in organic unity with world imperialism," wrote George Habash, but—following Mao Tse-tung—"there are enemies within the Arab and Palestinian communities in collusion with Zionism and imperialism, which can be identified by their class interests: the reactionary and big bourgeoisie classes."[33] Violence and terror will exacerbate the internal economic and cultural contradictions of Israel and lead to the PFLP goal of establishing "a progressive democratic structure in which the different racial and religious groups can co-exist." The PFLP suspicion of Fatah stemmed from the latter's original focus on Zionism in Palestine and its willingness to accept the support of Arabs who were not "progressive." PFLP theoreticians feared that Fatah might sell out if given a sufficiently attractive compromise package, such as a West Bank state.

The PFLP's chief radical competitor was the much smaller DFPLP. It claimed to have a more correct Marxist-Leninist interpretation of the Palestine situation than the PFLP. The DPFLP came into existence in February 1969, when some important political cadres split off from the PFLP leadership. Its violence capabilities were low. It was more committed to international socialism and less to Arab nationalism than the PFLP. In terms of instrumental doctrine the differences were even sharper. According to the Democratic Front itself, "the basic difference between the Democratic Front and the Popular Front is the refusal of the right-wing [Habash] leadership of the PFLP to analyze critically the reasons and causes that led to the military defeat of June 1967, under the pretext of refusing to interfere in the internal affairs of the Arab states and the Arab regimes. In this sense the PFLP has a position not dissimilar from that of Fatah."[34] The DPFLP also accused the PFLP of accepting money from the Iraqi Baath party, Egypt, and Saudi Arabia, while priding itself on being untainted by support from any Arab state. Spokesmen for the PFLP and Fatah noted a certain gap between the DPFLP's words and actions: for example, the PFLP, not the DLPFP,

33. The Popular Front for the Liberation of Palestine, "Theoretical Armament in the Battle of Liberation," translation of an article written by Dr. George Habash for "al-Taliʿah" magazine, mimeographed (Cairo: n.p., n.d.), pp. 9–11.

34. "Middle East for Revolutionary Socialism" 1, no. 1, mimeographed (London: Democratic Popular Front, 1970), p. 6.

had been responsible for the significant attacks on Arab and western imperialist interests outside Palestine; and the DPFLP, not the PFLP, had elected to join the armed Struggle Command under Fatah's domination, while the PFLP remained outside, even though Fatah continued to prohibit such attacks. It was clear that ideological radicalization had not eliminated elite factionalism; without it though, such factionalism might have been worse.

The Setbacks of 1970–71

In September 1970, the Jordan Army launched a massive counterattack against the growing guerrilla power in the kingdom. The guerrillas weathered the onslaught more successfully than their adversaries had predicted, but the number of civilian casualties ran to several thousand. In the following months, however, the Fatah-dominated guerrilla leadership acceded to royalist demands for dismantling of commando and militia organization in the cities; and by spring 1971, the guerrillas had been effectively penned up in the Jerash-Ajloun area of North Jordan. Nobody except the Fatah leadership was surprised when the Jordan army eliminated these last strongholds in July 1971, thereby removing the guerrillas as an effective force in Jordan for the immediate future. Nothing could more clearly indicate the desperate condition of the movement than the spectacle of *fedayeen* in flight across the Jordan River, surrendering to the Israelis to avoid extermination by the king's army. By the end of 1971 the resistance was not dead but its condition was critical. If it were to reemerge as a significant force in the Middle East crisis it would have to do so in a different form.

What went wrong? The resistance leadership was consistently unable to make the necessary decisions that would protect its independence and integrity, and it misjudged the dynamics of Arab interstate politics in the Middle East crisis.

Despite their considerable progress in structural and ideological terms, the Palestinians were unable to develop a sufficient degree of rational executive authority to confront their formidable adversaries. More important than the much-lamented divisions between resistance groups was the common failure to develop enough discipline and reponsibility among the rank and file of commandos, militia, and supporters. The leadership was unable to give this problem the highest priority that it required, given the preciously short "honeymoon period" of the resistance with Arab regimes. The guerrillas swaggering through Amman just before the September 1971 civil war seemed caught up by some primordial instinct for self-destruction. Instead of overthrowing Hussein they teased him; instead of establishing stronger links with non-Palestinian Arabs they frequently alienated them.

Fatah's strategy of cooperation with Arab governments was effective at first, as it bought time for the movement to establish itself. That this approach succeeded for as long as it did can be explained partly by the need for Israel's defeated neighbors to cultivate a morale-boosting distraction for their disillusioned citizens. But as the United States peace initiative, launched in summer 1970, gained momentum, these regimes had a new straw to grasp at and began to perceive the guerrillas as a serious liability rather than as a benefit. Two decades of bitter experience should have taught the Palestinians that state interests take precedence over national interests in the Arab world, yet they were still unable to act rationally in light of this knowledge. Fatah was stunned when President Nasser, pursuing the Rogers cease-fire initiative, closed the resistance radio stations in Cairo. Yasir Arafat thought until too late that he could share power in Jordan with King Hussein, and the leadership seemed so confused after the September showdown that it squandered the gains it had made as if it were ignorant of the realities of politics, yet it had been repeatedly warned at the highest levels of the consequences of its behavior.

In fairness to the leadership it must be stressed that the forces opposing the movement were in fact strong and pervasive. Certainly the United States, through its military assistance to Israel and Jordan, ensured that the main enemies of the Palestinians would maintain their superiority in armed strength. Israel's threats against Syria deterred any substantial assistance to the beleagured Palestinians. Iranian pressures in the Persian Gulf deterred Iraq. Within the ranks of the guerrillas themselves, agents and provocateurs sapped the strength of credibility of the movement. An Ataturk or a Nasser might not have fared better in Arafat's place.

Nevertheless, there was a distinct gap between the leadership's understanding of the situation and its ability to act. The Fatah and PLO leadership, while repudiating in general terms the traditional Palestinian leaders, had been unable to commit itself to a total and coherent radical strategy, nor had it severed the ties that bound it to regimes that could only tolerate it as a weak and nonradical movement, useful primarily for propaganda in the West. If the mainstream Palestinian leadership of this period showed a typical human weakness, it was not the conscious betrayal of ideals but rather a willingness to be co-opted into the company of the politically influential. The temptations of power and prestige dimmed the perceptions of danger that co-optation entailed.

The Resistance at the Crossroads

After the defeat in Jordan many observers felt that the Palestinians were finished as an effective political force. But the Palestinians still had powerful elements working in their behalf. First, Israel and the United States seemed prepared to maintain a status quo in the area that would keep alive the Palestinian issue and radicalism generally among the Arabs. Second, the Palestinians themselves seemed to have successfully resuscitated their national identity, and the idea of organized struggle appeared to be firmly implanted in the younger generation.

Two contradictory tendencies were evident in the convulsions of the Palestinian movement after the setbacks in Jordan, viz., intensified pressures from outside to "domesticate" it and, from inside, to "domesticate" it and, from inside, to "radicalize" it. On the one hand, Arab governments generally felt that the Palestinians should be under their control. While neighboring Arab states had protested the severity of Jordan's suppresion of the guerrillas, for example, they all had imposed some degree of restraints on guerrilla activities. On the other hand, the disasters they had suffered in Jordan in 1970–71 had convinced many influential Palestinians of the necessity for going underground to wage a campaign of terror, assassination, and sabotage against Israel and Jordan and against American interests in the area. For the intolerable constraints throughout the Arab states threatened the movement's legitimacy which derived essentially, of course, from an armed struggle. Those who favored a radical approach argued that (*a*) the resistance must go underground to preserve its independence from Arab governments, even "progressive" ones; (*b*) any other approach ultimately required acceptance of an unsatisfactory diplomatic settlement, such as establishment of a Palestinian entity on the West Bank that would forever silence the Palestinian claim to independence in all, or even part, of Palestine; and (*c*) Jordan in the short run and Israel in the long run were vulnerable to internal disruption through terror and violence, while neither were vulnerable to conventional force because of their outside protectors; and the great powers would respect nothing but violence.

The emergence of the Black September Palestinian group a year after the September 1970 civil war in Jordan exemplified and strengthened the radical tendency, and it gave a new emphasis to violence in terrorist form. Not only did the Black September strike at Israeli targets, notably in the operation against Israeli athletes at the 1972 Munich Olympics, but it also attacked Arab and American governmental targets with a directness and ferocity not previously evident in Palestinian activities. The assassination of the prime minister of Jordan, Wasfi Tell, in Cairo in November 1971 and the murder of two high American officials in Khartoum in March 1973 seemed to bear out the grimmest predictions of observers concerned with the failure of the United States and the international community to come to grips with the Palestinian problem. While the Black September initially had a mixed impact in the Arab states, it seemed to indicate that resistance to Greater Israel and her supporters would continue, and that the threat to "moderate" Arab regimes and to American petroleum interests would not soon disappear.

Five years after the June War it was not certain that the Palestinian resistance could develop the cohesion to direct it either toward a domesticated or a radicalized position. In the Arab world it is not just regimes that are underdeveloped—liberation movements are, too. The obstacles of particularism, distrust, fatalism, and sentimentality would not quickly disappear.

After the 1967 war the Palestinians were able to fashion a new political identity and reactivate their claims to self-determination in Palestine. Whether or not their goal of a secular, democratic, unitary state of Palestine was achievable, their emergence made it likely that Palestinian political claims in some form would be part of any future settlement. In the absence of a settlement, the likelihood of continued turmoil remained strong, with the possibilities of new suffering and peril for Israel, frustration and economic regression for the Arabs, further decimation of the Palestinian people, destruction of American interests, and continued risk of superpower confrontation.

CHAPTER 6

Conditions of Conflict between Nations: An Overview of Middle Eastern and North African Nations

ROGER H. HARRELL

Many have assumed at both the popular and professional levels that there is a direct linkage between the internal and external behavior of nations. The author of this chapter cites an international relations expert who finds, for example, an association between domestic and international conflict behavior. In effect, nations involved at home in domestic conflict are likely to become involved in international conflict, and vice versa. He cites another who suggests that external involvements are sometimes used to promote internal stability.

Such statements are, of course, commonly made concerning the Middle East. Nasser was frequently accused of involvement in international adventures, for example, in order to focus popular attention abroad rather than on Egypt's overwhelming domestic problems. Egypt's external involvements, in essence, promoted internal stability at home.

How much credence should one give to the quantitative examination of these observations?

Introduction

The almost constant conflict within the Middle East raises a number of questions. Most of them have been treated at great length. In this chapter I will give major attention to one of the several questions of conflict behavior that has not been treated as extensively as the others. It concerns the relationships between the three basic types of conflict in the area: conflict within nations (i.e., domestic conflict), general conflict (e.g., border clashes) between nations, and major conflict (i.e., wars) between nations.

Relationships of these sorts are known within the jargon of international relations as linkages. While studied elsewhere in some detail, linkages have only been touched upon as they relate to Middle Eastern conflict behavior.

Frame of Reference

In this study I will test propositions related to the central question of linkages between conflict behavior in one system (the nation) and conflict behavior in another system (the international or regional system).[1] I have limited the focus to the following three basic and theoretically linked propositions: (*1*) that an increase in conflict behavior within a nation is associated with an increase in the external conflict behavior of the same nation; (*2*) that internal conflict is significantly related to major external conflict; and (*3*) that general external conflict is significantly related to major external conflict. It will test these propositions against nonverbal (i.e., physical) conflict behavior within the Middle East.

The propositions are not new. Quincy Wright has suggested, for example, that war and preparation for war have frequently been used as a tactic to promote internal stability or order.[2] With a slightly different emphasis, Richard Rosecrance has supported the same proposed linkage: he refers to the association between domestic insecurity of elites (as manifested in domestic instability and

1. The proposed linkage between conflict within and between nations is only one aspect of a larger question frequently referred to as the domestic sources of foreign policy, or something equally vague. For example, see James Rosenau, ed., *Domestic Sources of Foreign Policy* (New York: The Free Press, 1967); and idem, ed., *Linkage Politics* (New York: The Free Press, 1969). The articles in these two works deal with the linkage question at both the theoretical and empirical level. In most of the empirical studies, the linkage between domestic and foreign data is not established. These studies do, however, suggest the numerous possible explanations of how political behavior within nations might influence the external behavior of that same nation. Who initiates the internal conflict behavior, for example, within nations? Where does it take place? What are the relative capabilities of the initiators? What was the internal response of the government? Another aspect of the general linkage proposition includes questions related to the direction of the influence—i.e., are the preconditions for internal conflict to be found in the international system, or are the preconditions for external conflict to be found within nations? These questions are certainly relevant and should be investigated *if* an overview, such as the present study, finds any significant correlations between internal and external conflict behavior.

2. Quincy Wright, *A Study of War,* 2nd ed. (Chicago: The University of Chicago Press, 1965), pp. 254, 828–29.

internal conflict) and international instability and war.[3] Nor are the propositions untested. Rudolph Rummel and Raymond Tanter, for example, did some of the first studies to investigate the possible existence of a link between internal and external conflict behavior. Rummel collected data for twenty-two types of events—both internal and external.[4] The time and space units of analysis covered by Rummel include seventy-seven nations for the years 1955–57. Tanter repeated Rummel's earlier work using the same types of events, but covering eighty-three nations for the years 1958–60.[5] Both Rummel and Tanter used similar sources of data—sources such as the *New York Times Index, Facts on File,* and *Deadline Data on World Affairs.* They found no evidence, however, to support the proposition that external conflict behavior was linked to internal conflict behavior.

At the global level, therefore, their analyses did not support this basic proposition. The global level, of course, includes a great number of nations, many of which have different sociocultural settings—all increasing the uncertainty of the validity of variables in cross-national comparisons! It should also be noted that their global level of analysis did not provide any information, naturally, regarding the possibility of linkages at the regional level, or in one region of the world and not in others.

Subsequently, using a regional approach, another author found that indeed, "Domestic disorder is a sufficient condition of foreign conflict behavior in Africa." [6] John Collins used types of events and sources of data similar to Rummel and Tanter, but selected only African nations for his study. His regional findings justify, therefore, not only reopening the question of linkages between internal and external conflict behavior, but also testing the proposition in other regions of the world, such as the Middle East and North Africa.

Using the same basic approach as Rummel, Tanter, and Collins, Robert Burrowes thereupon began to explore the linkage question,

3. Richard Rosecrance, *Action and Reaction in World Politics* (Boston: Little, Brown and Co., 1963), pp. 304–306.

4. For example, he collected data on antigovernment demonstrations, riots, general strikes, purges, revolutions, assassinations, guerrilla wars, number of military actions, and number of wars: see Rudolph Rummel, "Dimensions of Conflict Within and Between Nations," *General Systems Yearbook* 8 (1963): 1–50.

5. Raymond Tanter, "Dimensions of Conflict Behavior Within and Between Nations, 1958–60," *Journal of Conflict Resolution* 10 (March 1966): 41–64.

6. See John Collins, "Foreign Conflict Behavior and Domestic Disorder in Africa" (Ph.D. diss., Northwestern University, 1967).

this time in the Middle East.[7] Focusing on one nation (Syria), he tested the same linkage proposition. In addition, he investigated the possibility that internal conflict behavior might or might not correlate with the external behavior of a nation, depending on what other nation is being dealt with. This latter focus, taking profiles of nations, appears to be the most meaningful approach. In this study I apply it to the four major nations in the Arab-Israeli conflict area. In his early report, Burrowes investigated Syria's external behavior toward several nations in the Middle Eastern region. He did not find any significant correlation between Syrian internal and external conflict behavior toward other nations in the region.[8] In this study I provide an overview of the region in an effort to discover where the linkages might exist and to measure their strength, rather than taking the narrower more indepth approach used by Burrowes.

I have divided external conflict behavior into two basic types: border clashes (general external conflict) and the three wars of 1948, 1956, and 1967 (major external conflicts). Just as one examines the possibilty of an association between internal and external conflict behavior, one can also evaluate the possible association between major and general external conflict. The assumption here, however, is based on history as well as logic; it suggests, for example, that general external conflict (i.e., border clashes) can precipitate major external conflict (i.e., war). This approach, it is hoped, will add perspective to any statistically significant correlation that might be found between internal and external conflict, when viewed along with a correlation between two types of external conflict. In essence, is general conflict (i.e., border clashes) more strongly associated with internal conflict than it is with major external conflict (war)?

To test the three propositions, this study draws upon 218 units of analysis: 11 Middle Eastern and North African nations, each analyzed within 21 distinct yearly time segments from 1948 through

7. Robert Burrowes, "The Strength and Direction of Relationships between Domestic Conflict and External Politics: Syria, 1961–1967" (Paper prepared for delivery at the annual meeting of the Middle East Studies Association, Austin, Texas, 15–17 November 1968. Also see Robert Burrowes with Bert Spector, "The Strength and Direction of Relationships Between Domestic and External Conflict and Cooperation: Syria, 1961–1967" (Paper prepared for delivery at the Sixty-fifth Annual Meeting of the American Political Science Association, New York City, 2–6 September 1969).

8. Burrowes covered Syria and her relations with other nations in the region for the years 1961–67, using events and data sources similar to those used by Rummel, Tanter, and Collins.

1968, inclusive. The nations are Lebanon, Israel, Jordan, Syria, Iraq, Egypt, Saudi Arabia, Libya, Tunisia, Algeria,[9] and Morocco.[10]

The study deals only with physical conflict events; verbal conflict and other types of internal and external behavior are not considered in this analysis. With only minor modifications, the physical conflict events are similar to those used in the above-mentioned studies by Rummel, Tanter, Collins, and Burrowes. They are as follows: [11]

> INTERNAL CONFLICT events are demonstrations, political strikes, riots, political assassinations, terrorism, coups, mutinies, purges, guerrilla wars, civil wars, private wars and large-scale revolts.

The total number of internal conflict events considered in this study is 451.[12]

9. Algeria is considered for only eight yearly time segments (1961–68), because of the very high levels of internal conflict prior to achieving independence in 1962.

10. The nations that are not adjacent to Israel have not been involved in general external conflict (border clashes) with her, obviously, and thus the first and third propositions are not relevant. But these nations are included in order to test the relationship expressed in the second proposition, viz., between internal conflict and the three wars.

11. The selection of these events has been primarily influenced by Ted Gurr's studies of civil strife. In addition to using his categories of events, this study also has employed his method of measuring the magnitude of domestic conflict. Gurr's method of measurement arrives at a "Total Magnitude of Civil Strife" for each unit of analysis. This same type of measurement will be referred to in this study as internal conflict. This measure is based on the scope, duration, and intensity of each event. These three event characteristics are defined as follows: *scope* is the extent of participation by the affected population, operationally defined for this study as the sum of the estimated number of participants in all events for each unit of analysis; *duration* is the persistence of strife, indexed here by the sum of the spans of time of all events in each unit of analysis, whatever the relative scale of the events, expressed in days; *intensity* is the human cost of strife, indexed here by the total estimated dead in all events for each unit of analysis. Again with only minor adjustments, this study follows Gurr's scaling procedure and method for calculating the magnitudes in determining measurement of internal conflict for each of the 218 units of analysis. See, for example, Ted Gurr, "A Causal Model of Civil Strife: A Comparative Analysis Using New Indices," *American Political Science Review* 62 (December 1968): 1104–24.

12. The internal event statistics used in this analysis are based on three different data collection projects. First, the data for the period 1948–60 were collected by Ivo Feierabend and associates for their Data Bank of Political Instability Events. The major source of information for the Feierabend collection was *Deadline Data on World Affairs,* and included 176 internal conflict events for the units of analysis covered in this study. Feierabend's Data Bank of

Measures of external conflict are taken on two variables—general external conflict and major external conflict. They are operationally defined as follows:

GENERAL EXTERNAL CONFLICT is defined as a military encounter by the armed forces of one nation with the armed forces of another nation. It includes such events as the following: "Both Israeli and Jordanian authorities reported clashes in the Baysan Valley area. Jordan reported that Israel had suffered many casualties and has lost 4 military vehicles. Israel reported no casualties." This item is coded as a general external conflict event for both Israel and Jordan. All events of this type that took place during the three wars were not included.

MAJOR EXTERNAL CONFLICT makes reference to the occurrence of the three major Arab-Israeli wars in 1948, 1956, and 1967.

Measures of the general external conflict (border clashes) variable are the frequency of events for each of the 218 units of analysis. The measures of the major external conflicts (wars) reflect, of course, the occurrence (or nonoccurrence) of the three wars during each of the units of analysis. The data for all external conflict events were collected from the *Middle East Journal;* they include 305 events.

Analyses

In the first analysis, the three propositions are tested at the regional level. All eleven nations over each of the twenty-one yearly time

Political Instability Events and coding manual are available through the Inter-University Consortium for Political Research, Ann Arbor, Michigan. The second data collection project drawn upon for this study was Ted Gurr's Civil Strife Data Bank. His principal sources of data were the *New York Times Index, Newsyear,* and the *African Digest.* This study has used Gurr's data for the years 1961–64; his data included some 150 events for the units of analysis used here. The data and coding instructions used in this study were made available through the generosity of Ted Gurr from his Civil Strife Data Bank at the Center of International Studies, Princeton University. The third body of data for internal conflict events covers the years 1965–68; it was generated for this study. These 1965–68 data were drawn from the *Middle East Journal* and included 125 events. The use of different sources of data did result in distortions. For example, Gurr's data tended to contain more events than Feierabend's for the same units, and the data collected from the Middle East Journal contained more events per unit than did Gurr's. In the overall analysis, the errors were less than 15 percent; no adjustments for these differences were made in this survey. The use of these data for more precise and in-depth studies would, however, necessitate corrections.

segments are dealt with in this analysis. The second analysis tests the same three propositions, but considers only four nations which constitute an identifiable subregion. It derives from those nations which were clearly responsible for most of the general external conflict in the region, Israel, Egypt, Jordan, and Syria. The final analysis deals with the four nations of the subregion individually over the twenty-one time periods in an effort to determine the role of each nation in the conflict arena.

1. THE REGIONAL LEVEL

The first analysis is an attempt to find any relationships between the three types of conflict that exist for the region as a whole. Regarding the first proposition, the regional level of analysis rejects a relationship between internal conflict and general external conflict (border clashes). The basis for this rejection derives from the correlation coefficient indicated the Table 1.[13]

TABLE 1
All Nations: Correlation Matrix

	1.	2.	3.
1. Internal Conflict	1.00	—.03	—.10
2. General External Conflict		1.00	*.18*
3. Major External Conflict			1.00

Note: The italic product moment correlation coefficient is significant at the .01 level for 218 cases.

The evidence yields a correlation coefficient of —.03, indicating an almost total lack of association between the two types of conflicts.

13. The statistical technique used to determine whether or not any of the relationships between the types of conflict are significant is the product moment correlation. A correlation coefficient (r) must be at least significant at the .05 level to be considered even weak support for the propositions. In general, any correlation coefficients that are significant at the .05 level are considered to be weak support for the propositions, and any that are significant at the .01 level are considered to be moderate support. There are no correlation coefficients significant at the .001 level, which would be considered very strong support for any proposition. A .05 level of significance means that there are only 5 possibilities in 100 that the findings were due to chance, and significant at the .01 level means that there is only 1 possibility in 100 that the findings were by chance. All reference to significant associations then refer to statistical significance.

Regarding the second proposition, that internal conflict is related to major external conflict (wars), the correlation coefficient is also not statistically significant ($r = -.10$). This proposition is also rejected, therefore, at the regional level.

The third proposition, however, is supported ($r = .18$). The correlation between general external conflict (border clashes) and major external conflict (war) is considered moderate, and suggests that within the region as a whole there is increased general external conflict just prior to or after the major external conflicts. While certainly not profound, this finding does at least indicate that at the regional level of analysis the preconditions for, and consequences of, external conflict are most likely to be at the international level, and not within nations.

2. THE SUBREGIONAL LEVEL

At this level, it will be recalled, only the conflict behavior in, and of, Israel, Egypt, Jordan, and Syria are considered. The correlation coefficients for this group of nations are presented in Table 2.

TABLE 2
Subregional: Correlation Matrix

	1.	2.	3.
1. Internal Conflict	1.00	.10	−.18
2. General External Conflict		1.00	*.34*
3. Major External Conflict			1.00

Note: The italic product moment correlation coefficient is significant at the .01 level for 84 cases.

The evidence does not indicate a significant change in the relationships between the three types of conflict behavior in this more intense subregional conflict area. Again the first and second propositions are rejected, while support is found for the third. The strength of the relationship between general external conflict (border clashes) and major external conflict (war) is, however, greater in the subregion than it is for the region as a whole (at the subregional level $r = .34$). As pointed out above, the subregional focus is achieved by dropping from the analysis those Arab nations which did not engage in general external conflict with Israel. The purpose of this subregional analysis, then, is to get a more accurate measure of the structure of conflict for the most active nations in the area.

At this subregional level of analysis, the evidence suggests that there has been a tendency for the frequency of general conflict to be relatively low between the major external conflict events. A high level of general external conflict was sustained, however, during the period just after the June War (from June 1967 to December 1968), indicating a course, a change in the external conflict pattern for the area. The change in the structure of external conflict since 1967 is illustrated more clearly by the third analysis.

3. THE INDIVIDUAL NATION LEVEL OF THE SUBREGION

In the third analysis, the four nations included in the subregion are viewed individually over time. These longitudinal profiles are used to pinpoint more precisely which nations are primarily responsible for the correlation between general and major external conflicts and for the indicated change in this relationship since the June War (Table 3).

TABLE 3
Israel: Correlation Matrix

	1.	2.	3.
1. Internal Conflict	1.00	−.01	−.19
2. General External Conflict		1.00	*.47*
3. Major External Conflict			1.00

Note: The italic product moment correlation coefficient is significant at the .05 level for 21 cases.

All external events, of course, involved the behavior of both Israel and one of the Arab nations. The external conflict behavior for Israel represents its interaction with all of the Arab nations in the subregion, and consequently the profile for Israel generally reflects the sum of the profiles for the other nations if it were computed. The data for Israel, therefore, support the third proposition as one might expect given the subregional level of support for it (the third proposition was supported by an *r* significant at the .01 level using the subregional data, and by an *r* significant at the .05 level using the data for Israel—the difference is primarily due to the different number of cases used in the two different analyses, 84 and 21 respectively).

TABLE 4
Egypt: Correlation Matrix

	1.	2.	3.
1. Internal Conflict	1.00	−.08	−.05
2. General External Conflict		1.00	*.65*
3. Major External Conflict			1.00

Note: The italic product moment correlation coefficient is significant at the .01 level for 21 cases.

The interaction between Israel and Egypt is primarily responsible for the support of the third proposition. In fact, general external conflict takes place for Egypt more than any other nation almost exclusively during and immediately following the time periods in which the major external conflict events occurred. Table 4 indicates that the data for Egypt ($r = .65$) support the third proposition and reject the first and second propositions ($r = -.08$ and $r = -.05$, respectively). These data suggest that, for the most part, Egyptian border clashes with Israel are related to the outbreak of the major conflicts in 1948, 1956, and 1967. But the evidence also shows that Egyptian border clashes developed a new pattern after the June War.

TABLE 5
Jordan: Correlation Matrix

	1.	2.	3.
1. Internal Conflict	1.00	.41	−.09
2. General External Conflict		1.00	.35
3. Major External Conflict			1.00

Note: None of the above product moment correlation coefficients is significant at the .05 level for the 21 cases. An r of .42 is needed to be significant at the .05 level, and the above r of .41 is considered to be very weak support for the first proposition.

The data for Jordan do not support the third proposition, but they do show some association between the two external conflict variables ($r = .35$). What is of major interest in the case of Jordan, however, is that she is the only nation for which some support is found for the first proposition. The relationship between internal conflict and general external conflict is just short of being statistically significant ($r = .41$), and is due to the fact that Jordan had a much different pattern of general external conflict than either Egypt or Syria. Jordan had been more continuously involved in general external conflict and had more internal conflict during the periods between the wars than the other nations (excluding Syria). Thus, while the evidence is not strong enough to support the relationship between internal and external conflict, one hesitates to reject the proposition in the case of Jordan. The question remains open pending more evidence.

TABLE 6
Syria: Correlation Matrix

	1.	2.	3.
1. Internal Conflict	1.00	.15	−.33
2. General External Conflict		1.00	.08
3. Major External Conflict			1.00

Note: None of the above product moment correlation coefficients is significant at the .05 level for the 21 cases. An r of .42 would be significant at that level.

In the Syrian case, the third proposition is rejected ($r = .08$). Although it is not statistically significant, the strongest association is for the second proposition. The strength of this relationship results from the fact that Syria has had extensive internal conflict ever since the Arab-Israeli war in 1948 but has tended to have less during the periods in which the major external conflicts occurred. The lack of support for the first proposition resulted from Syria's moderate involvement in general external conflict, a tendency which continued after the Six-Day War in 1967. Syria increased its involvement in general external conflict after the June War, but nothing comparable to the dramatic and sustained increase that Egypt and Jordan experienced during this same period.

Selected Observations

Within the perimeters of this study, it is possible to comment on the existence or nonexistence of eighteen statistically significant findings. But not all of the findings are equally interesting.

1. THE RELATIONSHIP BETWEEN INTERNAL AND EXTERNAL CONFLICT

The evidence indicates that there was no correlation between internal conflict and the three Arab-Israeli wars of 1948, 1956, and 1967 in any of the nations located outside the subregion. The evidence also shows that the Arab nations which are not adjacent to Israel had not been significant actors in the Arab-Israeli conflict (except for verbal conflict, perhaps, which was not considered in this study). Moreover, external conflict in the subregion had no significant impact on the internal conflict of these Arab nations.

Within the subregion, a relationship between internal and external conflict was very weakly supported by the data for Jordan, indicating at least the possibility that general external conflict is associated with internal conflict. Thus, only in Jordan can one consider the internal to external linkage to be even possibly meaningful within the perimeters of this study. The internal conflict of Jordan, however, had been complicated by periodic clashes between commando groups and Jordanian forces after the June War. This prohibits generalizations about the long-run relationship between internal and external conflict in the Jordanian case.

2. THE RELATIONSHIP BETWEEN BORDER CLASHES AND WAR

Over the entire time period covered in this analysis, there was moderate support for the proposition that general and major conflicts are somehow linked. But after the Six-Day War in 1967, the two types of external conflict seemed to be independent of each other. The support for the proposition that linkages operate between border clashes and war derived primarily from the Israeli-Egyptian and Israeli-Jordanian interactions. The strongest support comes from the fact that there were relatively few border clashes involving Israel and Egypt during the interwar periods, while they were a constant factor between Israel and Syria. Israeli-Syrian border clashes represented 45 percent of Israel's total border clashes, versus 29 percent involving Israel and Jordan, and 20 percent involving Israel and Egypt.

A constant phenomenon in the periods between the wars of 1948, 1956, and 1967, the Israeli-Syrian border clashes provide no support for the proposition of linkages between border clashes and war. While Israeli-Jordanian border clashes also occurred during the entire period, they had a slight tendency to increase just prior to or after the wars, suggesting, therefore, weak support for linkages between border clashes and war. Israeli-Egyptian border clashes tended to occur, on the other hand, shortly before or after one of the major wars, providing strong support, therefore, for the case of linkages between border clashes and war. The three major Arab actors had, obviously, quite different patterns of general external conflict behavior prior to the Six-Day War in 1967.

3. BORDER CLASHES: A CONSTANT PHENOMENON AFTER 1967

After the Six-Day War of 1967, one of the most important characteristics of the conflict structure was that general external conflict (border clashes), when measured in event frequency, seemed to be an increasingly constant phenomenon. In the past, border clashes in the area had been primarily an escalation to, or a winding down of, a major conflict (except in the case of Syria). Data subsequent to the Six-Day War indicated that general external conflicts had a momentum independent of major external conflicts. In a broad sense, whatever the functions of external conflicts might have been in the past, the trend indicated the possibility that border clashes had assumed a new, or additional, function in the subregion. Only the following of several variables involved will be considered.

a) Commando Operations

The first area of inquiry is the increased presence of commando action in the subregion. Al-Fatah reported that it was involved in approximately 2,390 conflict events during 1969, while Israel reported some 10,000 incidents involving commando groups or individuals since the Six-Day War in 1967 (three-fourths of which took place in 1969).[14] The simultaneous increase in commando operations and border clashes in the subregion would be a useful relationship to investigate. Egypt and Jordan, for example, might simply have been competing for popularity with the more colorful and active commando groups, thus, their increased action on the borders. Israel, on the other hand, might have been increasing her involvement on the borders with Egypt and Jordan (and from time to time with Syria and Lebanon) because of her inability to identify and cope with the commando groups.

14. *The Christian Science Monitor,* 3 March 1970.

b) The United Nations Emergency Forces (UNEF)

Israeli-Egyptian general external conflict (border clashes) was of particular importance for the support of the third proposition, i.e., that linkages between border clashes and war were operative in the Middle East. Evidence prior to the Six-Day War supported this proposition. Following the Six-Day War, however, Israeli-Egyptian border clashes became a constant phenomenon, in effect, rejecting the correlation between general and major external conflict. But there was an obvious difference between pre- and post-June War conditions; for prior to the Six-Day War in 1967, the United Nations Emergency Forces (UNEF) stood between the two nations.

The background to this situation illustrates the early and subsequent relationship between the two types of external conflict. Between the 1956 and 1967 major conflicts, the UNEF was on the Israeli-Egyptian border exercising a certain inhibiting control over border clashes. In the meantime, however, general conflict increased between Israel and both Syria and Jordan; it was on these fronts, in fact, that general conflict events triggered the escalation that led to the major conflict in June 1967.[15] Once the escalation was underway, it was impossible for Egypt to stay behind the insulation provided by UNEF, so Egypt requested their removal. Based on past experience, there is no solid evidence that the presence of UNEF had or could prevent major conflicts. But there is evidence that UNEF can prevent, or at least hold to a minimum, general external conflict.

The presence of UNEF did prevent general conflict on the Israeli-Egyptian border, which suggests that placing similar forces on all Israeli borders—incidentally, on both sides—would be a step in the right direction to eliminate general external conflict. The suggestion poses a dilemma, of course: one has a choice of violating either the idea of sovereignty or the idea of peace.

Conclusion

The question of ending the major external conflicts goes much deeper and is much more complex. It involves past and present attitudes toward neocolonialism, deep cultural conflict, national security, and above all the issue of the Palestinian refugees. The structure of conflict in the area after the Six-Day War, as revealed in

15. See, for example, Michael Howard and Robert Hunter, *Israel and the Arab World: The Crisis of 1967*, Adelphi Papers, No. 41 (October 1967), 13–14.

the examination of the third proposition, suggests that there is a degree of independence between general and major external conflict. Any efforts to bring peace to the area should, therefore, consider this fact. In essence, reducing or removing border conflicts may well be a major step in reducing the probability of another major war in the area.

Appendix A

The figures in this appendix are for purposes of illustration only, and should be used with care. Figure 1 profiles the aggregate general external conflict for all the nations of the subregion. Figures 2–5 are used to illustrate two variables that have been measured on different scales and thus the areas enclosed by the curves are not comparable. For example, in figures 2–5 the vertical axis is used to measure the magnitude of internal conflict as well as the frequency of general external conflict. These illustrations do, however, permit the comparison of the high points on one variable with the high points on the other variable in time. The major external conflict events which took place in 1948, 1956, and 1967 can be located in the appropriate place on the horizontal axis.

FIGURE 1. Subregion: General external conflict, over time. Major external conflict occurred during the italicized time periods. The correlation coefficient for proposition three is .34 and is significant at the .01 level for 84 cases.

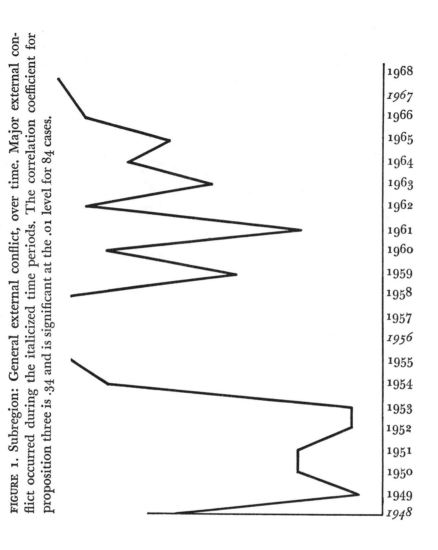

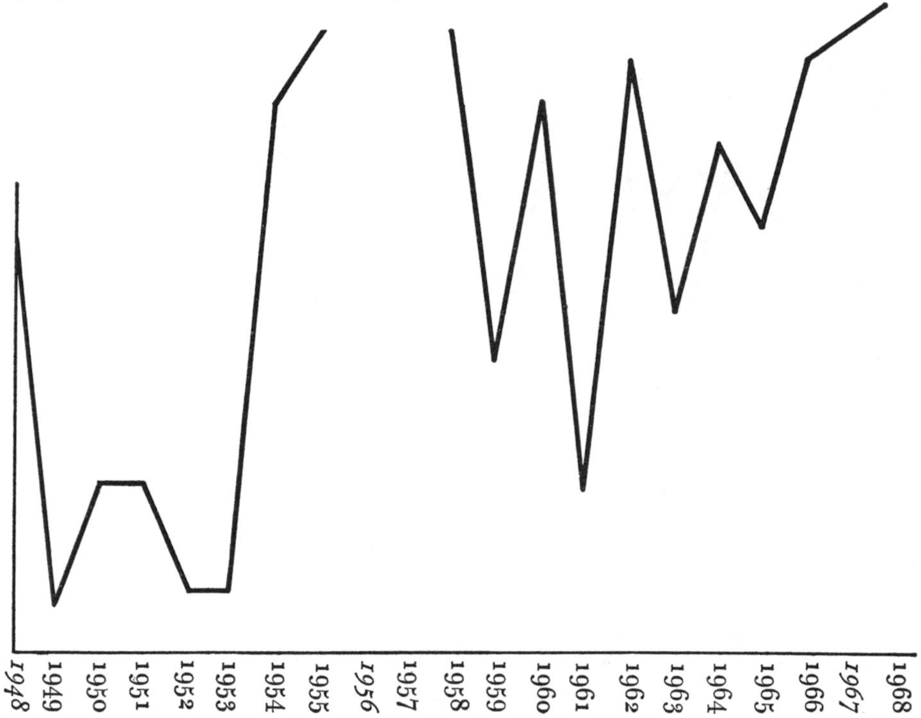

FIGURE 2. Israel: Internal conflict and general external conflict, over time. Major external conflict occurred during the italicized time periods. The correlation coefficients based on these same data are −.01, −.19 and .47 for propositions one, two, and three respectively.

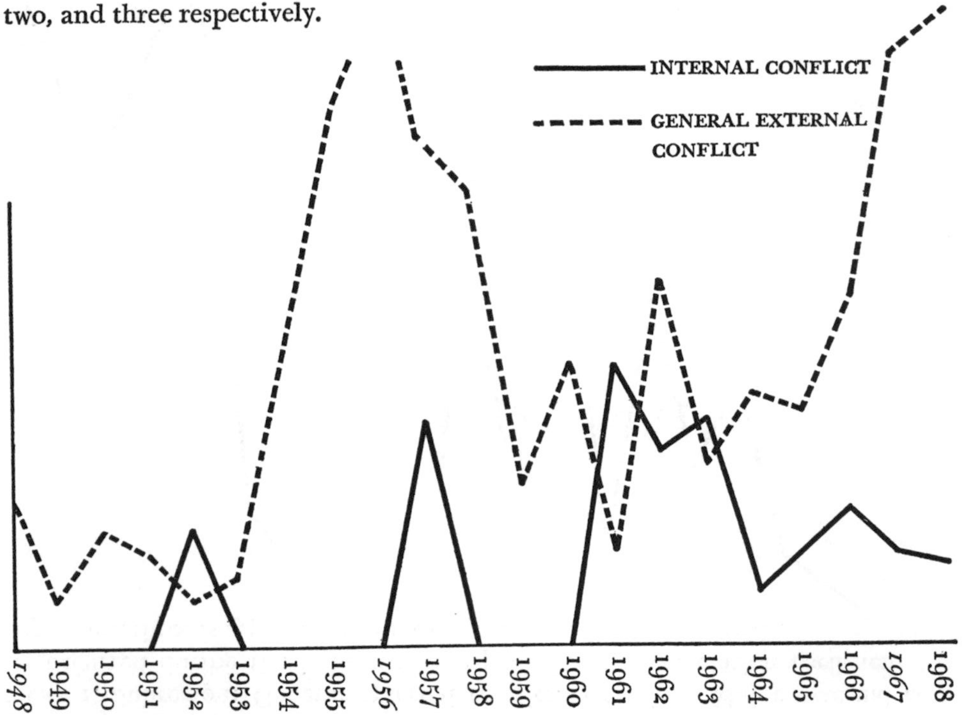

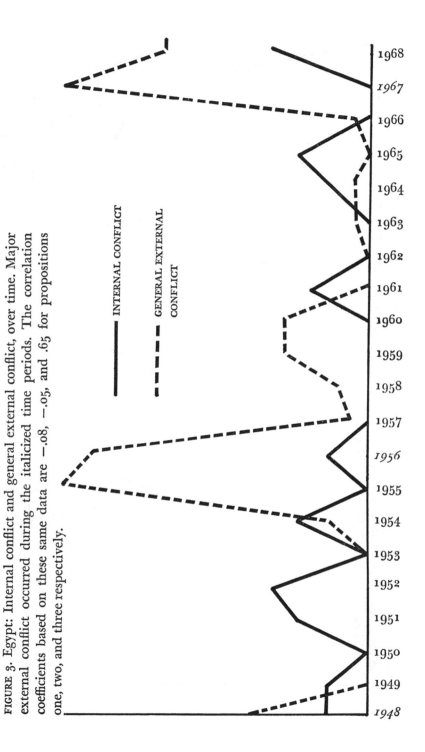

FIGURE 3. Egypt: Internal conflict and general external conflict, over time. Major external conflict occurred during the italicized time periods. The correlation coefficients based on these same data are −.08, −.05, and .65 for propositions one, two, and three respectively.

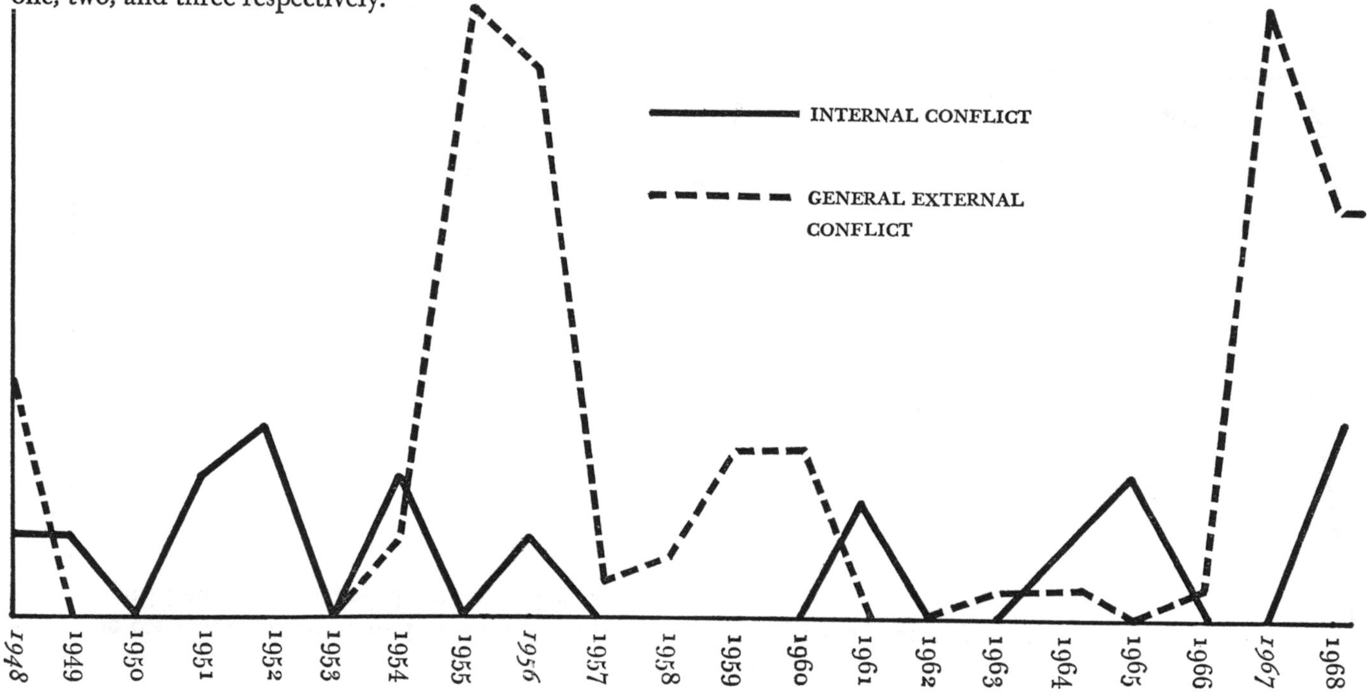

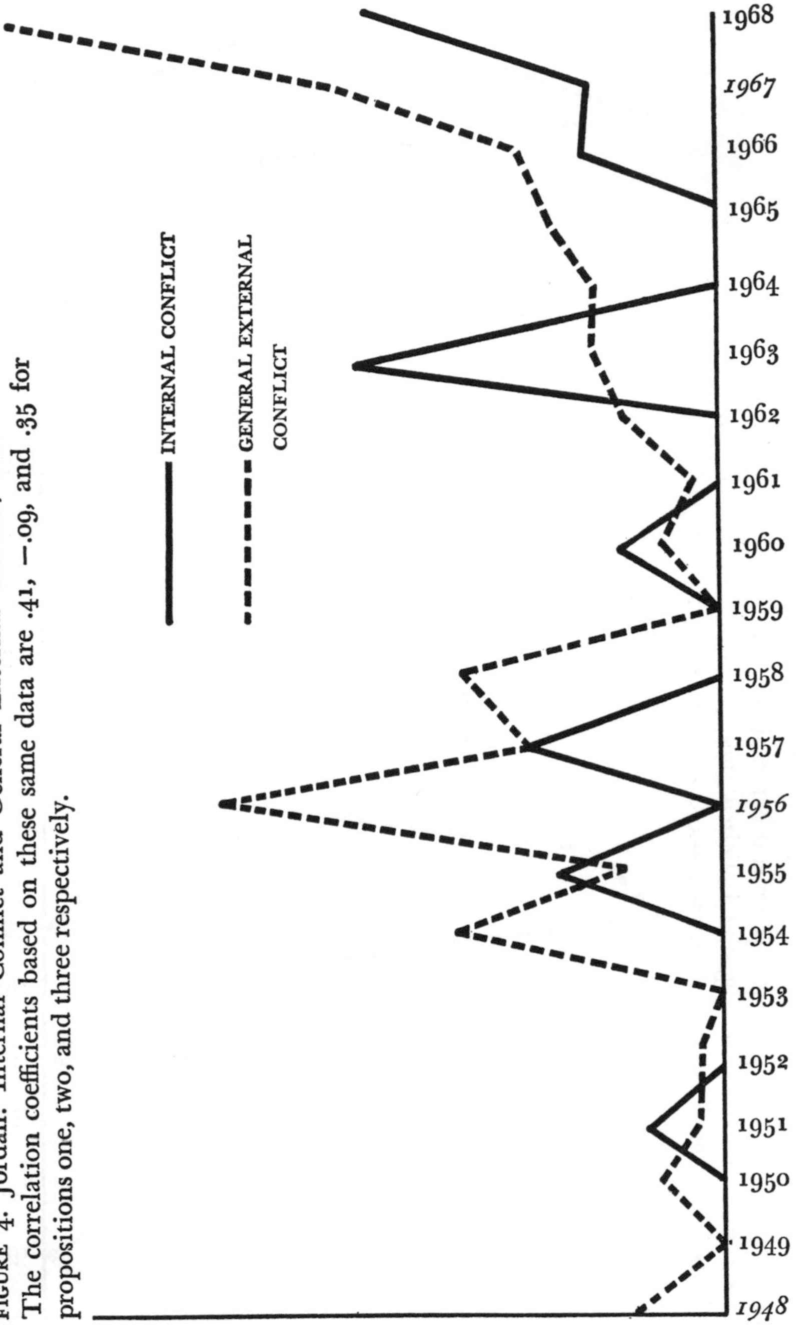

FIGURE 4. Jordan: Internal Conflict and General External Conflict, over time. The correlation coefficients based on these same data are .41, −.09, and .35 for propositions one, two, and three respectively.

FIGURE 5. Syria: Internal conflict and general external conflict, over time. Major external conflict occurred during the italicized time periods. The correlation coefficients based on these same data are .15, −.33, and .08 for propositions one, two, and three respectively.

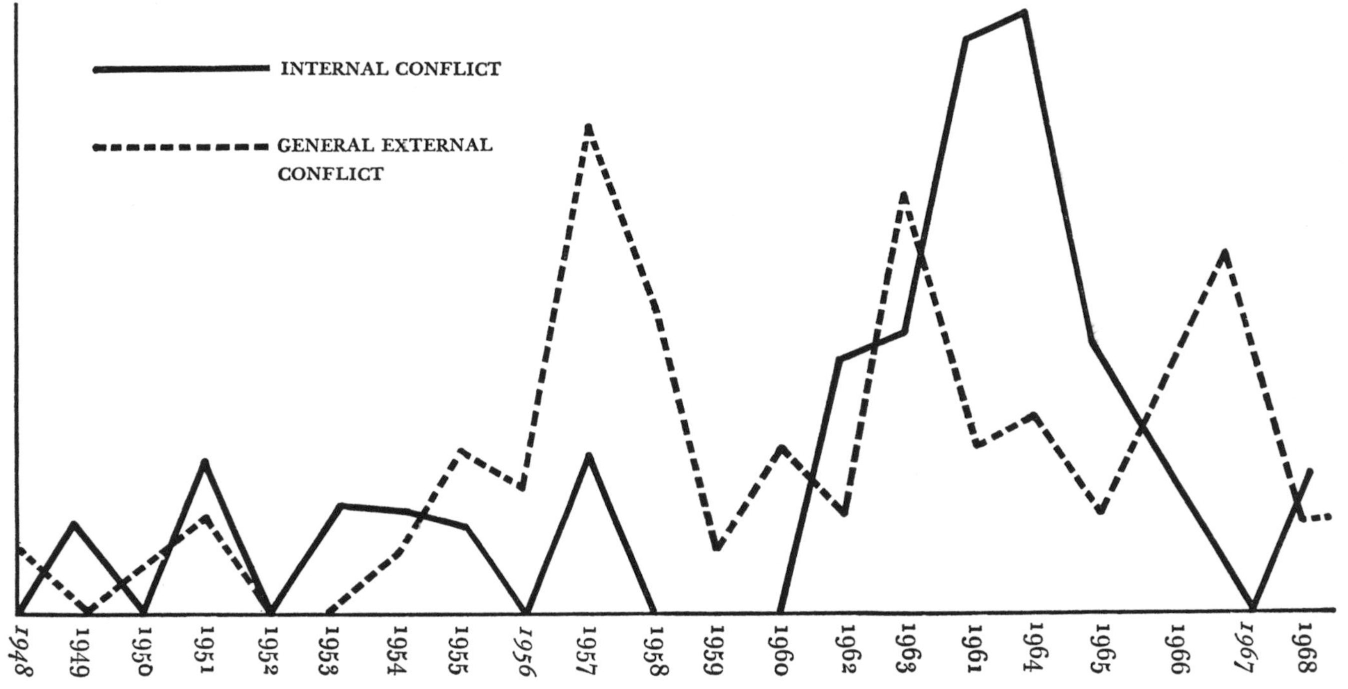

Part II

The International Political System: Interactions between Major Actors and the Middle East

CHAPTER 7

An Interaction Survey of the Middle East

CHARLES A. MC CLELLAND & ANNE ANCOLI GILBAR

Unlike some quantitative exercises, this study is understandable even to the uninitiated. It avoids the jargon of computerized analysis. As a quantitative measurement and evaluation of the foreign or external affairs of Middle Eastern states it offers new perspectives on the area.

The procedures of recording, coding, and counting the actions of nations can obviously be brought to bear on specific topics, as this chapter illustrates, in the study of international relations. Nevertheless, the authors remain dissatisfied with the state of the art. Ideally, Professor McClelland would like studies of this sort to have more than mere postdictive value. Indeed, this chapter hints that this is possible.

Middle Eastern states ranked high, for example, among the top actors in the international political system in 1966. Did this portend the June War? What are the portents of the present Middle East event flow? Given an even richer and more complete data file and experience, could computerized international event analysis provide valid predictive indicators?

The authors believe that the computerized approach to model construction and operation has the best prospects in current international relations theory development. They make a good case for their position. Indeed, they evaluate the fit of their quantitative findings in this study with some conclusions Middle East regionalists reached. How do the regionalists' "intuitive" interpretations stand up against quantitative analysis? This treatment alone, apart from its own direct contributions to the understanding of the area, justifies the inclusion of the chapter in this volume.

Computer Analysis and Regional Studies

The Middle East is, among other things, a special province of foreign-area specialists. The generalist's knowledge of public affairs does not extend satisfactorily to the countries of the Arab world as it seems to do in the case of American and European countries. Conventional images of individual motivations, social institutions, and political processes do not appear to work satisfactorily when they are applied to Middle Eastern affairs. Even members of the attentive foreign-policy public in the United States tend to remain in a state of quasi-mystification with respect to developments in public affairs in that part of the world while they do better at understanding such places as Germany, the Soviet Union, and China. This problem seems not to be strictly a result of differences of culture and language. For example, the attentive but nonspecialist American may feel more certainty and assurance in understanding Japanese affairs, despite the large culture and language differences, than in understanding Egyptian affairs.

The result of this is that it is difficult to strike up an interesting and informed discussion about the contemporary Middle East outside the circles of scholars whose speciality is that area. Probably, we could get together a more interesting conference involving American laymen on the antiquities than on the current international relations of the region. The one exception in all this is Israel and the Arab-Israeli conflict. The American image of Israel is strong and clear. The reclamation of the land since World War II is widely viewed in this country as a saga with romantic overtones. The steady stream of interesting writing, often in the form of the novel, treating the theme of the Israeli struggle against hostile nature and hostile neighbors has helped to form this image. About the only really popular fiction of the past two decades that has an Arabic locale (or perhaps it is more generally a Mediterranean locale) is Lawrence Durrell's *The Alexandria Quartet*,[1] but these novels, whatever authentic flavor they may contain, are extremely personal and entirely apolitical.

Further, Israel's motives of active self-defense, even including the policy of selective retaliation, make sense to American newspaper readers. That Israel has a small population and that the Arab nations have many times more people are facts that contribute to natural American sympathies for the underdog. We may tend to think we know more about the Arab-Israeli conflict than we really do. Only occasionally are we affected by some dissonance that throws that confident understanding into doubt. It arises almost always from the Arab side. One example is the Egyptian explanation that

1. 1st ed. (New York: E. P. Dutton & Co., Inc., 1957).

their defeat in the Six-Day War was the result of an unequal contest between Egypt and the United States. Most Americans cannot believe that they were a major party in the war and, therefore, they have to adjust psychologically by believing either that Egyptians really know better or that the latter have a distorted view of reality.

The American image of the Arab side of the conflict appears to have become increasingly negative. Arab irrationality, violence, and mob action are perceived elements of that image. Lurking within many American discussions of the Middle East crisis is an ultimate United States policy question: what will we do if the unremitting opposition of the Arab countries and their overwhelming populations finally wear down the Israelis through the process of attrition? Will the policy be to prevent a military defeat of Israel? What can prevent that outcome? The social, political, and economic phenomena of the Middle East are again bypassed. Only the small group of foreign area specialists in the universities and in the government keep their attention on the affairs of the area and thus maintain a virtual monopoly on the more fruitful inquiries.

Only rarely can a student of international relations whose specialization is not the Middle East break in on this monopoly and offer independent findings which tend to confirm or disconfirm the observations of the specialists or which develop information about the area not previously noted. Our attempt here is to do something on this order. Our claim to expert competence and to knowledge on the domestic aspects of public affairs of the Middle East countries is not far from zero. What is offered is an analytic approach to the measurement and evaluation of the foreign or external affairs of the Middle East countries. Our findings cover three topics: (*1*) comparisons of Middle East event output with that of the world as a whole and with that of other regions; (*2*) a tracing of the recent course of the Arab-Israeli conflict; and (*3*) some observations on the fit of our findings with some conclusions reached in the publications of Middle East analysts.

The necessary introduction to these findings is a brief description of the World Event/Interaction Survey. This is a research activity that concentrates on the external activities of all countries and records, codes, and analyzes quantitatively the international events that are reported in the news. The source of data in this study is the daily *New York Times*. The data collection runs from the beginning of 1966 to the present and contains over 40,000 items. The prime unit of analysis is the official act of a government directed abroad to another government. No attempt has been made to gather data or make analyses of events that are internal or domestic. The purpose of the research is to add substance to the idea of international systems as well as to show how international systems operate. Attention is focused on the development of models of international systems that will be expressed eventually as computer programs and that will reflect relationships and patterns of action in international relations. Thus, the level of research is that of the "big picture"—the larger aspects of international action and response. The work is behavioral in the same way that traditional diplomatic history is behavioral: the focus is on the flows of activity of nations as they attempt to control and direct affairs in international situations. The approach differs from that of diplomatic history only in that the analyses are quantitative and represent efforts to measure the patterns, variations, changes, and trends of contemporary international action.

The World Event/Interaction Survey (WEIS)

The World Event/Interaction Survey categorizes every recorded international act in one of sixty-three possible classes. In effect, there are sixty-three different specified ways a government can act toward another government. Various combined groupings of the sixty-three types are used; the most common of these is a category system consisting of twenty-two basic types of acts. Under this twenty-two-category system, *accuse* is considered a basic type and so also are *agree, request, warn,* and *threaten,* to name a few. Both verbal acts and physical acts are encompassed by the category system; both cooperative and conflictual types of acts are included (see appendix for complete listing).

The data are organized in chronological order. Computerization enables the researcher to select or delete any slice of time according to the requirements of a study. Because each specific act is associated with an initiator and recipient of the action, any part of the data may be selected, combined, or deleted according to the names of the nations or polities. For example, if all one wants to review is the record of exchanges of threats between the Soviet Union and China in the first six months of 1969, one can get that information directly and immediately from the computerized data collection. It is this flexible capability to select and to group that makes it possible to extract the Middle East international action from the whole collection for the purposes of the present study.

The source of information for the main WEIS data collection is, as previously mentioned, the *New York Times.* While there have been criticisms of the limitations of this source, comparative investigations of the selecting and reporting habits of other major newspapers have shown that there is no practical way to assemble a full and accurate record of international events from any one or any combination of public sources. The *New York Times,* whatever its bias and limitations, is better than most sources in providing a rough but useable record of indicators of the worlds' international activity. For the purpose of a worldwide survey which facilitates analyses of the proportions, distributions, fluctuations, changes, and trends in the flow of international events, the *New York Times* serves well.

Middle East Event Output Comparisons with the World as a Whole and Other Regions

Several possibilities exist in undertaking comparisons of the international activity of the Middle East with the international activities of other parts of the world. The first problem is to choose the Middle East countries to be included in the analysis. The countries chosen are those that the data show to be most heavily involved in the Arab-Israeli conflict and those that also have a relatively high rate of interaction with other Middle East nations and with the world. The various Arab Commando Forces have been included as a composite actor playing a direct and significant role in inter-Arab-Israeli relations. The actors included in the analysis are Iraq, United Arab Republic, Syria, Lebanon, Jordan, Israel, and Palestine Liberation Organization (PLO—the several commando groups).

With the foregoing definition in hand, it can be determined how the Middle East international actors compare, singly and as a group, with the other international actors of the world. The structure of the WEIS data collection makes it possible to rank the nations of the world in terms of their total foreign policy output. The rates of interaction can be determined on a comparative basis.

The most active sixty nations were ranked every six months beginning with 1966. Where the Middle Eastern nations place can be shown readily. During the first half of 1966 the United Arab Republic, Israel, Syria, Jordan, Iraq, and Lebanon were all on the list of the top sixty actors. Egypt ranked highest at number eight and

Lebanon was the lowest at fifty-seven. In the second half of 1966 Jordan's external action increased to place that country at twelve and Egypt's activity declined to ten. Israel's rank rose during the second half of 1966 to one, to lead all the Middle Eastern countries. Israel and Egypt ranked in the top ten thereafter through 1969.

During the June War in 1967 all the Middle East actors advanced in the rankings. Saudi Arabia's activity brought that country into the top sixty actors for the first time. After the war, all the Middle Eastern countries, except Israel and Egypt, fell to lower positions in the rank ordering. Israel and Egypt continued to hold high positions among the top ten actors. During 1969, there occurred a new upward movement by six of the Middle East states (excluding the PLO guerrilla forces and Saudi Arabia) towards the top of the rank order list. The Middle East nations have ranked high (within the group of the top thirty actors for the four-year period taken as a whole) among the main producers of international interactions. Moreover, no other regional grouping of nations outside the great powers is represented in the top ten list.

That the Middle East is a prime focus of world attention is shown by data which trace the flow of acts initiated by others and directed to the Middle East. To illustrate this, two time studies were conducted and compared. In the first a 4-year total of actions (January 1966 through December 1969) initiated by all 159 parties in the international system was obtained. Of the 25,760 acts for the period, 2,862, or 11.1 percent of the total, were directed to the Middle East countries, while Southeast Asia was the recipient of 1,925 or 7.46 percent. Of the 2,862 acts directed from the world to the Middle East, Israel was the recipient of 42.32 percent, the United Arab Republic of 25.13 percent, Jordan of 10.48 percent, and Syria, 6.92 percent. The same study was run for a 64-month period running from January 1966 through April 1971. Of the 39,121 acts for this new time span, 4,811 acts, or 12 percent of the total, were directed to the Middle East. Unlike the first time study, which ended at a time when the Middle East nations were still embroiled in the aftermath of the 1967 war, this time our data showed that Southeast Asia was gaining as the recipient of world attention because of the tension in that area of the world. Thus, as of May 1971, Southeast Asia was the recipient of 4,843 acts or 12 percent of the total acts in the international system, showing that in 1970 and 1971 the world's attention was directed almost evenly to the Middle East and Southeast Asia. Although world interest in Southeast Asia picked up, it was not at the expense of attention to the Middle East.

The 64-month study also showed interesting results concerning the Middle East countries themselves. Of the total acts directed from the world to the Middle East during the 64-month period, Israel was the recipient of 36.8 percent (a drop from the 4-year total), the United Arab Republic 22.6 percent (also a drop), Jordan 15.8 percent (a gain of 5 percent), and Syria remained relatively stable with 6.25 percent of the action. Thus, the Middle East nations individually received less attention from the world over the last 16 months of the second time study. The exception is Jordan, which gained more attention, most likely due to the problems with the guerrilla organizations beginning in September 1970.

It would seem that the Middle East is a high-level producer of international events with two countries, Egypt and Israel, initiating action as if they belonged in the company of the great powers. The Middle East countries taken together demonstrate an extraordinary capacity to displace the total flow of international activity so that in some periods almost 30 percent of the reported world action has originated in that region. In reciprocal fashion, a considerable proportion of the activity of the rest of the world has been directed to the Middle East.

The distinctive character of the Middle East is amplified when the patterns produced by three flows of actions are analyzed. These are the relationships of the volume of action (*1*) within the grouping of countries, (2) directed abroad, and (*3*) received from the rest of the world. A series of studies was made of this three-way relationship for the Middle East countries and for several other regional groupings as well, including Southeast Asia, Russia and Eastern Europe, and the United States and its allies on the Atlantic. The results of the comparisons are too cumbersome to report in detail but they converge on one arresting conclusion. One test of an international subsystem is the strength of the network of interactions among its members. Of the regional groupings studied, only the Middle East manifests a very strong flow of intragroup action, compared with the intragroup action of the other subsystems. Thus, in our comparisons, the Middle East qualifies as a subsystem much more prominently than any other grouping. The data show that the Middle East actors have a level of intragroup action almost double that of the United States and its allies and that of the Southeast Asian nations, and four times as much as the USSR and Eastern Europe intragroup action.

These findings suggest a strong subsystem autonomy in the Middle East that is not duplicated in other regions. It should be added that the WEIS collection is composed of "high level" or "official" political data and, therefore, our interpretation is that the Middle East subsystem, unlike others studied, appears to qualify as an international political subsystem.

With these data one is also able to compare the volume of action that a subsystem directs to the world and that it receives from the world community. It was found that each of the four subsystems directs more action to the world than to itself (see table 1). As can be seen from the table, the total world output toward a subsystem is *always less* than the subsystem's attention to the world. Thus it can be said that the Middle East as a subsystem directs and receives action at about the same rate as the other subsystems studied. However, it is still the strongest of all subsystems, exhibiting a greater rate of interaction within its own subsystem than any of the other subsystems studied.

TABLE 1

Subsystem Interaction, January 1966–April 1971

	MIDDLE EAST	WORLD	S.E. ASIA	USSR †	USA †
Middle East	3216	6398			
Southeast Asia		5958	1916		
USSR and Eastern Europe		4966		851	
USA and Atlantic Allies		11655			1830
World	4811	39121	4843	3400	8783

The next subject to be reported concerns the relationships between the Middle East and the four great powers. Considering all the acts initiated by the Middle East actors and directed to the four powers and vice versa, the Middle East group sends forth more international action than it receives from the United States and Britain, but receives more action from the Soviet Union and France than it directs to each of them. The highest level of interaction is maintained between the Middle East as a whole and the United States, with the Middle East nations giving to the United States twice as much attention as they receive.

More relevant detail is revealed if the total flow of international action is divided into Arab and Israeli components and into "friendly" and "hostile" groupings of actions.[2] Looking at the data in selected time periods, one discovers several interesting features in the event flow. In the relationship between Israel and the four powers, the volume of Israeli friendly acts directed to the Soviet Union in June of 1967 was greater than the flow of Israel's friendly acts directed to the other three powers; however, at the same time Israel's flow of hostile acts directed to the Soviet Union reached a peak. The Soviet Union's hostile action toward Israel rose in June of 1967, as might be expected. Friendly output by Israel to the United States was more than twice as great as Israeli friendly output to the other three powers combined, and the United States led the other great powers in directing friendly acts to Israel. From the June War to the present the United States has maintained this pattern of action toward Israel. In 1968 and 1969 the Israeli output of friendly acts directed to the Soviet Union, France, and Britain was close to zero. Hostile acts by Israel toward the Soviet Union showed an upward trend in 1969.

Of Israel's total hostile output to the 4 powers over the 64-month period, 41 percent was directed to the USSR and 32 percent to the United States. Of her total friendly output, Israel directed 76 percent to the United States, while the Soviet Union, France, and Great Britain were about equal in total Israeli friendly action received (12 percent, 11 percent, and 10 percent respectively).

One finds a surprising development when analyzing the Arabs' friendly output. After the 4-year study (ending in December 1969), it was found that the Arabs directed most of their friendly action to the Soviet Union. However, the 64-month data show a total of 57 percent of the Arabs' friendly output to the United States with only 25.5 percent to the Soviet Union, thus indicating a trend of friendlier Arab-American relations beginning in 1970. However, an analysis of strictly unfriendly output by the Arabs shows the United States receiving 71 percent of the output and the USSR only 13 percent. One can conclude that the Arab nations interact more with the United States than with the USSR and that more of this Arab-American relationship is hostile than friendly. Over time it is evident that there was a definite increase in the flow of hostile action

2. The WEIS categories can be divided into two general groups of behavior; the first 10 of the 22 categories can be grouped to form a cooperative category; the 12 remaining can be termed uncooperative or "hostile" types of behavior. For a complete listing of the 22 types of behavior see Appendix A at the end of this chapter.

from the Arab countries to the United States in June of 1967 and that it has since remained higher than for the other three powers.

The Fit of the Findings with Conclusions Reached by the Regionalists

Hisham Sharabi stressed a point concerning Arab relations with the United States and the Soviet Union. Our method of quantitative analysis can be related to Sharabi's observation about the relations between the Arab nations and the Soviet Union. He finds an example of a polarization in the relations of Syria and the USSR.

> Syria, for example, cannot tolerate friendly relations with the United States, and views with suspicion any Arab country having friendly relations with the United States. By the same token, Syria's natural orientation is toward the socialist states, principally the Soviet Union.[3]

According to our analysis, it is evident that Sharabi is correct in his interpretation. We found that the percentage of Syria's acts to the Eastern European socialist nations compared with her output to the world was 2 percent, to the USSR it was 4 percent, while her output to the United States was 9 percent. These numbers are misleading at first glance, but when broken down, it becomes evident that Syria's hostile output to Eastern Europe was just about 1 percent, to the USSR it was zero, but to the United States her hostile output was 14 percent. Thus, while at first it seems that Syria's interaction with the United States is greater than with the USSR, upon further analysis it is evident that this relationship is of a hostile nature on Syria's part and of a friendly nature with the Soviet Union, thus supporting Sharabi's contention.

The relationship between Syria and the Soviet Union bears on a proposition put forth by Walter Laqueur concerning the attention that the Soviet Union pays to the Arab states. Laqueur wrote that until recently it was Egypt which ranked highest as a recipient of Soviet attentions, but that increasingly, . . . [Egypt's] role in Soviet Middle East strategy is almost certain to decrease. Soviet attention

3. H. Sharabi, *Palestine and Israel: The Lethal Dilemma* (New York: Pegasus, 1969), p. 100.

is turning increasingly to other countries of the Middle East." [4] By defining attention as the sum of all international acts between actors, we find some evidence of the shift of Soviet attention in the Middle East as Laqueur suggests. From January 1966 to July 1968 the United Arab Republic led the Arab states as a recipient of Soviet international acts. Other Arab countries received little attention from the Soviet Union. Beginning in mid-1967, Syria began to receive more attention from the Soviet Union. By 1969 the United Arab Republic was still the leading recipient of Soviet acts but the number was less than in previous years, while Syria, Jordan, Lebanon, and Iraq all gained as recipients of actions by the Soviet Union. Thus it was found that Soviet attention is shifting increasingly away from the United Arab Republic to other Arab states, although the United Arab Republic continues to receive a fairly constant amount of attention from the Soviet Union.

The discussion now turns to the Arab-Israeli conflict—the most crucial phenomenon in the Middle East today. It is this conflict that may account mostly for our findings on the Middle East as a special political subsystem. There is no need to provide a background on the beginnings of the conflict. The history is long, the stories are old, and an international interaction analysis can apply only to some particular aspects of the struggle.

The most salient finding on the Arab-Israeli conflict concerns the trend in the hostilities between the two sides. Because of the nature of the WEIS data, it is not valid to compare violence levels in the Middle East over time—virtually no military conflict was coded during the June War period because of the WEIS policy not to code this kind of interaction during ongoing wars. Thus to compare the violence level in June 1967 with that in June 1970 would be incongruous. However, the data after June 1968 are indicative of all interactions in the Middle East including conflict, and it is on the span of data from June 1968 to April 1971 that this analysis focuses its attention.

As can be seen from the graph, figure 1, the conflict level rose fairly steadily from June 1968 through January 1970, when Israeli conflict reached a peak as Israel began attacking the Egyptian heartland. In April 1970 there was a sharp decrease in force, preceding an even sharper rise in May and June as President Nasser announced and implemented his war of attrition with Israel. September 1970

4. W. Laqueur, "Russia Enters the Middle East," *Foreign Affairs* 47, no. 2 (January 1969): 30.

shows markedly the effect of the Suez Canal cease-fire negotiated by United States Secretary of State Rogers in August—there are almost no conflict events for September, and as can be seen on the graph, conflict levels remained low for the remaining months of the study.

Malcolm Kerr has stated that "in midsummer 1968 it was possible to imagine that the Arab-Israeli War of 1967 might give rise to protracted and fairly stable although disagreeable impasse. . . ." [5] The flow of international action for the Middle East in 1968 does have some appearance of a stable but chronic conflict, but the data for 1969 fail to support the interpretation of a stable relationship. Not only is there an obvious escalation of violence but the phasing of action of the opponents also changes. The monthly records of military action by both sides show a very regular pattern from January 1966 through August 1968, but thereafter the variations in action and response become less ordered. The evidence suggests generally that the Arab-Israeli conflict took a new turn in 1969 and that whatever impasse settled in after the June War was disturbed seriously after March 1969. It is after this date, however, that one can say that Kerr's observation again has some validity, for as can be seen by the data, the relationship between the Arabs and Israel became more hostile but this hostility can be said to be stable; i.e., the rate of hostility, although high, is fairly constant.

Of the Middle East actors, Israel has maintained the highest level of reported military action during the sixty-four-month period of January 1966 through April 1971. It has generated more hostile behavior to the Arab nations than they have directed to Israel. Jordan, Egypt, and Syria have had the second highest recording of military violence. After the June War, Jordan became the most active opponent of Israel until the end of 1968. In 1969 Egypt's military activity increased to the level highest among the Arab states and remained at this high point until August 1970.

Michael Brecher, in his analysis on the Middle East as a subordinate system, holds that on a scale of intensity of conflict between the Arabs and Israelis, the United Arab Republic and Syria are in the lead followed by Jordan, Iraq, and Lebanon.[6] As noted above, the WEIS data yield different results. Syria and Lebanon alternate in

5. M. H. Kerr, *The Middle East Conflict,* Headline Series No. 191 (New York: Foreign Policy Assn., Inc., October 1968), p. 47.

6. M. Brecher, "The Middle East Subordinate System and Its Impact on Israel's Foreign Policy," *International Studies Quarterly* 13, No. 2 (June 1969): 123.

FIGURE 1. Arab-Israeli military conflict from January 1966 through April 1971.

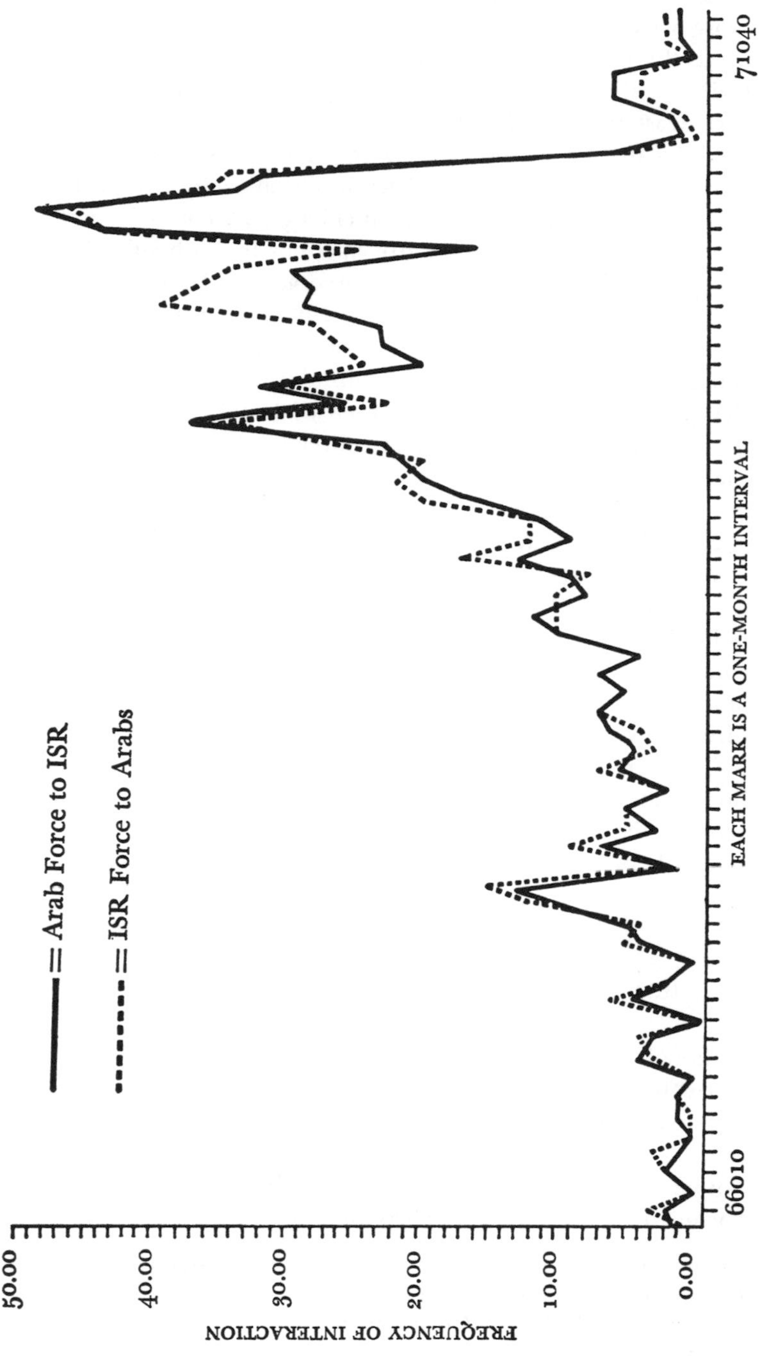

ranking the lowest in military actions, with Lebanon becoming more active militarily than Syria in the last half of 1969. We would place the United Arab Republic and PLO as the most active militarily in the recent period, with Jordan and Lebanon next and Syria least active militarily.

Characteristic of the Arab-Israeli conflict is Israel's policy of retaliation against the Arabs. Much has been written about this policy. Fred Khouri said "any border incident . . . could initiate a series of increasingly violent retaliatory actions by both sides." [7] Malcolm Kerr wrote that, "every threat uttered against Israel, whether or not it was accompanied by serious intent, and every commando raid . . . gave credence to the views of the Israelis' retaliation." [8] Because of current computer-programming limitations, the exchanges that would demonstrate how much of Israel's international action is retaliatory cannot be analyzed directly. The shortest time period that we can analyze, at present, is one month. Thus, month by month tracings permit only indirect evidence of some of the larger effects relating to Khouri's and Kerr's commentaries on the Israeli retaliation policy. In any case, there is not much argument on the point since Israel's spokesmen have often declared that a retaliatory policy has been followed in military strikes at the borders with Arab countries. We studied the relationship over time periods of one month between Arab accusations, warnings, complaints, and threats directed to Israel and Israel's record of acts of military activity, at least a part of which will be deemed retaliatory in character. The interesting finding, shown on figure 2, is that Arab verbal conflict activity (the record of accusations, warnings, complaints, and threats) generally decreases during the periods of intense Israeli military activity.

Conclusion

Although event-flow analyses of the type reported here are best suited to the description of large global effects in the patterns and changes of international politics, we have illustrated that the procedures of recording, coding, and counting the actions of nations can be brought to bear as well on more limited topics. If thoroughly documented and detailed chronologies—prepared, perhaps, by the

7. F. J. Khouri, "The Policy of Retaliation in Arab-Israeli Relations," *Middle East Journal* 20, No. 4 (Autumn 1966): 435–55.

8. Kerr, *The Middle East Conflict*, p. 16.

FIGURE 2. Arab verbal conflict with Israel versus Israeli military retaliation.

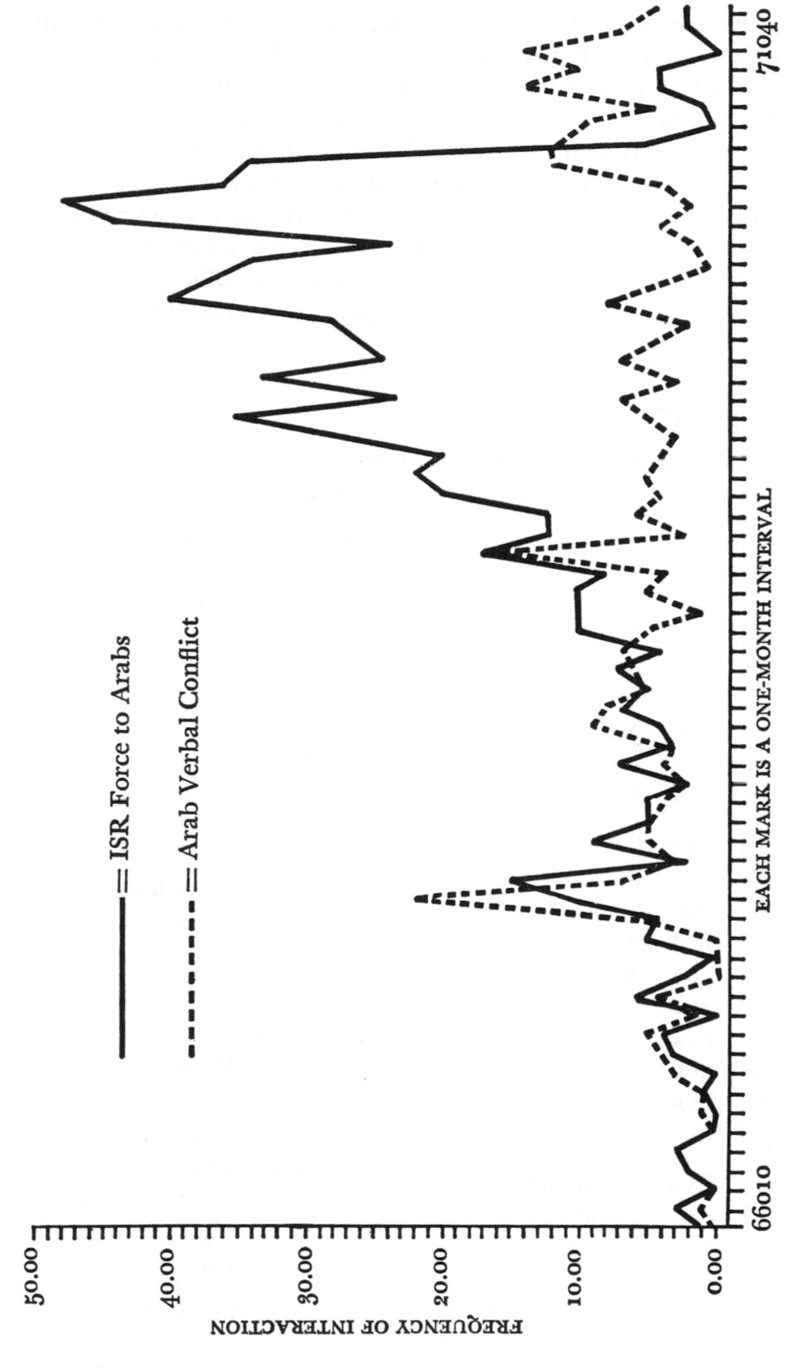

collaborative efforts of area experts—could be assembled from richer sources than newspaper reports, the techniques of international-event analysis of the general type illustrated in this chapter might well be put into play to yield insights and conclusions about the characteristics of international affairs in various regions and subsystems as well as to contribute to a more exact understanding of the structures and dynamics of general international relations. The computerized data file provides a resource of great potential value for the researcher working on foreign areas and in international affairs. The application to the flows of political events among nations is only one among a large number of possibilities.

Appendix A

Alphabetical Listing of Weis County Codes and International Behavior Category System

Number	Alpha	Actor
700	AFG	Afghanistan
339	ALB	Albania
615	ALG	Algeria
232	AND	Andorra
160	ARG	Argentina
900	AUL	Australia
305	AUS	Austria
053	BAR	Barbados
211	BEL	Belgium
266	EBE	Berlin/East
267	WBE	Berlin/West
145	BOL	Bolivia
571	BOT	Botswana
140	BRA	Brazil
355	BUL	Bulgaria
775	BUR	Burma
516	BUI	Burundi
811	CAM	Cambodia
471	CAO	Cameroun
020	CAN	Canada
482	CEN	Central African Rep.
780	CEY	Ceylon
483	CHA	Chad
155	CHL	Chile
710	CHN	China, People's Rep.
713	CHT	China, Rep. of
100	COL	Columbia
484	CON	Congo (Brazzaville)
490	COP	Congo (Kinshasa)
094	COS	Costa Rica
040	CUB	Cuba
352	CYP	Cyprus
315	CZE	Czechoslovakia
434	DAH	Dahomey
390	DEN	Denmark
042	DOM	Dominican Rep.
130	ECU	Ecuador
092	ELS	El Salvador
440	GUE	Equitorial Guinea (incl. Fernando Po)
530	ETH	Ethiopia
375	FIN	Finland

Number	Alpha	Actor
220	FRN	France
481	GAB	Gabon
420	GAM	Gambia
265	GME	Germany/Dem. Rep.
255	GMW	Germany/Fed. Rep.
452	GHA	Ghana
350	GRC	Greece
090	GUA	Guatemala
438	GUI	Guinea
110	GUY	Guyana
041	HAI	Haiti
091	HON	Honduras
310	HUN	Hungary
720	HOK	Hong Kong
395	ICE	Iceland
750	IND	India
850	INS	Indonesia
630	IRN	Iran
645	IRQ	Iraq
205	IRE	Ireland
666	ISR	Israel
325	ITA	Italy
437	IVO	Ivory Coast
051	JAM	Jamaica
740	JAP	Japan
663	JOR	Jordan
501	KEN	Kenya
731	KON	Korea/North
732	KOS	Korea/South
690	KUW	Kuwait
812	LAO	Laos
660	LEB	Lebanon
570	LES	Lesotho
450	LBR	Liberia
620	LBY	Libya

Number	Alpha	Actor
223	LIC	Liechtenstein
212	LUX	Luxemburg
721	MAC	Macao
580	MAG	Malagasy
553	MAW	Malawi
820	MAL	Malaysia
781	MAD	Maldive
432	MLI	Mali
338	MLT	Malta
590	MAR	Mauritius
435	MAU	Mauritania
070	MEX	Mexico
221	MOC	Monaco
712	MON	Mongolia
600	MOR	Morocco
698	MOM	Muscat and Oman
921	NAU	Nauru
790	NEP	Nepal
210	NTH	Netherlands
920	NEW	New Zealand
093	NIC	Nicaragua
436	NIR	Niger
475	NIG	Nigeria
385	NOR	Norway
770	PAK	Pakistan
095	PAN	Panama
150	PAR	Paraguay
135	PER	Peru
840	PHI	Philippines
290	POL	Poland
235	POR	Portugal
552	RHO	Rhodesia
360	RUM	Rumania
517	RWA	Rwanda
331	SAN	San Marino
670	SAU	Saudi Arabia
433	SEN	Senegal
451	SIE	Sierra Leone

Number	Alpha	Actor
830	SIN	Singapore
520	SOM	Somalia
560	SAF	South Africa
230	SPN	Spain
625	SUD	Sudan
572	SWA	Swaziland
380	SWD	Sweden
225	SWZ	Switzerland
652	SYR	Syria
510	TAZ	Tanzania
800	TAI	Thailand
461	TOG	Togo
052	TRI	Trinidad-Tobago
616	TUN	Tunisia
640	TUR	Turkey
500	UGA	Uganda
365	USR	USSR
651	UAR	UAR (Egypt
200	UNK	United Kingdom
002	USA	USA
439	UPP	Upper Volta
165	URU	Uruguay
328	VAT	Vatican
101	VEN	Venezuela
817	VTS	Vietnam/South
816	VTN	Vietnam/North
990	WSM	Western Samoa
678	YEM	Yemen
681	SYE	Yemen/South
345	YUG	Yugoslavia
551	ZAM	Zambia

Non-Governmental Actors

Number	Alpha	Actor
198	AFP	Alliance for Progress
699	ARL	Arab League
476	BIA	Biafra
397	EEC	Common Market
398	EFT	EFTA
396	NAT	NATO
199	OAS	OAS
599	OAU	OAU
697	PLO	Arab Commando groups
813	LAP	Pathet Lao
992	SEA	SEATO
818	VCG	Vietcong and NLF
394	WAR	Warsaw Pact
399	UNO	Any intl. org.
998	MLG	Any multilateral group
999	NSC	Not stated, unidentified target

1. YIELD
   - 011 Surrender, yield to order, submit to arrest, etc.
   - 012 Yield position; retreat; evacuate
   - 013 Admit wrongdoing; retract statement
2. COMMENT
   - 021 Explicit decline to comment
   - 022 Comment on situation—pessimistic
   - 023 Comment on situation—neutral
   - 024 Comment on situation—optimistic
   - 025 Explain policy or future position

3. CONSULT
   031 Meet with at neutral site; or send note; stay in same place
   032 Visit; go to; leave country
   033 Receive visit; host
4. APPROVE
   041 Praise, hail, applaud, condolences, ceremonial greetings, thanks
   042 Endorse others policy or position, give verbal support
5. PROMISE
   051 Promise own policy support
   052 Promise material support
   053 Promise other future support action
   054 Assure; reassure
6. GRANT
   061 Express regret; apologize
   062 Give state invitation
   063 Grant asylum
   064 Grant privilege, diplomatic recognition; de facto relations, etc.
   065 Suspend negative sanctions; truce
   066 Release and/or return persons or property
7. REWARD
   071 Extend economic aid (gift and/or loan)
   072 Extend military assistance; joint military exercises
   073 Give other assistance
8. AGREE
   081 Make substantive agreement
   082 Agree to future action; agree to meet, negotiate; accept state invitation
9. REQUEST
   091 Ask for information
   092 Ask for policy assistance; seek
   093 Ask for material assistance
   094 Request action; call for; ask for asylum
   095 Entreat; plead for; appeal to; help
10. PROPOSE
   101 Offer proposal
   102 Urge or suggest action or policy
11. REJECT
   111 Turn down proposal; reject protest demand, threat, etc.
   112 Refuse; oppose; refuse to allow; exclude

12. ACCUSE
- 121 Charge; criticize; blame; disapprove
- 122 Denounce; denigrate; abuse; condemn

13. PROTEST
- 131 Make complaint (not formal)
- 132 Make formal complaint or protest

14. DENY
- 141 Deny an accusation
- 142 Deny an attributed policy, action, role, or position

15. DEMAND
- 150 Issue order or command, insist; demand compliance, etc.

16. WARN
- 160 Give warning

17. THREATEN
- 171 Threat without specific negative sanctions
- 172 Threat with specific non-military negative sanctions
- 173 Threat with force specified
- 174 Ultimatum; threat with negative sanctions and time limit specified

18. DEMONSTRATE
- 181 Non-military demonstration; walk out on; boycott
- 182 Armed force mobilization, exercise, and/or display

19. REDUCE RELATIONSHIP (As Negative Sanction)
- 191 Cancel or postpone planned event
- 192 Reduce routine international activity; recall officials, etc.
- 193 Reduce or suspend aid or assistance
- 194 Halt negotiations
- 195 Break diplomatic relations

20. EXPEL
- 201 Order personnel out of country; deport
- 202 Expel organization or group

21. SEIZE
- 211 Seize position or possessions
- 212 Detain or arrest person(s)

22. FORCE
- 221 Non-injury destructive act; bomb with no one hurt
- 222 Non-military injury-destruction
- 223 Military engagement

CHAPTER 8

American and Soviet Defense Systems vis-à-vis the Middle East*

P. M. DADANT

The Middle East is, apparently, of special importance to the Soviet Union. On the one hand, it has intrinsic value for them—economic, political, and strategic. Perhaps, indeed, it is envisioned as a southern replica of its East European buffer states. On the other hand, the Middle East offers the Soviets an intermediate utility as a stepping stone for expansion into Africa and the Indian Ocean area.

In the meantime, the Middle East appears to have become of decreasing value to the United States. But that it will adopt a dovish attitude toward the Middle East need not follow, at least immediately, since American doves on Vietnam have become hawks on the Middle East. For the American commitment to the continued existence of Israel, unlike the commitment to Vietnam, is a vital factor within the American domestic political scene. It promises to remain the dominant Middle Eastern concern of the United States for some time.

Nevertheless, Soviet and American strategic positions in the Middle East are in obvious flux. What has replaced, for example, the American policy of containment in the Middle East? What new strategy has replaced the Dulles-conceived Northern Tier, Baghdad Pact, or CENTO? As strategic positions change, therefore, what are the implications in the international system—for the United States, for Israel? The author addresses himself to these kinds of problems in this chapter.

An Overriding Concern

It seems natural to many people that the Middle East should grip the attention of the world. This strategic area, credited by many as

* Any views expressed in this chapter are those of the author. They should not be interpreted as reflecting the views of The RAND Corporation or the official opinion or policy of any of its governmental or private research sponsors.

being the cradle of civilization, has been a hotbed for trouble since the dawn of that civilization. Forces spawned within the area and forces from without have surged back and forth through these barren deserts and fertile valleys. Even in this age of superpowers, of rockets to the moon, of nuclear energy and of worldwide pollution, the old Middle East remains important in international politics. To the two superpowers it presents opportunities, problems, dilemmas and, above all, a common danger.

The United States and the Soviet Union have one major concern in common in the Middle East: that any disturbance there does not escalate into an American-Soviet confrontation with its accompanying danger of all-out nuclear war. This common concern manifested itself most directly in 1967 when both major powers carefully avoided being drawn into the Arab-Israeli war. It has been evident since that Six-Day War in Soviet attempts to dissuade the Arab nations from renewing open warfare—this in spite of the willingness of the Soviet Union to furnish Arab nations with military supplies. It is also evident in attempts by the major powers to at least give an appearance of negotiating toward a Middle East settlement.

There can be no doubt that the danger of a United States–Soviet Union confrontation exists in the Middle East. Such a danger exists, of course, in any area in which the two nations have overlapping or conflicting interests, but it seems particularly acute in the Middle East because of the explosive nature of the situation and because the superpower relations in the area tend more and more toward those of patrons of opposing client states that are on the threshold of open warfare.

It appears difficult, however, to construct a credible scenario leading to superpower confrontation in the Middle East. The United States, for example, appears very unlikely to move into the area militarily, particularly in the wake of Vietnam; little else than the imminent collapse of Israel and overrunning of the land by Arab armies seems likely to cause a commitment of United States military force. If an Arab advance pursued such final objectives, however, Soviet participation would seem extremely unlikely, so that United States intervention in such extreme circumstances would probably not risk a United States–Soviet Union confrontation.

It is perhaps equally difficult to envisage the Soviets putting substantial military force into the Middle East. They have a history of not employing their own troops either at any distance from their territory or against states other than those they consider their own satellites.

That both powers would be drawn in and would pursue their respective courses until collision seems doubly unlikely. Mutual recognition of the confrontation danger lessens the probability of its occurrence even further. Active intervention by one superpower on behalf of a losing "client" might turn a losing military tide, for example, but might also insure against a threat to the other side so substantial as to bring in the opposing superpower.

Despite this, the dangers of confrontation cannot be dismissed. The United States has identified herself with a commitment to the existence of the State of Israel—a commitment that has not been formalized but to which many statements by government officials have attested. The Soviets, meanwhile, deepen their commitment to the Arab states by continued economic and military aid and have become deeply embroiled in the improvement of radical Arab forces—forces that have in the past proven themselves to be peculiarly beyond Soviet control. Many conceivable developments could create situations in which each superpower would find it hard to back away without unacceptable loss of prestige and influence in the area.

Heightening the nuclear danger is the future possibility of Israeli development of a nuclear weapon. Israel presently has undenied superiority in conventional war capability that makes it seem unlikely that she would resort to a nuclear threat, thereby opening the door for Arab cries for a counter-capability. Their Arab neighbors, however, outnumber the Israelis by nearly twenty to one, and the possibility of future meaningful increase in Arab coventional capabilities is always present. There can be little doubt that in dire circumstances Israel would use any threat she felt would insure her existence, and many observers have speculated that Israel may already have the capability to develop a nuclear weapon. Appreciation of this by the superpowers and Arab awareness of an Israeli nuclear potential could be a constant irritant in Middle East affairs in the next decade.

Barring a pronounced change in the political complexion of the area, or in the superpower interests and stated or implied commitments to Middle East states, this concern with avoiding a nuclear confrontation is certain to mark Soviet and American thinking about the Middle East through the 1970s. It must be like a heavy hand weighing on all other concerns in the area and tempering all superpower moves with respect to the Middle East.

Major Interests in the Middle East

In spite of the overriding concern with avoiding nuclear confrontation, other interests in the Middle East appear destined to prolong both Soviet and American involvement in the area. Not the least of these, of course, is the insistent Soviet drive toward expansion of Russian influence and extension of the Communist revolution. Russian desire to expand southward has a long history, formerly being based primarily on a desire for a warm water port that would be free of the stricture of the Bosporus. It took a heavy-handed turn when "Stalin in 1945 denounced the treaty of neutrality and non-aggression with Turkey and demanded joint Russian-Turkish management of the straits and the surrender of three provinces in the northeast adjacent to Soviet Armenia. With Red Army units still in Iran, he promoted the secession of Azarbayjan and Kurdistan in the northwest. Stalin's heavy-handed diplomacy deprived Russia of an opportunity to update the 1936 Montreux Convention, which regulated the use of the straits, and forced Russia to withdraw its troops from Iran with immense embarrassment, in the full international glare of the Security Council. It also drove Turkey, and later Iran, into intimate relations with the United States." [1]

Having alienated the states on her southern border, Russia in 1953 began a program to gain influence in the Middle East by backing at the United Nations the Arab claims in their dispute with Israel. Whether by crafty Soviet design or, as seems more likely, through opportunism, this program appears to be an outstanding success since "today, less than 17 years later, the Soviet Union has firmly established herself as a major power in the Middle East.[2] . . . Ironically, the western states themselves largely created the new opportunities for the Soviet Union." [3] First, when President Nasser in 1955 asked the United States for arms the Americans hesitated because they did not wish to provide Egypt with weapons that might lead to another Middle East war. As a result, Nasser "turned to the Soviet Union and [acquired] . . . (through the agency of Czechoslovakia) . . . about $250 million worth of . . . arms." [4] This was

1. J. C. Hurewitz, "Origins of Rivalry," in *Soviet-American Rivalry in the Middle East,* ed. idem (New York: Frederick A. Praeger, 1969), p. 5.

2. Robert E. Hunter, *The Soviet Dilemma in the Middle East Part I: Problems of Commitment,* Adelphi Papers, No. 59 (London: The Institute for Strategic Studies, September 1969), p. 1.

3. Ibid., p. 6.

4. Ibid., p. 6.

the modest beginning of a large-scale supply of Soviet Bloc arms to the "radical" Arab states. Second, the United States in 1956 withdrew its offer to help in financing the Aswan High Dam on the Nile. After some delay the Russians in 1958 extended their own offer and Egypt accepted. Third, the Eisenhower Doctrine, proclaimed in 1957, apparently alienated more Arabs than it impressed, being widely interpreted as outside interference in Arab affairs, and projected the Soviet Union as the only great power that seemed willing to support Arab nationalism and freedom from outside interference. When the United States sent 14,000 men to Lebanon in 1958, this view was strengthened and opportunities for Soviet arms sales in the Middle East increased.

"Since the Russians had no long-standing position to protect, they had little to lose and potentially much to gain by change and disruption in the Arab Middle East." [5] They apparently failed to understand the nature of Arab politics, however, and to appreciate the conflict between Communism and various Arab nationalist attitudes. In both Syria and Iraq the Soviets supported local Communists who moved too fast, overstepped themselves, and lost out to nationalistic forces. Their relations with Egypt, Syria, and Iraq fluctuated considerably as various Arab factions struggled for power and regimes changed in Syria and Iraq. In the mid-1960s the Arabs, spurred by competition for power within their own world, stepped up their anti-Israel activities. This presented new opportunities for the Soviet Union, whose aid and support were more in demand than ever. She sold arms to Arab states on very attractive terms in order to capture the market and gain whatever influence comes with being an arms supplier and increased her economic aid commitments. She also became vocal in supporting Arab causes.

At first the Soviets seemed perfectly safe in becoming more deeply involved in the Middle East. In fact, "until a few months before the Six-Day War—there was little evidence that the Soviet Union had begun to consider seriously that a policy of opportunism could also entail risks." [6] In early May of 1967, she apparently "warned" Syria and Egypt that Israeli troops were massing on the Syrian border, prepared to attack. Although patently untrue, these reports started a round of political escalation and military movements within the Arab states until Israel suddenly launched what she considered a preventive war on 5 June.

5. Ibid., p. 7.
6. Ibid., p. 9.

Midway in the crisis the Soviet Union seems to have realized that events were getting out of control and that total war in the Middle East also raised risks for the Soviet Union. She began trying to prevent war; but she was too late.

The Six-Day War initially appeared to ruin the Soviet position in the Arab world. Her seeming unwillingness to save her Arab clients from a sound thrashing at the hands of Israel—which may have been more inability than unwillingness—threatened to destroy all the recent gains in Soviet influence. In her eagerness not to lose the position she had gained in the Middle East, Russia undertook a massive rearming of the defeated Arab states. The Soviet position in the area was not only recaptured but increased as a result, although only at the expense of further increasing the Soviet commitment to and involvement in an area where, according to Malcolm Kerr, "it is not within the power of outsiders to adjust the flame under the pot." [7] Although her control of events in the area had just been proven to be marginal at best, the Soviet Union demonstrated that she is unlikely to give up her gains in the Middle East without a struggle; judging by past performance, she is almost certain to try to expand them at every opportunity.

The United States has consistently opposed Soviet expansion in all parts of the world. Alarmed by the rapid fall of all the Eastern European states to Soviet domination after World War II, the United States developed a policy of containment that attempted to ring Soviet Russia with states allied to and supported by the United States and pledged to resist Soviet expansion.

In the Middle East this took several forms. Military assistance to Turkey and Iran began during Marshall Plan years (1949–52), and expanded greatly after 1953. Individual mutual defense agreements were arranged with Turkey in 1951 and with Iran in 1952. Turkey was admitted to NATO on 18 February 1952. In 1955 the Baghdad Pact was formed by Turkey and Iraq with obvious United States support but without open United States membership; [8] this Pact was joined by the United Kingdom and Pakistan during 1955, and finally in November of that year by Iran. In January 1957 President

7. Malcolm H. Kerr, "Persistence of Regional Quarrels," in *Soviet-American Rivalry,* p. 228.

8. The United States was not a signatory to the Baghdad Pact nor to its successor, CENTO. However, she is an observer at CENTO Council Meetings and a member of the Military, Economic, and Anti-Subversion Committees. U.S., Department of State, "United States Defense Commitments and Assurances," August 1967, p. 15.

Eisenhower proposed the Eisenhower Doctrine, which was approved by Congress in March of that year. This Doctrine authorized the President "to undertake, in the general area of the Middle East, military assistance programs with any nation or group of nations of that area desiring assistance" and declared the United States "prepared to use armed force to assist any nation or group of nations requesting assistance against armed aggression from any country controlled by international Communism." [9] In 1959 the United States government entered into bilateral "Agreements of Cooperation" with Turkey and Iran.[10]

Initially, the Baghdad Pact seemed to promise success in blocking the Russians from expansion into the Middle East, even though it also tended to alienate states to the south. A coup in Iraq in July 1958, however, saw the Iraqi King and Prime Minister murdered. Iraq then swung away from its close ties with the West and withdrew from the Pact prior to its redesignation as the Central Treaty Organization (CENTO) in August 1959. CENTO has proved to be a very weak organization and without Iraq seems to have lost what meaning the Baghdad Pact had had.[11]

Although strongly suspicious of Russia because of her post–World War II policies, Turkey and Iran have softened their attitudes over the years. Both of these countries are now engaged in a normalization of relations with the Soviet Union, increasing their trade with Russia and, in the case of Iran, accepting Russian military supplies.

The old American policy of containment thus appears nearly defunct in the Middle East, with the Northern Tier both softening and being leapfrogged by Soviet inroads into Arab states. Yet America is unlikely to give up her attempts to thwart Russian expansion in this area. She still tends to view every expansion of Soviet influence as a threat to herself and to other nations of the free world, and to see such events as the invasion of Czechoslovakia in 1968 and announcement of the Brezhnev Doctrine as justifying that view. As a result of the Vietnam experience, America is developing a strong note of caution in her foreign policy and a pronounced reluctance to get drawn into entanglements that would again risk military involvement in any "peripheral" area. That the American view of the Middle East is vastly different from her view of Southeast Asia, however, was dramatically demonstrated in 1967

9. Ibid., p. 48.

10. Ibid., pp. 16–17.

11. Pakistan boycotted CENTO's military exercises and, for all practical purposes its ministerial conferences after the 1965 Indo-Pakistan war.

when innumerable Vietnam doves suddenly became Middle East hawks. Just how "peripheral" Americans might consider the Middle East in a new crisis in that area is a moot point.

Although less important than the possibility of nuclear confrontation and Russian expansion or American blockage of Soviet influence, other underlying interests in the Middle East strongly affect superpower attitudes toward the area. Oil, the primary Middle East resource, must be reckoned among the most important, both economically and strategically. As table 1 indicates, the Middle East

TABLE 1
World Crude Oil Production, 1971

COUNTRY OR AREA	THOUSANDS OF BARRELS PER DAY
Saudi Arabia	4,456.0
Kuwait	2,895.0
Iraq	1,692.0
Neutral Zone	551.0
Abu Dhabi	900.0
Qatar	429.0
Iran	4,514.0
Other Middle East	1,403.3
Middle East Total	16,840.3
USA	9,650.0
Venezuela	3,579.0
Canada	1,336.2
Other Western Hemisphere	1,505.5
Western Hemisphere Total	16,070.7
Western Europe Total	301.9
Libya	2,800.0
Algeria	603.0
Other Africa	2,174.6
Africa Total	5,577.6
Communist bloc Total	1,000.0
Asia-Pacific	1,698.0
World Total	40,588.5

Source: *The Oil and Gas Journal* 59, no. 52 (27 Dec. 1971): 72 ff.

supplied nearly 30 percent of the World's crude oil production in 1971. It is estimated that America has over $2 billion invested in the Middle East, nearly all in oil, and that America realizes an income of $1 billion per year from her oil interests in the area. Loss of this investment and favorable income could not be taken lightly.

The United States herself used less than 2 percent of the annual production of Middle East oil in 1970;[12] loss of this supply would hardly be serious and could easily be made up by increased domestic United States production. However, United States reserves are limited, and it is estimated that the future increase of these reserves will be outstripped by increasing consumption. Having access to the vast reserves of easily recovered Middle East oil may therefore become more important to the United States as the seventies progress.

The dependence of United States allies on Middle East oil may be more immediately crucial. As table 2 shows, much of Western

TABLE 2
Western Europe's Crude Oil Consumption vs. Imports from the Middle East

MILLIONS OF TONS

Country(s)	Crude Oil Consumption	Middle East Imports	Import as percent of Consumption
Benelux	59.3	53.6	90.4
France	86.6	45.5	52.5
West Germany	120.0	35.1	29.3
Italy	83.8	63.9	76.2
U.K	96.3	61.5	63.9
Scandinavia	65.3	18.4	28.2
Other Western Europe [a]	70.5	30.0	42.6
Total	581.8	308.0	52.9 (average)

Source: *Oil Statistics.* Middle East includes: Kuwait, Saudi Arabia, Iran, Iraq, Qatar, Neutral Zone, Egypt, Abu Dhabi, and other smaller producers.

[a] Includes: Greece, Ireland, Portugal, Spain, Switzerland, Turkey, Austria, and Iceland.

12. The Organization for Economic Cooperation and Development, *Oil Statistics: Supply & Disposal, 1970* (Paris: OECD, 1971), pp. 22–23 and 26 and the following pages.

Europe received over 50 percent of its crude oil supply from the Middle East in 1970, while Japan received over 85 percent of her crude oil from that area. Even with new discoveries elsewhere, this picture is not likely to change markedly. The demand for oil is increasing in all of the industrialized nations; oil imports to Western Europe were rising at an annual rate of 12 percent through 1970,[13] and those to Japan were increasing 22 percent per year.[14] Keeping the supply flowing appears vital to both the economies and the military machines of America's allies.

When the Arabs shut off the supply to the western nations in June 1967, Western Europe temporarily appeared to be in possibly serious difficulty. However, Iran increased her production and most of the rest of the shortage was filled from other areas in the world. Finding other markets lacking, the Arab nations soon relented and allowed shipments to the West to be resumed. Even if Russia could gain complete control of Middle East oil, therefore, she might have severe difficulty in turning off the supply to America's allies for any extended period.

Russia herself has been exporting large quantities of oil to her East European allies; but in recent years these countries have been looking elsewhere for oil. They have signed several barter agreements with Middle Eastern countries involving oil.[15] Even so Russia has little use for Middle East oil in the near future, although the picture is less clear for the longer run. Both Russian and Eastern European consumption is increasing rapidly, and some authorities feel that the Soviet Bloc as a whole may be an oil importer by 1980. A substantial increase in automobiles in the Communist nations could greatly aggravate the situation. Then, too, Middle East petroleum is much cheaper to extract than Soviet petroleum. In fact, one of the chief attractions of Middle East oil is its relatively low cost. Kuwait, for example, produced crude oil in 1967 for about one-eighth the cost of Venezuelan oil production and at about 5 percent of the cost of North American production.[16] Much of

13. *Oil Statistics,* p. 10.

14. Through 1967.

15. Due to the closure of the Suez Canal and lack of any tanker tonnage on either side, not many of these agreements have been implemented. In fact, the only sizeable delivery of Middle East oil to East Europe has so far been Iranian crude going to Rumania through the Israeli pipeline. Following their pro-Arab positions, the other East European countries have apparently refused to accept any oil transported through the Israeli pipeline.

16. T. T. Connors, *An Examination of the International Flow of Crude Oil, With Special Reference to the Middle East* (Santa Monica, Calif.: The RAND Corporation, P-4209, October 1969), pp. 61–62.

Southern Russia could be supplied from the Middle East. Soviet control of Middle East oil could also encourage further Russian encroachment into West European oil markets, toward which the Soviets have already made several moves.[17]

For the even more distant future, the Middle East still sits atop nearly 60 percent of the world's proven oil reserves.[18] In spite of recent discoveries elsewhere, it would seem unfortunate from the American point of view if such a valuable and extensive resource fell under control of unfriendly hands. From the Soviet viewpoint, a share in control of this vast resource and a share in the profits from Middle East oil must appear as at least an enticing by-product of any increase in influence in this area.

Another underlying interest in the Middle East, the Suez Canal, has lost much of its importance. In 1965 this vital waterway carried 225 million tons of supplies, about 75 percent of which was oil, and the flow was increasing by over 14 million tons annually.[19] However, the Canal was closed during the Six-Day War and has not yet been reopened. In the years that have elapsed, many changes have occurred. The initial impact of the closure was to raise the price of many goods in Western Europe and to decrease the availability of markets for Western European products. As one example, the tanker freight rate between the Persian Gulf and Rotterdam prior to June 1967 was $3.23 per ton; by September 1967 it was $16.50.[20] However, many alternative routes have been developed by now, and alternate means of transportation have improved, so that it is doubtful that an immediate and complete reopening of the Canal would have anything like the reverse impact that its closure had in 1967.

Most prominent among the new developments are the supertankers that are being added to the world's fleets. By the end of 1967, only 2 tankers over 200,000 deadweight tons were in service. By June 1971, there were 162 of them and another 261 on order.[21] At the same time, over one-fourth of the world fleet consisted of tankers with capacities of 150,000 deadweight tons.[22] The largest

17. The Soviet Union has moved in this direction regarding natural gas. Importing Iranian natural gas for consumption in southern Russia, the Soviet Union is able to export her own gas to West Europe at higher prices. Not only making a profit, the Soviet Union also obtains badly needed foreign exchange.

18. *Oil and Gas Journal*, pp. 72 and the following pages.

19. *The Middle East and North Africa, 1966–67*, 13th ed. (London: Europa Publications, 1967), p. 88.

20. *Navy Magazine*, September 1967, p. 19.

21. *Petroleum Press Service* 38, no. 10 (October 1971): 375.

22. The British Petroleum Co., Ltd., *Statistical Review of the World Oil Industry 1970* (London: 1971), p. 121.

tanker that could use the Suez Canal prior to 1967, on the other hand, was about 60,000 deadweight tons; over 50 percent of the world's ocean-going capacity is now in tankers that exceed that size.[23]

The supertankers would be unable to use a reopened Suez Canal without extensive widening and deepening, and therefore would have to continue to circumnavigate Africa to reach Western Europe from the Persian Gulf. A large part of the costs of ocean shipping, however, is in investment, insurance, port costs, and the like; adding transit distance has but small effect on the overall cost of a voyage.[24] In addition, crew requirements for the supertankers are usually no greater than for the smaller tankers, making the economies of scale substantial. It has been estimated, for example, that "a tanker with a capacity for 150,000 deadweight tons can move crude oil 5,000 miles at $1.69 per ton compared to $7.29 for a 10,000 deadweight ton tanker. Construction costs decrease with increasing tanker size from $220.00 per ton at 20,000 deadweight tons to less than $70.00 at 300,000 deadweight tons. Operating costs decrease, too, in particular with increased opportunities for automation. In fact, the *Tokyo Maru,* a tanker of about 135,000 deadweight tons, will be operated by a crew of 29, while tankers of 50,000 deadweight tons may use 35 men or more. As a result of such changes not only are detours around gateways like Suez cheaper than they were; they may, because of the limitations of the gateways themselves, be cheaper than the direct route." [25]

In addition to this, the Canal silts up quite rapidly and must be continually dredged when in operation. In the years since its closure, no dredging has been done; neither have any ships passed through the Canal, of course, and some believe that turbulence from ships causes much of the normal silting. No one is certain just how much silting has taken place, but one source estimated that as early as December 1967, four months of dredging would have been required before the canal could have been back to near its pre-1967 status.[26] By now the dredging operation could require a matter of years, and would be very expensive. With the heavy investments in mammoth

23. Ibid.

24. T. T. Connors, "Some Additional Data on Costs and Distance in Maritime Foreign Trade" machine copied.

25. A. H. Wohlstetter, "Strength, Interest, and New Technologies" (Paper delivered at the Ninth Annual Conference of the Institute of Strategic Studies on Military Technology, Elsinore, Calif., 28 September 1967).

26. "The Canal by Christmas," *The Economist,* 19 August 1967, p. 664.

tankers that could not use the canal without additional deepening and widening, lenders might be reluctant to invest in the canal's future.

The Soviet Union, on the other hand, may be quite interested in having the canal reopened. To her it would be very useful in furthering interests in the Persian Gulf and in areas bordering the Indian Ocean. That the Soviets are interested in the Indian Ocean was graphically illustrated by the extended visit of Russian warships to that area in 1968, when the cruiser *Dmitri Pozharsky,* a missile ship, and an antisubmarine escort ship visited ports in India, Pakistan, Ceylon, Aden, Somalia, and Persian Gulf ports.[27] The Soviet Union's unconditional and forceful support of India in the 1971 Indo-Pakistani war and her growing naval presence in the area are indications of the Soviets' deep interests in the Indian Ocean.

Without the Suez Canal, however, the Indian Ocean is not readily accessible to the Russians. Although the 1968 cruise was made by ships from the Soviet Pacific Fleet, Soviet Pacific Coast ports are severely handicapped by fog in spring and fall and by ice in winter.[28] Furthermore, the south coast of Arabia is over 6,100 NM from the nearest Soviet Pacific port. From more favorable ports on the Black Sea, the same destination is nearly 11,500 NM if one must transit the Mediterranean, exit at Gibraltar, and circumnavigate Africa. If the Suez Canal were available, on the other hand, Soviet ships sailing from the Black Sea would require only 3,200 NM to reach the same point. This short trip from warm-water ports on the Black Sea, close to the industrial heartland of the Soviet Union, would be much more attractive to the Soviets in pursuing economic interests or maintaining a military presence in the Indian Ocean area than any presently available options.

Soviet use of the Suez Canal prior to its closure demonstrates that the Canal would be even more widely useful to them than merely for maintaining their Indian Ocean interests. Before the June 1967 closure, for example, the Soviet Union was putting five to seven ships a month through the Canal with supplies for North Vietnam.[29]

The United States also has interests in the Indian Ocean and has

27. "Russia Moves Into Indian Ocean Area," *Los Angeles Times,* 8 March 1970.

28. U.S., Congress, House of Representatives, Committee on Armed Services, *The Changing Strategic Naval Balance USSR and U.S.A.* (Washington, D.C.: U.S. Government Printing Office, December 1968), p. 33.

29. Connors, *International Flow of Crude Oil,* p. 58.

maintained a Middle East Force since the end of World War II. Although it normally consists only of 2 destroyers and a flagship,[30] this small force has made many port visits throughout the Indian Ocean area in past years. Reopening of the Suez Canal would simplify America's job of maintaining this force, which is currently supplied from the United States East Coast via a route of nearly 11,000 NM around the southern tip of Africa. With the Suez reopened this trip could be cut to about 6,600 NM. Perhaps even more important, ships could easily be rotated to and from the Sixth Fleet in the Mediterranean if that were desirable. However, this decrease in distance from United States East Coast ports is not nearly as dramatic as the shortening of the route from the Black Sea to the Persian Gulf. On balance, it appears that at present the reopening of the Canal is more vital to Soviet interests than to those of the United States.

One ancient interest in the Middle East seems to be of questionable validity in today's world: highly regarded in past centuries as the land bridge between the Eurasian Continent and Africa, the Middle East now holds little attraction for this purpose. Only one north-south rail line runs through the area and part of that is currently unusable; good highways are also lacking. With today's technology, people and goods can be moved so cheaply by boat and so quickly by air that there would seem to be little reason to incur the expense of improving this land-bridge route.

Its central location in the Eurasian-African land mass does make the Middle East a valuable basing area, however. Air bases in particular would be useful to the Soviets in moving either cargo or military forces through the Middle East. Should the Soviet Union wish to supply quick and substantial military assistance to an African constituent, for example, airfields in the Middle East would be most convenient refueling bases. Only a few Soviet tactical-fighter aircraft presently have sufficient range to fly from a refueling base in, say, Yugoslavia to even the closest point in Africa, to say nothing of making it from a base in the Soviet Union. On the other hand, nearly any fighter aircraft could hop from a base near Baku in

30. According to *Newsweek*, 17 January 1972, p. 16, Washington has decided to "beef up the U.S. naval presence in the Persian Gulf." Even though the degree of this increase and the manner in which it is to be achieved are not yet known, it represents an important strategic move in the light of Britain's withdrawal from the region. *The London Times*, 7 January 1972, confirms that the United States was establishing a permanent naval base on Bahrain, occupying quarters that the British forces had occupied on the island. The United States had, of course, used British facilities when they were still on Bahrain.

southern Russia through an airbase in Iraq, then to either Jordan or Arabia, and on to Egypt and beyond if such routes were available. Cargo aircraft might find the same routes useful, perhaps with fewer stops, since their use would allow the aircraft to carry maximum loads.

New developments promise to decrease the importance of even that aspect of Middle Eastern lands. At the Paris air show in 1965, the Soviet Union displayed a huge new transport aircraft, the AN-22, capable of lifting some 88 tons for a distance of 3,100 mi., or 50 tons for 6,800 mi.[31] From bases in Southern Russia, these aircraft could reach all of Africa and Southeast Asia without a stop. A large fleet of these aircraft would give the Soviets tremendous new flexibility in moving supplies to distant places.

Naval bases in the Middle East can also be an asset, either in operating to the west in the Mediterranean Sea or to the south and southeast in the Indian Ocean. As the Soviets are already demonstrating with their use of the facilities at Alexandria and Port Said, the flexibility and staying power of the Russian fleet in the Mediterranean is greatly enhanced by access to ports on that sea. Ports such as Aden, on the other hand, give ready access to the Arabian Sea and, as British experience shows, can be valuable in extending seapower southward and eastward. From a base in this area (e.g., on the island of Socotra) the Russians could set up a permanent naval presence in the Indian Ocean, much as they have in the Mediterranean Sea.

For the United States, the Middle East is not on a north-south route but could be a stepping stone for east-west activities between the Atlantic-European region and the Indian Ocean area. The Indian Ocean, however, is on the opposite side of the globe from the United States; in fact, Ceylon is about the same distance by sea from Seattle through the Straits of Malaysia as it is from New York through Gibraltar and the Suez Canal. Airbases in the Middle East would be useful to the United States as refueling points in reaching areas in and around the Indian Ocean, but other routes can be used with no added difficulty if they contain comparable refueling bases, and in some cases would result in a shorter overall trip. From the United States to most of Africa, a route through the Middle East would be unnecessarily circuitous, although it could be used in getting to Ethiopia and other parts of Northeast Africa.

A naval base on the Mediterranean side of the Middle East is less

31. *Jane's All The World's Aircraft: 1969–70* (London: Jane's All The World's Aircraft Publishing Co., Ltd., 1969), p. 467.

important for the United States than for the USSR. The United States Sixth Fleet already operates out of Gaeta, Italy, and has demonstrated that it can maintain a permanent presence anywhere in the Mediterranean Sea. Prior to the Six-Day War, the Soviets had no available Mediterranean base. On the Indian Ocean side of the Middle East, however, a naval base has the same meaning for the United States as for the USSR. The United States Middle East Force currently operates out of Bahrain, a newly independent country in the Persian Gulf, where facilities of a British Royal Navy station had been used for logistics purposes prior to the British withdrawal. In the meantime, the United States has established its own permanent base on Bahrain. Without the facilities of such a port somewhere on the borders of the Indian Ocean, maintaining a permanent naval presence in that ocean would be extremely difficult if not impossible for either of the great powers.

The strongest United States interest in the Middle East—and potentially perhaps the most dangerous—is her identification with the continued existence of the State of Israel. Although never formalized, the commitment to this cause seems at least as strong in the United States as many commitments that have been the subject of treaties, as can be judged from the reactions to the Six-Day War. In March 1970, President Nixon stated that the United States would move to assure Israeli security if the balance of power in the Middle East were disturbed,[32] and Secretary of State Rogers said "we have no intention of jeopardizing the security of Israel." [33]

While trying to discover a way to reach a peaceful Middle East settlement that would assure Israel's security, the United States in 1967 assumed the role, abandoned by France after the Six-Day War, of principal supplier of major arms to Israel, first selling her some A-4 fighter-bombers to replenish wartime aircraft losses, and later selling her modern F-4 Phantom jets. The United States has simultaneously attempted to maintain firm and friendly ties with the moderate Arab states, such as Jordan, Lebanon, and Saudi Arabia, and to resume more normal relations with the radical Arab states in the area. Apparently feeling that the United States had become too closely identified with Israel, the Nixon administration in one of its first moves attempted to establish—or reestablish—an "even-handed" policy in the Middle East. This was immediately inter-

32. "U.S. Will Aid Israel if Power Balance is Upset, Nixon Says," *Los Angeles Times*, 22 March 1970, p. 1.

33. "Text of Statement by Rogers and Excerpts from his News Conference," *New York Times*, 24 March 1970, p. 14.

preted by some as an abandonment of Israel and hotly denounced. In the ensuing rhetoric, with raids and reprisals increasing in the Middle East and with the Soviets continuing to supply arms to the radical Arab states, the United States seems to have slipped reluctantly back to being the principal supplier of Israel. From a pragmatic viewpoint, if the United States is to pursue a dual policy of the survival of Israel and noninvolvement by United States military forces, the only feasible course seems to be to assure that Israel is strong enough to protect herself against all threats from her Arab neighbors. The great difficulty comes in trying to do this without further alienating the Arab states, further polarizing the Middle East and thus decreasing American influence in the area and backhanded promoting Soviet influence.

The Russians, on the other hand, are probably also anxious to preserve Israel as a state. They have used the Arab-Israeli struggle to great advantage in the last few years in gaining a strong foothold in the Middle East. Were Israel to disappear, the disunity between Arab states could blossom again, raising the dangers for the Russians that aiding one Arab nation would alienate others.

Expanding Soviet Naval Activities

The Soviet Navy has increased significantly since the end of World War II. According to a report prepared by the American Security Council and submitted to the House Committee on Armed Services in late 1968,[34] the USSR had commissioned 86 destroyers and 250 attack submarines in the preceding 20 years. These numbers compare to 14 destroyers and 45 attack submarines built by the United States during that period. The report stated that "two-thirds of the U.S. active fleet is over 20 years old. Only one-tenth of the USSR fleet is over 20 years old." [35]

Notable as this buildup is, it may be less significant than the increase in Soviet naval activity in the Mediterranean since 1964. Prior to that time Soviet naval vessels made only occasional visits to the Mediterranean and did not operate there on a sustained basis. Starting in about 1964 the Soviets began to maintain a constant presence in that sea with 3 or 4 naval vessels. By January 1967 there were 10 or 12 vessels in the Soviet Mediterranean Squadron; following the Six-Day War this fleet was rapidly expanded to about

34. *Changing Strategic Naval Balance.*
35. Ibid., p. 13.

35 vessels. "When this force was at its peak, it included a 15,000 ton guided-missile cruiser with 12 6-inch guns, 3 other heavy cruisers, 5 to 7 missile-equipped destroyers of the 4300-ton Kynda and smaller Kotlin class, 10 conventional and 2 nuclear powered submarines, 12 to 15 modern supply ships serving as floating bases in protected anchorages, and amphibious landing craft."[36] Admiral Sir John Hamilton, former commander in chief Allied Forces Mediterranean, stated that "the presence of this fleet is having a profound effect on men's minds. In this respect, it is contributing significantly to the rise of the Soviet influence in the Mediterranean area."[37]

The buildup continued during 1968 and 1969, reaching peaks of about 60 ships during exercises in November 1968 and April 1969 and 63 to 65 ships in August 1969. At the latter time, according to a United States Navy spokesman, there were 20 destroyers and other surface combat ships, 35 auxiliary and support ships, and 8 to 10 submarines operating with the Mediterranean Squadron.[38]

Two significant developments have accompanied this Soviet buildup in the Mediterranean. First, the Soviet navy must have learned techniques of refueling and replenishment without access to a major port. These techniques will help tremendously in divorcing the Soviet fleet from its home bases in the Soviet Union and giving it a wide-ranging capability.[39] Second, following the Six-Day War and perhaps as part of an agreement that sent some $2 billion worth of war supplies to Egypt to replenish her June 1967 losses,[40] the Soviets gained the use of storage and repair facilities, or nearly the equivalent of naval base rights, at Alexandria and Port Said. Use of these facilities is ideal from the Soviet viewpoint, avoiding the stigma of military bases on foreign soil—against which the Soviets have so often declaimed—while enormously increasing the flexibility and staying power of the Soviet Mediterranean Squadron.

Another possible expansion of Soviet Mediterranean activities also apparently arose as part of the political coin of reequipping the

36. Ibid., p. 31.

37. Ibid., pp. 31–32.

38. "Soviet Fleet Grows in the Mediterranean," *New York Times*, 20 August 1969, p. 12.

39. In 1969 the Pentagon reported a record number of 125 Soviet naval vessels away from home waters. See "Soviet Deploying Big Fleet Abroad," *New York Times*, 21 August 1969, p. 8.

40. Hunter, *Soviet Dilemma in the Middle East*, p. 12.

Egyptian military. Soviet pilots reportedly fly Soviet TU-16 aircraft (with Egyptian markings) from Egyptian airfields on surveillance missions over the United States Sixth Fleet.[41] If this appears to be principally an adjunct of naval activities in the Mediterranean, it is also a double-edged sword, representing as it does the equivalent of Soviet airbase rights in Egypt. The Russians are also reported to have facilities at other Egyptian airfields and "staging rights"[42] in Syria and Iraq.

Buildup of Soviet Naval activity has not been confined to the Mediterranean Sea. In February 1968, Admiral Sergei Gorshkov, commander in chief of the Soviet Navy, paid a ten-day visit to India. The following month the Soviet Squadron consisting of the cruiser *Dmitri Pozharsky* flying the flag of Admiral Amelko, commander of the Soviet Pacific Fleet, a missile ship, and an antisubmarine vessel visited both Madras and Bombay and proceeded to other ports around the Indian Ocean. Their 23,000 mile cruise was the longest by a Soviet naval squadron since 1945. In March 1969, three Soviet submarines, a subtender, and a tanker were reportedly seen off the coast of Ceylon.[43]

The number of Soviet naval vessels in the Indian Ocean apparently increased further in the meantime. At least two Russian task forces of 5 or 6 ships each reportedly entered the Indian Ocean through the Strait of Singapore and the Strait of Malacca in 1970, and the Australians supposedly shadowed such a task force off their west coast. A major combat vessel was in each of these forces. In addition, frequent reports of Soviet submarines have suggested to some that the Soviets may be deploying missile-bearing submarines in the Bay of Bengal.[44]

Some Indian observers seem to take for granted the Soviet Union's future status as a naval power in the Indian Ocean. One noted that the "arrival of the Soviet Navy means that for the first time since Vasco de Gama western naval supremacy is faced with a serious challenge." He added that "on the western Flank of India, the Soviet Navy's appearance will have incalculable effect on the Persian Gulf."[45]

41. Ibid., p. 13.

42. Ibid.

43. "Russia Moves into Indian Ocean Area."

44. Ibid.

45. *Changing Strategic Naval Balance*, p. 34.

United States and USSR Aid to the Middle East

In 1954 the Soviet Union began extending economic aid to underdeveloped countries, a practice the United States has been heavily involved in since World War II. There are, of course, aspects of humanitarianism in economic aid, particularly as practiced by the United States. There can be little doubt, however, that both superpowers have used their economic aid to one extent or another either in shoring up a buffer-zone defense against the other superpower or in an attempt to gain some measure of influence with the aided country. During the Marshall Plan, for example, a large part of United States economic aid went to Western Europe in a successful attempt to make the countries there economically viable so they could help protect themselves against spreading Communism.

Since the Soviets started from a more isolated position, their aid has comprised a more noticeable attempt to gain influence than has American aid. They have concentrated nearly two-thirds of their aid in the Middle East and South Asia, areas which the Soviets would undoubtedly like to incorporate into an enlarged Soviet defense system.

That aid can be humanitarian somewhat clouds the issue. That it has been used to extend systems of defense, however, implies that it can be an indirect measure of the importance a country attaches to a particular area. In the Middle East, because of the turmoil in the area, the ebb and flow of political power, and the other interests previously discussed, it must remain an uncertain measure. Nevertheless, some comparisons are enlightening.

United States aid to foreign countries continued after World War II. In the three years from 1946 through 1948, over $6.5 billion was granted outright to other nations, and loans extended totaled another $8 billion.[46] In the Middle East this assistance was all in the form of loans and the major recipients were Turkey with $44.5 million and Iran with nearly $26 million. The only other Middle East countries receiving appreciable aid in those years were the United Arab Republic with $18 million and Saudi Arabia with just over $14 million.

By the end of the Marshall Plan period in 1952, economic grants to the Middle East totaled over $250 million and loans had climbed

46. All data on U.S. foreign economic and military aid are from U.S., Department of State, Agency for International Development, U.S. Overseas Loans and Grants and Assistance From International Organizations, Executive Agreement Series, 29 May 1969 and 14 May 1971.

to nearly $330 million.[47] These were a small part of worldwide United States aid, however, most of which was going to rebuild our European allies during those years. The grants to the Middle East were only slightly more than 1 percent of worldwide United States grants and the loans were less than 3 percent of the worldwide total.

In the early 1950s, with the economic recovery of Europe essentially complete, the United States shifted its foreign aid to other areas of the world. During the Mutual Security Act period from 1953 through 1961, United States economic aid to less developed countries totaled nearly 90 percent of all United States foreign aid, whereas during the Marshall Plan period from 1949 through 1952, less than 25 percent of United States aid had been so directed. In the Middle East, United States economic aid increased perceptibly after 1953; it averaged about $190 million per year in grants and $200 million per year in loans from 1953 to its peak in 1966. As a percentage of worldwide United States economic aid, the amount extended to the Middle East appeared even more important, with grants averaging nearly 9½ percent and loans over 12½ percent of the worldwide totals.

As table 3 shows, Turkey has always been a special case for the United States, receiving about 37 percent of the economic aid for the entire Middle East region. This is in keeping with the concept of the Northern Tier which sought to build up Turkey and Iran as bastions against Communist expansion, the embodiment of the policy of containment in this region. The other Northern Tier country, Iran, received about 15 percent of the United States economic aid to the Middle East.

After 1966, however, United States economic aid to the Middle East decreased sharply. Grants to the area in 1970 totaled only $22.8 million, a mere 1.0 percent of the worldwide total. Although substanial loans were made to Israel ($50.9 million), Turkey ($71.0 million), and Iran ($46.7 million), total loans to the Middle East dropped to $183.7 million, about 7.3 percent of the worldwide total.

47. None of the figures quoted include any portion of U.S. contributions to international organizations, which amounted to nearly $4 billion from 1946 through 1968. In addition to general funds that may have been applied in part to the Middle East, such as the UN Development Program (U.S. contribution: $624 million) UN Children's Fund (U.S. contribution: $265 million) UN/FAO-World Food Program ($133 million from the U.S.) and the World Health Organization ($121 million from the U.S.), these contributions include some specifically earmarked for that area, such as $438 million for the UN Relief and Works Agency for Palestine Refugees.

USSR economic aid to the Middle East started only in 1954 and can therefore most appropriately be compared to the United States figures since 1953. Since 1954 Soviet Union credits and grants to Middle East nations, as shown in table 4, have totaled about $2.25 billion, less than 40 percent of United States economic aid during that period. However, total worldwide Soviet aid in those years was only $6.25 billion, barely more than United States aid to the Middle East alone. Aid to the Middle East, then, has been over 35 percent of the total worldwide Soviet program, indicating the relative importance the Soviets have attached to gaining a foothold in this area of the world.

TABLE 3
United States Economic Loans and Grants to Middle East Nations
(In Millions of Dollars)

NATION	1953–70 LOANS	1953–70 GRANTS	TOTAL 1946–70 LOANS	TOTAL 1946–70 GRANTS
Iran	570.5	438.8	596.3	455.3
Iraq	26.0	27.8	26.9	28.3
Israel	772.0	282.8	907.0	369.3
Jordan	31.3	564.7	31.3	569.9
Kuwait	50.0	—	50.0	—
Lebanon	16.5	71.2	18.1	73.0
Saudi Arabia	12.0	27.1	31.1	27.5
Syria	24.0	36.0	24.0	36.4
Turkey	1,310.4	1,058.7	1,439.9	1,198.8
UAR	608.4	291.1	619.1	293.0
Yemen	—	42.9	—	42.9
CENTO	18.3	35.3	18.3	35.3
Regional*	18.3	271.0	18.3	273.7
Total M.E. (Less Regional)	3,439.4	2,877.0	3,762.0	3,129.7
Total Worldwide	31,241	37,839	42,751	60,207

Source: "U.S. Overseas Loans and Grants and Assistance from International Organizations," Agency for International Development, May 14, 1971.
* Includes Near East and South Asia.

In addition to this aid directly from the USSR, nations in the Middle East have received economic assistance from Communist states in Eastern Europe, undoubtedly extended in many cases at the urging of the Soviet Union. The area has received nearly half of Eastern Europe's total foreign economic aid, which has added another $1 billion of Communist aid to the Middle East.

TABLE 4

USSR and Eastern Europe Economic Credits and Grants to Middle East Nations

(In Millions of Current U.S. Dollars)

NATION	USSR TOTAL 1954–68	EASTERN EUROPE TOTAL 1954–68
Iran	508	331
Iraq	184	—
Syria	233	169
Turkey	210	8
U.A.R.	1,011	562
Yemen	92	17
Total M.E.	2,238	1,087
Total worldwide	6,296	2,460

Source: U.S. Department of State, "Communist Governments and Developing Nations: Aid and Trade in 1968," RSE-65, Sept. 5, 1969, p. 3.

As shown in table 4, the lion's share of this aid has been given to the United Arab Republic, which has been the recipient of nearly half of all USSR and Eastern European aid to the Middle East. In the last few years, however, as Iran's memories of post–World War II faded and she began to pursue a rapprochement with the Soviet Union, that country has also received considerable aid from the USSR and her European satellites. Of the total of $840 million extended to Iran from the Soviet Union and Eastern Europe, $450 million was negotiated in 1968.[48] This makes Iran by far the second

48. Two hundred million dollars of this was a credit from Czechoslovakia that was not finalized until 1969. U.S., Department of State, "Communist Govern-

largest recipient of Communist bloc aid in the Middle East.

Economic assistance is not the only kind of aid given to the Middle East by the superpowers. Perhaps more pertinent to defense issues is the amount of military aid extended to the area, and in this activity both the United States and the Soviet Union have been heavily involved, although with some essential differences.

In her military assistance program the United States has extended about $4 billion in grants and over $650 million in credit assistance to nations in the Middle East.[49] Ninety-six percent of the grants, however, have been given to the two Northern Tier countries of Turkey and Iran—75 percent to Turkey alone, as indicated in table 5. Prior to 1968, nearly 70 percent of the nonclassified credit assistance to the area had also been extended to the Northern Tier, in this case all to Iran. Aside from Turkey and Iran, United States military aid to the Middle East has been only in the neighborhood of $160 million in grants and, prior to 1968, about the same amount in credit assistance.

Furthermore, the United States has professed and apparently followed a policy of trying to maintain an arms balance in the Middle East nations—between Israel and her Arab antagonists, and among the various Arab states. A large part of her military assistance, for example, had gone to Iraq and Jordan. In the meantime, even sales of military equipment to Israel have been held to a minimum, and at times refused. In March 1970, for example, the United States government announced that it would "hold in abeyance for now" an Israeli request to buy more modern aircraft, saying that, "in our judgement, Israel's air capacity is sufficient to meet its needs for the time being." [50] The United States has also tried to extract an agreement from the Russians to limit arms shipments to the Middle East in an effort to curtail military activities in the area and lessen the chance of a full-scale resumption of hostilities.

The Russians have refused this overture, however, and have continued their supply of arms to the so-called radical Arab states, to whom nearly all of their military assistance has been given. The United Arab Republic, Syria, and Iraq are the principal recipients of this Soviet military aid. The Soviets make no announcements of the amount of their military assistance, of course. Already sub-

ments and Developing Nations: Aid and Trade in 1968," RM-RSE-65/69 series, no. RSE-65, 5 September 1969, p. 3.

49. These figures do not include credit assistance and grants to Israel, Jordan, and Saudi Arabia. Aid to these countries has been classified since 1968.

50. "U.S. Will Aid Israel."

TABLE 5
U.S. Military Assistance Program
(Chargeable to Foreign Assistance Act Appropriations)
Credit Assistance and Grants to Middle East Nations
(In Millions of Dollars)

	1970		TOTAL 1946–70	
NATION	CREDIT ASSISTANCE	GRANTS	CREDIT ASSISTANCE	GRANTS
Iran	70.0	15.2	504.1	830.4
Iraq	—	*	—	46.7
Israel	†	—	†	—
Jordan	†	1.0	†	53.2
Kuwait	—	—	—	—
Lebanon	—	0.1	—	9.0
Saudi Arabia	†	0.5	†	35.1
Syria	—	*	—	0.1
Turkey	—	116.6	—	2,939.4
U.A.R.	—	—	—	—
Yemen	—	—	—	*
CENTO	—	0.1	—	1.0
Regional ‡	114.9	—	271.6	790.9
Total M.E. (Less Regional and Classified)	70.0	133.5	504.1	4,705.8
Total, worldwide	286.0	522.0	1,856.0	34,856.0

Source: "U.S. Overseas Loans and Grants and Assistance from International Organizations," May 14, 1971.
* Less than $50,000.
† Data classified. Credit assistance to Israel prior to 1968: 23.9.
Credit assistance to Jordan prior to 1968: 12.9.
Credit assistance to Saudi Arabia prior to 1968: 123.0.
‡ Includes Near East and South Asia.

stantial prior to the Six-Day War, Soviet arms shipments to the Middle East suddenly bounded upward in the months following that war as they hurried to replace a large portion of the equipment that had been destroyed or captured by the Israelis. It is estimated that between 80 and 100 percent of the lost army and air force equipment was replaced by the USSR and that the equipment supplied to Egypt alone was perhaps "worth as much as $2,000 million if measured in terms of the cost of providing similar Western equipment." [51] While Egypt has been by far the largest recipient of Soviet military aid in the Middle East, current arms levels balanced against the losses of the Six-Day War indicate that sizable aid has been extended to Syria and Iraq as well.[52]

Even by the more rigorous standards of modern warfare in Europe, the equipment supplied to these Arab states by the Soviets is not obsolescent. Many are of a type still in active Soviet inventories, and some have been supplied to the Middle East nations before the Russians have given similar weapons to their Eastern European satellites. Among the modern Soviet weapons in Egypt are T-54 and T-55 medium tanks, Mig-21, Mig-23, Su-7 fighter-bombers, and Su-11 interceptors, OSA and KOMAR boats with STYX surface-to-surface missiles[53] and SA-2 and SA-3 air-defense missiles.[54]

The major portion of Soviet military aid to the Middle East was apparently intended to rebuild the armies that were so badly shattered in the Six-Day War. This is particularly true in the case of Egypt. The Soviet's best interests would undoubtedly be served if the Egyptian forces were to be more effective when and if the full-scale battle with Israel were rejoined for a fourth time. They may also wish that the Egyptian army is *seen* to be more fit, as an added deterrent to Israel.

The quick installation of the "missile belt" west of the Suez Canal in 1970 implied a sharp alteration in Soviet intent, however. The SA-3 surface-to-air missiles, the latest addition in the United Arab Republic at that time, are perhaps the most significant for our present discussion. The SA-3 is reportedly designed to operate against low-altitude aircraft and would therefore be a significant addition to the SA-2 system (which the Israelis have proven time and again to be ineffective against low-altitude flights). The first shipments were reportedly accompanied by about 1,500 Soviet troops, and their introduction encouraged speculation that the

51. Hunter, *Soviet Dilemma in the Middle East,* p. 12.

52. *The Military Balance, 1970–71* (London: The Institute for Strategic Studies, 1970), pp. 40, 44.

53. Four of these missiles sank the Israeli destroyer *Elath* in 1967. See *New York Times,* 23 October 1967, sec. 1, p. 8; and *New York Times,* 24 October 1967, sec. 1.

54. *The Military Balance,* p. 45; *New York Times,* 19 March 1970, sec. 1, p. 2.

Russians may be moving to establish in Egypt a complete air-defense system manned by Russians.[55]

These 1,500 military personnel that allegedly accompanied the first SA-3 missiles brought the reported total number of Soviet military personnel in Egypt to about 4,500.[56] (In addition to this some 600 Soviet military personnel are reported to be in Syria.)[57] Soviet military personnel in Egypt apparently had a primary function of training and advising the Egyptian army, where they were reported to be present down to battalion level.[58] The troops with the SA-3s may also have been intended to train Egyptians to man these missiles.

In July of 1972, the USSR suffered a severe reversal in the Middle East when President Sadat of the Arab Republic of Egypt ordered the withdrawal from his country of Russian "military advisers and experts," and placed Soviet bases and equipment under exclusive Egyptian control.[59] According to reports, approximately 20,000 Russian military advisers, pilots, and missile crews were removed from Egypt within the next few weeks, leaving only about 300 Soviet military instructors in that country.[60] Nevertheless, Soviet warships continued to use the naval bases at Alexandria, Mersa Matruh, and Port Said,[61] and the USSR's strategic position in the Mediterranean was not greatly weakened. Because of the importance of Egyptian bases to Russian interests in the Middle East and beyond, the Soviets will doubtless strive to maintain and improve their rights to military use of these bases but perhaps not at the cost of incurring increased risks by supplying even more powerful arms.

A dilemma faces both the Soviets in any further attempt to rebuild the armed forces of the radical Arab states in the Middle East and the United States in its attempt to maintain Israeli strength to a point where the Israeli's can protect themselves against any Arab onslaught. Both of these attempts may increase the danger that Middle East warfare may be renewed and that the superpowers, as a consequence, might be dragged into an unwanted confronta-

55. "Israelis vs. Arabs: Comparison of the Weapons and Forces of Antagonists in the Mideast," *New York Times*, 24 March 1970, p. 14.

56. Three thousand were previously reported in Hunter, *The Soviet Dilemma in the Middle East*, p. 14.

57. Ibid.

58. Ibid.

59. *New York Times*, 19 July 1972, p. 1.

60. *New York Times*, 6 August 1972, p. 14, and *New York Times*, 2 October 1972, p. 9.

61. Ibid.

tion. In Egypt, more effective forces could tempt the Egyptians into a new adventure, perhaps through miscalculation or overconfidence, as a new attempt to capture wider Arab support and secure an Egyptian-led Pan-Arabism. New arms in Israel, claimed to be needed to counterbalance growing Egyptian capabilities, seem to make possible more daring and sometimes more devastating raids into Arab territories. This also serves to raise the temperature in the Middle East and, although intended to deter the Arabs by demonstrating Israeli superiority, could serve to goad them into the very actions that neither the Israelis nor the superpowers want. In spite of these dangers, military aid will apparently continue. It may be given reluctantly, but Middle East clients clamor for it and the diverging and conflicting superpower interests seem to demand it. Holding it to "safe" levels and types will be a major challenge in the seventies.

Geographic Accessibility and Superpower Deployments

From the viewpoint of either the United States or the Soviet Union, the Middle East remains an area that is not easy to reach with military forces in an emergency. Ships from the United States east coast must make over a 5,000-mile voyage to reach the Middle East. At 15 knots, troop ships would require more than 28 days to cover this distance. Not only is the voyage long, but the last 2,100 miles must be made through the relatively narrow confines of the Mediterranean Sea. During that part of the trip the ships would be exposed to possible actions by the Soviet Mediterranean Squadron, to submarines in the Mediterranean, and to aircraft attack from neighboring land bases. Even if the Sixth Fleet could control the sea lane, the threat from land-based air attack might require that all ships be escorted and might mean that some losses would be suffered.

From the west coast of the United States to the nearest point in the Middle East—the southeast coast of Arabia, an unlikely place for United States action—is over 12,000 miles. To reach Iran or Israel, where United States involvement might seem more likely, requires further sailing through confined waters in the Gulf of Oman and the Persian Gulf on the one hand, or the Gulf of Aden and the Red Sea on the other. Ships in these waters could also be exposed to ground-based air attack, and furthermore would not have the benefit of protection from the Sixth Fleet.

Transport aircraft such as the C-141 and the C-5 give the United States another option for moving forces to the Middle East, although air movement also involves problems. The shortest route from the United States to Israel, for example, passes over France, Italy, and Greece. Given the current attitude of the French government, permission to make such flights over France is questionable. The flight could be routed further south over Spain, but again overflight rights are doubtful and at best might require extensive negotiation. Still further south the planes might pass through the Straits of Gibraltar and make the entire flight over water, but this would expose them, too, to the threat of possible enemy land-based air opposition. Without escorts these transport aircraft might be excessively vulnerable to enemy air activities and to sea-based surface-to-air missiles.

True, the United States Sixth Fleet has been the dominant force in the Mediterranean Sea for more than 20 years. Two or three aircraft carriers are part of its normal compliment of some 50 or more ships. As we have seen, however, increases in the Soviet Mediterranean Squadron have overtaken the Sixth Fleet numerically. Although the Soviet Squadron operates without aircraft carriers, it does have many missile-launching ships and several submarines and could perhaps call upon Badger bombers for added support. The Sixth Fleet may possess adequate firepower to remain the dominant force in the area, but its position has become uncertain and its movements are no longer free from possible challenge.

If it were unchallenged by the Mediterranean Squadron, the Sixth Fleet could be a significant force in the Middle East. Its guns, missiles, and aircraft represent a sizable attack force by Middle East standards. On the other hand, the aircraft carriers themselves might be likely targets for fighter-bomber attack from nearby land bases. If forced to stand off at some distance for its own safety, the Sixth Fleet could lose part of its attack potential and perhaps a large part of its psychological effect.

The United States land forces closest to the Middle East are in West Germany, from where they could reach the Middle East in a few hours by airlift. The air route in this case is also uncertain, however, since any route to the south must pass over either Switzerland or Austria, both countries whose neutrality the United States would undoubtedly be anxious to respect. A swing to the west around Switzerland raises the French overflight question, while a much longer route around France and Spain poses all the formerly discussed problems about flying the length of the Mediterranean.

The United States has one other military asset that could be applied to the Middle East. The Sixteenth Air Force, a part of the

United States Air Forces, Europe, has its headquarters in Spain and operates from bases in Italy, Greece, and Turkey. Although some of these bases are close enough to allow actions over a large part of the Middle East, political problems raised in recent years pose a question as to whether the United States would be willing—or even able—to use these bases for this purpose.

For the Soviet Union, the Middle East is an immediate southern neighbor. Yet she, too, could find the area not really accessible. Although Turkey and Iran have softened their attitude toward the USSR and are increasing their trade with her, their memories of post-World War II activities leave them distrustful of intimate association. For the Russians, the case of Turkey is particularly important because the Turks control the Bosporus. That narrow exit from the Black Sea must be the passageway for any Soviet seaborne forces launched from Russia's good southern ports. Through that waterway a four- or five-day sail would reach the areas along the Eastern Mediterranean.

The international status of the Bosporus was agreed in the Montreux Convention, which stipulates that nonmilitary vessels have free passage through that strait and that military vessels have free passage during peacetime, provided that Turkey is given forty-eight hours notice. The Turks for their part seem anxious to preserve their control of the strait by observing the letter of the convention. The Russians, on the other hand, frequently abuse the apparent intent of the convention by submitting many prior notices which they fail to fulfill. Even so, it is questionable how far the Russians would be willing to go against Turkish wishes in moving forces through the Bosporus to the Middle East, particularly during a war.

By land and by air the Soviets seem to be cut off from most of the Middle East by the two countries of the Northern Tier. Should they decide to violate Turkish or Iranian air space, on the other hand, even short-legged Russian fighter aircraft could reach other areas in the Middle East from bases in the Transcaucasia area. Transport aircraft would need only a fraction of their range capabilities on this route; the only need for the new AN-22 would be its ability to lift large and heavy military equipment.

The transport aircraft need not be restricted to flights that violate the air space of Iran or Turkey; their range would allow them to use a route over Yugoslavia and the Mediterranean, although this might expose them to sea-based or land-based opposition. Many short-legged fighter aircraft in Russian forces, however, would be unable to make the flight from a refueling base in Yugoslavia to airbases in the Middle East.

In spite of this seeming isolation, the Russians, as we have seen, have established a significant presence in the Mediterranean Sea and now operate with de facto military-base rights in Egypt. To the east they are increasing their activities in the Indian Ocean, doubtless hoping to be the major power in that area after the British withdrawal.

Conclusions

In the wake of the Vietnamese war, the United States is less likely than at any time in the last thirty years to become embroiled in any military activities overseas. In spite of considerable private investments in and income from Middle East oil, America may be unwilling to resort to miltary force to preserve those investments. In a sense, there seems to be a trend in some quarters to degrade the importance to the United States of the Middle East, especially with the devaluation, if it may be called that, of the Northern Tier.

The Northern Tier in the Middle East, once highly regarded by the United States as the successful embodiment in that area of the policy of containment, has lost much of that charm. Not only have Turkey and Iran softened their attitudes toward the Soviet Union, but the physical Soviet presence in the Mediterranean, in Egypt, and in the Indian Ocean demonstrates that the Northern Tier leaves much to be desired as a barrier against Communist expansion. Although Turkey will likely remain important as the Eastern anchor of NATO, the Middle East as a whole may appear to become less critical to United States defense, much as the Suez Canal has receded in importance in American eyes.

With regard to Israel, however, United States attitudes seem remarkably different. Although she may assess the threat to Israel in different terms than do the Israelis themselves—as in the recent case of holding in abeyance a decision to sell more warplanes—the United States appears unwilling to let Israel be overwhelmed by her Arab neighbors. This may continue to be true through the seventies, even though the United States may seem to view Israeli independence as ever less closely tied to threats to American freedom.

The Soviets, by contrast, have seemed increasingly interested and involved in the Middle East. Frustrated for years in their drive to the south, they may feel that despite the reversal in Egypt, they have found a key to unlock the southern door. Although their initial objective may have been only to decrease American influence in the area, they have undoubtedly gone beyond that and see their own influence substantially increased. As they have found, they may have disappointingly—and sometimes dangerously—little control over events in the Middle East, but the Soviets are unlikely to give up easily a position they have gained at great cost. Despite the hazards, they may be induced to take further steps to protect and improve that position.

The Middle East appears to be of special importance to the Soviets. Initially the key to their extension of meaningful power into the Mediterranean, it also forms a base for expanding into Africa and the Indian Ocean area, and the Russians may be expected to exploit opportunities that arise for moving out from that base. In the likely Soviet view, the Middle East may be a desirable part of the overall USSR defense system and a cornerstone in the extension of that system southward.

Because of the volatile nature of the Middle East, however, Russian gains in this area have obviously not yet been solidified. Although she will direct her efforts to that end, the Soviet Union may still display considerable caution because of the latent danger of a confrontation with the United States.

CHAPTER 9

The American-Soviet Mediterranean Confrontation and the Middle East*

CIRO ZOPPO

Khrushchev launched the first positive Soviet steps toward becoming a globally mobile power in 1955 by initiating Soviet military aid programs to several countries in the Third World, among which Egypt was one of the first recipients. In the meantime, Soviet naval power in the Mediterranean has grown to such an extent that it could strongly inhibit, if not interdict, United States naval action in the Mediterranean.

An expert on arms control and strategic problems, the author weighs other factors that would influence any American-Soviet confrontation in the Mediterranean, such as a separate and distinct French policy for the Mediterranean; changing NATO attitudes—e.g., Italian, Greek, and Turkish—toward United States support of Israel; and the potential for land-based Soviet aircraft and missiles around the Mediterranean.

As we enter the 1970s the political instability of the Middle East is foreboding because it raises the danger of a confrontation between the United States and the Soviet Union. The United States is aligned, almost reluctantly, with Israel, and the Soviet Union with Israel's Arab neighbors, Egypt, Syria and Iraq, protagonists of an undeclared war. The fundamental issue of this war is Israel's right to exist as a nation created a generation ago to solve yet another political problem forged by Hitler in Europe. Until now, the Arabs have been unclear about their primary objective, whether to destroy Israel or contain her. Both rhetoric and policy have fluctuated between these quite different goals.[1]

* This chapter is based in part upon the author's "Soviet Ships in the Mediterranean and the U.S.—Soviet Confrontation in the Middle East," *Orbis* 14, no. 1 (Spring 1970): 109–28.

1. For an elaboration see Malcolm H. Kerr, "Regional Arab Politics and Conflict with Israel" in *Political Dynamics in the Middle East,* ed. Paul T. Ham-

The United States and the Soviet Union, on the other hand, are clearly concerned about their political influence in the Arab East. For the Soviet Union, control of this region would represent an important achievement in her bid for world leadership. For the United States, the denial of such control would be an important way to contain her superpower rival.

But the United States does not enjoy the freedom of action the Soviet Union bought when she jettisoned Israel, after briefly supporting the newly established state. Experience has shown that the objectives sought by Washington in the Middle East—eliminating military conflict from the region, maintaining access to Arab oil, limiting Soviet influence, and guaranteeing the security of Israel—have often been conflicting, and the resulting dilemmas remain unresolved.[2] Apart from losing whatever influence the United States retains in the Arab world, especially with Jordan, Saudi Arabia, Tunisia, and Morocco, the main threat to the United States national interest is the danger of a conflict with the Soviet Union that could escalate to nuclear war.

The development of operational multiple and independently targeted nuclear warheads and the increased accuracy of missiles may eventually undermine the current deterrent stability between the superpowers. The political impact of such technological changes, however, may not be felt for several years. Meanwhile, the fact that the United States and the Soviet Union are each capable of unacceptable retaliation against the other is a potent brake to escalation. A real danger of escalation would seem unlikely short of the imminent collapse of Israel—which could trigger a United States military intervention—or further Israeli expansion that threatened the Soviet Union's chief client Arab state, Egypt, with another humiliating defeat and more territorial losses.

The superpowers are keenly aware of the risks of nuclear war and have recently reached important strategic arms control agreements. In May 1972 President Nixon went to Moscow to sign agreements limiting the offensive and defensive strategic nuclear forces of the United States and the Soviet Union.[3] Previously both countries had

mond and Sidney Alexander (New York: American Elsevier Publishing Co., 1972).

2. The constraints on U.S. policy choices in the Arab East are discussed in William B. Quandt, "United States Policy in the Middle East: Constraints and Choices" in Hammond and Alexander, *Political Dynamics*.

3. Three documents were signed in Moscow on 26 May 1972: a strategic arms limitation agreement, treaty to limit antiballistic missiles (ABM), and an interim

taken steps to prevent nuclear mishaps that could lead to wrong perceptions of intentions. On 30 September 1971, the United States and the Soviet Union formally agreed to notify each other immediately if a nuclear weapon got out of control, by accident or a madman's design. They have committed themselves to immediate notification if either side suddenly found its early warning systems jammed or if radars showed unidentified and potentially hostile objects approaching.[4] The United States and the Soviet Union have also signed an agreement to improve the direct communication link (the hot line) between Moscow and Washington by relying on satellites, and they have begun talks to reach an informal understanding on how to avoid incidents involving their warships and aircraft.[5]

What is ambiguous, however, and hard to predict often moves history decisively. Miscalculation resulting from incomplete or false information is a very real threat to decision-makers in time of acute international crisis. The situation in the Middle East is volatile. Confusing signals are easily generated, as painfully demonstrated by the attack on a United States communications ship by the Israelis during the Six-Day War.

At the very outset of that war, it is true, the Soviets promptly got on the hot line to Washington to declare that they would not intervene directly with troops if the United States also abstained from military intervention. But what if United States ships had been hit by fire suspected of being Egyptian or Soviet, or clearly Soviet—the hot-line message notwithstanding? Moreover, for the United States at least, this problem is intensified by having to coordinate actions with many allies, like France, Britain, Italy, Turkey, and Greece; and with Spain which hosts United States naval and air bases.

All these countries have policies toward the Arab-Israeli conflict at variance with those of the United States, in particular with respect to the contingency use of military force in the Mediterranean. Only a clearcut attack against NATO could pull them all together in support and coordination with the United States.

agreement on offensive missiles. Texts may be found in the *New York Times*, 27 May 1972.

4. *Los Angeles Times*, 1 October 1971.

5. *New York Times*, 8 September 1971. In recent years there have been more than 100 reported incidents at sea involving U.S. and Soviet ships. Soviet and U.S. military aircraft continually overfly each other's warships to photograph armaments and follow their movements. On 28 September 1971, a U.S. Navy patrol plane was fired upon by a Soviet warship in the Sea of Japan.

The very stability alleged to exist in the strategic balance may make the superpowers more willing to risk conventional conflict during a confrontation.

Certainly the doctrine that the participation of the United States or the USSR in limited conflict inevitably raises the risk of a nuclear war has been modified by word and deed. The United States has intervened in local conflict with Communist regimes in Korea and Vietnam, in which Soviet aid was extensive and Soviet personnel participated covertly as technicians. The Soviets have in the process modified their military doctrine by de-emphasizing the inevitability of escalation from local conflicts in which the United States and the Soviet Union are involved.[6]

More to the point, the Soviets have been creating air transport, conventional strike forces, and naval forces that endow them with a capability to intervene in conventional conflicts away from their borders. Although this new military capability may not straightaway lead to the achievement of political goals, it permits them to take advantage of opportunities for penetration where before their intention might have been frustrated or inchoate. Most dramatic has been their permanent deployment of a flotilla in the Mediterranean. Soviet ships roaming this landlocked sea have heightened tensions in the already combustible Middle East. The deployment of such forces in a region where Soviet political objectives are ambitious and where the United States has long deployed a naval force of her own underscores Moscow's willingness to pursue a higher-risk policy in the area.

The Soviet naval buildup has evoked considerable United States and European concern.[7] It should be emphasized, however, that Soviet interest in the Mediterranean is not novel and that the increase in Soviet naval forces has been taking place for several years. The beginnings of the current buildup go back to at least the 1964 Cyprus crisis, and the number of Soviet vessels was greatly expanded in 1967 following the Six-Day War.[8] Historically, the Soviet presence is the latest episode in a chain of events that spans two centuries and includes recurrent Russian preoccupation with

6. Thomas W. Wolfe, *Soviet Strategy at the Crossroads* (Cambridge: Harvard University Press, 1964), pp. 119–24.

7. See, for example, *New York Times,* 13 and 29 May 1969, 18 January, 25 April, 27 May 1971; *Moderne Welt,* 16 December 1969; *Washington Post,* 19 December 1969 and 18 February 1970; and *Christian Science Monitor,* 19 March 1970, *New York Times,* 25 March 1973.

8. F. M. Murphy, "The Soviet Navy in the Mediterranean," *U.S. Naval Institute Proceedings,* March 1967.

the Dardanelles. Real Soviet success in penetrating the Arab East had its genesis in 1955, with the Soviet-Egyptian arms deal, but active Russian interest in the region considerably predates this event.

Past Russian Attempts to Control the Straits

Although it is the first recorded in this century, the Soviet deployment in the Mediterranean has several Czarist precedents.[9] In 1770 a Russian flotilla of forty vessels was dispatched to the Mediterranean to aid the Greeks in revolt against their Ottoman overlords. It remained until 1774, at the conclusion of the Treaty of Kuchuk Kainarji. In 1798 Russia again sent ships to the Mediterranean, this time through the straits, to fight against Napoleon. In 1806 a Russian squadron of fifteen vessels entered through Gibraltar, to fight Turkey as well as France. A year later the squadron failed in an attempt to force passage through the Dardanelles. Thereafter, the Mediterranean saw only sporadic Russian naval activity.

As is the case today, a Mediterranean presence was but one manifestation of Russian aspirations in the Middle East. The sixty-odd Soviet ships [10] now occasioning concern recall a long history of Russian attempts to break out of the Black Sea. Efforts to control the straits or open them to secure Russian passage have involved war and diplomacy punctuated by numerous treaties.[11] The 1936 Montreux Convention still governs passage through the straits.

During World War I, the Russians succeeded in extracting from the Allies a commitment that if they won, Russia would get control of the Dardanelles. The Sykes-Picot Agreement of April–October 1916 was concluded in the form of diplomatic notes exchanged between the governments of Britain, France, Russia, and later, in April 1917, Italy, in which the claims of each country for the territories of the Ottoman Empire were recognized by the others. The

9. A general discussion of Russian naval ambitions in the Mediterranean is found in Nicholas V. Riasanovsky, *A History of Russia* (New York: Oxford University Press, 1963). The Soviet navy did operate there during the Spanish Civil War from 1936 to 1939 but with few vessels and pursuing a different role.

10. Forty to seventy Soviet combat and support vessels plus ten to twelve submarines, depending on the season, are on station in the Mediterranean. *New York Times*, 5 July 1971, and 25 March 1973.

11. Navarino in 1827; Unkiar-Skelessi in 1833; Constantinople in 1841; Paris in 1854; London in 1871; Berlin in 1878; and in this century Lausanne and Montreux.

straits and the south shore of the Black Sea in Turkey were to go to Russia. With the fall of the Czar, the Bolsheviks repudiated the agreement. But once firmly in power, they also tried to achieve control. A secret understanding with Nazi Germany would have achieved this goal had Hitler not invaded the USSR.[12]

At war's end, the objective remained compelling. In 1946 Stalin strongly pressured Turkey for revision of the Montreux Convention, with the object of putting troops on the Bosporus "to guarantee its protection."[13] These pressures coincided with unsuccessful Soviet attempts to gain UN trusteeships over Cyrenaica, part of Italy's former colony Libya,[14] and the Dodecanese Islands.[15] At the time, Yugoslavia had not yet defected from the Soviet orbit, the Greek civil war was raging, a Communist takeover in Italy was a real possibility, Turkey was unaligned, and NATO did not exist. Had all the pieces of the mosaic fallen into place, the Soviet Union might have become the dominant Mediterranean power.

Cultivation of the Arabs is more recent, although it predates World War II. After the establishment of the Communists in Russia, the focal point of Soviet interest continued to be Turkey, Iran, and Afghanistan. The universal pretensions of Communist doctrine, however, extended Moscow's gaze beyond.

Early Soviet Political Penetration of the Arab East

Because Russian territorial expansion had not touched the Arab countries, the Soviet Union escaped association in the Arab mind with the imperial powers. This, together with the nature of Arab nationalism, created for the Soviets the opportunity to capitalize on anti-Western feelings and to penetrate the area politically. Soviet interest in the Middle East, although it fluctuated, continued during the USSR's defensive isolation of the 1920s, the political alliances with the "capitalist" powers of the 1930s, and the collusion with Nazi Germany. It greatly increased after the defeat of the Axis powers.

12. A detailed account of Soviet attempts to negotiate with the Nazis the establishment of a base for land and naval forces within range of the Bosporus and the Dardanelles is in R. J. Sontag and J. S. Beddie, eds. *Nazi-Soviet Relations, 1939–1941* (Washington: Department of State Publication 2023, 1948).

13. *New York Times,* 12 and 18 August and 29 and 30 September 1946.

14. Ibid., 20 and 22 January 1946; and J. Byrnes, *Speaking Frankly* (New York: Harper & Brothers, 1947), p. 76.

15. *New York Times,* 4 March 1946.

As early as December 1917, Lenin launched an appeal addressed "to the toiling Muslims of the East," telling them to throw off the chains of European imperialism.[16] The famous Baku Congress of 1920 codified this approach into policy, so that Stalin would write in *Pravda* on 9 August 1921, that "the victory of the proletariat cannot be a lasting one unless the nonsovereign nations and colonies are emancipated from the yoke of imperialism."[17]

British dominance of the area was, however, the most important factor curbing Soviet diplomacy in the Arab East. Even after their nominal independence from Britain in 1930, neither Egypt nor Iraq would admit Soviet Russia to diplomatic relations. The remaining Arab states in their quasi independence were easily controlled by France and Britain.

Not surprisingly, in 1924 Moscow recognized King Husayn of the Hijaz with great alacrity,[18] and when he abdicated in 1926 and Ibn Saud became King of Saudi Arabia, the Soviet Union became the first power to recognize this kingdom in the holy land of Islam.[19] In 1929 the Soviet government negotiated a treaty of friendship and commerce with feudal Yemen, which was renewed in 1939. The heads of Soviet diplomatic and commercial missions at this time, as well as most of their staff, were Soviet "Muslims" who ostentatiously professed their religion, even making the yearly pilgrimage to Mecca.[20]

Wherever the Soviets could not establish diplomatic relations they sought contacts by means of commercial missions or business firms such as Arcos, Shark, and Textilimport. These operated in Egypt, Syria, and Palestine and were also used as cover for intelligence operations.[21] Starting in 1927, regular shipping services were instituted between Odessa and the Arabian coast, and passage was offered to Muslim pilgrims at nominal fares.[22] Moreover, Communist

16. *Survey of International Affairs* (London: Royal Institute of International Affairs, 1928), p. 359.

17. For an account of the Comintern-sponsored Baku Convention, see Adam B. Ulam, *Expansion and Co-existence: A History of Soviet Foreign Policy, 1917–1967* (New York: Praeger, 1968), pp. 121–25.

18. *Times* (London), 7 October 1924.

19. *The Middle East* (London: Royal Institute of International Affairs, 1950), p. 46.

20. *Oriente Moderno* (Rome) 9 (1929): 613; 19 (1939): 290.

21. A discussion of Soviet intelligence activities in the Middle East during this period is in D. J. Dallin, *Soviet Espionage* (New Haven: Yale University Press, 1955).

22. *Oriente Moderno* 7 (1927): 281, 504; 9 (1929): 327–28.

parties were organized wherever possible in the Arab countries and Palestine, although none became markedly successful in the early period. The largest and most effective, the Communist party of Syria and Lebanon, produced some able cadres, including Khalid Bakdash, perhaps today's most influential Communist leader in the Arab world.[23]

Temporarily confused during World War II, Soviet diplomacy toward the Middle East refocused its efforts and had established formal relations with almost all important Arab states by war's end. The wartime alliance with the Western powers had enabled the Soviets to propagandize among the Arabs to an unprecedented degree. With decolonization in the area inevitable, the Middle East was finally open to significant Soviet penetration.

The USSR bitterly denounced any attempt by the Western powers to draw the Arab governments into Western defensive arrangements, while supporting nationalist demands that would further dislodge Western influence.[24] Malenkov, in a report to the Cominform in September 1947, reassured colonial and dependent countries that the Soviet Union would pursue a policy of unswerving support of those countries engaged in fighting "for their national liberation from the yoke of imperialism." [25] Concurrently, Moscow fostered the growth of neutralism in the Middle East, notably in Syria and Egypt, where because of the traditional distribution of power, neutralism favored Soviet policy.

Still, at the time of Stalin's death in 1953, no definite, comprehensive Soviet program for the Arab East had yet evolved, nor had the Soviet Union gained a sure foothold in the region. The turning away from Israel and the bid for the friendship of nationalist Arab leaders was undoubtedly the most portentous step taken. The subsequent Soviet success in exploiting the Arab-Israeli conflict needs no elaboration.

This briefly sketched historical background puts in perspective recent Soviet activity in the Mediterranean, and underscores that Russian aspirations in this region are long standing, transcending questions of ideology. The distinction today is that "ideology" serves Moscow's cause without the opprobrium of "imperialism."

23. For a discussion of Communist parties in the Middle East, see W. Z. Laqueur, *Communism and Nationalism in the Middle East* (New York: Praeger, 1956).

24. A convenient documentation is in *New Times* (Moscow), issues from 15 January 1946 through 24 October 1951.

25. Cominform, *For a Lasting Peace, For a People's Democracy* (Belgrade, 1 December 1947).

The Soviet Search for Strategic Mobility

To the historic Russian quest for control of the straits and the Communist contest for influence in the Arab East must be added a new factor—Soviet ambition to gain strategic mobility. All three factors are relevant to United States policy in the Mediterranean and the Middle East.

In the military context, the increased Soviet presence in the Mediterranean is not an isolated event. It is the most dramatic manifestation of Soviet efforts to achieve strategic mobility in the naval sphere. The immediate consequence is a challenge to United States naval supremacy.[26]

To achieve this objective, for the last 10 years the Soviet Union has expanded its naval forces, and has been developing ships and techniques which would allow its navy to operate in a self-sustaining way at long distances from home ports.[27] The Soviet Union now has the second largest navy in the world. Its merchant fleet constitutes about 7 percent of the world's merchant ships and more than 4 percent of the world tonnage.[28]

The first steps toward becoming a globally mobile power were taken under Khrushchev and coincided with the initiation of Soviet military aid programs to several countries in the Third World in 1955.[29] Egypt was one of the first recipients of such aid.

26. For an analysis supporting this view, see Christoph von Imhoff, *Duell im Mittelmeer: Moskau Greift nach dem Nahen und dem Mittleren Osten* (Freiburg: Verlag Rombach, 1968). For a dissenting view, emphasizing the defensive aspects of the new Soviet strategy, see Robert W. Herrick, *Soviet Naval Strategy: Fifty Years of Theory and Practice* (Annapolis: U.S. Naval Institute, 1968). See also Drew Middleton, "New Missile Cruiser's Added to Soviet Mediterranean Fleet," *New York Times*, 25 March 1973.

27. George W. Herald, "The Soviet Naval Challenge," *The New Leader*, 31 March 1969.

28. Soviet merchant marine tonnage has tripled since 1960 and is expected to double once more by 1980. See "Summary of Major Naval, Maintenance and Military Forces," *U.S. Naval Institute Proceedings*, May 1971, and Office of the Secretary of Defense, News Release No. 278, 29 March 1968, and Donald W. Mitchell, "The Soviet Naval Challenge," *Orbis*, Spring 1970. These vessels, when combined with the most modern fishing fleet—devoted to intelligence gathering as much as fishing—and the world's largest submarine fleet, give the Soviet Union a knowledge of currents, ocean depths, and other nautical data that equals or surpasses that of any other nation.

29. For a discussion of the development of the mobility of Soviet general-purpose forces, see Thomas W. Wolfe, *The Soviet Quest for More Globally Mobile Military Power* (Santa Monica: The RAND Corp., RM-5554-PR, December 1967).

Under Stalin, the USSR had pursued a policy essentially directed toward consolidation of Soviet influence and control on the periphery of the Russian nation.[30] Khrushchev reshaped military policy to support a political strategy that committed the Soviet Union to global competition with the United States. Toward the end of Khrushchev's tenure of power, there appeared signs of an increasing Soviet interest in developing a capability for amphibious landing and for airlift. Coupled with the deployment of equipment and accompanying technical personnel, this has led to the creation of potential logistical bases in distant areas—an asset for the time when political developments might permit their use.[31] During the Cyprus crisis in 1964, Soviet naval infantry was reactivated as a force.

The search for strategic mobility and self-sufficiency on the high seas was probably intensified by the humiliating experience of the Cuban missile crisis of 1962.[32] The Soviet navy was then unequipped to concentrate sufficient and appropriate naval forces to interpose between the United States Navy and Soviet missile-carrying merchantmen. Under Khrushchev's successors, the growth and improvement of the naval arm has continued. A notable innovation has been the construction of helicopter carriers. Two are now operational. One of them, the *Moskva,* underwent its sea trials in the Mediterranean and seems to have become a permanent part of the Soviet Mediterranean fleet.[33] Its sister ship, the *Leningrad,* has also seen service there. These carriers could be used either in an amphibious assault role for antisubmarine warfare or in a command function.

The Soviet navy has been equipped with significant surface-to-surface missile capabilities. The Egyptian patrol boat that sank the Israeli destroyer *Elath* in 1967 by missile fire was a Soviet-built ship. Surface-to-air missiles are also deployed on Soviet surface ships. The traditional emphasis on submarines has also persisted. The Soviet Union has already exceeded the United States in active surface ships and has near-parity in nuclear submarine strength. The SALT agreements acknowledge this parity in strategic nuclear

30. Vernon Aspaturian, "Moscow's Foreign Policy," *Survey,* October 1967, p. 55.

31. For a discussion of Soviet naval development under Khrushchev see Thomas W. Wolfe, *Soviet Power and Europe, 1945–1970* (Baltimore, Md.: The Johns Hopkins Press, 1970), pp. 188–94.

32. What the Cuban experience may have taught the Soviets is analyzed in "The Bear Learns to Swim," *The Economist,* 18–24 May 1968. See also Mitchell, *The Soviet Naval Challenge,* pp. 131–32.

33. *Christian Science Monitor,* 18 March 1970.

submarines.[34] Virtually all of the more than 2,000 operational naval vessels have been constructed since World War II. The current construction program emphasizes well-equipped smaller ships and auxiliaries, nuclear submarines, and qualitative improvements in weaponry.

Soviet leaders have made it clear that nothing less than a conspicuous and commanding presence on the oceans of the world will satisfy the aspirations of the Soviet Union as a global power. Since July 1967, just a few weeks after the Arab-Israeli June War, all the country's leading admirals have proclaimed the doctrine that Soviet seapower would no longer limit itself to the coastal defense of the homeland but must be prepared to extend its reach. That they have acquired "an oceanic vision" is clear from the remarks of Admiral Sergei Gorshkov, the Soviet fleet commander. "The flag of the Soviet Navy," he has said, "now proudly flies over the oceans of the world. Sooner or later, the United States will have to understand that it no longer has mastery of the seas." [35] Gorshkov and other Soviet admirals made similar and equally emphatic statements at the time of *Operation Okean,* in April and May, 1970, the largest Soviet naval maneuvers ever undertaken, with ships plying the Barents, Atlantic, Mediterranean, and the seas of Japan.[36]

The conviction that Soviet seapower has extended its reach to remote areas of the world's oceans, to cruise and patrol whenever the defense of the national interest requires it, confers an unprecedented role on the Soviet navy. The concept itself is new to the Soviet political vocabulary.[37] The most striking example of the

34. There is some disagreement about these figures in the *Military Balance, 1972–1973* (London: Institute of Strategic Studies) and *Jane's All the World's Fighting Ships, 1972–1973.* According to Secretary of Defense Laird, Soviet shipyards have been completing six to eight "yankee" class nuclear submarines (424-foot, 16-missile) every year. At this rate, the Russians could match or exceed the U.S. Navy's 41-submarine Polaris Poseidon force by 1974. U.S. shipyards will complete about 20 additional nuclear submarines by 1974. By then the Soviets are expected to complete 70 nuclear submarines. Norman Palmar, "Soviet Navy Pulls Even in Nuclear Sub Might," *Washington Post,* 4 October 1970. See also Laird statement, *New York Times,* 14 October 1971 and Admiral Hyman Rickover's testimony before Congress, *New York Times,* 27 September 1971.

35. Quoted in NATO's *Fifteen Nations,* June–July 1968, p. 12. Similar statements have been made by Marshal Zakharov, Soviet Chief of Staff. See *Izvestia,* 5 April 1969.

36. A compilation of statements in the Defense Ministry's newspaper *Krasnaya Zvezda* (Red Star) and the Soviet Navy's monthly *Morskoi Sbornik* (Naval Collection) is in *U.S. Naval Institute Proceedings,* May 1971.

37. Wolfe, *The Soviet Quest,* p. 10.

operationalization of this doctrine is the Soviet naval presence in the Mediterranean. The new strategic outlook has led the Soviet Union to insist that the Mediterranean and the Middle East are to be regarded as within its security sphere.

The attempt to make the Middle East a permanent sphere of Soviet influence was first implied by Brezhnev in a speech to the honor graduates of the military academies on 5 July 1967, in the wake of the June War.[38] On 5 November 1968, Foreign Minister Gromyko explicitly maintained that the area was within the Soviet security sphere and that the Soviet navy was in the Mediterranean by right. In an interview with *L'Unità,* the Italian Communist party paper, Gromyko argued that because the Soviet Union was a Black Sea power it was also a Mediterranean power and as such concerned with the peace and security of a region in direct proximity to its borders.[39] Since then, this thesis has been reiterated often by Soviet admirals and leading Soviet commentators.[40] In the most recent edition of Marshal Sokolovski's *Military Strategy* it is made clear that the purpose of the Soviet navy is to act aggressively against other naval forces and their support lines as well as to intercept enemy vessels on the high seas.[41] The Soviet Mediterranean fleet has such an operational doctrine, and its activities exemplify these declarations.[42]

The seriousness of purpose with respect to the Mediterranean is suggested by the fact that this sea has been used extensively as a training area by the Soviet navy. Although the Mediterranean squadron has been in existence for just over four years, almost all

38. *Current Digest of the Soviet Press,* 26 July 1967, pp. 3–6.

39. *L'Unità* (Rome), 5 November 1968.

40. Cf. Vice-Admiral Smirnov, "The Soviet Navy in the Mediterranean," *Red Star,* 12 November 1968, translated in *Survival,* February 1969; L. Kosolov, "U.S.S.R. Presence Insures Peace in the Mediterranean," *Izvestia,* 12 November 1968; and the interview with Nikolay Sergeyev, Chief of the Main Staff of the Soviet Naval Forces, by Enzo Roggi of *L'Unità,* 13 February 1969; Admiral Gorshkov, *Morskoi Sbornik* (Naval Review), March 1972.

41. V. D. Sokolovski, ed., *Voennaia strategiia* (Military strategy) 3rd ed. (Moscow: Voenizdat, 1968), pp. 362–68. Selected translations by Lilita Dzirkals.

42. In 1967 alone, according to the Turkish Foreign Ministry, 157 Soviet vessels transited from the Black Sea to the Mediterranean. Many of these were warships, with the total varying from 31 surface combat ships, 13 submarines (some of them nuclear), and several intelligence ships, closely shadowing the U.S. Sixth Fleet, in the summer of 1967, to a total of 45 in April 1969, to 52 in March 1970. See *Washington Post,* 12 April 1969; Institute for the Study of the USSR, "The Soviet Fleet in the Mediterranean," *Bulletin,* p. 37, and *Christian Science Monitor,* 19 March 1970.

admirals have served with it.[43] Evidently, Moscow wants to make sure that the squadron commander can always be replaced by an officer familiar with the region.

There is other evidence to suggest that the Soviet presence in the Mediterranean is a permanent feature of the situation in the Middle East. The USSR has agreements with littoral Arab countries permitting its navy to berth regularly at Latakia in Syria, and Port Said and Alexandria in Egypt. It may, eventually, get the right to develop Mers-el-Kebir in Algeria, the once formidable French naval base that guards, or threatens, access to Gibraltar. Premier Kosygin visited Morocco and Algeria in the fall of 1971 and his trip was used to emphasize the interest the Soviet Union has in the Mediterranean.[44]

The Soviets have also made overtures to Malta,[45] even to Spain.[46] At the start of 1972, a Soviet economic mission visited Prime Minister Mintoff to discuss possible agreements on construction and repair of ships.[47] The Soviets have put a squadron in the Indian Ocean. Reportedly, they have approached India for basing rights presumably to ensure the security of that area once Britain removes its naval forces from East of Suez.[48] In any case, Prime Minister Lee Kwan Yew announced, in March 1970, that Singapore would open its docks to the Soviet navy for repairs, replenishment, and refueling berths, on a commercial basis.[49] These moves would further strengthen the Soviet position in the Middle East, although as long as the Suez Canal remains closed, Soviet vessels in the Indian Ocean

43. *Bulletin*, p. 40.

44. *New York Times*, 11 October 1971. Military cooperation between the Soviet Union and Algeria goes back to the Secret Treaty of 1963, put in abeyancc when Ben Bella fell in 1965 but renewed when Boumedienne visited Moscow in 1966. The Soviet Union supplies Algeria with Mig-21 jet fighters, Komar-type boats equipped with Styx rockets, tanks, and artillery. Every year 600 Algerian pilots are trained in the Soviet Union and Soviet instructors staff flying schools in Algeria.

45. *Christian Science Monitor*, 11 August 1969. They have denied that they are interested in establishing an air and naval base there. *New Times*, 7 November 1969 and *New York Times*, 18 August 1971.

46. Rolf Gortz, "Madrid flirtet mit Moskau," *Die Welt*, 8 November 1969. Spain has opted to renew the U.S.–Spanish base accord instead. *New York Times*, 7 August 1970.

47. Paul Hofmann, "If British Go, Maltese Ask, Who'll Help Us?" *New York Times*, 8 January 1972.

48. *Christian Science Monitor*, 22 May 1969, and Guido Gerosa, "Will the Indian Ocean Become a Soviet Pond?" *L'Europeo* (Milan), November 1970.

49. *Los Angeles Times*, 11 March 1970.

are at a disadvantage. The reopening of the canal is a constant feature of Soviet proposals for resolving the Middle East conflict.

In the spring and summer of 1971, the Soviets both intensified the tempo of their public justifications for the Soviet naval presence in the Mediterranean and floated two arms-control proposals: one a revival of a nuclear-free zone in the area, the other a vague suggestion that the Soviet Union might be willing to discuss the mutual reduction of fleets "plying the seas for long periods at great distances from their own shores." [50] The latter was responded to by the United States but seemingly to no avail.[51]

The "indisputable right" of Soviet ships to cruise the Mediterranean was reaffirmed in a spate of official statements and articles in Soviet journals.[52]

During the same period, there was great activity by the Soviet Mediterranean squadron,[53] which was visited by the highest-ranking Soviet military officials. Soviet defense minister Marshal Grechko, accompanied by General Yepishev, chief of the Army and Navy political directorate, and the chief of the Soviet Navy Admiral Gorshkov, boarded the Soviet cruiser *Dzerzhinsky* to take part in naval exercises in the Mediterranean in June and to consult with commanders of the Soviet Mediterranean squadron.[54]

Also in June, a Soviet broadcast beamed a commentary to Turkey in which the establishment of a nuclear-free zone in the Middle East and the Mediterranean was proposed. The commentary stressed that ships in the Mediterranean had nuclear weapons aboard, and that a nuclear-free zone would greatly reduce the danger that coun-

50. Brezhnev in an election meeting in Moscow's Bauman Election District, on 12 June 1971. *Current Digest of the Soviet Press,* 13 July 1971. See also *Izvestiia,* 29 August 1972 and *New Times,* September 1972. This proposal was repeated by him in October 1972.

51. *New York Times,* 3 February 1972.

52. "A Hostile Course," *Red Star,* 26 April 1971; I. Bobkov, "Fleets in the Mediterranean: The Historical Perspective," *Voyenno-istorichesky zhurnal,* in *Current Digest of the Soviet Press,* 2 March 1971; D. Volsky, "The Mediterranean and Peace," *New Times,* July 1971; and M. Korenevskiy and M. Novikov, "The Mediterranean Squadron," *Krasnaya Zvezda,* July 1971.

53. This increase of activity is illustrated by the fact that whereas in 1964 the Soviet squadron had registered 650 ship-days at sea in the Mediterranean, in 1970 the figure was 20,000: U.S. officials, as reported by Drew Middleton, "NATO Moves to Build Up Forces in Mediterranean," *New York Times,* 29 May 1971.

54. M. Loshchits, "In the Mediterranean Squadron," *Red Star,* 15 June 1971, and *New York Times,* 14 June 1971.

tries in the Middle East and the Mediterranean would be "dragged into great international military disputes." [55]

A nuclear-free zone was proposed by the Soviet Union in the early 1960s, but the proposal had then been quietly shelved. If seriously considered, its impact on the military and political situation in the Mediterranean and the Middle East today would be quite different. In addition to the Limited Test Ban, the Nuclear Nonproliferation Treaty is also in effect. Saliently, Israel (a party to the LTB) is reluctant to adhere to the NPT and is generally believed to have the capability to develop an indigenous nuclear force in relatively short time. Negotiations on such a zone would have the effect of increasing United States political pressures on Israel to join the NPT. Moreover, if the Soviet and United States Mediterranean fleets were to be "denuclearized," it is obvious that United States carriers and Polaris submarines could be singularly affected.[56] Much depends on how the 1972 Strategic Arms Control Agreements affect the deterrent role of the Sixth Fleet.[57]

In any case, the basic position of the Soviet Union, as stated by General Party Secretary L. I. Brezhnev, could consolidate and would further legitimize the Soviet naval presence in the Mediterranean. In his report to the Twenty-fourth Communist Party Congress on 30 March 1971, Brezhnev stated that his "country is prepared to participate, together with the other powers that are permanent members of the Security Council, in the creation of international guarantees of a political settlement in the Near East. After this is achieved, it would be possible . . . to consider further steps aimed at a military detente in this whole area, *in particular, steps aimed at transforming the Mediterranean into a sea of peace and friendly cooperation."* [58]

On 12 June Brezhnev amplified his meaning by emphasizing that although the United States concern about Soviet ships in the Mediterranean was the product of "a double standard in evaluating one's

55. Radio Moscow, in Turkish, to Turkey on 24 June 1971.

56. The earlier Soviet proposal was made in May 1963 and focused on Mediterranean basing for Polaris submarines. The Soviet proposal is in *U.S. Documents on Disarmament,* 1963, pp. 187–93. The U.S. reply of 24 June 1963, in the negative, is in Ibid., pp. 242–43.

57. The U.S. Navy Program submitted for fiscal 1972 speaks of a need to maintain nuclear parity with the Soviet Union by means of Polaris submarines. *New York Times,* 3 September 1971.

58. *Pravda* and *Izvestia,* 31 March 1971, as translated in *The Current Digest of the Soviet Press,* 20 April 1971, p. 11. Italics mine.

own actions and the actions of the other side," and that the Mediterranean was "the Soviet Union's doorstep," the Soviet Union was prepared to resolve the problem of a United States and Soviet naval presence in the Mediterranean "on an equal footing." [59]

It is difficult, as yet, to assess the Soviet commitment to these probings in the arms-control area. Meanwhile, the Soviet presence in the Mediterranean obviously serves Soviet Middle East diplomacy and Soviet military objectives against NATO and is also concrete evidence of the shift in Soviet naval strategy to global pretensions.

Improved Soviet-Turkish Relations

As noted, Czarist and Soviet rulers have been keenly aware of the importance of the Dardanelles and have repeatedly attempted to gain direct or indirect control over this strategic waterway.

In a nuclear war such control could be easily emasculated. But in large-scale conventional conflict or a severe Mediterranean crisis, passage through the Dardanelles could become the Achilles' heel of any Soviet naval operation in the Mediterranean. A Soviet commander operating in the Eastern Mediterranean would be vulnerable if the straits were blocked by Turkey. Whether such an eventuality occurs depends to an important degree on the circumstances of the crisis or conflict. The prime consideration, however, is that the state of relations between Turkey and the Soviet Union will decide whether the Soviet navy will have freedom of passage through the Dardanelles. Turkey is the sole legal guardian of the straits as part of its national territory.

The Montreux Convention assures Soviet warships and merchantmen free transit through the straits, but the passage of all ships is strictly controlled by a complicated system of regulations under Turkish sovereignty. Turkey has the right to deny passage to the warships of all powers, including those of the Black Sea, if it is under the threat of war or at war.[60]

Soviet naval units in the Mediterranean have the capability of maintenance and replenishment at sea.[61] But neither modern technology nor friendly Arab ports can completely eliminate the con-

59. *Current Digest of the Soviet Press,* 13 July 1971, p. 24.

60. League of Nations, Treaty Series, *Convention Concerning the Regime of the Black Sea Straits* 17 (Lausanne, 20 July 1936), pp. 213–41.

61. L. L. Lemnitzer, "The Strategic Problems of NATO's Northern and Southern Flanks," *Orbis,* Spring 1969, and *Washington Post,* 14 December 1970.

straint that Turkish control of the Straits places on the operations of the Soviet fleet west of the Bosporus. Good relations with Turkey are obviously crucial to Soviet freedom of maneuver.

Soviet-Turkish relations have dramatically improved during the last several years as a result of the East-West détente and the worsening of relations that have occurred between Turkey and the United States, following the 1964 Cyprus crisis. Once grounded in deep suspicions bordering on hostility, Soviet-Turkish relations are now characterized by guarded cordiality.

Following Stalin's death, Soviet leaders reversed their previous antagonistic stance toward Turkey and tried to cultivate neighborly relations. The USSR formally withdrew both its claim to Turkey's eastern provinces, Kars and Ardahan, and its demand for a military presence on the Bosporus. This change in Moscow's policy removed two important sources of Turkish anxiety. However, early Soviet pressures and the cold war had pushed Turkey out of its neutrality into close collaboration with the West and eventually into membership in NATO. No real opportunity for Moscow to exploit the doctrine of peaceful coexistence with respect to Turkey arose before the Cyprus crisis.

Even if the Cyprus dispute had not taken place, the East-West détente might have resulted in a greater measure of flexibility in Turkey's foreign policy. Domestically, the development of a highly vocal opposition and its unprecedented criticism of Turkey's relations with the United States were making the Turkish government wary of a foreign policy that appeared excessively dependent on Washington. Nevertheless, it was the strong disagreements between Turkey and the United States over United States policy toward Cyprus during and following the 1965 crisis which gave the Soviets their first real opportunity to change the course of Soviet-Turkish relations. A secret letter sent by President Johnson to Prime Minister Inonu on 5 June 1964, when a Turkish invasion of Cyprus seemed imminent, is generally regarded as a watershed in Turkish-American relations. The American president stated bluntly that if Turkish forces landed on Cyprus and the Soviet Union chose to respond militarily, Turkey could not count on the United States coming to her defense.[62]

In May 1964 the Turkish government had declined an invitation extended to the Turkish foreign minister to visit Moscow to discuss

62. The letter and Inonu's reply were released by the White House on 15 January 1966. The texts are published in *Middle East Journal* 10, No. 3 (Summer 1966): 386.

the Cyprus issue. The reason given was that the Soviet position on Cyprus was hostile to Turkish interests. Following the Johnson letter, however, Prime Minister Inonu accepted a renewed invitation and in early November dispatched his foreign minister to the Soviet Union for a week of discussions. The visit led to a Soviet volte-face on the Cyprus dispute. A joint communique issued at its end stated that *enosis*—or the reunification of Cyprus with Greece—was not the proper solution. Instead, the Greek and Turkish Cypriot communities on the island should be largely autonomous. The new Soviet stance amounted to a nearly complete acceptance of Turkey's position in the dispute.[63] A restatement of the Soviet position on Cyprus by Podgorny on the occasion of Makarios' visit to the Soviet Union in June 1971 said that a settlement in Cyprus must lead to the cooperation of all Cypriots within the framework of a sovereign, independent, and territorially integral state.[64] This implied qualification on the original understanding has been denied by Moscow in response to Turkish protestations.

In January 1965 President M. Nicolai Podgorny first visited Turkey. During his visit the Turkish government informed the United States that it would be unable to participate in the American-sponsored multilateral nuclear force, and a few days later it rejected a NATO request for increased force levels.[65] Podgorny was followed, in May, by Soviet Foreign Minister Gromyko, who had discussions with the Turkish president, the prime minister, and the foreign minister. In August Turkish Prime Minister Urguplu went to the Soviet Union for still another round of high-level discussions.

The turning point in the changing relationship between the two countries came in December 1966, when for the first time since the Bolsheviks seized power in Russia a Soviet head of government visited Turkey. On 20 December as he arrived in Ankara, Premier Kosygin stressed Soviet support for the Turkish position on Cyprus and paved the way for further agreement with the Turks.[66] Thus the 1964 Cyprus crisis was the catalyst for the rapprochement that has characterized Turkish-Soviet relations in recent years.

The dialogue has since been extended to other matters of mutual interest. By 1968 the veritable procession of Soviet dignitaries to

63. The joint communique was published in *Pravda*, 5 November 1964, and translated in *Current Digest of the Soviet Press*, 2 December 1964, p. 18.

64. *Tass International* (Moscow), 2 June 1971.

65. *Le Monde* (Paris), 15 January 1965.

66. *Cumhuriyet* (Istanbul), 21 December 1966.

Turkey was being augmented by the exchanges of journalists, technicians, and cultural and trade missions. Turkey and the Soviet Union agreed on a border demarcation long in dispute, and on a joint hydroelectric power project on their common frontier. A Moscow-Ankara air link was also established.

Equally significant has been the increase in trade and the beginnings of a Soviet aid program intended to forge closer economic ties between the two countries. As a consequence of the visit to Moscow of Turkish Prime Minister Demirel, in 1967, and of many Turkish and Soviet economic missions, trade has increased sharply. The USSR has committed more than $200 million in low-interest credits and grants to Turkey for various industrial projects.[67] To administer this program it has established an economic aid mission in its embassy in Ankara.

Declining United States military and economic aid levels [68] have strengthened this trend, and the improved relations have weathered several changes of government in Turkey. Even the conservative press and right-of-center elements in Turkish politics, most outspoken in their distaste for the Russians, have come to support efforts to promote amity with Moscow. There has also been substantial amelioration in Turkish relations with the Communist satellite states in Europe, and Turkey's diplomacy is now distinctly more favorable to the Arab position in the Middle East.

The 12 March 1971 "coup by communique" by the Turkish military replaced the Justice party government of Premier Demirel with a coalition government led by Nihat Erim, at the head of a cabinet of "technocrats," but it did not alter, basically, Turkish foreign policy. Turkey's diplomacy continues to pursue an independent course while remaining committed to NATO and seeking increased participation in the Common Market.

There has been, nevertheless, a leaning back toward the United States. In fact, President Sunay declared after the coup, "There is no doubt that the Turkish nation is very much in favor of the Government's pro-American policy. . . . As for NATO, it is the greatest guarantee of peace that exists today. My fondest wish is that

67. Ibid., 8 July 1968, and U.S., Department of State, *Communist Governments and Developing Nations: Aid and Trade in 1968,* Research Memorandum RSE-65, 5 September 1968, p. 3.

68. Even loans have been curtailed. According to the Turkish State Planning Organizations, U.S. AID has canceled $7,720,000 in project loans previously agreed to with Turkey, *Cumhuriyet,* 12 March 1971.

Turkey's association with NATO will continue and I can assure you that the vast majority of the Turkish nation shares this view." [69] United States military aid has been increased somewhat,[70] but with economic aid remaining at minimal levels.[71]

However, Soviet economic aid has also continued apace,[72] along with assurances that the Soviet Union attaches great importance to friendly Turkish-Soviet relations—a statement by Soviet foreign minister Gromyko—in the wake of President Makarios' visit to Moscow in June 1971.[73]

The Turkish government has recognized Communist China, signing an agreement permitting Chinese commercial-airline stopovers in Turkey on the way to Rumania.[74] The rationale advanced for recognition noted that the recent understandings between the United States and the Soviet Union could upset the balance of power between the superpowers that allows for Turkey's independent stance. In the past, some Turks have expressed fear that the SALT talks might lead to secret agreements that could damage Turkish national interests. Thus the recognition of "the third superpower, China," opens an option that enables Turkey to continue its "balance policy." [75] Reportedly, the Turkish foreign ministry had wanted to make contacts with Communist China in 1963 and 1964 during the premierships of Inonu and Urgulpu, but the electoral victory of the Justice party in 1965 aborted this initiative.[76]

Other expressions of Turkish attempts to underscore independence in foreign policy have been the official denials by the Ministry of Foreign Affairs that the United States was permitted, in 1970, to transit sixty-five F–105 jets through Turkey on the way to Jordan,

69. Interview with C. L. Sulzberger, *New York Times,* 27 August 1971, and *New York Times,* 14 October 1971.

70. U.S. Military aid to Turkey for fiscal 1971 was $148 million. *Yeni Gazete,* 29 July 1971. The United States also sold Turkey two submarines at token prices; *Pulse,* 2 July 1971.

71. Twenty-five million dollar forty-year program aid loan at 2 percent for the first 10 years and 3 percent thereafter. *Yeni Gazete* or *Pulse,* 27 July 1971.

72. A second iron/steel complex is to be built with Soviet assistance. *Yeni Gazete,* 1 July 1971.

73. *Pulse,* 21 June 1971.

74. *Cumhuriyet,* 5 August 1971.

75. *Milliyet,* 14 August 1971.

76. The recognition of Communist China was not without controversy in domestic Turkish politics with ousted Premier Demirel leading the opposition. See *Cumhuriyet,* 9 August 1971 and 11 August 1971; and *Son Havadis* and *Milliyet,* 10 August 1971.

as claimed by some Beirut and Cairo newspapers,[77] and the Foreign Ministry's periodic affirmations that Turkey enforces the Montreux Convention "with care and impartiality." [78]

Thus, at minimum, the rapprochement between Turkey and the Soviet Union has resulted in scrupulous Turkish application of the Montreux Convention. Soviet naval units moving between the Black Sea and the Mediterranean can count on unhampered passage through the Dardanelles. Turkey has even acceded to Moscow's request that Soviet submarines en route to the Mediterranean be allowed to enter the Bosporus an hour or more before first light, although the Convention restricts passage for submarines to daylight hours.[79]

By and large, the Soviet presence in the Mediterranean has not been viewed by the Turkish government and the Turkish public with the alarm it would have produced only a few years ago. The prevalent attitude, especially among the leftist opposition, is that the Soviets have as much right to enter the Mediterranean as the Americans. Because of United States support of Israel, the reasoning goes, it is the United States that has, in fact, opened the Mediterranean to the Soviets.[80]

If Soviet military deployments are careful not to appear to threaten Turkish security, it should be possible for Soviet diplomacy to isolate United States and Turkish interests. Consequently, feeling more secure at the straits, the Soviet Union can exploit its presence in the Mediterranean to further its Middle Eastern objectives.

The Role of France in the Mediterranean and the Arab Response

The military key to Soviet access to the Mediterranean is at the Dardanelles, but the ultimate fate of the Soviet naval challenge may be decided in the Western Mediterranean. It is there that the policies of European countries—France in particular—abutting on the Mediterranean, and their relations with Arab countries of the

77. *Cumhuriyet*, 20 August 1971.

78. Ibid., 21 June 1971.

79. *New York Times*, 27 January 1970.

80. See, for example, Sukru Esmer, "Russian Expansion on the High Seas," *Ulus* (Ankara), 29 April 1968.

Maghreb, may decisively affect the military and political balance between the United States and the Soviet Union in the Mediterranean.

Just as Soviet ships operating in the Mediterranean must be concerned with freedom of passage through the straits, conversely United States naval units must have unhampered passage through the narrows of Gibraltar. Whether they do or not—and whether they have anchorage and back-up shore facilities in the Western Mediterranean—depends as much on the relations that France, Italy, and Spain have with Algeria, Morocco, Tunisia, and Libya as on the relations that the United States and the Soviet Union have with these European and Mediterranean countries.

Agreements or understandings with Greece, Spain, Italy, and France about United States Sixth Fleet operations relating to the Arab-Israeli conflict go a long way toward defining the political and military utility of the United States naval presence in the Mediterranean.

Crucial variables are the degree and kind of access or denial given the Soviet Union to air and shore facilities in the Arab states of North Africa and what the United States does vis-à-vis the Soviet presence. Should the United States decide to redeploy out of the Mediterranean, unilaterally or reciprocally by agreement with the Soviet Union, the effect on the policies of European countries could be profound.

Currently, these Mediterranean and European countries have defined their policies for the Mediterranean almost exclusively in terms of the Middle-East confrontation primarily, and in the case of France and Spain with special attention to their relations with the Maghreb. Even France's policy—the only one which explicitly defines itself as "Mediterranean"—cannot escape a definition constrained by the Arab-Israeli conflict and the history of its relations with the Arab countries of the Mediterranean littoral.

This is the result not only of the absence of rivalry or contest with the other European powers washed by the Mediterranean, but also because France cannot offer an alternative to either the Soviet Union or the United States if it required standing up to either in relationships of power.

Although since the aftermath of the Six-Day War France's Mediterranean policy has been viewed favorably by most of the Arab states, French aspirations of leadership in the Mediterranean have been rejected in principle. Support for the denuclearization of the United States and Soviet Mediterranean fleets, or their withdrawal, has not been seen as creating a power vacuum to be filled by France.

To the contrary, Algeria and Tunisia have, for example, specifically criticized French expectations that the French navy would replace the American and Soviet naval presence in the Mediterranean.[81] Even so, France's Mediterranean policy has been viewed positively by most of the Arab states of the Mediterranean, although they have tended to regard it almost exclusively in terms of the Arab-Israeli confrontation, with little reference to French ambitions for leadership in the Mediterranean region. What is France's Mediterranean policy and where does it fit into the United States–Soviet naval confrontation in the Mediterranean?

The divergence of national interests between the United States and its European allies has been most dramatic with France, and Vietnam aside, most acute concerning the Middle East and the Mediterranean. Although in a future Arab-Israeli conflict selective denial of the use of facilities by Turkey is likely, by Spain (not a NATO ally), perhaps by Italy and Portugal, though maybe not Greece, the United States has no expectations that it would be allowed to use French naval infrastructure. This is because since the final period of de Gaulle's tenure of office, France has sought to be recognized as the major European power in the Mediterranean and has insisted that it has the right to participate in the definition of the terms of agreement between Israel and its Arab enemies,[82] on an equal footing with the United States, Britain, and the Soviet Union. As for defining the security of the Mediterranean, France believes it should play the leading role, especially in the Western Mediterranean. There, France has been expounding the advantages of nonalignment not only to Morocco, Tunisia, and Algeria, but also to Spain, Italy, and Libya.[83] In February 1969, the French foreign minister, in a speech in Madrid, underscored the necessity of keeping the Mediterranean free of Soviet and American political control and endorsed the Spanish suggestion that both Soviet and United States fleets be withdrawn from the Mediterranean.[84]

The Spanish foreign minister returned the visit several months later, and a military agreement between the respective general staffs

81. Compare the remarks of Mohammed Masmoudi, Tunisia's foreign minister, in an article published in *Jeune Afrique,* 22 September 1970, and the reportage by *Le Monde,* 5 February 1970.

82. A useful discussion of French Mediterranean policy is Edward A. Kolodziej's "French Mediterranean Policy: The Politics of Weakness," *International Affairs* (London), July 1971.

83. Ibid., p. 510.

84. *Le Monde,* 7 February 1969.

for contingency planning, arms production, and military exercises (with joint use of Spanish and French territory) was signed.[85] This led to more talks on Mediterranean security in the fall of 1970.[86]

The importance attached to the Mediterranean in French security and foreign policies is made apparent by the attention given it by the leading members of the French government. French defense minister, Michel Debré, in a policy speech before the Institut des Hautes Etudes de Defense Nationale, in June 1970, devoted a good deal of attention to the Mediterranean. He conceded that the situation in the Mediterranean might require France to take action in concert with other nations, and that the Mediterranean had changed from "a European sea" to one that was also African, American, and Soviet. But then he stressed that this change, by modifying the basis of French security, demanded a new and active approach for the defense of French national interest. French national interest requires that "the Mediterranean, at least in its Western part, [be] a peaceful area, that our national interests there [be] respected, and that it remain open to our influence." [87] France, he argued, must promote common efforts with the Arab countries of the Maghreb, Spain, Italy, and even Greece and countries of the eastern Mediterranean, to avoid "excessive external influence" in the Mediterranean region.[88]

President Pompidou has been at once more specific and equally forceful in his definitions of France's future role. He has noted the importance of the conventional navy and its mission—short of nuclear war. It is clear that he values its political role. The navy, he points out, is important in maintaining the prestige and the political influence of France, particularly in the Mediterranean. For he sees the Mediterranean as very important to France not only because it washes French shores for considerable lengths but because it is also France's gateway to North Africa and the African continent.[89]

85. *Le Monde,* 23 June 1970.

86. *Le Monde,* 26 October 1970.

87. Michel Debré, "Les Principes de Notre Politique de Defense," *Revue de Defense Nationale,* August–Septembeer 1970.

88. Ibid. See also the remarks of France's Secretary of State for Foreign Affairs, Jean de Lipkowski, in Athens, *New York Times,* 30 January 1972.

89. These concepts were outlined by M. Pompidou in his speech in France's chief naval base, Toulon, on 19 June 1971, on the occasion of the national military maneuvers in the South East. *Le Monde,* 20, 21, and 22 June 1971. What unencumbered passage to North Africa means for France is suggested by the fact that six Arab countries (Algeria first of all) supply France with 90 percent of oil imports.

More concretely, the French Navy in the Mediterranean is being reorganized as an autonomous operational command. A squadron of about twenty-five ships, including several conventional submarines and the aircraft carrier *Arromanches,* and destroyers, antisubmarine forces, minesweepers and support vessels will also be given additional capability from land-based air.[90]

The French squadron, although modest by comparison with either the Soviet or United States squadrons, by being placed under an autonomous commander who receives his orders directly from Paris is obviously organized to function in times of Mediterranean crises primarily. It does not serve strategic purposes like the French Atlantic squadron but as now constituted it endows the French government with the organizational beginnings for a more flexible arm to promote French naval policy in the Mediterranean.[91]

Although the diplomatic style has changed, the French government's current policy objectives in the Mediterranean seem to be, in the main, a continuation of de Gaulle's policy and of his conviction that France must maintain her "historic role" in the Middle East and North Africa.[92] To achieve these goals, France continues in her attempts to counterbalance the United States and the Soviet Union in the Mediterranean by her military presence, by diplomatic maneuvers to prevent close alignment of other Mediterranean countries with either superpower, and by promoting arms sales to Spain, Greece, and the Arab countries, especially those of the Maghreb.

The most dramatic example of how France has functioned as an additional, sometimes alternative, arms supplier—giving Arab regimes increased opportunities for foreign policy stances that appear to be independent of superpower influence—has been the sale of French Mirage aircraft to the revolutionary government of Libya in December 1969.[93]

90. *Le Monde,* 3 July 1971. To relate this squadron to total French naval forces, see also "France," in *Jane's Fighting Ships, 1972–1973,* p. 96 and the following pages.

91. See, for example, Jacques Isnard, "Le Plan Naval a Long Terme," *Le Monde,* 21 July 1971.

92. My purpose is not to discuss the complex of relations between the European Mediterranean states and the Arab East but rather to indicate those aspects of such relations that bear upon the Soviet and U.S. naval involvement in the Mediterranean. For a discussion of historical and recent relations between France, Italy, and other European countries with Arab states, see Pierre Rondot, "Western Europe and the Middle East," in Hammond and Alexander, *Political Dynamics.*

93. *New York Times,* 17 December 1969.

Under public criticism of the sale Foreign Minister Maurice Schumann stated before the French Senate Foreign Affairs Committee that there was no French policy of arms sales, as such, to the Middle East, but a Mediterranean policy. The French government, he said, did not consider Libya to be directly involved in the Arab-Israeli conflict. Arms deliveries would not be made in the immediate future, and guarantees would be forthcoming on the use of the aircraft.[94] The alternative to Soviet influence provided by the sale of French military aircraft was stressed by other government commentators. The eventual impact of Libya's federation with Egypt and Syria, approved by referendum 1 September 1970, on this agreement is not yet clear. But the agreement does provide for joint military command and authority to deploy troops against Israel. The contract for the sale of French combat aircraft to Libya forbids transfer to a third country and provides for suspension and cancellation.[95]

Pompidou's policies differ from de Gaulle's in their reemphasis on conventional naval power rather than one-sided reliance on nuclear submarines, a willingness to relax arms embargoes to the countries involved in the Arab-Israeli conflict, and a desire to improve relations with Israel and not only with the Arab countries. His application of policy is distinguished from his predecessor's by lack of firmness in dealing with the increasing economic and political blackmail of the Maghreb countries. This policy of "discreet impartiality" toward all Mediterranean countries to avoid damaging existing relations with Arab countries has resulted in futile attempts to reconcile irreconcilable positions. Policy initiatives against French economic interests during 1971 underscore the French diplomatic failures in Morocco, Libya, and especially Algeria.

Algeria's decision to nationalize French oil companies on 24 February 1971 illustrates the limitations of Pompidou's "Mediterranean policy." Morocco has also pursued "moroccanization" of French interests and Spain has officially deplored French criticism of the Burgos trial. There have also been problems with Libya. The

94. *Le Monde,* 28 January 1970.

95. *Le Monde,* 10 November 1970. On 16 February, the French Foreign Ministry issued a declaration reminding Libya of the conditions on the sale of the Mirages. The declaration was issued after an interview by Qadafi in which he told the Tunisian news agency, "we are free to use as we wish the arms we buy. . . . The Mirage are not the only aircraft in the world." *Arab Report and Record,* 15–18 February 1971.

arms deal negotiated with the government headed by Colonel Qadhafi, in December 1969, was hailed as the first step to more important agreements with the Libyan regime, in the cultural and economic fields. But the radical positions taken by Tripoli in the Middle East conflict and the oil negotiations have not helped relations, and there is no longer any talk of closer cooperation. Since the agreement of Libya, Sudan, Egypt, and Syria to unite, Schumann's statement that "far from constituting a way around them such eventualities would set the clauses of the sales contract in motion," has been forgotten.[96]

France can congratulate itself on the fact that Egypt has been more favorable to France than Algeria in the matter of the oil nationalizations and has been more moderate in general on the Middle East conflict.[97] A large number of French technicians will be needed in Libya to keep the Mirages running, and they provide some insurance that the planes will not be used on the Middle East front. However, these problems have aggravated relations between France and other Mediterranean countries. Aside from Black Africa, French diplomacy cannot point to any successes in other areas. One reason has been France's low profile in international conflicts. France was content to sit back and watch the efforts made by the United States to implement the Rogers Plan. Only if France were able to speak for the entire Common Market could it hope to wield greater influence in the Middle East talks, but the other members of the EEC are far more favorable to Israel than is France. The softening of Gaullist antagonism toward Israel may stem from hopes of strengthening French arms sales[98] and more importantly from attempts to counteract French diplomatic failures in the Maghreb.

Nevertheless, France's strongly condemnatory stand toward Israel after the Six-Day War, its diplomatic support for the Arab position

96. *Le Monde* (Weekly Section), 25–31 March 1971. In fact, Dassault has given priority to the production of the 100 Mirages for Libya at the expense of the French air force. The first six training planes have been delivered, and it is expected that the majority will be delivered in 1972 and 1973. Libya will not be able to form an operational squadron until next year. *Le Monde,* 27 April 1971.

97. Al-Ahram al Iqtisadi, 1 February 1971.

98. French arms sales abroad are broadly based and have increased over the years to the point where France is third, after the United States and the Soviet Union, as exporter of arms in the world market. Jacques Isnard, "French Arms Exports," *Survival,* April 1971. About 70 percent of exports have been in the aeronautical sector. *Le Monde,* 20–21 June 1971.

at the Four-Power talks and in the United Nations, and its arms embargo to Israel have predisposed Arab governments toward France's Mediterranean policy.[99]

In terms of a call for a naval withdrawal of the United States and the Soviet Union from the Mediterranean and reaction to French initiatives, the Arab states may be grouped into two categories: Syria, Lebanon, Egypt and Libya; and Tunisia, Algeria, and Morocco.

As early as February 1968, the Egyptian press gave support to the withdrawal of all foreign naval forces from the Mediterranean —although it qualified the circumstances for the withdrawal of Soviet forces.[100] This support of the French position may have been merely posturing, given Egypt's utter dependence on Soviet military assistance.

Lebanon's position has been understandably cautious. Its security and internal integrity have been sustained traditionally by the Western military presence in the Eastern Mediterranean. Withdrawal of the Sixth Fleet would further and severely undermine this Western presence, already undercut by the increasing vulnerability of United States naval forces in the Eastern Mediterranean caused by the increase in Soviet military capability in that area. At the same time France has expressed its willingness to shoulder this responsibility.[101] Pro-Western Lebanese would be likely to support an assertive French Mediterranean posture.[102]

Although Libya, under the Qadafi regime, has become strongly nationalistic, and the French constraints on the use of the Mirages sold to Libya have been a periodic source of friction, Libyan policy is not incompatible with the general outline of French Mediterranean goals.

The Libyan government is not on record as favoring French

99. Examples of the Arab government's appreciation of French Middle East policy are: by the Arab League—*Arab Report and Record,* 1–15 March 1970; by Lebanon—*Le Monde,* 19 May 1971 and *Arab Report and Record,* 16–30 June 1971; by Morocco—*Le Monde,* 10 February 1970; by Egypt—*Arab Report and Record,* 1–15 November 1970, and 16–30 April 1971.

100. *Akhbar al-yom,* February 1968.

101. French Secretary of State for Foreign Affairs, Jean de Lipkowski, in Beirut for a private visit and later a meeting of French Ambassadors in the Middle East, assured members of the Lebanese Parliament's Foreign Affairs Committee on 23 June that France would not remain idle if Lebanon were "exposed to danger," and also said on the following day, according to Beirut Radio, that "the purpose of our presence here is to guarantee Lebanon's independence." *Arab Report and Record,* 16–30 June 1971.

102. *Le Monde,* 19 May 1971.

Mediterranean policy. On the other hand, in terms of Mediterranean strategy, Libya's policy of eliminating foreign bases on Libyan territory and of encouraging Malta to do the same is congruent with the thrust of French Mediterranean policy.

The Arab countries of the Western Mediterranean have been more forthright and generally favorable toward the basic French position. Among the reasons is that France articulates its own plans primarily in terms of the actions of these countries, and Italy and Spain.[103] Algeria has been the most forceful in proposing the withdrawal of the navies of non-Mediterranean powers.[104] Tunisia [105] and Morocco [106] have been more cautious, probably because of concern about their relations with the United States.

For example, Tunisia has assessed the probability that Soviet and American warships would leave the Mediterranean to be low for the foreseeable future. It has called, however, for a stronger European presence in the Mediterranean to establish a balance, but in terms of economic and technical assistance, not military aid.[107]

Morocco's relations with France were greatly eroded by the Ben-Barka affair, which resulted in a five-year breach of relations. These were restored in 1969. But by then French economic and military aid had been largely replaced by United States assistance. A United States communications base has been established. These events have inhibited stronger espousal of French initiatives about the Mediterranean.

Algeria, because of its location and special historical and post-independence relationships with France, is considered by the latter to be the linchpin of France's Mediterranean policy. President Boumedienne was actually among the first to call for a withdrawal of all non-Mediterranean naval forces. The concessions made by the French government—the very strong pressures by French oil interests notwithstanding—were because of in a not inconsiderable degree the awareness that the alternatives might so alienate the Algerian government as to seriously undermine Mediterranean policy.

With the settlement of Algeria's border disputes with Tunisia and Morocco in 1970, French relations with the Maghreb countries have

103. Michel Debré, "The Principles of our Defense Policy," *Survival*, November 1970.

104. Interview by *Le Monde* with President Boumedienne 6 January 1970.

105. Interview by *Le Monde* with Tunisian Foreign Minister Mohammed Masmoudi, 27–28 June 1971.

106. Interview by *Le Monde* with King Hassan at the end of his visit to Paris, 10 February 1970.

107. *Survival*, December 1970.

a better chance of leading to the expected outcomes in French Mediterranean policy. Algeria remains strongly disposed toward neutralizing the Mediterranean from superpower naval presence.

French failures have not deflected France from continuing to aspire to a leadership role in the Mediterranean, especially in the West. The French Foreign Minister, Maurice Schumann, has summarized France's position well.

> France changes neither doctrine nor language, whether the visitor received in Cairo is named William Rogers or Nikolai Podgorny. What is, actually, the present situation in the Mediterranean? It leads back to a basic assessment: the chance for a lasting settlement in the Middle East does not increase when a very great power acts on its own though it is . . . with intentions most worthy of being encouraged. Why? Because the spectacular deployment of one presence and one influence attracts the rival power, and consequently intensifies the rivalry between powers. . . . Does this mean that it would be in the power of France, or of all the Mediterranean countries, to change the situation? Assuredly not. The economic and political vitality of the United States and the Soviet Union forbids them . . . to ignore the importance of this traditional arena of conflict of influence. . . . But on the other hand it is certain that among the powers, those which border on the Mediterranean and France, the most important among them have an even greater responsibility by reason of their geographical location and their political and economic influence in the Middle East. . . .

Without the presence of France, Schumann has emphasized, which exemplifies "a policy of independence and impartiality in the Middle East," the chances for increasing the division of the Mediterranean would be multiplied. This would intensify, in turn, the risk of confrontation. Precisely at a time when some Mediterranean countries might be tempted to join one side or the other (Libya for example) it is most useful for France to affirm her independent and peaceful presence. France does not accept the division of the Mediterranean. On the contrary, it believes in inevitable cooperation among all riverain countries. "France has made rendezvous with the only future whose face has not been scarred by war and distorted by hate."[108]

108. Ambassade de France, Service de Presse et d'Information, *Address Delivered by Maurice Schumann, French Minister of Foreign Affairs, before the National Assembly,* 9 June 1971.

Implications for United States Policy

Soviet ships permanently on station in the Mediterranean are one of the more dramatic indicators of the changed environment affecting NATO and United States freedom of maneuver in the Middle East, yet at first no action was undertaken by the United States to cope with the Soviet naval challenge. Not until the Soviet flotilla increased manyfold, in 1967, did members of NATO, especially Italy, begin to feel uneasy and to raise the issue at NATO Council meetings. Although air surveillance was talked about,[109] it took the invasion of Czechoslovakia to galvanize the United States and NATO into action. An air surveillance group became reality, and a special NATO naval force for the Mediterranean was organized to become operational whenever needed. As in the air unit, the naval members are the United States, Britain, and Italy, with Turkish and Greek participation.

These measures are palliatives, however. They do not meet the challenge in the Mediterranean, where the Soviet naval presence has permanently altered the local situation militarily and politically. On the military side, the Soviet presence complicates the defense of NATO's southeastern flank, inhibits United States military initiative in Middle East crises and conflicts, and increases the chances of inadvertent escalation from local conflict. The likely inhibitions on United States actions are well illustrated by the behavior of the Sixth Fleet during the initial phase of the Six-Day War. Most of the United States fleet was in the Western Mediterranean when the crisis broke. It immediately observed three important restrictions: (*1*) no premature departures from scheduled port visits; (*2*) deliberate and visible retention of its amphibious forces in the central Mediterranean, at Malta; and (*3*) purposeful retention of United States naval forces south of Crete and well clear of the prospective

109. *New York Times,* 18 May 1967; *Christian Science Monitor,* 13 November 1967. Measures to be undertaken to meet the Soviet naval threat in the Mediterranean continue to be mainly at the level of discussion. In May 1971 a communique issued at the end of a meeting of the NATO Defense Planning Committee talked of a more effective defense of the Mediterranean. Britain has proposed that the standing or special naval force now deployed once or twice a year remain in being as a combat group. Although the Mediterranean was the focus of concern at the meeting, the only concrete actions were the pledge by the United States to station an additional helicopter carrier with the Sixth Fleet and to increase the latter's number of operational days at sea and improve the quality of electronic detection equipment on the aircraft aboard its two attack carriers. *New York Times,* 29 May 1971.

area of action.[110] Soviet naval forces were in the Eastern Mediterranean, being reinforced through the straits, with some units on the way to Egyptian ports.

Admittedly, the operational capability of the Soviet Mediterranean fleet is curtailed by the Turkish control of the straits, the blocking of the Suez Canal, and Britain's control of Gibraltar. Moreover, the Sixth Fleet and the Italian, Greek, and Turkish navies together certainly outnumber the Soviet squadron. However, the Egyptian navy matches in number of ships the Turkish navy, and is more modern. Of the three NATO European navies on the spot, only the Italian navy is not predominantly composed of obsolescent warships. Even United States vessels are, on the average, less modern than their Soviet counterparts.[111] France's naval contribution to the defense of the Mediterranean is undercut more seriously by French Mediterranean policy than by the relative obsolescence of its warships.[112]

A more serious drawback is the Soviet fleet's seeming lack of air cover. The Soviet navy has no carriers and there are no Soviet airfields near the shores of the Mediterranean. The military, aware of this shortcoming, has sought to surmount it by creating an operational doctrine that emphasizes missile-carrying submarines and missile-carrying aircraft. This, they contend, would permit Soviet naval units and aircraft to attack United States and NATO carriers without entering the zone of antisubmarine and air defenses of the carrier force.[113]

A direct United States–Soviet conventional confrontation in the Mediterranean would not be free from potential escalation to the nuclear level. In this extreme, United States land-based airpower may be neither immediately available nor sufficient in numbers. A confrontation in the Mediterranean raises the specter of possible fighting on other NATO fronts. The aircraft in NATO presumably have their target assignments elsewhere. Their diversion to the

110. For a more detailed account of Sixth Fleet deployment at the time, see J. C. Wylie, "The Sixth Fleet and American Diplomacy," in *Soviet-American Rivalry in the Middle East*, ed. J. C. Hurewitz, Proceedings of the Academy of Political Science, Columbia University, March 1969.

111. *Washington Post,* 18 February 1970.

112. See, for example, Schumann's insistence that the Middle East, hence the Mediterranean, necessarily become "a zone of peace and neutrality sheltered from the competition of all the major powers" in his speech before the Twenty-sixth Session of the United Nations General Assembly on 28 September 1971. Ambassade de France, Service de Presse et d'Information, No. 71/66.

113. Sokolovski, *Voennaia strategiia.*

Mediterranean could leave targets uncovered, degrading the NATO military posture on the central front, and this risk might make it difficult to convince NATO commanders to redeploy their aircraft. It would also take time to reach available fields in the vicinity of the Soviet fleet because NATO aircraft could not overfly Austria, Switzerland, and maybe even France.

In a desperate situation the Soviet Union could commit long-range aircraft from southern Russia and Bulgaria, or transfer them to Syrian and Egyptian fields via Iraq.

The carrier-based aircraft of the Sixth Fleet—two carriers with 100 strike aircraft apiece—is a formidable force. Its effectiveness is contingent, however. The potential availability of land-based Soviet aircraft and the existence of Soviet submarines in the area may hobble the offensive use of the carrier craft. The number of planes available to strike at Soviet ships will depend on how many aircraft will be necessary to defend the carriers themselves against air and submarine attacks, the strength of inhibitions against using aircraft with a nuclear mission in a conventional mode, the relative distance between the contending fleets, the types and number of land-based craft available to each side, and the political constraints operating at the time of battle.

Clearly, a host of imponderables would operate in the event of a naval confrontation between the United States and the Soviet Union. But the thought is compelling that in situations of limited conventional conflict in the Middle East, Soviet ships could strongly inhibit—if not interdict—United States naval actions in the Mediterranean.

In ambiguous situations tending toward escalation to nuclear confrontation, the Soviet force could play an anti-Polaris role with its helicopter carriers—e.g., the *Moskva* and the *Leningrad*—and threaten United States Sixth Fleet carriers with its submarines. This last is the threat taken most seriously by United States naval commanders in the Mediterranean.[114] The recent decision to acquire a "home" base for the Sixth Fleet in Greece [115] increases fleet vulnerability. The Sixth Fleet was stationed in the Mediterranean in the 1950s to complement SAC, and presumably still has a nuclear mission. Should hostilities break out, Soviet nuclear submarines could, at the very least, target the French *force de frappe,* or threaten countercity strikes against France and Italy. But it should be clear

114. Admiral Rivero, NATO Commander, South, in a press interview in Naples, *Le Monde,* 20, 21 April 1969.

115. *New York Times,* 8 March 1972.

that nuclear war and large-scale conventional warfare in the Mediterranean—the latter threatening to escalate quickly to the former—are unlikely contingencies and offer questionable justification for an operational doctrine for either the Soviet Mediterranean flotilla or the Sixth Fleet.

It is more reasonable to assume that the likely contingencies in which the Soviet naval presence will play an important role will not only be ambiguous but sufficiently limited, from a military viewpoint, to preclude extensive engagements of the kind broached above. The Soviet naval presence creates a Soviet capability more likely to threaten or inhibit possible American deployments than to engage in combat. This purpose is primarily political, inhibiting military actions. For this purpose, the Soviet Mediterranean fleet is adequate even now.

In the past, the utility of the Sixth Fleet went beyond its NATO nuclear role. It was political as well as conventional in the military sense. One need only recall the freedom of action the United States enjoyed, politically as well as militarily, at the time of the Lebanese crisis to realize the telling changes that have taken place in the Mediterranean region. With a Soviet fleet in these waters, it would be perilous to attempt an operation such as the landing of United States Marines in Lebanon in 1958, or a similar operation to aid Israel.

In 1958 there were no Soviet fleet units in the Mediterranean. The cold war was on and Turkey, already in NATO, unqualifiedly supported United States foreign policy actions in the Middle East. The staging area for the United States troops who landed in Lebanon was in Turkey. The United States proceeded from the assumption that Turkish territory was available for United States use and was not disappointed by the Turkish government's reaction. It had no overflight problems in that or any other Mediterranean NATO country, including France.

Would such unencumbered United States intervention be possible in present circumstances? Putting aside whether any Arab government would be likely to request United States aid, the answer must be no. Turkish territory may not be available as a staging area,[116] if for no other reason than that the United States and Turkish positions diverge on what policy should be toward the Arabs. In fact, the use of their territory by the United States in

116. See for example the remarks by former Turkish Prime Minister Demirel in *Yeni Gazete*, 27 November 1968, and *Pulse*, 20 August 1971.

1958 has become the subject of acrimonious political debate among the Turks. Thus they have already drawn the distinction between contingencies affecting NATO and those in the Middle East. Using Italian facilities in a situation not explicitly affecting NATO would also be problematic.[117] France—seeking to forge an independent Mediterranean role—might be even less likely to cooperate. Constraints on United States actions in the Mediterranean could become severe.

The Soviet Union's strategic military position in the region has been weakened by Sadat's new Egyptian policies starting with the events of July 1972, but not decisively. Soviet naval vessels continue to use Egyptian ports, although the terms under which they are used appear to have changed. The Soviets evidently no longer exercise direct control over any facilities.[118] In operational terms, however, the Soviet Mediterranean squadron has probably not been seriously affected. Also Syrian ports remain available, and in the Persian Gulf, Iraqi and Yemeni ports.

The Soviet political position in Egypt has clearly been shaken and weakened, but it is likely that Moscow does not regard this entirely as a setback.[119] Basic Egyptian dependence of the Soviet Union remains an unalterable fact of life. Arms deliveries have continued, but at a pace now more firmly controlled by the Soviet Union. Egypt has no alternatives. Possible West European arms suppliers have not materialized. Egypt cannot maintain its forces without continuing large-scale Soviet support. And the Soviet Union appears willing to give it. There are reports that Soviet personnel have been returning to Egypt on a reduced scale.[120] It has been reported also that the highly sophisticated Soviet SA-6 air defense missile system, reportedly removed in July 1972, has returned to Egypt, manned by Soviet personnel. Nevertheless, the Soviet presence is vastly reduced and is most unlikely to reassume the dimensions of the 1970–72 pe-

117. Italy has a policy of maintaining a "presence" in the Arab countries of the Mediterranean littoral, chiefly through trade and commercial and cultural ties, while at the same time maintaining friendly relations with Israel. Before the Libyan coup Italian exports to Libya equaled those to the Soviet Union. *Lo Spettatore Internazionale,* July–December 1966, p. 311. For the various positions taken by Italian political parties in the wake of recent events in the Middle East and Soviet naval expansion see *Corriere della Sera,* 5, 6, 30 November 1970, 2 and 18–20 February 1971, and 6 June 1971, and 11 and 15 August 1971.

118. *New York Times,* 8 August 1972.

119. "Sadat and the Soviet Union," Anthony McDermott, *The World Today,* September 1972.

120. *Foreign Report,* 1 November 1972.

riod.[121] This reduces Soviet influence but increases the freedom of maneuver available to the Soviet Union. An Egyptian decision to resume fighting is now less likely to entangle the Soviet Union and Soviet prestige.

The Soviet squadron represents a permanent Soviet presence in the Mediterranean and a firm commitment to the Arabs. Soviet ships in Egyptian ports routinely inhibit Israeli air strikes and remind the average Egyptian that the USSR is involved in his country's fate.[122] Soviet ships roaming the Mediterranean also expand the confrontation of the superpowers beyond Europe and bring into question the military boundary between the Soviet and American spheres of influence. It remains to be seen whether a naval balance of power between the Soviet Union and NATO and the United States—leading to mutual deterrence—can be achieved before another conflict between the Arabs and Israel or another Cyprus crisis spreads to envelop NATO.[123] The asymmetry of the commitments by Washington and Moscow in the region make such an eventuality very real.

121. *U.S. News & World Report,* 31 July 1972.

122. See for example the statement by Hasan Rajab, supervisor for research and information for Akhbar al-Yom (Cairo) as reported in *The New Middle East,* November 1969, p. 24.

123. A thorough discussion of the meaning of Soviet policy for the Mediterranean is in Curt Gasteyger, "Moscow and the Mediterranean," *Foreign Affairs* 46, No. 4 (July 1968).

CHAPTER 10

The Third World and the Middle East since the Six-Day War*

SAMIR ANABTAWI

Both Arabs and Israelis have focused considerable effort upon wooing the Third World to their respective sides in the Arab-Israeli conflict. Arab participation in Afro-Asian and Pan-African affairs, on the one hand, and Israeli technical aid programs in Africa and Asia, on the other, are cases in point. Both claim a measure of success for their efforts, but the Arabs have had the advantage. During and after the Suez crisis of 1956, for example, a highly vociferous and active nonaligned grouping backed them.

In the meantime, what has the Third World's reaction been? Was it as active on the Arab-Israeli issue during and after the 1967 war, for example, as it was during and after the 1956 war? Is it now sitting on the sidelines while the big powers play their game in the Middle East? If so, is this in turn a measure of Israeli success? The author evaluates these kinds of problems carefully in this chapter.

The United Nations, seized since its inception with what it still terms the "Palestine Question," devoted enormous energies and resources prior to the Six-Day War in 1967 in seeking an amicable solution to the problem. The Third World also played an important role in Middle Eastern politics. This study focuses on the role of the Third World in the Middle East since the Six-Day War—and the role of the United Nations, since they are inextricably related. What role has the Third World played in the Arab-Israeli conflict since 1967, and why?

* The term "Third World" is used throughout this chapter to denote the non-Communist Afro-Asian countries. Where distinctions are necessary, the non-aligned states are indicated separately.

The Decline of the Third World Grouping

There is no doubt, of course, that the prevailing patterns of world politics are substantially different from those that characterized the period shortly after World War II.[1]

1. SYSTEMIC AND GREAT POWER VARIABLES

The bipolarity which was then current could only be said to subsist today in the sense that, militarily speaking, both the United States and the Soviet Union have a destructive capacity far more overwhelming than that of any other combination of world powers.[2] But the old forms of alignment wherein the world was viewed as essentially divided into two camps, endlessly braced for mortal combat, have given way to a diffusion marked by varying degrees and complexities of interpenetration between systemwide and regional axes of conflict, and between global and regional issues. What in essence is present today is a discordant international system distinctive in having "elements of both congruence and discontinuity." [3] The frigid climate of cold war has been warmed by the recognition on the part of the United States and the Soviet Union, particularly after the Cuban Missile Crisis, that the avoidance of further confrontations was so compelling that cooperation was essential in seeing to it that local wars did not escalate into major conflicts.

The impact of this transformation on the practice of nonalignment has been drastic. It meant that those newly independent states which had since nationhood championed the cause of neutralism could not as they once were able to do posit themselves in the middle of a bipolar spectrum and enhance their prestige and effectiveness by pursuing a policy of a "play-off," and by toying with the expectations of the great powers in their competition vis-à-vis the small.[4]

1. For a good summary of approaches to studies of the international system, see Richard B. Gray, *International Security Systems* (Ithaca, Ill.: F. E. Peacock Publishers, Inc., 1969).

2. Raymond Aron, *Peace and War* (New York: Doubleday, 1966).

3. Oran Young, "Political Discontinuities in the International System," *World Politics* 20 (1968): 370.

4. Works on nonalignment and neutralism are now legion. Among the most cited are, Laurence Martin (ed.), *Neutralism and Non-alignment* (New York: Praeger, 1962); Peter Lyon, *Neutralism* (Leicester: Leicester University Press, 1963); Cecil V. Crabb, Jr., *The Elephant and the Grass* (New York: Praeger, 1965). For a very useful collection of articles and essays on the subject see

Rather they had to adjust to a constantly shifting situation which saw a progressive convergence of great power interests, at times so much so that they very nearly acted in concert to ward off the claims of the minor ones.

Adding to the decline of neutralism, perhaps, has been the diminution in the political and military worth of the Third World in the eyes of the United States and the USSR resulting in part from a decrease of emphasis on alignment and the rewards that accrued from it. In other words, whereas the nonaligned countries were once important because the great powers regarded them as important, they are now less significant precisely because the great powers regard them as less significant.[5] The early and once intense rivalry between the United States and the Soviet Union to bring the uncommitted states of the world into their respective alliance orbits seems to have at least abated. Indeed, the impression one derives would suggest that, far from seeking to add to their military responsibilities, they seem anxious to shrink whatever commitments they presently have and bring them more in harmony with their resources, resources which are increasingly being claimed for the satisfaction of internal social needs and the amelioration of domestic conditions.

2. THIRD WORLD VARIABLES

But if systemic and great-power variables contributed to the decline of neutralism, various factors and considerations in Asia and Africa lent their weight also.

a) Decline in Charismatic Leadership

Foremost among these, perhaps, is the decline in charismatic leadership and the coming to the fore of an elite far less given to exaggerated rhetoric and pompous pronouncements and much more attuned to problems of political and social development. Gone from power are the Sukarnos and Nkrumahs, and with them has gone a propensity for foreign adventurism and the acquisition of the trappings of prestige. They have been supplanted by a different body

Julean Friedman, Christopher Bladen and Steven Rosen (eds.), *Alliance in International Politics* (Boston: Allyn and Bacon, 1970).

5. On the reasons why the Great Powers used to regard the nonaligned countries as important, see my article "Neutralists and Neutralism," *The Journal of Politics* 27 (1965): 351–61.

of policy-makers considerably more performance-oriented and eager to press on with the tasks of economic construction, without the distractions of unnecessary foreign involvements. They still profess, of course, an attachment to certain principles, but in their advocacy there is lacking some of the earlier fervor or ideological élan. And nowhere does neutralism have standard bearers of the stature of Nehru and U Nu, who could endow it with a reflected respectability stemming from the immense personal prestige which they enjoyed among statesmen of their times.

Related to this is the simple fact that nearly every major member of the Third World, be it nonaligned or not, has had to contend in recent years with issues and problems so urgent and vital to its national makeup that it could ill-afford to channel energies to other concerns. Indonesia has yet to recover from the internal strife that recently beset it. Nigeria has barely begun the task of binding the wounds from a civil war that very nearly maimed it. India has still to overcome the deep cleavages that divide its parties and leadership. The United Arab Republic is desperately trying to cope with the situation that confronts it. And Pakistan failed to resolve the fissiparous tendencies within it. Just exactly what remedial bearing could the staunch advocacy of neutralism have on these thorny problems must be a source of bewilderment to those charged with their countries' destinies.

b) Neutralism Reevaluated

The jealous regard for sovereignty on the part of the new states of Asia and Africa and the fear that entanglements with certain powers might bring back the shackles of an imperial past (and which very nearly consecrated neutralism as an ideology) has been somewhat abated. This is not to say of course that they are no longer zealous in safeguarding their independence or are insensitive to hints of its compromise, but merely to suggest that their earlier obsession with colonialism which almost instinctively caused them to shun some ties with great powers has mellowed considerably. And with this came less of a disposition to regard independence and nonalignment as inseparable and mutually inclusive.

c) Security vs. Neutralism

Events of the past decade have shown that the road to security was not necessarily the outgrowth of an espousal of nonalignment or of the assumption of a policy of aloofness from East-West cold war rivalries. The rise of new powers and the multiplication of local and regional conflicts have tended to render neutralism as an ineffective and perhaps even an irrelevant sanctuary from regional wars and limited engagements which were neither instigated nor approved by the great powers. In the final analysis, for instance, India's advocacy of nonalignment did not insulate her from the onslaught of Chinese forces in 1962 or from being embroiled in a war with Pakistan in 1965 and 1971. In fact, the Chinese military successes at the expense of India culminated in a more realistic appraisal of neutralism and brought home the realization that, after all is said and done, the cause of political independence and territorial integrity was so paramount as to justify the abandonment of certain other principles and doctrines, no matter how dear they may be. Nehru's comment that it was merely "a compulsion of events which has made (India) accept Western military aid," [6] was only another way of saying that the vagaries of international life could not be met by the faithful pursuit of policies along rigid ideological lines.[7]

d) *The Shift from United Nations General Assembly to Security Council*

Contributing to the decline of neutralism, there has been a progressive diminution in the influence of the Afro-Asian States in the United Nations, owing to a shift of emphasis within the organization's component parts. There was a time when the General Assembly seemed to reign supreme as the principal organ of the United Nations. This was, of course, contrary to the intentions of the framers of the charter who endowed the council with the primary responsibility for the maintenance of peace, and thus enshrined, albeit in institutionalized forms, the nineteenth-century Concert System wherein the great powers constituted the "board of directors" of the world. That this concept of collective guardianship failed to materialize in the aftermath of World War II is now a matter of history. The lack of unanimity which attended the council's deliberations and the repeated employment of the veto by the Soviet Union virtually paralyzed it. It was almost natural in such

6. Peter J. Fliess, *International Relations in the Bipolar World* (New York: Random House, 1968), p. 148.

7. "In time, India has come to lean heavily on the United States and the Soviet Union for defense against China." That the Soviet Union has also provided India with military assistance is not so much indicative of the vindication of neutralism as a viable policy as merely a reflection of the fact that on this particular matter Soviet and U.S. interests happened to coincide. Ibid.

circumstances for attention to be focused on the General Assembly whose powers were added upon through the adoption of a plan incorporated in the Uniting for Peace Resolution of 1951 authorizing the assembly to make recommendations on matters previously deemed within the exclusive province of the council. The United States was the prime mover behind the resolution,[8] not only out of concern for the success of the international organization, but also because it was certain in its belief that it could muster the necessary two-thirds votes in the Assembly on matters vital to its interests. Of the sixty-odd member-states the United States could then very nearly always count on the support of the Latin American and Western European groupings plus the endorsement of some Asian and African friends and allies to boot.

With the gradual and, at times, quite substantial increase in United Nations membership following the rapid decolonization of Asia, and particularly of Africa, the capacity of any power to command a ready majority on questions other than those replete with platitudes has substantially narrowed. The consequence of this transformation was to endow those newly independent states with a leverage disproportionately greater than their intrinsic power would merit, which they further magnified by a certain tendency to cast their ballots as a group.[9] Within a setting based on the twin principles of majoritarianism and the sovereign equality of all states, the big powers found themselves in the ironical, though by no means novel, position of having to court the small. Aside from whatever benefits such a relationship allowed each to exact from the United States and the USSR, it had certain positive results both to the UN and the world at large. By their staunch advocacy of nonalignment, many of the Afro-Asian states succeeded in (*a*) preventing the world from being further polarized into two hostile camps; (*b*) often toning down some of the more militant policies of the two super powers; (*c*) preventing the UN from becoming nothing more than a contentious arena of the cold war; (*d*) reconciling opposing viewpoints through compromise draft-resolutions; (*e*) playing an important role in UN peace-keeping activities, and (*f*) calling attention

8. Dean Acheson, *Present at the Creation* (New York: Norton and Co., 1969), p. 443.

9. For some studies on voting in the Assembly see Hayward R. Alker, Jr. and Bruce M. Russett, *World Politics in the General Assembly* (New Haven, Conn.: Yale University Press, 1965); Robert E. Riggs, *Politics in the United Nations* (Urbana, Ill.: The University of Illinois Press, 1958); Thomas Hovet, Jr., *Africa in the United Nations* (Chicago: Northwestern University Press, 1963).

to the pressing needs and aspirations of the bulk of humanity residing in the underdeveloped world.

While the Afro-Asian states still continue to perform such salutary functions, there has been a perceptible diminution of their influence because of a political shift away from the assembly and a return to the Security Council. The revitalization of the council derived, in part, from the qualitative changes in United States and USSR relationships resulting from the Cuban missile confrontation and fundamental transformations in the international system alluded to earlier. The shift to the council was spurred on by mechanical considerations: transacting business in the assembly had become increasingly cumbersome as the body increased its membership over the years. Moreover, the United States and the Soviet Union had become increasingly aware that the issues which in the end separated them were so weighty and vital that reconciliation or accommodation would be enhanced through discussions within the more intimate, even though at times rancorous, setting of the council, without the distractions which the small states generate.

3. THE FRAGMENTED THIRD WORLD

Contributing to this transformation was the eventual realization that, far from being a coherent entity, the so-called Third World was indeed terribly fragmented. All too often, the term *Afro-Asian* or *Third World* had been used in such a way as to signify a closeness and an affinity beyond what could be properly justified. It is true, of course, that a shared history of colonial experience, an antipathy to racial discrimination, a jealous regard for national sovereignty, a similarity in economic life-styles, have all tended to create bonds which have prompted Asian and African leadership to speak in unison on particular issues before international forums. But it is equally true that beneath these affinities lie such vast differences of religion, race, culture, language, institutions, and political aspirations, that they have progressively manifested themselves in acrimonious discussions, regional disputes, and sometimes local wars.[10] Indeed, the divisions have been so severe that they often were detrimental to UN peace-keeping efforts, an area of activity to which the Afro-Asian states were looked upon as potential major contributors. Nowhere was this more poignantly demonstrated than

10. In the case of the African states, see, I. William Zartman, *International Relations in the New Africa* (Englewood Cliffs, N.J.: Prentice Hall, 1966).

in the Congo, where the UN had dispatched its peace-keeping forces, many of which came from Africa. But the early consensus was heavily undermined by the outbreak of rivalries and factionalism among those states, which had been in the forefront of those championing the UN endeavor. At one point, so intense was the bickering among the African countries, and so heated were their exchanges, that they shook the very foundations of the UN structure and very nearly caused the entire UN effort to collapse.[11]

By the mid-1960s it had become apparent that aside from their demand for more aid from the developed countries and their call for greater liberalization in the latter's tariff and trade policies, the areas of agreement among the Afro-Asian states had become smaller and smaller. Even the solidifying bond of anticolonial sentiment had come to acquire less and less of a relevance with the shedding of imperial colonial domains. In fact, the consensus that they still manifested regarding the liquidation of the remnants and consequences of empire has at times been expressed in such vehement and intemperate terms that they bared themselves open to the charge of gross irresponsibility. No matter how sympathetic and understanding one may be to their hatred of the present regime in Rhodesia, for instance, the repeated calls on the part of the African states for Britain to use force to suppress Ian Smith's government, and their efforts to condemn her for not succumbing to their will, can hardly be viewed as being either balanced or mature. The United Nations was, after all, founded to maintain peace and security and not to subvert it by fomenting disorder in the heart of Africa. For whatever one may think of the present internal conditions in Rhodesia or of their long-range consequences, it would be stretching the point to argue that they currently constitute a threat to international peace and tranquility.

The Third World and the Six-Day War

It is essentially within such a context that the role of the Third World during and after the Middle East crisis in 1967 has to be viewed. Systemic variables, preoccupation with domestic concerns, numerous quarrels, vituperative rhetoric, local conflicts, and much more conspired against its playing a constructive role during those ominous days of May 1967.

11. Perhaps the most succinct analysis of their role in the Congo is to be found in Catherine Hoskyns, *The Congo Since Independence* (London: Oxford University Press, 1965).

1. EARLY PHASES OF THE CONFLICT

The Middle East had been for quite some time a powder keg. It did not require the peculiar gift of political prescience to recognize that the region was again on the brink of disaster. And yet the Third World stood by seemingly immobilized as though it were suddenly afflicted with paralysis. Within the United Nations, and even outside of it, its representatives, nearly always in the thick of debates, were remarkably mute. And aside from the usual call for restraint, the impression one derived during the period from mid-May until the outbreak of open hostilities in June was one of gross timidity.

Yet surely this could not altogether be attributed to dissension and strife within Asia and Africa, or to the mood of political withdrawal that they evoked. Neither could it be argued that the Middle East was looked upon with marginal concern. After all, the bulk of Asian exports and imports passed through the Suez Canal. Moreover, there were the extensive ties that linked the Middle East to Asia and Africa. Some could arouse intense passions where matters pertaining to the holy land were concerned.[12] Furthermore, the Middle Eastern antagonists had nurtured associations with a number of Afro-Asian states. Finally, they were aware of commitments each of the two superpowers had made to their respective wards in the region and of the consequences that a war would bring even to those outside of it.

The ironic and simple fact is that the relative silence of the Afro-Asian world during the early phases of the crisis, far from being caused by a sense of indifference, was prompted by their very involvement, and by their appreciation of the range of issues at hand. They fully recognized, particularly as events began to unfold, that the vital interests of the great powers were at stake, and they anticipated pressures being brought to bear to align themselves with them. In such circumstances, they felt that the appropriate course to follow was essentially one of patience, waiting until the complexities of the situation unraveled themselves.

Until the outbreak of open conflict, the immediate questions which attended the crisis were: (*1*) the withdrawal of the UN Emergency Force, (*2*) the subsequent Egyptian blockade of the Straits of Tiran to Israeli shipping, and (*3*) the utilization of whatever mechanisms were available both within and outside of the UN to prevent the situation from deteriorating to the point of war.

12. For a very interesting account of relations between, say, Pakistan and the Arab states, see M. Ahmad, *Pakistan and the Middle East* (Karachi: Kitabi Markaz, 1948).

a) Withdrawal of the United Nations Emergency Force

There is little doubt that the overwhelming majority of the Afro-Asian states shared in the general dismay expressed in various world quarters about the removal of UN troops, the United Nations Emergency Force (UNEF). It was common knowledge that UNEF had been a principal element in the maintenance of an atmosphere of relative tranquility along the Egyptian-Israeli border and were therefore quite mindful of the immediate and long-range consequences that its withdrawal would have on the region. Furthermore, they were appalled to see that the complex and magnificent edifice of peace-keeping which the UN had built should in the end prove so fragile. They knew that its destruction was bound to have grievous implications for future UN activities and would ultimately further weaken its capacities as a sentinel of world peace.

Constitutional and theoretical intricacies aside, there were real and compelling reasons for supporting the Secretary-General's decision to comply with Cairo's request for the removal of UNEF. To begin with, the United Arab Republic was not just any ordinary state, but a key member of the Arab world and a principal actor in Afro-Asian circles. For some time it had been a major supporter of national liberation groups.[13] Its capital has been for centuries the intellectual center of Islamic scholarship and the seat of its oldest university, Al-Azhar. The United Arab Republic was also among the earliest advocates of neutralism and its president, Nasser, ranked with Nehru and Tito as a pillar of nonalignment.

It should also be borne in mind that the membership of the UNEF Advisory Committee, as specified in its enabling resolution, consisted of seven states, three of which were Asian, namely Ceylon, India, and Pakistan.[14] And as of May, 1967, troops for UNEF were supplied by four members of the committee and three nonmembers —Denmark, Sweden, and Yugoslavia—whose representatives were

13. There were particularly close political sympathies between Egypt and the Indian subcontinent, owing in part to the large Muslim population in South Asia, stretching as far back as the early twenties. These were often expressed in the form of various resolutions adopted by the Indian Congress party and, of course, The Muslim League supporting Egypt, as well as other Arab states, in their struggle for complete independence. See Werner Levi, *Free India in Asia* (Minneapolis: University of Minnesota Press, 1952); Sisir Gupta, *India and Regional Integration in Asia* (London: Asia Publishing House, 1964); William Roy Smith, *Nationalism and Reform in India* (New Haven, Conn.: Yale University Press, 1938); J. C. Kundra, *Indian Foreign Policy 1947–1954* (Gronigen [Netherlands]: J. B. Wolters, 1955), p. 36n.

14. The others were Brazil, Canada, Colombia, and Norway.

also involved when the Secretary-General consulted with the advisory committee on May 18.[15] In other words, of the ten delegates at least four (the Ceylonese, Indian, Pakistani, and Yugoslav) would have been ready to comply with the Egyptian request.

Of the approximately 3,400 men comprising the UN contingent, more than 1,500 were supplied by India and Yugoslavia, whose governments quickly notified the Secretary General of their intention to remove their troops upon learning of the Egyptian request.[16] Both countries of course have had particularly close relations with Cairo, and it would have been unthinkable for them to jeopardize their warm ties by endorsing measures aimed at delay. Indeed, there are indications that the Yugoslav and Indian governments were advised of Egypt's intentions prior to its formal request to U Thant.[17]

Finally, it was recognized that no UN peace-keeping group could continue to discharge its mission without the consent and cooperation of the state concerned. In any event, discussion of the matter had been rendered academic only a few days later by the United Arab Republic's deployment of military units on the Israeli frontier.

b) Blockade of the Straits of Tiran

Afro-Asian attitudes regarding the question of the Straits of Tiran were, quite understandably, mixed. The bulk of them sympathized with the United Arab Republic's assertion of sovereign rights over Sharm El-Sheikh and its adjacent islands. But when it came to the matter of blockade and to the denial of passage to Israeli ships through the Gulf of Aqaba, opinions varied. The issue was tangled in a web of international legality. Of those that did make pronouncements on the subject before and subsequent to the outbreak of war, India, Indonesia, Pakistan, and Afghanistan, among others, wholeheartedly supported the Arab position that it was within the sovereign rights of the United Arab Republic to take such measures as it deemed necessary in defense of its legitimate national interest. The Indian delegate restated his government's position, expressed as far back as 1957, that the Gulf of Aqaba was an inland sea and entry into it lay within the territorial waters of the United Arab

15. "Issues Before the 22nd General Assembly," *International Conciliation,* September 1967/No. 564, p. 15n.

16. UN Document A/6730/Add.3.

17. *New York Times,* May 21, 1967, p. 3.

Republic which had unquestionable sovereignty over it. No state or group of states, he said, should attempt to challenge that sovereignty.[18]

c) Attempts to Avert War

All this notwithstanding, they were quite mindful of the ominous consequences that the closure of the straits to Israeli shipping was bound to have, particularly after reports circulated of Egyptian minelaying in strategic sea lanes leading to the port of Elath, and upon learning that the Israeli government would consider this an act of war. Still, they were hopeful that prudence and restraint would prevail until such time as a modus vivendi could emerge through the intercession of third parties and the good offices of the UN and its Secretary General.

Complicating this approach, however, was an awareness that so-called third parties were not altogether impartial. The major Western maritime powers, led by the United States, insisted that the Gulf of Aqaba was an international waterway that should remain open to international navigation. Taking the contrary view, the Soviet bloc provided staunch backing for the Egyptian position. And those states outside of the two major orbits that had not taken a stand did not seem anxious to step forward and become embroiled in a matter tangential to their central concerns. There was, of course, the International Court of Justice to which the entire matter could have been submitted for judgment. In point of fact, however, the entire issue had become so political that while it still technically could have been subject to juridical scrutiny, it had for all intents and purposes gone beyond this stage.

There remained, therefore, only the intercession of the UN whose options progressively narrowed as time went on, first by the withdrawal of UNEF and then by the coolness of the Israeli government toward the reactivation of the Egyptian-Israeli Mixed Armistice Commission (EIMAC), which had been established pursuant to the terms of the Egyptian-Israeli Armistice Agreement. It was hoped that EIMAC would provide a limited form of UN presence in the area to keep the antagonists apart. Israel, however, had long since denounced EIMAC; it had for some years refused to have anything to do with it.[19]

18. For summaries of the debates within the Security Council and the General Assembly see *UN Monthly Chronicle,* June and July 1967.

19. *UN Monthly Chronicle,* June 1967, p. 8.

All that seemed left was the personal intervention of the Secretary General. The Afro-Asian states were, therefore, delighted when U Thant decided to undertake his mission to Cairo. The expectation was that perhaps personal diplomacy might succeed where other approaches failed, and they entertained the hope that others would curb their compulsion to speak out lest his mission be jeopardized.

They, therefore objected strongly to the convening of a Security Council meeting on 24 May which Canada and Denmark had called. With the exception of Japan, all of the Afro-Asian states represented on the council regarded such a move as both premature and inopportune. Ethiopia, Mali, Nigeria, and India took great pains to point out that council action at this stage would be precipitate and that any discussion at this juncture could only complicate the Secretary General's tasks.[20] Besides, neither Israel nor the United Arab Republic, the principal parties concerned, had seemed anxious for a Security Council debate. Indeed, of the six meetings held by the Council from 24 May to 3 June none was requested by any of the Arab states or by Israel.[21]

Given such circumstances, the Afro-Asian states were content to allow any initiatives to pass to other members of the council, a disposition which was further accentuated by the increasing revelation of great power commitments to their Middle Eastern client states. They spoke little and proposed less. In fact, during the entire discussions held by the Security Council prior to the outbreak of conflict, Ethiopia intervened five times, India only four, while Mali and Nigeria each a bare three.[22]

2. THIRD WORLD REACTION TO THE SIX-DAY WAR

Curious as it may seem, this inclination toward reticence was not checked, at least not initially, by the eruption of open hostilities between Israel and several of the Arab states on 5 June. To begin with, none of the active belligerents involved requested consideration of the matter by the Security Council, each seemingly confident in allowing the battlefield to determine the course of events. Early

20. Ibid., pp. 9–10. India seemed particularly irritated at not having been consulted about the holding of such a meeting. See *Washington Post,* 26 May 1967, p. A20.

21. Arthur Lall, *The UN and The Middle East Crisis, 1967* (New York: Columbia University Press, 1968), p. 109.

22. Ibid., p. 108.

reports emanating from the region were mixed and made it difficult to ascertain who among the combatants had launched the first attack. Finally, it was generally recognized that for the council to be successful it had to have the agreement of the great powers and the compliance of the warring parties themselves.

It was apparent from the start of the council debates that the United States and the Soviet Union were poles apart. The former merely wished for the council to issue a call for a cease-fire, while the latter wanted to couple this with a condemnation of Israel and a demand for a withdrawal of forces to positions held on 4 June. In such circumstances, there was little that the Afro-Asian states could do. It was not possible to seek a compromise resolution since both great powers were unyielding in their stands. Furthermore, the Afro-Asian states themselves were divided and exhibited varying degrees of concern. India, which had close ties with the Arab world and with Egypt in particular, together with Mali, a member of the Casablanca grouping, favored the Soviet position.[23] Ethiopia and Nigeria, on the other hand, evinced a preference for the American approach. The deadlock was ultimately resolved, not so much by a process of debate and reasoned conversion as by developments on the battlefield. The rapid advances which Israeli forces were making on all fronts caused the Soviet Union to drop its demands and to join in a unanimous call for a cease-fire on June 6.[24]

But despite the council's action, compliance from all parties was slow in coming, and the Security Council felt constrained to issue two additional calls on 9 and 12 June demanding that all hostilities should "cease forthwith" and condemning "any and all violations of the cease-fire." [25] No difficulty attended these repeated injunctions nor the spate of humanitarian resolutions calling for respect of various conventions relating to the treatment of prisoners of war and the facilitation of the return of refugees to their homes.

3. THIRD WORLD REACTION SINCE THE SIX-DAY WAR

The disintegration of consensus quickly took place, however, when, the cease-fire having been effected, the Soviet Union submitted a revised draft resolution [26] containing two operative paragraphs. The

23. In their statements the delegates of India and Mali joined those of Bulgaria and the U.S.S.R. in condemning Israel as an aggressor state.

24. Security Council Resolution 233 (1967).

25. Resolutions 235 and 236 (1967).

26. UN Document S/7951/Rev. 2, June 13, 1967.

first condemned "Israel's aggressive activities and continued occupation" of Arab lands, while the second demanded her immediate and unconditional withdrawal from the conquered territories.

a) The Third World and the United Nations Resolutions

In separate votes, India, Mali, Bulgaria and the USSR favored both provisions, while Ethiopia and Nigeria endorsed only the second. The rest of the membership abstained and the resolution failed to receive the requisite majority. Given this rebuff, the Soviet Union issued a request for the convening of an emergency special session of the General Assembly in accordance with Article 11 of the charter.[27]

In some ways, the call for an assembly session came too soon. Inactive as the Afro-Asian states may have been, it is quite possible that had the deliberations of the council been a little more protracted they might have become somewhat more aggressive in seeking a scheme which could have commanded the support of the major powers. The likelihood of this having come about is indicated by the fairly constructive suggestions made by the Indian delegate on at least two occasions during the course of the debate. In his judgment there were four steps for the council to take: (*1*) to reinforce its call for a cease-fire and to order the withdrawal of all armed forces to positions held prior to the outbreak of hostilities; (*2*) to reactivate and strengthen existing UN machinery in the area to insure observance of the cease-fire; (*3*) to consider whether the Secretary General should dispatch a personal emissary to the Middle East with a view to reducing tensions; and (*4*) to contemplate further measures aimed at stabilizing peace in the region within a framework based on the sovereignty of all states concerned and the just rights of the Palestinian people.[28] All of these proposals, it will be remembered, were subsequently incorporated in a council resolution the following autumn on the basis of which negotiations between the Big Four got under way, and launched the mediation efforts of Ambassador Gunnar Jarring. But in the passions of the moment, there was little hope that they would succeed.

Not that the atmosphere surrounding the assembly proved any more conducive to settlement. On the contrary, the acrimony which characterized the council's discussions was magnified by the much

27. The Soviet Union did not wish to invoke the Uniting for Peace Resolution of Nov. 1950, whose legal validity the U.S.S.R. has always denied.

28. *UN Monthly Chronicle,* July 1967, pp. 18, 19, 29.

larger confines of the assembly within whose halls charges and counter charges were hurled. And the rigidities that they engendered were further intensified by the embittered and lengthy pronouncements which resounded from the lips of the scores of foreign ministers, prime ministers, and heads of state who descended upon UN headquarters in New York.

The Soviet Union took the lead in championing the Arab cause by seeking to marshall world opinion to the view that Israel had committed a premeditated act of aggression against her Arab neighbors and was refusing to withdraw from their lands. The obvious thing for the UN to do, so the Soviets argued, was for it to condemn such aggression and to demand the immediate and unconditional evacuation of Israeli troops from conquered soil. For the UN to pursue any other course, it was pointed out, would be to undermine the principles of the charter and to sanction the use of force as a method of settling disputes.

The United States, on the other hand, persisted in its position that while withdrawal of Israeli troops should in the end take place, it must at the same time be coupled with an overall agreement which would finally bring the nearly twenty years' dispute between the Arabs and Israel to an end. Were the Assembly merely to call for an immediate and unconditional withdrawal as the Arabs and Soviets would have it, then the situation would only revert to the precarious peace and brinkmanship which the region has for some time known. As such, direct negotiations were essential between the parties concerned to settle once and for all the longstanding issues of the past.

The likelihood of either position prevailing in the assembly was, from the outset, quite slim. For one thing, the majority of members was unwilling to censure Israel for her attack. There was a fairly widespread belief that, while Israel's actions were indeed illegal, they were not altogether unreasonable, and that while she may have fired the first shot, she did not start the war. Such an attitude was in the main the result of their recollections of the intemperate and inflammatory speeches of Arab spokesmen immediately preceding the war. And, as it subsequently became apparent, such a view was not merely confined to Western circles. A good number of Afro-Asian states refused to endorse the call for Israeli condemnation in the Soviet draft resolution when it was put to a vote.[29]

It also seemed fairly certain that neither side could, given the

29. See the voting tabulations on this and other drafts in ibid., pp. 78–79.

pressures operating on various delegations, muster the necessary two-thirds vote which in this instance meant the support of more than eighty states. The United States was apparently quite mindful of this for it did not put its draft resolution to the test. Finally, it was realized that even if one side managed to have its way in the assembly, all indications were that compliance would not be forthcoming from either of the belligerents involved.

As such, compromises were sought: On 4 July, the assembly had before it two draft resolutions, one submitted by Yugoslavia and a group of other nonaligned states, and another introduced by 18 Latin American states.[30] The Yugoslav draft dropped the call for condemnation featured in the Soviet proposal and concentrated instead on a call for immediate withdrawal and a request that the Secretary General both directly and through the designation of a personal representative seek ways for the resolution's implementation. The Latin American draft, on the other hand, while also calling for withdrawal, linked it with an end to all forms of belligerency between Israel and her Arab neighbors. It also requested the Security Council to continue to consider on an urgent basis the situation in the Middle East. Valiant as these efforts may have been, both drafts failed to receive the requisite two-thirds vote. The vote on the Yugoslav draft was 53 to 46, with 20 abstentions, while that on the Latin American draft was 57 to 43, with 20 abstentions.

The vote on the proposed Yugoslav resolution produced some interesting alignments. All the Moslem states, from Morocco and Mauritania in the West to Indonesia in the East, voted for it. They were joined by the Communist bloc, including Cuba, and by the majority of non-Moslem Afro-Asian states. But it also drew support from members with political ties to the United States, namely France, Greece, Japan, and Spain. Significantly enough, however, it failed to receive the endorsement of a substantial number of African states, ten of whom abstained, while eight opposed it.[31] This was all the more remarkable considering that many of those states were members of the French Community and had been since independence susceptible to the influence of France which favored the Yugoslav proposal.

The Latin American draft produced no surprises. It elicited the

30. A/L.522/Rev. 3 and A/L.523 respectively.

31. These were Botswana, Gambia, Ghana, Lesotho, Liberia, Madagascar, Malawi and Togo. The abstainers were Central African Republic, Chad, Dahomey, Ethiopia, Ivory Coast, Kenya, Niger, Rwanda, Sierra Leone, and Upper Volta.

support of nearly all the states that had opposed the Yugoslav resolution and the affirmative votes of some of the African states that had previously abstained. Conversely, it met with the opposition of those that had favored the Yugoslav draft.

Aside from various humanitarian measures, the only politically significant draft adopted by the fifth emergency special session of the assembly was one introduced by Pakistan declaring efforts by Israel to alter the status of the city of Jerusalem as invalid and calling upon Israel to rescind them. The resolution was passed by a vote of 99 to 0, with 20 abstentions.[32] All of the Latin American states endorsed it, partly because of their long-held belief that annexation of territory by force of arms was contrary to international legal norms, and partly because of the position of the Vatican which was then calling for the internationalization of Jerusalem. Being predominantly Catholic countries it would have been difficult for them to have gone against the wishes of the pope. It is nevertheless somewhat ironic that the only issue on which such an overwhelming consensus prevailed should prove itself to be precisely the one regarding which Israel has been most intractable. Indeed, hardly a week went by when the Israeli government declared, for all intents and purposes, its unwillingness to abide by the wishes of the assembly.[33]

Still, the assembly debates were not altogether useless. Out of the many speeches, behind-the-scenes negotiations, and various proposals there emerged certain common outlines which paved the way to future agreement. These were that Israel should in the end withdraw her troops from occupied Arab lands; that all belligerency between her and her neighbors should cease; that the sovereignty of all states in the region be recognized; that a just settlement of the refugee problem ought to be sought; that all waterways should be open to all shipping without discrimination; that UN machinery be reactivated in the area; and that the Secretary General both directly and through the designation of a personal representative should do all in his powers to effect a settlement. All of these proposals were, of course, incorporated in the now celebrated council resolution of November 1967 proposed by Lord Caradon.

32. Res. 2253 (ES-V), 4 July 1967. Israel did not participate in the vote on the grounds that the issue of Jerusalem was "outside the legal competence of the General Assembly." *New York Times,* 5 July 1967, p. 1. The United States was among the abstainers.

33. See the text of Foreign Minister Abba Eban's letter to U Thant in *New York Times,* 12 July 1967, p. 14.

b) The Third World and the First Cease-Fire

Salutary though the acceptance of these principles by the great powers was, they nevertheless merely succeeded in deferring for future bargaining the most thorny of the issues at hand. In an effort to win the necessary concurrence for the resolution, the British representative couched its contents in such general and, sometimes, vague terms that it was destined ultimately to conflicting and at times seemingly irreconcilable interpretations. Without a doubt, of course, a certain measure of ambiguity in the resolution had to be contrived, or else its chances for passage would have diminished with each increase in specificity. And it is really a testimony to the diplomatic skills of its sponsor that the resolution tackled the complex questions in the manner that it did and still managed to command the consensus of the council's membership.

Be that as it may, no sooner had the resolution been adopted than the parties directly concerned began to ascribe to its contents certain tendentious meanings more suited to their respective interests and likings. The Arab states, on the one hand, hailed the resolution as a call for a total and immediate Israeli withdrawal from occupied lands and as an affirmation that any territorial adjustments of frontiers would be minor; that termination of all belligerency did not entail recognition of Israel or direct negotiation with her; and that a "just" settlement of the refugee problem meant an unrestricted choice for the Palestinians to return to their land if they so wished. Israel, on the other hand, was quick to point out that while the resolution did demand a pullback of Israeli forces from conquered territories it did not explicitly call for withdrawal from *all* occupied areas, nor did it spell out *when* such withdrawal was to take place. The settlement of such questions, it was argued, could only be arrived at through direct negotiations between the parties concerned without interference from the great powers or even the UN.[34] As to other matters covered by the resolution, they too would be the subject of bargaining within a framework of mutually recognized sovereignties.

Given such a polarity of viewpoints, the prospects for the resolution of differences seemed from the outset quite remote. It was recognized that the attainment of any settlement, interim or otherwise,

34. For a concise summary of the Israeli position see Shabtai Rosenne, "Directions for a Middle East Settlement—Some Underlying Problems," *Law and Contemporary Problems* 33, Winter 1968, No. 1 (The Middle East Crisis: Test of International Law).

would require not only an inordinate amount of skillful mediation on the part of the Secretary General's special representative (Gunnar Jarring), but the active cooperation of the two superpowers as well. The prevailing impression was that if left to themselves the Arabs and Israelis were unlikely to come to terms and that therefore it was essential for the United States and USSR to apply sufficient pressure on their respective wards in the region to bring them to heel. However, what was perhaps lacking in such thinking was the realization that the degree of influence and control which great powers have over client states is far from complete and that, furthermore, in certain circumstances the influence which small states could in turn exert on their patrons is not altogether miniscule. In other words, even if in this instance the two superpowers were in accord on the terms for a Middle East settlement, compliance from the states directly concerned would neither be automatic, nor assured.

In any event, consensus among all parties was not forthcoming, despite the valiant efforts of Jarring. For nearly two years he shuttled between various capitals seemingly to no avail. But the world was not discouraged, taking solace from the belief that deplorable though the situation was, fruitless negotiation was preferable to war.

c) The Third World and the War of Attrition

Such thoughts, however, were quickly dissipated when in an effort to refocus attention on the urgency of the Middle East situation and in fear that the continued relative tranquility on the Suez Canal would ultimately lull the world into indifference and thereby cause the cease-fire lines to harden into permanent boundaries, Egyptian President Nasser declared in the spring of 1969 that the cease-fire was null and void. He further stated that the Egyptian armed forces would henceforth embark on a "war of attrition" aimed at exhausting Israeli troops along the canal. Open hostilities ensued, with Israeli retaliating through heavy aerial strikes with United States–built Phantoms against Egyptian military, and ultimately industrial, targets both along the canal as well as inside the Nile Delta. The object of these raids in the Israeli view was not only to impede any Egyptian preparations for another war, but also to break the will of the Egyptian people and make them sue for peace.[35] So intense became the engagements that Secretary General U Thant felt impelled to report to the General Assembly in the fall of 1969 that

35. *New York Times*, 17 January 1970.

for all intents and purposes "war [was] being waged throughout the area, short only of battles between large bodies of troops." [36]

Dangerous as the situation was, it became even more fraught with ominous possibilities when in response to deep Israeli penetration of Egyptian skies the Soviet Union acceded to an urgent Egyptian request for more advanced weapons to ward off Israeli incursions. In March 1970, Soviet technicians began installing and manning SAM-3 ground-to-air missiles at various points within Egypt. Furthermore Russian pilots were reportedly flying advanced Mig-23 fighter-bombers in order to provide a protective umbrella over vast areas of Egyptian territory.

In other areas of the cease-fire between Israel and her Arab neighbors events were equally bleak. Israeli planes and troops frequently struck against bases of Palestinian guerrillas who had become an important factor in the Middle East equation as well as an increasing source of discomfort to Israel. These raids were not merely confined to Jordan and Syria, but also extended to Lebanon which even though it did not participate in the June War was nevertheless becoming increasingly drawn into the circle of violence and counterviolence owing to the attacks which the Palestinians planned and launched from its soil against Israeli border settlements and broader world interests. Indeed, some of these reprisals proved quite severe, as in the nearly total destruction of Lebanon's civilian air fleet at Beirut's internationl airport.

d) The Third World and the 1970 Cease-Fire

In an effort to halt this drift into deeper crises, United States Secretary of State William Rogers proposed in the summer of 1970 the establishment of a temporary cease-fire for at least ninety days during which Egypt, Israel, and Jordan would, through intercession of UN mediator Gunnar Jarring, formulate a plan for the implementation of the Security Council's November 1967 resolution. Such a plan would have to be based on the twin principles of mutual acknowledgment of sovereignty on the part of all states concerned and on Israeli withdrawal from territories occupied in the June War. Furthermore, it would be understood that neither side would use the cease-fire period to bolster its military posture at the front.

Acceptance of the Rogers plan posed difficulties for both sides.

36. GAOR, *Introduction to the Annual Report of the Secretary General*, 24th Session, 1969, Supplement No. 1A (A/7601/ Add. 1).

For Israel it meant an agreement in principle to withdraw from occupied territories, a position which was repugnant to a substantial segment of the Israeli public and to certain factions within Premier Golda Meir's coalition government. For Egypt and Jordan it entailed recognition, tacit or otherwise, of Israeli sovereignty, something which several Arab states and Palestinian guerrillas were loathe to accept.

Given the risks, it was understandable that response to the American initiative was slow in coming. But in due course, first Egypt, then Jordan, and finally Israel concurred, and on 7 August 1970 the cease-fire took effect.[37]

Ironically enough, however, no sooner had the guns fallen silent in the Suez Canal area than full-scale civil war raged in Jordan between Palestinian guerrillas and Jordanian forces. Syria threatened to, and actually did for a brief period, intervene on the side of the Palestinians, while Israel massed some of her armored units along the Jordan River and declared that she could not remain indifferent to political and military shifts on her eastern front. Meanwhile, the United States Sixth Fleet in the Mediterranean was placed on alert and the possibility of American involvement was not altogether ruled out. The Soviet Union responded to these developments in bellicose terms, and the spectre of a confrontation between the two superpowers again loomed large. But the crisis soon eased, partly because of the exercise of self-restraint and mainly due to the subjugation of the Palestinian guerrillas by the Jordanian army. Still, the situation remained precarious, and it was this realization which ultimately prompted Secretary of State Rogers to launch his proposal for an interim settlement.

Conclusion

The Afro-Asian states' reaction to all these developments has been by and large somewhat distant and aloof. They had become even more entrenched in their belief that in the final analysis the entire problem and its solution fell squarely in the domain of the superpowers and those directly concerned. They could, of course, exhort, appeal, plead, urge, prod, and even on occasion censure. And this

37. The cease-fire was twice extended, then allowed to lapse. However, it has been observed and has generally been quite effective, even though there were charges made by Israel regarding the movement of additional surface to air missiles by Egypt into the Canal sector, contrary to prior understandings.

they had done on numerous occasions both within and outside of the confines of the UN.[38] But there is noticeable a certain detachment which is even greater than that which they displayed immediately preceding and following the June War. The Arab States, and particularly Egypt, have, quite naturally, sought to mobilize the support of the Third World by appealing to Afro-Asian solidarity and to the religious bonds of Islam. The response to these invocations has, however, been faint and far from unanimous.[39] Even the fire at Al-Aqsa Mosque failed to ignite the necessary fervor and to bring on more than a temporary closing of ranks. Indeed, the divisions which characterized the Islamic conferences in Morocco and Saudi Arabia still stand in sad relief to the optimism that was then gushing from the minarets. And aside from occasional expressions of sympathy and support which the Arab states have received from Asia and Africa, the role of the Third World has been essentially passive: to sit in judgment on the great powers and to mourn with the oppressed in their distress.

38. Well over 35 separate resolutions relating to the Mid-East crisis have been passed by the UN General Assembly and Security Council since 14 June 1967.

39. At the Foreign Ministers' Conference of the OAU in Addis Ababa in 1970 seven African States abstained from endorsing a message of "total solidarity and sympathy" to the UAR in its confrontation with Israel. These were Dahomey, Gabon, Lesotho, Swaziland, Rwanda, Sierra Leone, and Malawi. *New York Times,* 2 March 1970, p. 36. A few months earlier, several African states actually voted against a UN General Assembly resolution (Res. 2535 B) reaffirming the "inalienable rights of the people of Palestine." These were Botswana, Chad, Gabon, Gambia, Liberia, Malawi, Rwanda, and Swaziland. A much larger number of Afro-Asian states abstained, namely Burma, Cameroon, Central African Republic, Ethiopia, Ghana, Ivory Coast, Japan, Kenya, Laos, Lesotho, Madagascar, Nepal, Niger, Philippines, Sierra Leone, Togo, Uganda, and Upper Volta. *UN Monthly Chronicle* 7, No. 1, January 1970, pp. 89–90.

Part III

American Policy Formation for the Middle East Forces at Work in a Domestic System

CHAPTER 11

Domestic Influences on United States Foreign Policy in the Middle East: The View from Washington

WILLIAM B. QUANDT

Perhaps no other area of American foreign policy has focused on itself as much domestic interest and attempts at influence as the Middle East. The oil interests and Zionists rank highest in the popular mind as Middle Eastern lobbyists. But this view is only partially correct, according to the author.

Pressure *is not the word to describe efforts of oil companies, for example, to affect American policy in the Middle East. Rather, they appeal to interests and attempt to explain problems of the oil industry. Operating quite differently from pro-Israeli groups, the oil companies pursue a low-key strategy. They themselves have very little effect, in essence, on Arab-Israeli issues.*

The Arab-Israeli conflict has had a way of dominating other American interests in the Middle East during the past two decades. The question is whether or not it will continue to do so in the 1970s. Will the Middle East itself be viewed as vital to United States interests in the 1970s, for example, as it had been earlier? Are there new domestic factors that will influence United States policy decision-making in the Middle East in the present decade? The author looks at the total problem.

Introduction

The process by which foreign decisions are made is complex and often perplexing, not only to outside observers but also to the participants themselves. When this awkward process, dominated by bureaucratic rivalries, the rhetoric of "national interest," and the pressures of interest groups, Congress, and the press, is applied to the formation of policy for the Middle East, the results are often particularly opaque. Of the numerous issues of concern to the

United States in the Middle East, the Arab-Israeli conflict has a way of dominating other interests, in large part because of its intractability, its potential for violence, and the conflicting interests and emotions surrounding it. Consequently, a study of the formulation of United States policy toward the Arab-Israeli conflict, with particular attention paid to domestic influences, serves to illustrate the general problems of decision-making in complex organizations in all their variety, richness, and confusion.

Middle East Policymakers

To understand how American policy in the Middle East is made, it is necessary to break down the image of the United States government as a unitary rational actor. In fact, the number of relatively high-level officials engaged in writing memos, reports, speeches, and analyses of the Arab-Israeli problem probably exceeds fifty in Washington alone. At least four major departments within the executive branch deal with Arab-Israeli affairs and each of these contains subdivisions which differ among themselves as to appropriate policies.

At the center of the policy-making process are the president and the White House staff. The president has ultimate responsibility for foreign affairs, but he is limited in the degree to which he is able to keep abreast of all of the problems requiring his attention. Nor is his staff large enough to do the entire job. Consequently, the White House is primarily the recipient, the collator, and finally the arbiter of the suggestions, recommendations, and studies that are produced throughout the government. In addition to the president himself, the other major actors dealing with Arab-Israeli affairs on the White House staff are the White House coordinator, or national security affairs adviser—McGeorge Bundy under President Kennedy, Walt Rostow under Johnson, and Henry Kissinger under Nixon—and his assistants for the Near East, North Africa, and South Asia. Most presidents also choose to have a minority affairs adviser on their staff, a post that has included in its functions the responsibility of dealing with American Jewish groups sympathetic to Israel. Under President Truman, David Niles filled this role, as did Myer Feldman for Kennedy and Harry MacPherson for Johnson. Needless to say, the advice the president receives from his own staff is often inconsistent.

The State Department, as the executor, and, at times, formulator of policy on the Arab-Israeli conflict, has at its disposal the largest number of experts on the Middle East. The secretary of state himself, and often his under-secretaries as well, are likely to become closely involved in the making of Middle East policy. The area expertise, however, lies at a lower level in the department, particularly in the Bureau of Near East and South Asian Affairs; in the Intelligence and Research division (INR); with the ambassadors and representatives in the various Middle East countries; and on the Policy Planning Staff or the Planning and Coordination staff as it has been called since 1970. In addition, the delegate to the United Nations and the Bureau of International Organizations in the State Department frequently become involved in Middle East problems. Finally, the Agency for International Development (AID) may play an important part in decisions concerning economic assistance to Middle East countries.

The Near East and South Asia bureau is presided over by an assistant secretary of state and his deputy assistant secretaries for the countries of the Near East. In addition, each major country or region has a country director—one for Egypt, the Fertile Crescent countries, the Arabian Peninsula, and one specifically for Israel and for Arab-Israeli affairs. The North African countries of Morocco, Algeria, Tunisia, and Libya are dealt with by the assistant secretary for African affairs and country directors under him. The country directors remain in close touch with United States embassies in their areas of responsibility, and are heavily involved in day-to-day problems. The Intelligence and Research branch, which is also organized along regional and country lines, is expected to work on more general, less immediate problems, providing both background information and estimates of trends into the future.

The Department of Defense also gets in on the act of policymaking on Arab-Israeli problems. Military questions are only part of the concern of the Department of Defense, but it is here that they speak most authoritatively. Three groups within the Pentagon should be distinguished. First, the office of the secretary of defense is frequently consulted on matters of high-level policy. Second, the Joint Chiefs of Staff are also brought into the picture on matters involving military aid and on operational questions. Regional expertise on the Middle East, however, is primarily found in the International Security Affairs (ISA) branch, where a deputy assistant secretary for the Near East and South Asia heads a group of specialists on Arab-Israeli problems. ISA and the Joint Chiefs of Staff at times reach quite dissimilar conclusions on such matters as military aid.

Finally, the intelligence services, including the Central Intelligence Agency (CIA), the Defense Intelligence Agency (DIA), and the National Security Agency (NSA), play an important role in gathering and evaluating information concerning the Middle East. While none of these agencies takes an official stand on policy alternatives, the process of collecting, analyzing, and reporting on developments in the area has a major impact on the perceptions and understanding of the parts of the government which are involved in making policy.

The importance of cataloging these subdivisions within the White House, the State Department, the Department of Defense, and the intelligence community is that these units represent the closest things to unitary actors in the bureaucratic game of politics. Individuals within these subdivisions interact frequently with each other, less frequently with other agencies, and as a result often hold rather similar opinions. Consequently, papers are often drafted by individuals in these units and purport to represent "the ISA position," the "Joint Chief's position," or the opinion of the Bureau of Near Eastern Affairs in the State Department. Policy-makers often refer to alternative courses of action by the name of the sponsor of that position. Particularly in the early stages of examining alternatives, it is not unusual for ISA, the Secretary of Defense, the Joint Chiefs, the regional bureau, the Secretary of State, and the White House staff to be pushing for quite different policies.

Outside the circle of official policymakers in the executive branch lie several other important groups. Congress, of course, plays an important role in the making and unmaking of policy in the Middle East, as does the press. Arab-Israeli issues have the peculiar property of raising passions and interests of many Americans, and consequently organized interest groups try to play a role in determining United States policies. Most noteworthy of these groups are a variety of pro-Israeli and Zionist groups, oil companies, several pro-Arab organizations, and representatives of cultural and religious groups with interests in the region. Perhaps more important than these formal organizations are influential individuals with special access to the president, congressmen, or the secretary of state. These may include large campaign contributors, friends of the president, or simply prominent Americans in public and private life. Beyond these specific points of contact, of course, lies American public opinion at large, occasionally, if not always, exercising a determining influence on foreign policy.

The Influencing of Policy Decisions

The study of power and influence lies at the core of contemporary political science, and yet widespread dissatisfaction and disagreement exist with respect to these concepts. Just as the concept of the government as a unitary, rational actor is misleading, so also are the terms *power* and *influence*. A first step toward clarifying these concepts requires some elaboration of the scope and the means of influence.

No single individual or interest group is able to affect the whole range of decisions that constitute United States policy toward the Arab-Israeli conflict. The major issue areas that should be distinguished are composed of policy decisions concerning diplomatic-political positions, economic aid, and military assistance. Diplomatic-political decisions involve questions of supporting policies favored by Israel or the Arabs; using pressure and inducements to alter the policies of parties to the dispute; concluding alliances or reaffirming close ties; and sending high-ranking officials on visits.

Examples of policy decisions in the economic realm are the granting of aid, credits, and favorable terms for loans. In the past, the United States has tried to use aid as an instrument of policy by offering to help construct the High Dam at Aswan in Egypt and by providing surplus wheat to the United Arab Republic. At frequent intervals, the Congress has been interested in providing aid to Israel to build a desalting plant, and the Israelis have received large sums of economic aid to improve their balance of payments situation.

Military assistance is frequently seen as a key element of United States policy in the Middle East, but until recently the United States had tried to avoid becoming a major supplier of arms to Arabs or Israelis. In the past few years, however, Israel, Jordan, and Saudi Arabia have been heavily dependent on the United States for arms, and both Presidents Johnson and Nixon have had to confront the issue of whether to provide high performance aircraft and other sophisticated military equipment to Israel in the face of Arab displeasure.

The means available to interest groups or private citizens for influencing various parts of the bureaucracy with respect to these issue areas are remarkably diverse. Generally speaking, influence attempts involve some combination of threat and promise, often coupled with an appeal to national interests. Direct pressure may come in the form of a threat to withhold campaign contributions, to withdraw political support on a wide range of policy issues, or to attack the government directly through the press and other mass media. Alternately, persuasion may involve the trading of favors, promises of future support, and cooperation on unrelated issues. A very important ingredient in the efforts of interest groups is to raise the saliency of the problems they are concerned with, to define alternatives, and to arouse public opinion.

The relationship between interest groups and government officials is more complex than a simple mechanistic model would suggest. Of the many parts of the government dealing with Arab-Israeli affairs, the State Department, Congress, and the White House are the most frequent targets of direct influence attempts by domestic groups. Policy alternatives are generally known to be favored or opposed by interested parties, and the actions of groups and individuals are frequently anticipated by decision-makers. The expectation of negative reactions to specific policies may serve to eliminate an otherwise promising initiative, without the interest group ever being heard from. At times, however, the government officials take the step of calling in representatives of pro-Israeli organizations or of oil companies.[1] Their views are solicited, explanations are given, and frequently the occasion is used to try to convince the representatives of these interests to understand the government's position and to explain it to their members or supporters. Lobbying, then, is very much of a two-way street, a bargaining process in which the interest groups—and through them public opinion—are as much the target of persuasion as is the government.

Interest Groups

Pro-Israeli organizations and individuals sympathetic to Israel have for over two decades made efforts to influence United States policy on Arab-Israeli issues. Attention has been paid to cultivating relationships with the White House, in Congress, and with the mass media.

1. For example, in early 1970, after a U.S. initiative opposed by Israel, the Assistant Secretary for Near Eastern and South Asian Affairs, Joseph Sisco, took the initiative in calling a meeting with representatives of the Conference of Presidents of Jewish Organizations to explain U.S. policy. See the *Jerusalem Post*, 16 January 1970, p. 2.

The State Department also frequently hears from pro-Israeli groups but is generally less responsive than the elected officials. Requests are made for political, economic, and military support of Israel, and protests are lodged against policies seen as too pro-Arab. The greatest successes of the pro-Israeli groups lie in influencing elected officials to make declarations of political support for Israel and in generating sympathy on the part of the American public at large for Israel. On specific issues of economic and military aid, the record of successful lobbying is less positive.[2]

Oil companies operate quite differently from pro-Israeli groups. Oil is widely recognized to be an interest of growing importance for the United States in the Middle East, for its input to the European economy, for its favorable contribution to the United States balance of payments, and for direct U.S. consumption. Oil companies per se generally pursue a low-keyed strategy of explaining what is at stake in the Arab world. Appeals to public opinion and to Congress are not generally made. Instead, contacts are kept open with the State Department, the Pentagon, and the White House. *Pressure* is hardly the word to describe the efforts of oil companies with respect to Arab-Israeli issues. Rather, appeals to interests and attempts to explain problems of the oil industry highlight the efforts of oil representatives. Without a public voice, the oil companies do not carry as much weight as the pro-Israelis. In addition, they are less ambitious, trying merely to temper the United States position on the Arab-Israeli conflict and pushing for particular favors from the Administration when oil problems arise. The radical Arab states are not helped by oil company efforts in their relations with the United States. On the contrary, whatever influence oil companies have tends to work in favor of Saudi Arabia, Kuwait, and Iran.

The other organized interests concerned with Arab-Israeli affairs are either too weak to weigh heavily on the scales of policy-making or limit themselves to very narrow issues. Numerous pro-Arab groups exist, and their representatives at times talk with officials, but their constituency is limited and their impact is modest.[3] Groups

2. On 30 January 1970, shortly after Jewish leaders had convened in Washington to discuss reactions to recent U.S. policy initiatives, President Nixon announced that within one month he would announce his decision on whether to sell Israel more Phantom and Skyhawk jet aircraft. The timing of this announcement, but not the final decision, reflected the influence of this interest group.

3. On occasion, Under Secretary of State Elliott Richardson received pro-Arab groups, including a delegation led by John Davis, ex-head of UNWRA, in late January 1970.

with cultural or humanitarian concerns may be effective in maintaining United States government concern with American cultural institutions and with the plight of Palestinian refugees. But no one is arguing strongly against these interests, and few major policy choices are involved.

The general image of the policy-making process is thus one of numerous competing groups within the bureaucracy pushing for alternative policies. Some parts of the government are in closer contact with interest groups and more responsive to public opinion than others, and this may be reflected in their preferred alternatives. Pro-Israelis press for a wide range of decisions, often in a public manner, while oil companies deal rather quietly with a more limited range of topics. While communications among all of these actors are frequent, the result of the process at any given time will heavily depend upon external factors, especially developments in Soviet policy and in the Arab-Israeli conflict itself. Some recent examples may help to clarify the interactions within the government and between government agencies, interest groups, and public opinion.

United States Policy since the June War

Since the Arab-Israeli war of June 1967, United States policy has occasionally shifted from a very close identification with fundamental Israeli positions toward a somewhat more evenhanded stance. At critical points, domestic factors have had some impact upon the decisions of policy-makers, generally in the direction of restoring closer United States–Israeli ties.

1. DIPLOMATIC INITIATIVES

Within days of the outbreak of the war, several important guidelines for policy were laid down. First, Israel should not be required to withdraw from occupied Arab lands in the absence of a full peace settlement. There would be no repeat of 1957, for fear that a return to armistice agreements would once again prove unstable and another round of war would ensue.

Second, despite some irritation that Israel had preempted in the June War, there was a strong feeling that President Nasser was largely to blame for the war and that he should be made to pay a substantial price for recovering the Sinai.[4] In addition, American officials were generally relieved that Israel had been able to win the war rapidly without outside help. The worst imaginable situation for the United States, it was widely believed, would be an imminent Israeli defeat that would put pressure on the United States to intervene. The combination of these fears and perceptions led United States government officials to conclude that it was in the American interest to keep Israel strong—primarily as a way of reducing the need for American involvement in the Middle East at a time when Vietnam was absorbing most of the energies of top officials.

The guidelines for American policy—no Israeli withdrawal without peace and maintenance of Israeli military strength—were easily adopted, in part because of the overwhelmingly pro-Israeli tone of United States public opinion at the time of the war. One high-level official reported a leading pollster's comment that during the war public opinion had rarely been so united on any foreign policy issue as in support of Israel. President Johnson and many of his top advisers—Walt Rostow, Eugene Rostow, Arthur Goldberg, and McGeorge Bundy—seemed to share this generally sympathetic feeling toward Israel. With such agreement among the top leadership, Congress, pro-Israeli interest groups, and public opinion at large, the Johnson administration was under little pressure to do anything immediately other than to work for international acceptance of the idea that Israel should not be required to withdraw in the absence of peace. On 19 June President Johnson made a major policy address in which he set forth the elements of a "package settlement," and over the next few months American diplomats worked to have these principles incorporated in a United Nations resolution. The 22 November 1967 resolution was sufficiently ambiguous that all parties, albeit with reservations, could accept its terms. Once the resolution was adopted and Ambassador Gunnar Jarring had begun his contacts with the Arabs and Israelis, United States diplomacy limited itself to behind-the-scenes efforts to induce flexibility into Arab and Israeli positions. The United States never fully supported all Israeli positions, but points of disagreement were not publicly voiced.

By the fall of 1968, debate within the Johnson administration was under way concerning the wisdom of adhering to a policy of limited involvement in defining the terms of settlement. The ten-

4. This attitude was clearly reflected in President Johnson's speech of 19 June 1967.

sions between Arabs and Israelis were rising, moderate Arabs were being put on the defensive throughout the Arab world, the Palestinian commando movement was growing, and Israeli terms for a settlement were hardening. Two Israeli contentions were increasingly questioned: first, the forces at work in the area did not seem likely to lead to peace in the absence of outside intervention; second, Israel's early disclaimer of any desire for territorial acquisitions was being eroded by the facts of life of administering new areas. Consequently, in November 1968, the United States, in accord with State Department recommendations, took the initiative of clarifying its position on territorial withdrawal in the context of peace. Secretary of State Dean Rusk is reported to have told Egyptian Foreign Minister Mahmoud Riad that as part of a total settlement Israel should withdraw to the old international frontier between Palestine and Egypt. Similar, though less precise, assurances had been given to the Jordanians earlier in the year. Despite these modest initiatives, however, the United States government was unwilling to announce publicly its preferred terms for a settlement. It should be noted that these initiatives were not the result of domestic pressures, least of all from oil companies—although Johnson did see two presidents of oil companies after the war—but rather stemmed from a concern with developments in the region and the apparent drift toward renewed war.

President Nixon came to office with several alternatives open to him. He could pursue the Johnson policy of relative detachment from the conflict. Or he could become more actively involved in the search for a diplomatic settlement by talking with the Soviets, the British, and French, and directly with Arabs and Israelis. Finally, he could limit his initiatives to the search for partial, ad hoc means of reducing tensions without trying for an overall settlement. Very early in his administration, Nixon seems to have consciously decided to engage the United States more actively in the search for peace. In doing so, he appeared willing to risk alienating the Israelis by taking positions that they found objectionable. If the United States were to get out in front of the Israelis, without fully losing their confidence, and if the Soviets would do likewise with the Egyptians, perhaps minimally acceptable terms for a settlement could be found. In any case, even if the effort were to fail it seemed to be worth trying.

In April 1969, over strenuous Israeli objections, United States–Soviet talks on the Middle East officially began. Over the next few months various proposals were presented by both sides. Some areas of agreement appeared, but two major points stood out as matters of contention. The United States government refused to say explicitly that Israel should withdraw from all Arab territory in return for peace, and the Soviets refused to commit themselves to specific language on Arab obligations toward Israel after a settlement. Each side tried to get the other to reveal the minimum terms of its fall-back position. Meanwhile, Arab and Israeli interests were being effectively presented to the United States government by the representatives of the concerned countries. Once again, domestic forces played little role in the conduct of these negotiations other than to caution the United States side not to strain unduly its relations with Israel.

By the fall of 1969, a series of incidents led to a growing concern on the part of the United States that its position in the Arab world was deteriorating. The prolonged crisis in Lebanon, strong expressions of anti-Americanism in the Arab world following the delivery of Phantom jets to Israel in September, and the overthrow of the monarchy in Libya in that same month all served as danger signs. Sometime in October it was decided that the United States should go ahead and publicly reveal its fall-back position calling for virtually complete Israeli withdrawal in the context of a peace settlement. Several objectives might thereby be served. First, the Soviets might eventually be willing to push their clients to make concessions and this could marginally increase the chances for a settlement. Second, the United States would not seem quite so firmly tied to Israel as most Arabs believed, and this might give some encouragement to moderate Arab leadership. Third, this would put the Israelis on notice that their increasing appetite for territory would not receive United States support, a position long stressed in private but never taken too seriously by Israel. On 28 October a proposed working paper of ten points dealing with an Egyptian-Israeli settlement was given to the Soviets. On 9 December Secretary of State Rogers gave a somewhat overdue speech that revealed much of the content of the proposals. Finally, on 18 December on the eve of the Arab Summit Conference at Rabat, the United States presented a proposed Israeli-Jordanian plan in the Big Four talks in New York.

Behind these gradual changes in United States policy during 1969 lay a concern with developments in the Arab world and with the rising level of violence between the Arabs and Israelis. Domestic factors played a relatively small role directly in making these assessments. In early December, President Nixon did meet with American businessmen with interests in the Middle East and with links to the oil industry, and he was presumably warned of the erosion of the United States position in the Arab world. It would be quite inaccurate, however, to link Secretary Rogers' speech to any pressures brought to bear by these businessmen. The rationale for taking the steps outlined by Rogers had been developed long before, and Rogers himself appears to have become convinced of its soundness. The regional bureau of the State Department was clearly the strongest supporter of these initiatives, since it had been pushing for such proposals for over two years without success.

After Rogers delivered his speech he was strongly criticized by American Jewish groups for endangering Israel and for undercutting her bargaining position. At least two major pro-Israeli delegations talked to Rogers at length during December and January. One may assume that he used the occasion to inform them of his reasons for giving the speech, and that they did much of the listening after having lodged their initial complaints. Further efforts to pressure the United States government to change its policy took place in early 1970, with concentration on influencing the President directly.[5] Those active in this effort were the Conference of Presidents of Major Jewish Organizations and Jewish Republicans led by Max Fisher, a Detroit industrialist who served President Nixon as White House adviser on urban affairs.

The response to Secretary Rogers' speech and to the United States proposals on the part of pro-Israeli groups virtually insured that no further pro-Arab initiatives would soon be taken. American policy can afford to be at odds with Israel to some degree, but in the absence of obvious benefits from adopting an evenhanded position, the administration would find it difficult to put further pressure on Israel. This, in part, does stem from a concern with the level of domestic opposition than can be mounted by pro-Israeli groups. Republican administrations have traditionally felt less vulnerable on this score—it is estimated that Nixon received only 17 percent of the Jewish vote in 1968—but any politician, particularly in an election year, will try to avoid alienating an articulate and influential minority, as the 1972 elections demonstrated. Thus, domestic factors do seem to enter into consideration by defining bound-

5. On 8 January 1970, the President of the World Jewish Congress Dr. Nahum Goldmann, stated that: "The Jews in America still live under the illusion that the Truman era continues—but it does not. There is no Jew in America now who can phone the President at any time." *Jerusalem Post,* 9 January 1970, p. 8.

aries beyond which it seems imprudent to step. This restriction of the scope of possible initiatives has been the most visible effect of domestic factors over the past few years and generally seems more important than the influence of domestic factors in bringing acceptance of favored policies. It is easier to limit the scope of new departures and to inject notes of caution than it is to obtain all that one wants.

While Secretary Rogers' speech and proposals of late 1969 remained the basis for United States policy for a settlement during the following two years, efforts were nonetheless required on the diplomatic front to keep the Arab-Israeli conflict from deteriorating into full-scale war. These initiatives were prompted by developments in the region and by the growing Soviet involvement in the conflict rather than by domestic pressures. In the spring of 1970, direct contacts with Egypt's President Nasser were made, reflecting a departure from the earlier American approach of dealing with Egypt through the USSR. Encouraging Egyptian responses, plus rapid escalation of the military conflict along the Suez Canal, prompted a new United States peace initiative on 19 June 1970. Essentially the proposal called for a limited stand-still cease-fire and indirect negotiations aimed at reaching a settlement along the lines sketched in the 22 November 1967 UN resolution. After one month of intense bilateral negotiations with Israel and Egypt, the United States was able to persuade both parties to accept the proposal. A cease-fire went into effect during the first week of August 1970.

Within days of the cease-fire, accusations were being made, especially by Israel, that Egypt was introducing new military equipment into the stand-still zone. Nearly two weeks were required for the United States to confirm that there had been significant violations of the cease-fire by Egypt, and by that time Israel had also technically violated the agreement. Consequently, the United States worked primarily to keep the two parties from resuming the fighting and to agree to indirect negotiations through Ambassador Jarring rather than trying for a return to the status quo ante. Movement toward peace talks was disrupted in September 1970 by the outbreak of fighting in Jordan between Palestinian commandos and Jordanian troops. Both the United States and Israel made signs of willingness to intervene in the fighting after Syrian troops entered Jordan. Before any such actions were taken, the brief civil war was brought to an end under pressure from President Nasser on 27 September. The following day, Nasser died of a heart attack, ushering in a new era of uncertainty in the Middle East.

Once the Egyptian regime under President Anwar al-Sadat had recovered from Nasser's death, new United States diplomatic moves were launched to get negotiations started. Sadat proved to be surprisingly conciliatory and flexible, which was greatly appreciated by United States officials. Sadat not only accepted the idea of indirect talks, but also in February 1971 he officially stated that Egypt was prepared to make peace with Israel in return for full Israeli withdrawal from the occupied territories and a settlement of the Palestinian refugee problem. In addition, Sadat proposed that as a first step toward a full peace settlement, the Suez Canal should be reopened. The United States welcomed this suggestion, and served as intermediary in subsequent negotiations on the topic with Israel during the spring of 1971.

As part of these diplomatic initiatives, the United States exerted some influence on Israel to be more forthcoming on terms of a settlement. First, Israel agreed to accept the United Nations security resolution as the basis for peace. Second, Israel used the word "withdrawal" in describing her obligations in a settlement. Third, Israel reluctantly agreed to talk to Egypt through Jarring and the United States rather than directly.

By mid-1971, expectations were running high that a United States–sponsored peace agreement between Egypt and Israel was impending. Secertary of State Rogers visited Cairo just as Sadat was ousting his allegedly pro-Soviet advisers, adding to speculations that peace was just around the corner. Sadat was reportedly told that the United States was pleased with his willingness to end the conflict with Israel and that he should now be patient while the United States "delivered" Israel. Israel, however, was in no mood to be delivered, and Assistant Secretary Joseph Sisco was told so in no uncertain terms when he visited Israel in July. The United States was unwilling at this point to use heavy-handed pressure to force Israel to comply, and thus ended for all practical purposes the United States peace initiative. The degree to which domestic politics influenced United States decisions at this time is unknown, but certainly the Israelis knew that they could afford to hold out against United States pressure until 1972. Then, in an election year, the President would be very reluctant to take an anti-Israeli position. The United States government must have also realized that Israel could outwait the Nixon Administration, and that the stakes simply did not seem to warrant a major arm-twisting effort. Consequently, the initiative was allowed to die a slow death in the remainder of 1971 for lack of White House support.

This development should have resulted in a dramatic setback for United States policy in the Arab world, leading to a sharp polarization between a United States-backed Israel and Soviet-supported Egypt. Other factors, however, intervened to confound such predictions. Washington and Moscow began to talk of detente with respect to major issues of arms control and European security. The Middle East was rapidly losing significance for the Soviet Union in comparison to these areas of interest and the possible dangers of United States–Chinese rapprochement. In addition, the Soviets were unable to help Egypt resolve the conflict with Israel by peaceful means and were unwilling to help Cairo make war. By mid-1972, President Sadat, clearly under great domestic pressures, made a daring historic decision to expel Soviet military personnel from Egypt.

Sadat's dramatic action caught the United States in the midst of an election campaign. Until then, virtually no candidate had discussed the Middle East in terms other than the degree of support for Israel. Senator George McGovern came under severe attacks for being allegedly soft on Israel, and in response he tried to outbid his rivals by claiming that he would be the first President to visit Israel while in office, would favor recognition of Jerusalem as Israel's capital, and would provide Israel all the arms it needed. With the exception of Congresswoman Shirley Chisholm, no candidate even mentioned other aspects of the Middle East conflict such as the issues raised by Palestinian nationalism.

On the Republican side of the campaign, President Nixon was basking in the glow of virtually having been endorsed by the Israeli Ambassador to the United States. Without engaging in rhetoric on the Middle East, the Nixon Administration had done an immense amount to bolster Israeli military might, and it was no longer talking to Sadat about Israeli withdrawal. The word had gone out from the White House that no initiatives would take place in the Middle East before election time. Thus, when Sadat's decision to oust the Soviets occurred, Washington was surprised, pleased, and incapable of responding because of the constraints of domestic politics. No response, of course, may have been a very wise policy in such a confusing situation, but in this case it was less a calculated decision than an imperative of election year politics in which a Republican incumbent for the first time had hopes of winning as much as forty percent of the Jewish vote. It was not until early 1973, after the elections were over and a settlement of the war in Vietnam had been achieved, that the Nixon Administration once again turned its attention to Middle East policy.

2. MILITARY AND ECONOMIC DECISIONS

In addition to the diplomatic dimensions of United States policy, military and economic issues have arisen in connection with the Arab-Israeli conflict. The June War put an end to major French shipments of arms to Israel. In particular, jet aircraft on order from France were placed under embargo. Israel consequently turned to the United States as the only country that might be willing to satisfy her demand for arms.

In January 1968, Premier Levi Eshkol visited the United States and argued strongly that Israel should be allowed to purchase fifty Phantom jets. President Johnson apparently agreed in principle but did not announce the accord immediately. As the election campaign of 1968 got under way, however, every major candidate, including McCarthy, Kennedy, Humphrey, and Nixon, felt compelled to declare himself in favor of selling the Phantoms to Israel. An issue that might have remained in the shadows for some time to come consequently gained in salience. As pressures mounted, Senator Symington got into the act by making it a condition of passing the military aid bill that the United States sell Phantom jets, which happen to be built in his home state, to Israel. Finally in October President Johnson announced that the sale had been agreed upon with Israel.

Within the foreign affairs bureacracy there had been strong opposition to selling Phantoms to Israel at that time. The secretary of defense, the International Security Affairs bureau of the Pentagon, the regional bureau of the State Department, members of the White House staff, and analysts from the CIA were all reported to have opposed the sale or at least to have insisted that the United States receive some quid pro quo from Israel. In the end, however, the president made the decision, and his own motives are, of course, unknown. It would not be unreasonable to suppose, however, that he recognized the political advantages of the decision.

The Nixon administration abided by the Johnson agreement, and Israel received the first shipment of Phantoms in September 1969. That same month, Israel's Prime Minister Golda Meir visited the United States and reportedly asked for substantial economic and military assistance. The request received careful study in ensuing months, but no immediate decision was made.

The dilemma facing the Nixon administration was acute, particularly after having put forward proposals for the resolution of the Arab-Israeli conflict that were meant to be balanced. If the

United States were to gain any credit from the Arabs, it would have to resist the pressures to grant further aid to Israel. On the other hand, if Israeli confidence were to be maintained, and if domestic pressures were to be reduced, it would seem wise to grant Israel some of its requests.

Apart from domestic pressures to sell jets to Israel, a theme frequently heard is that if Israel is to retain military superiority several years hence, decisions must be made today to provide her with advanced aircraft. The underlying fear is that some day the Arab countries will become sufficiently strong to pose a real threat to Israel. The United States government would feel under great pressure to aid Israel if she were being defeated, and to avoid this unpleasant prospect many officials would prefer to insure Israeli military superiority, not just to guarantee a military "balance." The urgency of aiding Israel then becomes closely tied to estimates of actual and potential Soviet (and French) aid to the Arab states and to judgments of Arab ability to use their weapons effectively.

For the President to refuse Israel's request for jets in 1970, several conditions in the international environment would have had to occur. First, the Arabs and/or Soviets would have to show some interest in United States proposals for a political settlement. Second, there would have to be a reduction in the level of fighting along the cease-fire lines. Third, the Soviet Union would have to limit the shipment of arms to the Arab states. In the absence of any of these developments, there was little incentive for the President to refuse to sell arms to Israel, even though he could politically afford to do so. The issue was less one of insurmountable pressures being brought to bear than of a lack of incentives for resisting those modest pressures that do exist.

During the first half of 1970, the first two of these three conditions were realized. Arab hints of receptiveness to a United States peace initiative, combined with veiled threats against United States interests if more Phantom jets were supplied to Israel, led President Nixon to a decision announced on 23 March that Israel's request for 25 Phantoms and 100 Skyhawks had been turned down on an "interim basis." This bitter pill for the Israelis was sweetened by the grant of $100 million in economic aid. The administration's decision set off a cry of protest, particularly in the United States Senate. These domestic pressures raised the cost to the administration of pursuing its evenhanded policy, but were not great enough to bring about a major change in the absence of regional developments that seemed to threaten Israel's security.

When a cease-fire went into effect in August 1970, Israel's supporters were outraged by alleged Egyptian violations of the standstill provisions of the agreement. When the administration was finally able to confirm that there had been violations, a decision was made to "rectify" the situation by supplying Israel with weapons to counter the newly constructed missile sites in Egypt and with a small number of new planes. In addition, economic credits totaling $500 million was requested from the Congress for Israel. The combination of intense public and congressional concern for Israel's security, plus Soviet and Egyptian military developments, were sufficient to bring about this extremely important shift in United States policy toward increased aid for Israel.

Domestic Influence on Middle East Policy: The Policymaker's View

How are the efforts of organized interest groups, the sentiments of the public, and the representations of influential individuals seen by policy-makers? As one would anticipate, there is no unanimity of opinion. Those sympathetic to Israel tend to stress the role of oil companies and financial interests in influencing policy decisions. Those who view the Arab side with more concern emphasize the strength of the Zionists and other pro-Israeli groups and individuals.

Within the government, however, there is general agreement that oil companies are not very high powered in their efforts to influence policy on the Arab-Israeli conflict. Oil company executives similarly stress their lack of effectiveness on Arab-Israeli matters.

Organized Zionist pressures, on the other hand, are seen as a problem whenever the United States and Israel strongly differ over appropriate policy. The efforts of these groups are often discounted, however, because of their mechanical and sponsored nature. For example, after the United States condemnation of the Israeli attack on the Beirut airport in December 1968, the executive branch received many letters of protest. But a large number of the letters had an identical text, the same misspelling of the assistant secretary's name, and suspiciously similar signatures. They did not count for much as a genuine reflection of public opinion.

Personal contacts with the president and with individual congressmen are generally seen as the most effective means for attempting to influence policy. Congressmen, many of whom are relatively ignorant of the issues involved in the Arab-Israeli conflict, are often easily persuaded to support Israeli positions. The White House is more able to withstand such pressures. A recent example was the suggestion that Israel should be given $40 million in aid to construct a desalting plant. The White House, after preliminary analysis, recommended against the project. Congress, however, insisted on appropriating funds for the plant.

Another example of congressional action on Arab-Israeli issues is the nearly unanimous support given by the United States Senate in June 1970 to Israel's request for arms. Noting the growing Soviet activity in the United Arab Republic, seventy-six senators urged the president to announce his intention "to provide Israel with the aircraft so urgently needed for its defense." An analysis of those who signed this letter reveals that only the members of the Foreign Relations Committee showed a tendency not to support Israel on this issue. By contrast, all twelve senators who had received substantial honoraria for speaking engagements from pro-Israel groups during 1969 signed the letter.[6] In addition to genuine concern for Israel's security, it would seem that some senators were quite aware of the political benefits of identifying with a pro-Israel cause.

Policy-makers will generally argue that their own decisions are made by calculations of national interest rather than in response to domestic pressures. But by the very nature of United States interests in the Middle East—generally defined as the avoidance of a United States–Soviet confrontation, the maintenance of Israel's security, the limitation of Soviet influence, the continued flow of Arab oil to Europe, and the achievement of a peaceful settlement of the Palestine problem—the appeal to interests does little other than to highlight the dilemmas for United States policy-makers. Ideally, American officials would like to have good relations with both Israel and the Arabs; they would like to reduce tensions and achieve peace; they would like to see Soviet influence in the region reduced; and they would like to have access to the oil and communications and transport routes of the area. These objectives, of course, are not always compatible. Consequently, domestic forces can serve to define priorities and to facilitate the determination of trade-offs. The priority accorded to Israel in American Middle East policy would probably be less in the absence of the efforts of domestic groups concerned

6. *Congressional Quarterly,* 29 May 1970, p. 1376, reports that "Jewish organizations in 1969 paid out more money for speaking engagements by U.S. Senators than any other interest group; twelve Senators, most of them liberals, received $29,250." Muskie received $11,000; Bayh $3,800; McGee $3,000; Ribicoff $2,500; Harris $2,500; and Tydings $1,500.

with Israel's welfare. Because public opinion generally favors Israel, Israel's security has become an important concern of the United States in a way that is not true for France or Great Britain. Still, this concern does not generally dictate specific policy decisions as much as it defines boundaries beyond which no American administration will step. For example, to take a remote case, it is inconceivable that the United States would support the Palestinian commando groups and their announced goal of creating a democratic, nonsectarian state for Jews and Muslims in Palestine. A few American groups of the New Left support this policy,[7] but there is no chance that the United States government will go this route.

Probably the most important domestic factor in United States policy-making in the Middle East consists of the widespread predisposition among officials and the general public to favor Israel over the Arab states. This is not the result of specific pressures by pro-Israeli groups or the Zionist lobby, but rather it reflects the fact that for over two decades Israel's side of the story has been heard repeatedly in the press, in schools, and in other mass media. Since many Americans, including policy-makers, take for granted the merits of the Israeli case, it is not often necessary for pro-Israeli groups to use heavy-handed pressure. Instead, they need to define issues, to keep Israeli security at the forefront of attention, and to provide political favors for specific congressmen. When this is done, the rest can be left to friendly predispositions toward Israel and to the effective Israeli Embassy in Washington. President Johnson and his close advisers were not the object of pressure by pro-Israeli groups largely because they agreed with these groups on most basic issues.

Despite the closeness of United States–Israeli relations, strains could result from a whole host of issues. This might include a general disenchantment with Israel as an occupying power on the part of some segments of American public opinion. A 1969 poll conducted by the Greenwich College Research Center showed that university student opinion in the United States has become rather surprisingly unsupportive of Israel. Fifty percent were opposed to arms aid to Israel in the event of war, with only twenty-two percent in favor; sixty percent said they did not favor continued United States support of Israel. Late in 1970, *Newsweek* reported that in response to the question, "What should the U.S. do if Israel seemed in danger of being defeated by Arab armies?" forty-two percent of

7. For a controversial account, see Seymour M. Lipset, "The Left, the Jews and Israel," *Encounter*, December 1969.

the respondents said "stay out," thirty-two percent said "send equipment," and only fourteen percent said "send troops." [8]

Whether this indicates a gradual shift in public opinion away from Israel is not clear, but the reaction in the United States to the Vietnam War has certainly made Americans cautious about becoming directly involved in foreign conflicts. This post-Vietnam sentiment may have a strong influence on United States foreign policy in many areas of the world. It is not inconceivable that this would lead to a lessening of United States involvement in efforts to resolve the Arab-Israeli conflict, particularly if Soviet activity remains muted.

Possible Future Policies

A policy of consciously avoiding United States involvement in the Arab-Israeli conflict would require a reduction of arms supply and a limitation on diplomatic efforts to resolve the dispute. Two domestic factors might encourage this development. First, the reaction to the Vietnam War could serve as a constraint on United States involvement elsewhere. Second, a lessening of concern for Israel's security on the part of United States public opinion because of Israel's overwhelming military superiority might facilitate this decision to disengage.

Several regional developments might also encourage this development. For example, a reduction in the sense of crisis in Arab-Israeli affairs, habituation to the current level of violence, or any stabilization of the status quo could lower the attention paid to the Middle East momentarily. A reduced Soviet presence would greatly facilitate United States disengagement. Alternately, an aggressive, expansive Israel, self-sufficient in arms, possessing and perhaps brandishing nuclear weapons, would probably not receive much United States support or sympathy, and thus United States involvement in the Arab-Israeli dispute might subside as long as Israel remained the dominant military power.

A second possible policy for the United States might be that of evenhanded involvement in the Arab-Israeli dispute. The domestic forces working for this policy are rather weak but would primarily reflect added weight from pro-Arab and oil interests within and outside the government. If indeed an energy crisis develops in the

8. *Newsweek*, 14 December 1970. Other poll results are given in Hazel Erskine, "The Polls: Western Partisanship in the Middle East," *Public Opinion Quarterly*, Winter 1969–70, pp. 627–40.

United States in the late 1970s, there may be pressures to resolve the Arab-Israeli conflict in order to try to assure the stable supply of Arab oil to United States consumers.

A third policy that might emerge over the next few years would be closer United States relations with Israel. Generous arms supply, political support, and economic aid would be given Israel, while few efforts would be made to deal with the "radical Arabs." The domestic forces working in this direction would include a heightened pro-Israeli tone in United States public opinion, a development that might occur if Israel's security really seems threatened. The overthrow of moderate regimes in Arab countries and the creation of a credible Arab or Soviet threat to Israel would raise the pressures for adopting such a policy of polarization. In the adoption of this policy, domestic forces would probably play a larger role than in the first two. But even here, the effectiveness of domestic pressures would themselves be partly a function of regional developments.

Conclusion

This survey of United States Middle East policy has tried to destroy the myth of all-powerful Zionist or oil lobbies as major factors in the decision-making process. While the lobbies per se are largely relics of the past, the interests they represent are nonetheless substantial and may in fact become increasingly important in Middle East policy making in coming years. The Jewish vote and Jewish campaign financing are up for grabs between the two parties to a degree never before seen in American politics. The pattern of Jews supporting liberal Democratic candidates and civil rights causes is being eroded, as more Jewish voters become part of the establishment and see their interests well served by the Republican party. These voters, who cannot be taken for granted by either party, may look to policy toward Israel as a key factor in deciding their vote. For many Jewish voters, who feel torn between a traditional Democratic orientation and the self-interest of voting Republican, a candidate's stand on Israel may be of great importance. This will do little to improve the quality of public discourse on Middle Eastern affairs, especially in election years, and it may tie the hands of elected officials once in office.

While a strong stand supporting Israel has not destroyed the United States posture in the Arab world, it has certainly complicated relations and restricted opportunities. This may have been unfortunate in the past, but the interests at stake were mainly financial and not of overwhelming importance in any case. For those who worried about Arab oil, the response was always that the United States was fortunate not to be dependent upon imports of Arab oil and, besides the Arabs had to sell oil to the West for lack of alternative markets. Suddenly, however, these comfortable truths are being challenged by the emergence of an energy crisis and dire predictions that by 1980 the United States will be importing nearly half of its oil supply, much of it from the Middle East. This may occur precisely at a time when the Arabs will have alternative markets to choose from. Thus, competition for oil could be intense and certainly not devoid of political overtones.

If domestic politics and energy needs develop along predicted lines, the United States may find itself in the late 1970s facing exceedingly difficult choices in its Middle East policies. The myths of past decades concerning the power of the Jewish vote and the oil interests may begin to take on reality, not in crude mechanistic ways, but because of very real concern for Israeli security among United States voters and equally real energy requirements. The hope for United States policy makers, of course, is that choices will not have to be made between "pro-Israeli" and "pro-Arab" policies, for the United States should not have to sacrifice either set of interests for the other. A settlement of the Arab-Israeli conflict would greatly ease these dilemmas for the United States, and for this reason, as well as obvious humanitarian and strategic considerations, such a settlement will doubtless remain a high priority objective of any United States Administration, although uncertainty will persist as to the best means to that end.

While peace in the Middle East is always an elusive goal, the United States is better capable of contributing to its attainment, despite the handicaps of domestic politics, than any other outside power. The room for maneuver may be small, but it is likely to remain, awaiting the efforts of statesmen able to combine domestic and foreign policy interests on behalf of a policy of peace in the Middle East.

CHAPTER 12

Congress and American Middle East Policy

GEORGE KENT

Charging that the role of Congress has been limited to legitimizing and endorsing the foreign-policy decisions of the executive branch, Congress passed the National Commitments Resolution of 1969. In June 1971, it was revealed that the administration had indeed systematically misled Congress as the United States was entering into the Indo-Chinese conflict. Will Congress, therefore, seek to assert itself to guide or constrain the president's hand in the Middle East, something which it obviously failed to do in Indochina?

Historically, Congress has exercised very little influence over foreign policy in the Middle East. It has given far less attention, in fact, to the Middle East than one might expect, since Israel should generate considerable congressional interest. Congress's failure may have been due, of course, to recognition that it apparently could not exercise any real initiative in Middle East policy.

If Congress now succeeds in exerting significant control over foreign policy, could it mean a perceptible change in foreign policy in the Middle East? The author focuses on the congressional role in the Middle East, moving through history to the present.

Even within its limited authority in foreign affairs, the Congress of the United States has given little official attention to the Middle East. A compendium of laws passed through the Ninetieth Congress shows only one entry specifically devoted to the region, the legislation of the Eisenhower Doctrine in 1957.[1] Other actions have been taken, however, and they are worth recalling.

1. U.S., Congress, Senate and House, Committee on Foreign Relations and Foreign Affairs, *Legislation on Foreign Relations* 91st Cong., 1st sess., 1969. The legislation of the Truman Doctrine in 1947, "An Act to Provide for Assistance to Greece and Turkey," is not counted. For our purposes, the Middle East consists of the Arab States and Israel.

The purpose of this study is to review the legislative action of the United States Congress in relation to the Middle East. Rather than tracing the activities of particular congressmen or the legislative histories of the many bills on the Middle East that have been offered through the years, this study focuses specifically on those bills which have passed. These passed bills provide the most meaningful characterization of the will of the Congress as a whole.

Palestine Resolutions

In the Zionist view, the British Balfour Declaration of 1917 provided the legal foundation for the encouragement of large-scale Jewish immigration into Palestine. Using language similar to that of the declaration, in 1922 the Sixty-seventh Congress of the United States resolved

> That the United States of America favors the establishment in Palestine of a national home for the Jewish people, it being clearly understood that nothing shall be done which may prejudice the civil and religious rights of Christians and all other non-Jewish communities in Palestine, and that the holy places and religious buildings and sites in Palestine shall be adequately protected.[2]

This resolution gave the strongest possible endorsement of the Balfour Declaration and thus for the legitimacy of the Zionist movement.

The 1922 resolution was incorporated into a resolution introduced into the House of Representatives on 27 January 1944, which, following the American Zionist Biltmore Program, proposed

> That the United States shall use its good offices and take appropriate measures, to the end that the doors of Palestine shall be opened for free entry of Jews into that country, and that there shall be full opportunity for colonization, so that the Jewish people may ultimately reconstitute Palestine as a free and democratic Jewish commonwealth.[3]

2. P.L. 67–73. U.S., *Statutes at Large,* vol. 42, p. 1012 (hereafter cited 42Stat. 1012). Also in Ralph H. Magnus, ed., *Documents on the Middle East* (Washington: American Enterprise Institute, 1969), p. 40.

3. Richard P. Stevens, *American Zionism and U.S. Foreign Policy* (New York: Pageant Press, 1962), p. 38. Stevens is by no means neutral on the issues, but he is careful in his documentation and in his analysis. His work contrasts with

The general public, American Zionist organizations, and the Congress all strongly supported this Palestine resolution. The Chairman of the House Committee on Foreign Affairs, Sol Bloom, was himself an ardent Zionist. The administration, however, opposed the resolution on the grounds that passage would be "prejudicial to the successful prosecution of the war." [4] As a result of administration pressures, the Palestine resolution was shelved in both House and Senate committees.

Pressure for consideration of the resolution was resumed in late 1944. Partly because of the influence of Senator Robert Wagner of New York and partly because of the upcoming election, in October President Roosevelt issued a statement strongly favoring the Zionist cause ("if elected I shall help to bring about [the realization of a] free and democratic Jewish commonwealth"). The House Committee on Foreign Affairs approved a weakened version of the Palestine resolution on 28 November 1944.[5]

After the election, the president returned to his former position of opposition. He explained in a letter to Senator Wagner on 3 December 1944:

> Here is the only trouble about additional action by either House in regard to Palestine at this time. There are about a half a million Jews there. Perhaps another million want to go. They are of all shades—good, bad and indifferent.
>
> On the other side of the picture there are approximately seventy million Mohammedans who want to cut their throats the day they land. The one thing I want to avoid is a massacre or a situation which cannot be resolved by talking things over.
>
> Anything said or done over here just now would add fuel to the flames and I hope that at this juncture no branch of the Government will act. Everybody knows what American hopes are. If we talk about them too much we will hurt fulfillment.[6]

The campaign to secure favorable congressional action began once again in February 1945 when Representative Geelan of Connecticut introduced a Palestine resolution identical with the unamended Compton resolution of the previous session. Representa-

the vigorous anti-Zionist argument by Fadhil Zaky Mohamad, *Congress and Foreign Policy: A Cast Study of the Role of the U.S. Congress in Shaping the American Stand Toward Palestine* (Baghdad: Ministry of Culture and Guidance, 1965).

4. Stevens, *American Zionism,* p. 51.

5. Ibid., pp. 60, 84.

6. Ibid., p. 85.

tive Emanuel Celler of New York also introduced a similar measure. In May and June 1945 a number of bills were offered calling for "U.N. guardianship of the repatriation of Hebrews in Europe, with Palestine under new administration as a free state." Some also asked for membership of Palestine in the UN, with the United States to use its good offices to this end. All of these bills remained unreported by the Foreign Affairs Committee.[7]

Renewed efforts in October 1945 resulted in the introduction of measures calling upon the United States to

> use its good offices to the end that the doors of Palestine shall be opened for free entry of Jews into that country, and that there shall be full opportunity for colonization, so that they may reconstitute Palestine as a free and democratic commonwealth in which all men, regardless of race or creed, shall enjoy equal rights.[8]

Both the House and Senate passed a slightly amended version of the resolution in December 1945. After having made a number of compromises, "the Zionists thus secured the passage of a resolution to which they had no objections and which marked the end of a campaign undertaken in February 1944." [9]

On 14 May 1948 the new sovereign state of Israel was established, with the recognition of the United States granted by President Truman within minutes after the declaration of its birth. No official action was taken at the time by the Congress.

Support for the existence of the State of Israel was implicit in all congressional action from 1948 onward, and it was frequently made explicit. In 1968, in honor of Israel's twentieth anniversary, the Senate reconfirmed its endorsement of the Palestine resolution by agreeing that:

> Whereas the people of the United States, speaking through the President and the Congress, favored restoration of an independent Jewish nation in Palestine; and
>
> Whereas resolutions expressing support for that objective were adopted by the Sixty-seventh, Sixty-ninth, Seventy-ninth, Eighty-first, and Eighty-fifth Congresses. . . .
>
> *Resolved,* That the Senate of the United States extends its congratulations to the people of Israel on this anniversary and

7. *Congressional Quarterly* 2 (1946), pp. 698–99.
8. Stevens, *American Zionism,* p. 110.
9. Ibid., p. 116.

best wishes for continued progress and expresses the hope that the nations of the Near East may soon meet as neighbors, in negotiations which will lead to peace. . . .[10]

Refugees

In the late 1930s and early 1940s sharp debates arose both in and out of Congress over the question of admission to the United States of refugees from Hitler's Europe. Between 1933 and 1945 about 250,000 Jewish and other European refugees reached safety in the United States, a number larger than that reaching Palestine or any other country. Although many felt that there was still more space in the United States, prevailing domestic attitudes prevented lifting of the highly restrictive immigration quotas. Many congressmen expressed their support for Jewish settlement elsewhere by signing a petition calling on President Roosevelt to urge Britain to ease Jewish immigration to Palestine. The Palestine resolution of 1945 commended the president for his attempts to open Palestine to greater numbers of Jews. Although immigration to the United States was limited, the Congress did provide some material assistance. In June 1940 an unemployment relief appropriation bill was amended to include $50 million for the purchase of American agricultural, medical, and other supplies for refugee relief.[11]

Neither the public nor the Congress ever seriously argued that Arab refugees might be welcomed into the United States. But the Congress has been active in providing material support for the Palestinian Arabs. When the United Nations General Assembly passed a resolution on 19 November 1948 calling for voluntary contributions for their relief, the Congress responded with an authorization for up to $16,000,000.[12] When on 8 December 1949 the General Assembly authorized the establishment of the United Nations Relief and Works Agency for Palestine Refugees in the Near East (UNRWA), the Congress passed the United Nations Palestine

10. Approved 2 May 1968. See U.S., Congress, Senate, *Congressional Record*, 90th Cong., 2nd sess., 2 May 1968, pp. 11538–41; or U.S., Congress, Senate, *Journal*, 90th Cong., 2nd sess., 1968, p. 342.

11. David S. Wyman, *Paper Walls: America and the Refugee Crisis 1938–1941* (Amherst: University of Massachusetts Press, 1968), pp. 59, 117, 299, *passim*.

12. P.L.81–25, 63Stat.16, approved 24 March 1949. See U.S., Congress, Senate, Committee on Foreign Relations, *A Decade of American Foreign Policy: Basic Documents, 1941–1949*, 81st Cong., 2nd sess., 1950, pp. 855–56.

Refugee Act of 1950 authorizing an initial contribution of up to \$27,450,000.[13] The Mutual Security Act of 1951, anticipating that specific projects would be undertaken "for the relief of refugees coming into Israel," authorized additional funds for this purpose for fiscal 1952.[14] Amendments passed in 1952 provided funds for 1953.[15] Additional amendments in 1953 authorized funds for fiscal 1954 and also called for a congressional study of the refugee situation.[16] According to the resulting report of the Special Study Mission to the Near East, the United States contribution to the United Nations refugee program up to 30 June 1953 amounted to \$109,450,000, 58 percent of the total.[17]

The Mutual Security Act of 1954 repealed the preceding Mutual Security Acts and, starting with a clean legislative slate, authorized an appropriation of up to \$30 million for Palestine refugees.[18] Additional funds were authorized by the Mutual Security Act of 1955, and the program was continued by the acts of 1956, 1957, 1958, and 1959.[19] In the Mutual Security Act of 1960, however, in addition to authorizing up to \$16,500,000 for UNRWA, the Congress attempted to tighten control of the funds by adding

> Sec. 407. In determining whether or not to continue furnishing assistance for Palestine refugees in the Near East, the President shall take into account whether Israel and the Arab host governments are taking steps toward the resettlement and repatriation of such refugees. It is the sense of the Congress that the earliest possible rectification should be made of the Pales-

13. Title III of the Foreign Economic Assistance Act of 1950, P.L.81–535, 64Stat.203, approved 5 June 1950. See U.S., Congress, House, Committee on Foreign Affairs, *Mutual Security Legislation and Related Documents,* 83rd Cong., 1st sess., 1953, 125–27.

14. P.L.82–165, 65Stat.375, approved 10 October 1951. See *Mutual Security Legislation,* p. 7.

15. P.L.82–400, 66Stat.142, approved 20 June 1952; and P.L.82–547, 66Stat.652, approved 15 July 1952.

16. P.L.83–118, 67Stat.152, approved 16 July 1953. See *Mutual Security Legislation,* pp. 38, 40.

17. U.S., Congress, House, Committee on Foreign Affairs, *The Arab Refugees and Other Problems in the Near East,* 83rd Cong., 2nd sess., 1954, p. 3.

18. P.L.83–665, 68Stat.832, approved 26 August 1954.

19. P.L.84–138, 69Stat.283, approved 8 July 1955; P.L.84–726, 70Stat.555, approved 18 July 1956; P.L.85–141, 71Stat.355, approved 14 August 1957; P.L.85–477, 72Stat.261, approved 30 June 1958; and P.L.86–108, 73Stat.246, approved 24 July 1959.

> tine refugee rolls in order to assure that only bona fide refugees whose need and eligibility for relief have been certified shall receive aid from the Agency and that the President in determining whether or not to make United States contributions to the Agency should take into consideration the extent and success of efforts by the Agency and the host governments to rectify such relief rolls. . . .[20]

Similar conditions were specified in the Foreign Assistance Act of 1961, which replaced most of the legislation of the Mutual Security Acts.[21] From 1948 to the end of 1962 the United States had contributed over $307 million for the Palestine refugees.[22]

No new funds for Palestine refugees were authorized in the Foreign Assistance Acts of 1961, 1962, 1963, or 1964, but funds were appropriated on the basis of prior authorizations. The 1965 Act specified that the United States contribution to UNRWA for calendar 1966 should not exceed $15,200,000.[23] The Foreign Assistance Act of 1966 provided for a contribution to UNRWA in fiscal 1967 of up to $13,300,000, but on the condition that the Agency

> take all possible measures to assure that no part of the United States contribution shall be used to furnish military assistance to any refugee who is receiving military training as a member of the so-called Palestine Liberation Army.[24]

While restraint had been advocated, the June War moved the United States to increase its contribution to UNRWA:

> The United States contributed $24,200,000 for the fiscal year 1967, of which $22,200,000 was for the Agency's regular program, including about $8,900,000 in Public Law 480 food commodities and $13,300,000 in cash. The United States contribution to the regular program represented about 64 percent of total contributions made to the Agency by all governments for

20. P.L.86–472, 74Stat.134, approved 14 May 1960.

21. P.L.87–195, 75Stat.424, approved 4 September 1961.

22. U.S., Congress, Senate, Committee on Government Operations, *Report of a Study of United States Foreign Aid in Ten Middle Eastern and African Countries,* 88th Cong., 1st sess., 1963, p. 402.

23. P.L.89–171, 79Stat.653, approved 6 September 1965.

24. P.L.89–583, 80Stat.795, approved 19 September 1966. When some of these organizations took control of UNRWA camps in Lebanon in November 1969 a number of Congressmen considered cutting off funds to UNRWA, but "refrained because of the danger of weakening Beirut's effort to regain control of the camps." *Near East Report* 13, No. 24 (26 November 1969): 115.

1967. The remaining $2,000,000 contributed by the United States in 1967 was a special contribution due to the emergency situation arising from the hostilities of June 1967.[25]

No new authorizations or conditions were established in the Foreign Assistance Acts of 1967 or 1968. In the Foreign Assistance Act of 1969 the condition established in 1966 was amended to read:

> No contribution by the United States shall be made to the United Nations Relief and Works Agency for Palestine Refugees in the Near East except on the condition that the United Nations Relief and Works Agency take all possible measures to assure that no part of the United States contribution shall be used to furnish assistance to any refugee who is receiving military training as a member of the so-called Palestine Liberation Army or any other guerrilla type organization or who has engaged in any act of terrorism.[26]

The 1969 act authorized increases of $1 million for fiscal 1970 and another $1 million for fiscal 1971 specifically for the expansion of short-term technical training courses. These amounts were later appropriated.[27] In recent years the basic annual contribution from the United States to UNRWA has been on the order of $22 million.[28]

The question of Jewish refugees was raised once again in early 1969 when, following executions in Iraq, a number of bills were introduced with a view to helping Jews leave Arab countries, but none of these bills reached the floor of the Congress.

The Eisenhower Doctrine

On 5 January 1957 President Dwight Eisenhower asked Congress for authorization to provide assistance to the nations of the Middle East to defend themselves against Communism.[29] The debate and

25. U.S., Congress, House, Committee on Foreign Affairs, *The Continuing Near East Crisis,* 91st Cong., 1st sess., 1969, p. 10.

26. P.L.91–175, 83Stat.805, approved 30 December 1969.

27. P.L.91–194, 84Stat.5, approved 9 February 1970; and P.L.91–619, 84Stat. 1856, approved 31 December 1970. These may be found in *United States Code: Congressional and Administrative News,* 91st Cong., 2nd sess., 1970, pp. 4, 2178.

28. See U.S., Congress, House, Committee on Foreign Affairs, *The Near East Conflict, Hearings,* 91st Cong., 2nd sess., 1970, pp. 126, 311. For more specific figures, see the chapter on "Questions Concerning the Middle East" in the annual *Yearbook of the United Nations.*

29. Magnus, *Documents on the Middle East,* pp. 86–93.

the hearings on the proposal were intensive.[30] The program was related to the United States efforts to induce Israel to withdraw from territories occupied in the 1956 Suez war, and according to one report, "one of the untold secrets of the day was that Democratic Floor Leader Lyndon B. Johnson deliberately held up a final vote until the Israelis had worked out an agreement on the terms of their withdrawal." [31] Finally in March both houses passed, and the president signed, the House Joint Resolution to Promote Peace and Stability in the Middle East. It authorized the president to provide economic and military assistance to the nations of the Middle East, and asserted that the United States "is prepared to use armed forces to assist any nation or group of such nations requesting assistance against armed aggression from any country controlled by international communism." [32] The doctrine was warmly endorsed by Iraq, Lebanon, and Libya, and given more reserved support by Saudi Arabia, Yemen, and Israel. It was first invoked in April 1957 when the Sixth Fleet was ordered to the eastern Mediterranean in support of King Hussein of Jordan.[33]

Desalting Plants

The idea of assisting in the construction of a power and water desalting plant in the Middle East has been discussed and debated in both houses of the Congress for years. In December 1967 a sense of the Senate resolution was adopted which endorsed the Eisenhower-Strauss proposal for plants to provide water and power for both the Arabs and the Israelis. It was hoped that the project would facilitate peaceful cooperation in the region. But the will to cooperate was also a prerequisite. The State Department objected to the plan on the grounds that political reconciliation between the

30. U.S., Congress, House, Committee on Foreign Affairs, *Economic and Military Cooperation with Nations in the General Area of the Middle East, Hearings on H.J.Res. 117,* 85th Cong., 1st sess., 1957.

31. "The Eisenhower Doctrine," *Near East Report* (April 1969), p. A–18.

32. P.L. 85–7, 71Stat.5, approved 9 March 1957. See *Legislation on Foreign Relations*, pp. 641–42; or Magnus, *Documents on the Middle East,* pp. 93–94.

33. Nadav Safran, *The United States and Israel* (Cambridge: Harvard University Press, 1963), pp. 247–48. A number of accounts of the dispatch of American Marines to Lebanon in 1958 (by George Lenczowski, Frederick Schumann, and others) suggest that the action was based on the Eisenhower Doctrine legislation, but official American statements of the period do not support this view. Authorization was found in the United Nations Charter, but not explicitly in the Eisenhower Doctrine.

Arabs and the Israelis would be necessary before any such regional economic development project would be feasible.

The project foundered. Through 1968 and 1969, however, the idea was revived in the form of a proposed desalination plant in Israel. In April 1969 Congressmen Rosenthal and Frelinghuysen offered an amendment to the 1969 Foreign Assistance Act proposing such a project, and an identical proposal was offered in the Senate by Gaylord Nelson in August 1969. The proposal called for the construction of a prototype dual purpose power and water-desalting plant in Israel, to produce 40 million gallons of water a day. The United States would contribute up to $40 million.

The proposal was approved by both houses, but with the authorization reduced to $20 million and became a part of the Foreign Assistance Act of 1969.[34] Once again, however, the State Department disapproved the project. The department based its opposition on budgetary and technical grounds, and denied that there were any political implications in the decision. The administration did not include the project in its budget or in its foreign-aid request, but the Congress nevertheless appropriated $20 million for a prototype desalting plant in Israel.[35]

Economic Assistance

The United States has sponsored extensive economic assistance programs, both loans and grants, to all of the major countries of the Middle East. From 1949 through 1963 Lebanon received about $80 million, Syria received $95.7 million, and Libya received over $150 million. Tunisia received about $300 million through this period, and Jordan received about $325 million. Grants and loans to Egypt amounted to about $890 million. Israel received nearly the same amount, about $879 million, mostly in outright grants.[36] "On a per capita basis of the recipient country, this is probably the highest rate of American aid given to any country."[37]

The Congress does not have direct control over country-by-country allocations of foreign assistance monies, but it can make

34. P.L.91–175, 83Stat.805, approved 30 December 1969.

35. *Near East Report* 13, No. 17 (20 August 1969), and 13, No. 24 (26 November 1969); P.L.91–194, 84Stat.5, approved 9 February 1970.

36. *Report of a Study of United States Foreign Aid,* pp. 43, 54, 76, 95, 123, 147. Additional data on economic and military assistance to the Middle East may be found in *Near East Report,* September 1966, p. C–9.

37. Safran, *The United States and Israel,* p. 278.

recommendations. In 1963, following a detailed study, Senator Ernest Gruening recommended that the United States economic assistance programs for Jordan and Tunisia should be continued at the same or higher levels, while the programs for Syria and Libya should be stopped. It was also recommended that continued aid to Egypt should be conditioned on Egypt's complying with the terms of the United Nations settlement of the Yemen dispute, and on Egypt's ceasing "production of missiles, warplanes, submarines, and other implements of war clearly designed for aggressive purposes." The creation of a United Nations Middle East Peace Corps to work with the refugees was also proposed.[38] These recommendations do not seem to have had any effect.[39]

The Congress exercises its prerogatives with respect to foreign assistance by imposing restrictions on allocations. Primarily because of Arab discrimination against Jews, the foreign assistance legislation since 1959 has regularly included an amendment withholding aid from countries which discriminate against Americans on the grounds of race or religion.[40] Because of its concern with the closing of the Suez Canal to ships trading with Israel, in 1960 the Congress amended the Foreign Assistance Act to show its opposition to providing aid to countries engaged in boycotts and blockades.[41] In 1965 the Congress passed an amendment to the Export Control Act of 1949 to limit the extent to which American firms could cooperate with the Arab boycott against Israel.[42] The Foreign Assistance Act of 1965 limited sales to the United Arab Republic under the authorization of the Agricultural Trade Development Act of 1954.[43] Beginning in 1965 the Foreign Assistance Acts specified that no assistance should be furnished to the United Arab Republic unless the president found it to be essential to the national interest of the United States. In 1968 it was required that economic assistance be withheld from underdeveloped countries in

38. *Report of a Study of United States Foreign Aid,* p. 13.

39. U.S., Congress, House, Committee on Appropriations. *Foreign Assistance and Related Agencies Appropriations for 1968, Hearings, Part 2,* 90th Cong., 1st sess., 1967, pp. 571–648, *passim;* U.S., Congress, House, Committee on Foreign Affairs, *The Continuing Near East Crisis,* 91st Cong., 1st sess., 1969, pp. 29–32.

40. *Near East Report,* October 1965, p. C–5.

41. *Near East Report,* August 1967, p. B–21.

42. P.L.89–63. See "The Arab Boycott Involves Americans," *Near East Report,* May 1965; "The United States Acts Against the Arab Boycott," *Near East Report,* October 1965; and "The Arab Boycott Today," *Near East Report,* August 1967.

43. P.L.89–171, 79Stat.653, approved 6 September 1965. Also see P.L.89–2, 79Stat.4, approved 11 February 1965.

an amount equivalent to their expenditures on sophisticated weapons' systems, but Israel and a few other allies were excepted from these provisions.[44]

Partly because of the war, in 1967 the Congress considered a protectionist bill which would reduce the cotton quota from Egypt and the Sudan and transfer it to American producers. The House passed the bill (HR 10915) in October 1967 and the Senate passed it in July 1968. The administration opposed it, however, on the grounds that it would unnecessarily politicize a purely economic matter. President Johnson vetoed it in August 1968.[45]

The Congress has regularly provided funds for schools and hospitals in the Middle East. The Appropriation Act for 1970, for example, included the following allocations: [46]

American University of Beirut, Lebanon	$9,490,000
American University in Cairo, Egypt	200,000
Weizmann Institute, Israel	2,500,000
Merkaz Lechinuch Ichud, Israel	1,900,000
Amana Ulpenat B. A., Israel	600,000
Hadassah (expansion of medical facilities in Israel)	4,850,000
Hospital and Home for the Aged, Zichron-Yaakov, Israel	650,000
Beth Yaacov Avat Girl's School	1,200,000
Educational Center of Galilee	800,000

Military Assistance

In 1950 the United States, Britain, and France signed a tripartite declaration which, while recognizing that "the Arab states and Israel all need to maintain a certain level of armed forces for the purposes of assuring their internal security and their legitimate self-defense," affirmed their intention to limit the flow of arms into the area.[47] Britain and France eventually withdrew their adherence to the declaration, but it has been claimed "it remains the foundations of U.S. policy for the Near East." [48] Between 1946 and 1967 the United States furnished military assistance in the following

44. P.L.90–249, 81Stat.940, approved 2 January 1968.

45. *Congress and the Nation, Vol. II, 1965–1968* (Washington: Congressional Quarterly Service, 1969), pp. 96, 113.

46. P.L.91–194, 84Stat.5, approved 9 February 1970.

47. Magnus, *Documents on the Middle East,* pp. 163–64.

48. *The Continuing Near East Crisis,* p. 13.

amounts: Syria, $0.1 million; Lebanon, $8.8 million; Israel, $41.6 million; Iraq, $46.7 million; Jordan, $67.4 million; and Saudi Arabia, $258.4 million. The United Arab Republic has not received any military assistance from the United States.[49] From these figures it appears that the United States has been more concerned with supporting the traditional regimes in the disputes among the Arab states than with supporting Israel in the Arab-Israeli conflict. Extensive military assistance has been supplied to Jordan and to Saudi Arabia as well as to Israel, both before and after the 1967 war.

The Congress has rarely taken specific official actions with respect to military assistance in the Middle East. While the Eisenhower Doctrine of 1957 gave the president the authorization of the Congress to undertake such programs, they had begun well before that time and were unaffected by that legislation. In the Foreign Assistance Act of 1968, the Congress did express its views on the sale of Phantom jets to Israel:

> It is the sense of the Congress that the President should take such steps as may be necessary, as soon as practicable after the date of enactment of this section, to negotiate an agreement with the Government of Israel providing for the sale by the United States of such number of supersonic planes as may be necessary to provide Israel with an adequate deterrent force capable of preventing future Arab aggression by offsetting sophisticated weapons received by the Arab States and to replace losses suffered by Israel in the 1967 conflict.[50]

On the day after the passage of the act, President Johnson instructed Secretary of State Dean Rusk to begin negotiations for the sale of the Phantoms to Israel. The sale of fifty phantoms was announced on 27 December 1968. The first of the jets was delivered to Israel in September 1969.

Occasionally there has been explicit legislation, as in the Special Foreign Assistance Act of 1971 which authorized up to $30 million in additional military assistance for Jordan and up to $5 million in additional military assistance for Lebanon.[51] The specific figures which appear now and again, however, do not provide good mea-

49. Ibid.

50. P.L.90–554, 82Stat.960, approved 8 October 1968. Also in *Legislation on Foreign Relations,* p. 84.

51. P.L.91–652, 84Stat.1942, approved 5 January 1971. This may be found in *United States Code: Congressional and Administrative News,* 91st Cong., 2nd sess., 1970, p. 2281.

sures of overall flows since most arms supplies go around rather than through the Congress, or they pass through the Congress without being broken down and examined.

In an amendment to the Foreign Military Sales Act, it was declared that

> It is the sense of Congress that (1) the President should continue to press forward urgently with his efforts to negotiate with the Soviet Union and other powers a limitation on arms shipments to the Middle East, (2) the President should be supported in his position that arms will be made available and credits provided to Israel and other friendly states to the extent that the President determines such assistance to be needed in order to meet threats to the security and independence of such states, and (3) if the authorization provided in the Foreign Military Sales Act, as amended, should prove to be insufficient to effectuate this stated policy, the President should promptly submit to the Congress requests for an appropriate supplementary authorization and appropriation.[52]

The Congress is usually not quite so explicitly and so thoroughly openhanded. The record as a whole, however, shows that the Congress has never imposed meaningful controls or conditions on the supply of military assistance to the countries of the Middle East.

Conclusions

Four distinct but interrelated impressions emerge from a review of the United States congressional actions in relation to the Middle East over the last half a century. First, the Congress has overwhelmingly favored Israel over the Arab states. There has been a consistent pattern of sympathy and support, first for the establishment and then for the continuation of the state of Israel. A second, less obvious finding is that the Congress favors Israel more than the executive branch favors Israel.[53] Both of these findings might be attributed to the greater responsiveness of the Congress to public opinion, in contrast to the executive branch, which is more concerned with

52. P.L.91–672, 84Stat.2054, approved 12 January 1971. See *United States Code,* p. 2395.

53. The same observations were reported in July 1970 by I. L. Kenen who, after praising the Congress' long history of support for Israel, remarked that "regrettably, its views have not always been accepted by the Executive Branch." *The Near East Conflict,* p. 74.

strategic considerations and which tends to be more responsive to oil and other business interests.

The third observation is that, in spite of its great significance for United States interest, the Congress has given little attention to the Middle East. This may be attributed to its lack of real power in foreign affairs, but the Congress does not seem to have pressed up to the limits of its power. This inattention is directly related to the fourth, highly significant finding: the Congress has not and apparently cannot exercise any real initiative in Middle East policy. The sidetracking of the Palestine resolution in 1944, the rejection of the proposed desalination plants, and the veto of the attempt to reduce the Egyptian and Sudanese cotton quotas all illustrate the fact that, where the executive branch and the Congress disagree, the executive regularly prevails. Rather than disagree, however, the executive often simply avoids confrontations with the Congress. Secretary of State Dulles did not consult with the Congress in 1956 when the United States withdrew its support for the construction of the Aswan dam in Egypt. In 1964 President Johnson, undoubtedly anticipating that Congress would react negatively to such a proposal, induced the International Monetary Fund to loan $40 million to Egypt.[54] The Congress has exercised little influence over economic assistance programs and practically none over military assistance programs. The most significant thing about congressional action with respect to the Middle East is what it has not done.

In his address calling for the legislation of the Eisenhower Doctrine, the president promised that under certain conditions the Congress would be consulted:

> If, contrary to my hope and expectation, a situation arose which called for the military application of the policy which I ask the Congress to join me in proclaiming, I would, of course, maintain hour-by-hour contact with the Congress if it were in session. And if the Congress were not in session, I would, of course, at once call the Congress into special session.[55]

In July 1958 President Eisenhower requested neither advice nor consent, but simply informed the Congress that American Marines had been sent to Lebanon.[56] The president mentioned the legisla-

54. "U.S. Allies Irked on Loan to U.A.R.," *New York Times,* 28 May 1964, pp. 1, 9; "U.S. Denies it Forced Fund to Help Cairo," *New York Times,* 29 May 1964, p. 4.

55. Magnus, *Documents on the Middle East,* p. 92.

56. Ibid., pp. 95–97.

tion of 1957 in his radio-TV statement explaining the action, but only in quoting its declaration that "the United States regards as vital to the national interest and world peace the preservation of the independence and integrity of the nations of the Middle East." [57] Although the action in Lebanon was based on provisions of the United Nations Charter rather than on that legislation, the president *had* indicated recognition of an obligation to consult with the Congress during this kind of crisis. The promise of January 1957 seems to have been intended more to expedite congressional legitimization of presidential authority than as a recognition of any genuine congressional authority.

In this respect, the Eisenhower Doctrine was a precursor of the Tonkin Gulf resolution. Both were targets of the National Commitments Resolution of 1969 which belatedly recognized that, so far as foreign policy is concerned, the role of Congress has been limited to that of legitimizing and endorsing the decisions of the executive branch.[58] The pattern has been fully confirmed by subsequent events, including in particular the revelation in June 1971 of the ways in which the administration systematically misled congressional leaders and committees during the United States entry into Indochina. The lack of influence has always been due as much to the Congress' own failure to assert itself as to executive initiative, demonstrated again in 1971 when, even in the face of the new disclosures, the Congress remained reluctant to exercise its own judgment to guide or constrain the president's hand.[59] If the Congress is the organ of government most responsive to the people, its failure to exert significant control over foreign policy, in the Middle East as well as in Indochina, provides a clear demonstration of the impotence of the public-at-large in influencing foreign policy.

57. U.S., Department of State, "United States Dispatches Troops to Lebanon," Radio-TV Statement by Dwight D. Eisenhower, Dept. of State Bulletin 39, No. 997 (4 August 1958), p. 185.

58. Cf. James A. Robinson, *Congress and Foreign Policy-Making,* rev. ed. (Homewood, Ill.: Dorsey Press, 1967); J. William Fulbright, *The Arrogance of Power* (New York: Vintage, 1966), pp. 44–55; Erwin Knoll and Judith McFadden, eds., *American Militarism 1970* (New York: Viking Press, 1969); Jacob K. Javits, "The Congressional Presence in Foreign Relations," *Foreign Affairs* 48, No. 2 (January 1970), pp. 221–34.

59. *Time,* 28 June 1971, p. 16, observed, "The revelation of the Pentagon papers angered war critics on Capitol Hill, who claimed vindication for their long-held feeling that Congress had been misled by the Executive Branch. . . . Yet the Congress made no immediate move to grasp control of the war from the Nixon Administration."

Appendix

Major Measures Passed by Congress Dealing Explicitly with the Middle East

Bill or Resolution Type	Number	*Date of Approval*	*Public Law* Cong.No	*Statutes at Large* Vol:Page	*Description*
H.J.Res	73	Sept. 21, 1922	67- 73	42:1012	Endorsement of Balfour Declaration
S.Con.Res.	44	Dec. 19, 1945	79 —	59: 848	Palestine Resolution
S.J.Res.	36	Mar. 24, 1949	81- 25	63: 16	Aid via UN to Palestine Refugees
H.R.	4046	June 23, 1949	81-119	63: 232	Appropriation for P.L.81-535
H.R.	7797	June 5, 1950	81-535	64: 203	Aid via UN to Palestine Refugees
H.R.	7786	Sept. 6, 1950	81-759	64: 763	Appropriation for P.L.81-535
H.J.Res.	302	July 31, 1951	82- 97	65: 149	Appropriation for Pal Refugees
H.J.Res.	320	Aug. 29, 1951	82-132	65: 208	Appropriation for Pal Refugees
H.R.	5113	Oct. 10, 1951	82-165	65: 375	Aid via UN to Palestine Refugees
H.R.	7005	June 20, 1952	82-400	66: 142	Mutual Security Act of 1952
H.R.	8370	July 15, 1952	82-547	66: 652	Appropriation for Pal Refugees
H.R.	5710	July 16, 1953	83-118	67: 152	Mutual Security Act of 1953
H.R.	6391	Aug. 7, 1953	83-218	67: 478	Appropriation for P.L.83-118
H.R.	9678	Aug. 26, 1954	83-665	68: 832	Mutual Security Act of 1954
H.R.	10051	Sept. 3, 1954	83-778	68:1219	Appropriation for P.L.83-665
S.	2090	July 8, 1955	84-138	69: 283	Mutual Security Act of 1955
H.R.	7224	Aug. 2, 1955	84-208	69: 435	Appropriation for P.L.84-138
H.R.	11356	July 18, 1956	84-726	70: 555	Mutual Security Act of 1956
H.R.	12130	July 31, 1956	84-853	70: 733	Appropriation for P.L.84-726
H.J.Res.	117	Mar. 9, 1957	85- 7	71: 5	Eisenhower Doctrine

S.	2130	Aug. 14, 1957	85-141	71: 355	Mutual Security Act of 1957
H.R.	9302	Sept. 3, 1957	85-279	71: 601	Appropriation for P.L.85-141
H.R.	12181	June 30, 1958	85-477	72: 261	Mutual Security Act of 1958
H.R.	13192	Aug. 28, 1958	85-853	72:1100	Appropriation for P.L.85-477
H.R.	7500	July 24, 1959	86-108	73: 246	Mutual Security Act of 1959
H.R.	8385	Sept. 28, 1959	86-383	73: 717	Appropriation for P.L.86-108
H.R.	11510	May 14, 1960	86-472	74: 134	Mutual Security Act of 1960
H.R.	12619	Sept. 2, 1960	86-704	74: 776	Appropriation for P.L.86-472
S.	1983	Sept. 4, 1961	87-195	75: 424	Foreign Assistance Act of 1961
H.J.Res.	234	Feb. 11, 1965	89- 2	79: 4	Restrict Agricultural Aid to UAR
H.R.	10871	Oct. 20, 1965	89-273	79:1002	Foreign Assistance Appropriation
H.R.	7750	Sept. 6, 1965	89-171	79: 653	Foreign Assistance Act of 1965
H.R.	15750	Sept. 19, 1966	89-583	80: 795	Foreign Assistance Act of 1966
S.	1872	Nov. 14, 1967	90-137	81: 445	Foreign Assistance Act of 1967
S.Res.	155	Dec. 12, 1967	90 —	— —	Desalination Plants
H.R.	13893	Jan. 2, 1968	90-249	81: 936	Foreign Assistance Appropriation
S.Res.	284	May 2, 1968	90 —	— —	Congratulations on Israel's 20th Anniversary
H.R.	15263	Oct. 8, 1968	90-554	82: 960	Foreign Assistance Act of 1968
H.R.	19908	Oct. 17, 1968	90-581	82:1137	Foreign Assistance Appropriation
H.R.	14580	Dec. 30, 1969	91-175	83: 805	Foreign Assistance Act of 1969
H.R.	15149	Feb. 9, 1970	91-194	84: 5	Appropriation for P.L.91-175
H.R.	17867	Dec. 31, 1970	91-619	84:1856	Appropriation for P.L.91-175
H.R.	19911	Jan. 5, 1971	91-652	84:1942	Special Foreign Assistance Act
H.R.	15628	Jan. 12, 1971	91-672	84:2053	Foreign Military Sales Act Amendment

S. -Senate Bill, S.J.Res. -Senate Joint Resolution, S.Con.Res. -Senate Concurrent Resolution, S.Res. -Senate Resolution, H.R. -House Bill, H.J.Res. -House Joint Resolution, H.Con.Res. -House Concurrent Resolution, H.Res. -House Resolution

OTHER REFERENCES

Congress and the Nation, Vol. II, 1965–1968 (Washington: Congressional Quarterly Service, 1969).

Congressional Quarterly.

Congressional Record.

Eisenhower, Dwight D. "United States Dispatches Troops to Lebanon: Radio-TV Statement," *Department of State Bulletin,* Vol. XXXIX, No. 997 (August 4, 1958), p. 185.

Fulbright, J. William. *The Arrogance of Power* (New York: Vintage, 1966)

Javits, Jacob K. "The Congressional Presence in Foreign Relations," *Foreign Affairs,* Vol. 48, No. 2 (January 1970), pp. 221–234.

Journal of the Senate.

Knoll, Erwin and McFadden, Judith (eds.), *American Militarism 1970* (New York: Viking Press, 1969).

Magnus, Ralph H. (ed.). *Documents on the Middle East* (Washington: American Enterprise Institute, 1969).

Mohamad, Fadhil Zaky. *Congress and Foreign Policy: A Case Study of the Role of the U. S. Congress in Shaping the American Stand Toward Palestine* (Baghdad: Ministry of Culture and Guidance, 1965).

Near East Report.

New York Times, May 28, 29, 1964.

Robinson, James A. *Congress and Foreign Policy-Making,* Revised Edition (Homewood, Illinois: Dorsey Press, 1967).

Safran, Nadav. *The United States and Israel* (Cambridge: Harvard University Press, 1963).

Statutes at Large of the United States of America.

Stevens, Richard P. *American Zionism and U. S. Foreign Policy* (New York: Pageant Press, 1962).

Time. June 28, 1971.

U. S. Congress. House. Committee on Appropriations. *Foreign Assistance and Related Agencies Appropriations for 1968, Hearings, Part 2* (Washington: Government Printing Office, 1967).

U.S. Congress. House. Committee on Foreign Affairs. *The Arab Refugees and Other Problems in the Near East* (Washington: Government Printing Office, 1954).

U. S. Congress. House. Committee on Foreign Affairs. *The Continuing Near East Crisis* (Washington: Government Printing Office, 1969).

U. S. Congress. House. Committee on Foreign Affairs. *Economic and Military Cooperation with Nations in the General Area of the Middle East, Hearings on H.J.Res. 117* (Washington: Government Printing Office, 1957).
U. S. Congress. House. Committee on Foreign Affairs. *Mutual Security Legislation and Related Documents* (Washington: Government Printing Office, 1953).
U. S. Congress. House. Committee on Foreign Affairs. *The Near East Conflict,* Hearings (Washington: U. S. Government Printing Office, 1970).
U. S. Congress. Senate. Committee on Foreign Relations. *A Decade of American Foreign Policy: Basic Documents, 1941–1949* (Washington: Government Printing Office, 1950).
U. S. Congress. Senate. Committee on Government Operations. *Report of a Study of United States Foreign Aid in Ten Middle Eastern and African Countries* (Washington: Government Printing Office, 1963).
U. S. Congress. Senate and House. Committee on Foreign Relations and Foreign Affairs. *Legislation on Foreign Relations* (Washington: Government Printing Office, 1969).
United States Code: Congressional and Administrative News.
Wyman, David S. *Paper Walls: America and the Refugee Crisis 1938–1941* (Amherst: University of Massachusetts Press, 1968).
Yearbook of the United Nations.

CHAPTER 13

Elite American Newspaper Opinion and the Middle East: Commitment versus Isolation

CHARLES H. WAGNER

Beginning in the middle 1960s, disengagement became the new mood of the United States. To examine this phenomenon, the author of this chapter employs a quantitative editorial content analysis of three elite American newspapers, the New York Times, *the* Los Angeles Times, *and the* Washington Post. *Why these? The author selected them because they are "opinion leaders" that influence the formulation of American foreign policy as well as "reflectors" of their reading public. His sample period extends from 1967 through 1969, during which disengagement had become a well-established phenomenon in the United States.*

Actually, disengagement per se was not in itself the research object. Rather, the author sought to determine whether the American mood of disengagement applied to the Middle East; whether it was as intense vis-à-vis the Middle East as, say, Southeast Asia; and, among other considerations, whether it was only military disengagement, or something more. In effect, did the Middle East enjoy "special" consideration both within the neo-isolationist framework and the American press?

Introduction

In the middle 1960s, the United States began its pendulum swing away from the internationalism that had characterized its foreign policy for over two decades. Disengagement was the new mood. Prior to the 1968 elections, Mr. Nixon noted that "weary with war, disheartened with allies, disillusioned with aid, dismayed at domestic crises, many Americans are heeding the call of the new isolationism." [1]

1. Richard M. Nixon, "Asia After Viet Nam," *Foreign Affairs* 46, No. 1 (October 1967): 123–24.

Despite the fact that the mood of disengagement was obviously one of the most powerful social forces operating on the American scene of that period, there have been but few attempts to systematically and quantitatively study this phenomenon across time. The present chapter hopes to meet the challenge by means of a quantitative editorial content analysis of three elite American newspapers, the *New York Times* (NYT), the *Los Angeles Times* (LAT), and the *Washington Post* (WP).

Just how difficult this "disengagement" phenomenon is to work with as it relates to the Middle East should be apparent in the following list of central questions to which this study hopes to respond:

1. How does the attitude of disengagement toward the Middle East, and particularly the Arab-Israeli conflict, compare with attitudes toward other areas, say Southeast Asia?
2. More specifically, what disengagement/commitment *themes* recur in newspaper editorials dealing with the Middle East?
3. How may disengagement/commitment attitude differences, or "abberations" among the three newspapers vis-à-vis the Middle East be explained?
4. What are the implications of this survey's findings for the formulation of American foreign policy?

Procedure and Methodology

The selection of the newspapers used in this survey was made partly on the basis of intuition and expert opinion and partly on the basis of availability of materials.

1. SELECTING MATERIALS FOR ANALYSIS

What is an elite newspaper, and which ones qualify for this distinction? De Sola Pool has offered answers to both of these questions:

> The *Times* (of New York) has long been regarded as *the* American "prestige paper": . . . these prestige papers are read by public officials, journalists, scholars, and business leaders. They seldom have large circulations yet they have enormous influence.[2]

2. As cited in Bernard C. Cohen, *The Press and Foreign Policy* (Princeton: Princeton University Press, 1963), p. 136.

Bernard Cohen, from whose work the above has been cited, further enumerates what he considers to be the elite papers:

> There can be no question that the *New York Times* is of prime importance; but it has distinguished company on the desks of foreign policymaking officials, very few of whom limit their consumption to one or even two newspapers: the *Washington Post,* the *New York Herald Tribune,* the *Wall Street Journal,* the *Christian Science Monitor,* the *Baltimore Sun,* the *Washington Evening Star.*[3]

Of the newspapers cited by Mr. Cohen, three were readily available—the *New York Times,* the *Washington Post,* and the *Christian Science Monitor.* The first two papers were selected for analysis, but the third was omitted because its editorials were qualitatively different from those of the *Times* and the *Post.* Instead, the *Los Angeles Times* was selected. Undoubtedly the most prestigious paper published on the West Coast, it was readily available for use. Additionally, it is a "Republican" newspaper, as opposed to the *Times* and the *Post* which are both listed as "Independents."

It should be stressed at this point that only the unsigned (and, therefore, unsyndicated) newspaper editorials were used in this study. It was felt that they would give the clearest and most direct picture of a particular newspaper's editorial stance or personality. The justification for the use of the so-called elite press seems evident. It influences and is, in turn, influenced by the most important segment of the American public—those whom Elihu Katz has called the opinion leaders: "Influences stemming from the mass media first reach "opinion leaders" who, in turn, pass on what they read and hear to those of their everyday associates for whom they are influential." [4]

There is, of course, also substantial evidence to suggest that newspapers attune their editorial views to their reading publics. Nevertheless, in terms of impact on the formulation of American foreign policy, the press' most direct and immediate influence in this area is probably with congressmen, rather than *through* the American voting public, according to James Reston: "What influence the press has on the conduct of foreign policy often comes indirectly, not through the mass of the people, but mainly through the Con-

3. Ibid.

4. Elihu Katz, "The Two-Step Flow of Communications: An Up-to-Date Report on an Hypothesis," in *Human Behavior and International Politics,* ed. J. D. Singer (Chicago: Rand McNally, 1965), p. 293.

gress of the United States . . . . the reporter and the Congressman are often natural allies."[5]

In summary, therefore, the editorial content analysis of this study will, in part, reflect editorial personality—where it exists—and, in part, the attitudes of the reading public.

2. THE RESEARCH DESIGN

Turning now to the question of techniques and methodology, it is necessary to describe the manner in which the questions with which this paper is concerned have been measured and operationalized through the general procedure labeled content analysis.

a) What is Content Analysis?

There are many definitions of content analysis. According to three early practitioners in the field, it "is a technique which aims at describing, with optimum objectivity, precision, and generality what is said on a given subject in a given place at a given time."[6] In keeping with the notion of measurement, the concept of frequency must be added to the above definition: we are not only concerned with what was said, but how many times what was said was repeated over a given time period. The frequency of reiteration of articles or themes of a particular "direction" is, then, an indicator of intensity of a particular opinion.

b) The First Content Analysis Taxonomy

Actually, we have used two content analysis taxonomies. The first and most general one considered the entire editorial as the "coding unit"[7] and was employed to measure disengagement/commitment attitudes on a region-by-region basis. Every unsigned editorial[8]

5. "The Press and Foreign Policy," *Foreign Affairs* 44, No. 4 (July 1966): 566–67.

6. Harold D. Lasswell, Daniel Lerner, and Ithiel de Sola Pool, *The Comparative Study of Symbols* (Stanford: Stanford University Press, 1952), p. 34.

7. For an explanation of content analysis jargon see Richard Budd, Robert Thorp, Lewis Donohew, *Content Analysis of Communications* (New York: Macmillan, 1967), p. 57.

8. The NYT, LAT, and WP all devote three columns on the lefthand side of one of their editorial pages to "unsigned" editorials, which represent the newspapers' views on many issues. The LAT's Saturday editorials do not follow this pattern; hence, in order to keep the sample strictly parallel, consideration of Saturday's editorials for all three newspapers was omitted.

page (except Saturday's) of all three newspapers analyzed was searched, from May 1967 to December 1969,[9] for articles which carried opinions on United States international involvement in the Middle East, East or West Europe, Asia, Africa, Latin America or the world in general. Once a relevant editorial was found, it was carefully read in order to determine its overall direction (i.e., its message content) according to one of four disengagement/commitment categories.

The first of these categories was called military commitment. Articles whose opinion direction was predominantly characterized by a call for an initial, continued, or increased involvement of United States military material, personnel, or diplomatic support (which called for a specific action) in a particular conflict situation was placed in this category. Conversely, an article whose opinion direction was predominantly characterized by a call for an initial noninvolvement or a decreased (negotiated or otherwise limited) involvement of United States military material, personnel, or diplomatic support action in a particular geographic region was placed in a category labeled military disengagement.

Brief acquaintance with the data indicated that nonmilitary disengagement and commitment categories were needed to obtain a complete and meaningful picture of newspaper opinion on United States international involvement. If an article were predominantly characterized by themes urging increased foreign aid and technical assistance, foreign trade, cultural exchange or innocuous diplomatic gestures toward a particular geographic region, it was recorded as a non-military commitment article. If the article urged decreased foreign aid and technical assistance, etc.—which rarely occurred in fact—it was recorded as a non-military disengagement article.

To sum up, the data generated from this first content analysis taxonomy would, then, indicate the intensity of a particular newspaper's attitude toward both military and nonmilitary commitment and disengagement of the United States to, or from, the Middle East, East and West Europe (considered together), Asia, Africa, Latin America, or the world in general for a particular time period.

9. Since this chapter is primarily concerned with U.S. involvement in the Middle East, it was decided that the time period from just prior to the June War to the end of 1969 would be a relevant sample to work with. The disengagement phenomenon had become well established within the U.S. by this time.

c) The Second Content Analysis Taxonomy

The second and more specific content analysis taxonomy utilized the *theme* to measure the intensity of specific opinion on United States commitment versus disengagement vis-à-vis the Middle East. A content analysis theme may be defined as "an assertion about a subject matter. Thus it is a sentence (or a sentence-compound), usually a summary or an abstracted sentence, under which a wide range of specific formulations can be subsumed." [10]

The commitment-versus-disengagement themes on the Arab-Israeli crisis used in this second taxonomy are listed below:

1. United States should give economic/technical aid or trade to Israel.
2. United States should give economic/technical aid or trade to Arab(s).
3. United States should give, sell, etc., military material to Israel.
4. United States should give, sell, etc., military material to Arab (s).
5. United States should make a formal military alliance with Israel.
6. United States should restrain, warn, or threaten an Arab state or USSR.
7. United States should restrain, warn, or threaten Israel.
8. United States should not force a negotiated settlement of Arab-Israeli crisis.
9. United States should mend diplomatic relations with an Arab state.
10. United States should give the Arabs more even-handed treatment.
11. United States should seek a negotiated settlement of Arab-Israeli crisis.
12. United States should not give economic/technical aid or trade to Israel.
13. United States should not give economic/technical aid or trade to Arab (s).
14. United States should not give, sell, etc., military material to Israel.
15. United States should not give, sell, etc., military material to Arab(s).
16. United States should not make formal military alliance with Israel.

10. Budd, Thorp, Donohew, *Content Analysis of Communications.*

Observations based on Findings from the First Taxonomy

The region-by-region survey of commitment/disengagement attitudes provides some interesting findings which lead to the following observations.

1. SOME OVERALL COMMENTS

Referring to the questions posed at the outset, the data generated by this survey overwhelmingly confirm the assumption upon which this paper was predicated; i.e., there was a very pronounced attitude trend toward United States military disengagement. On the average, 55 percent of all editorials urged military disengagement. Furthermore, this trend was almost entirely linked to specific world regions and specific crises. An average of only 9 percent of all military disengagement themes called for a disengagement from the "world in general." Approximately 80 percent of the military disengagement themes were linked to the so-called Third World, an indication of how much this area (as opposed to Europe and the developed countries) had become an arena of conflict.

But the new isolationism was obviously quite different from the old variety. An average of 29 percent of all editorials urged the continuation or initiation of nonmilitary international commitments; only 16 percent urged a posture of military commitment. The idea of substituting economic aid and trade for military commitment was reiterated many times. The idea that the problems of the Third World were economic rather than political and social (certainly, a tenuous proposition) was quite popular. In the wake of the Six-Day War, for example, the LAT suggested that the receipt of United States economic assistance by Middle Eastern countries would help "mitigate the effects" of war and "make peace in the region more realizable." [11]

Finally, some general remarks on internewspaper differences are in order. The LAT is, overall, far more hawkish than the other two papers. This posture undoubtedly relates to several "givens," including a more conservative reading public, a declared Republican orientation, and, possibly, a generally lower level of interest in international relations. One hesitates to generalize from the limited research done in this study, but the fact that the LAT accounted for only 21 percent of the editorials coded in this study seems to con-

11. LAT, 11 June 1967, p. 39.

firm the general hypothesis put forth by Johan Galtung to the effect that more information and involvement with international affairs increases sensitivity to conflict and international welfare problems.[12] The NYT and the WP were fairly close to each other in their overall opinion posture. Both were more dovish than the LAT; the WP, however, manifested a 10 percent greater military commitment oriented posture than did the NYT. Oddly enough, the data indicate that the WP contained 40 percent more coded editorials than did the NYT. Perhaps being based in Washington, would explain its larger interest in international commitment versus disengagement. Certainly, the normalized data indicate a wider spread of interest among all world regions on the part of the WP in comparison with the other two papers.

With these general propositions in mind, the presentation of a region-by-region, internewspaper comparison may proceed.

2. ASIA: MILITARY COMMITMENT VERSUS DISENGAGEMENT

The most immediate and interesting observation that can be made from just a cursory glance at the graphs relates to the relative intensity levels of editorial activity by region. The amount of attention given to Asia—particularly Vietnam—far outstripped that given to other geographic regions.

It should be stressed that none of the papers advocated a sudden military withdrawal from Asia. Even the NYT, whose disengagement profile on Asia far surpassed that of the other two papers, believed that an honorable disengagement from Vietnam did not mean total American disengagement from Asia. Treaty commitments and our own self-interest give the United States a "share in collective responsibility" for that part of the world.[13] Generally speaking, however, disengagement themes centered on "mainland" Asia. All three papers sooner or later urged limiting our commitments to Vietnam and Thailand and noninvolvement in Cambodia and Laos; and all three advocated a negotiated withdrawal posture vis-à-vis Vietnam. Articles urging continued military commitment to the Philippines, Japan, and Australia were to be found in all three papers.

There were some distinct dissimilarities in newspaper attitudes

12. Johan Galtung, "Social Position, Party Identification and Foreign Policy Orientations," in *Domestic Sources of Foreign Policy,* ed. J. N. Rosenau (New York: Free Press, 1967), p. 159.

13. NYT, 16 July 1968, p. 48.

toward Asia. The LAT started with a hawkish attitude on Vietnam which generally decreased over time while its disengagement posture increased. Fifty-three percent of all LAT disengagement editorials were, however, devoted to Asia—which was more than for the WP (at 35 percent) and even came close to the NYT's 67 percent disengagement posture. As might be expected, the NYT—whose overall military commitment profile was much smaller, percentage wise, than that of the WP and NYT—was the least military commitment oriented toward Asia. The WP fell in between the more hawkish LAT and the NYT in this regard.

Finally, it is rather remarkable that editorial frequencies on commitment and disengagement in Asia vary markedly at two-month intervals. The trend lines for all three papers surveyed resemble the teeth of a jagged saw! This phenomenon is related to the fact that editorialism (and news reporting) is highly responsive to major domestic and international events. Checking back through the coding sheets, for example, it was found that the high peaks correspond to controversy over domestic protests, bombing halts, and Vietnam elections—all related to Southeast Asia. Other major events, both internal (the presidential elections, riots, and strikes) and external (the Czech Crisis and the Six-Day War) clearly drew attention away from Vietnam during the months in which they occurred.

3. THE MIDDLE EAST: MILITARY COMMITMENT VERSUS DISENGAGEMENT

It is highly instructive to compare the Asia findings with those of the Middle East, since the Vietnam War is undoubtedly directly related to the rise of neo-isolationism. Although the Middle East received about the same amount of editorial attention as did Europe, Asia received as much attention as Europe and the Middle East combined. Clearly, United States newspapers attached far less interest to United States involvement in the Middle East than to events in Asia.

Most interesting was the initial hawkish reaction, both qualitative and quantitative, of the newspapers during May and June of 1967. All three newspapers urged that Israel be supported diplomatically on the closure of Tiran, and all three suggested that the United States should continue to supply Israel with military material. Only the NYT, however, opined that the United States should "militarily intervene," if the situation warrants that action because of "continued Arab aggression." [14] As one might expect, in light of Israel's quick and easy victory, military commitment editorials fell off somewhat and were increasingly balanced by disengagement editorials. Furthermore, many of the military commitment editorials which followed were qualitatively different from the initial ones in that they suggested continued military or diplomatic support for Israel, if and only if certain contingencies were operative —e.g., increased Soviet aid to Arab countries. By July 1968, the NYT was supporting the sale of the defensive Hawk antiaircraft missile to Israel; but it believed that the United States should not sell Phantom jets for fear of instigating a "new round in the Middle East arms race" at a time when Jarring was "striving for a breakthrough in his peace mission." If, however, the Soviets were to sell additional weapons to Egypt, the United States should sell more to Israel.[15]

As early as July 1967, the LAT was already editorializing on the area within the framework of cold war considerations when it suggested that the United States should sell arms to Israel, Jordan, and Saudi Arabia "to keep the balance of power" and to "prevent the USSR from selling arms" to Jordan and Saudi Arabia. The action was considered "unfortunate but necessary." [16] And, although the WP was not willing to go as far as the LAT, it did suggest that "Congress should give the President authority to aid the Arab countries' economic development" in order to forestall loss of all influence.[17]

In light of what has already been said, one should not be too surprised to find statistical differences manifested in the three newspapers' orientation toward the Middle East The NYT had both qualitatively and quantitatively shown a larger military and nonmilitary commitment posture toward the Middle East. This posture cannot be explained only in terms of a large Jewish reading public sympathetic to Israel, since the LAT, which was much less committed to the area, has a similar reading public. This attitude difference is particularly significant in light of the fact that the NYT was the first elite American newspaper to adopt a military disengagement stance on the Vietnam war. Clearly, there is an editorial personality difference between the two papers. Interestingly, the WP's quantitative Middle East stance was mid-way between that of the other two papers, but closer to the LAT than to the NYT.

14. NYT, 29 May 1967, p. 46.
15. NYT, 10 July 1968, p. 46.
16. LAT, 21 July 1967, p. 48.
17. WP, 28 June 1967, p. 38.

4. OTHER GEOGRAPHIC REGIONS: MILITARY COMMITMENT VERSUS DISENGAGEMENT

The normalized data reveal average military commitment levels toward East and West Europe to be slightly lower than those toward Asia and the Middle East, while average disengagement levels toward Europe were low—particularly compared with those for Asia. Certainly, Europe is still considered more vital to the security of the United States, as evidenced by all three papers' continued militant support for the existence of West Berlin. Except for the Czech Crisis (about which the United States could do very little) and some routine rumblings from West Berlin, Europe remained relatively quiescent during the period of this study; hence, editorial activity was sparse.

On the disengagement side of the ledger, it should be pointed out that not many of the frequencies counted here had to do with withdrawal of troops from Western Europe—particularly after the Czech Crisis. Rather, a large percentage of these editorials were concerned with the possibility of ABM and MIRV disarmament with the Soviet Union. The two peaks of disengagement activity in March and April 1969 were not related to a single crisis. A culmination of issues—including discontinuation of air bases in Spain, withdrawal of aid and support for Greece, arms limitations, and NATO troop levels—simply converged during this time period.

One of the more surprising findings was the paucity of editorializing on Latin America, an area closer to our own backyard. Undoubtedly, the geopolitical predominance of the United States coupled with the disinclination of several Latin American governments to do business with Communist powers, and vice versa, goes a long way toward explaining this neglect. The level of nonmilitary commitment (foreign aid, etc.) to Latin America was, on the average, the second lowest for all geographic regions. Perhaps disillusionment with the Alliance for Progress (which largely failed in its anticipated economic and social objectives) and the relative political quiescence of Latin America explain this phenomenon.

The extreme lack of editorializing on United States relations with Africa probably related to the tacit United States–Soviet disengagement from the area since the Congo Crisis. Furthermore, the newspapers regularly suggested that the area was more in the province of Western Europe whose proximity and former colonial ties with Africa are still operative.

If nothing else, the commitment/disengagement data on the

world in general neatly illustrate the difference in attitudes among the three newspapers. Many of the disengagement editorials in the NYT and WP relate to the ABM debate; a number of them did, however, relate to the conventional military posture of the United States. At the same time, the military globalism of the LAT is readily apparent.

Observations Based on Findings from the Second Taxonomy

Returning now to the Middle East area, the thematic content analysis on American commitments in the Arab-Israeli conflict showed: (*a*) a generally pro-Israeli tone, (*b*) a preoccupation, nonetheless, with the achievement of a negotiated settlement and, (*c*) the opinion differences in greater detail among the three newspapers in the survey. That the thematic findings were generally pro-Israeli should be evident. In summary, it should be noted that while the positive economic aid theme usually applied to the region as a whole, the positive military aid theme applied exclusively to Israel, except in one instance in the LAT. Both the positive and negative military alliance themes applied to Israel. The negative economic aid theme applied exclusively to the Arabs, while the negative military aid theme (usually couched in voluble language) applied mostly to Israel, since Arab countries were seldom seriously considered for such aid.

Only small degrees of difference exist among the three newspapers on American involvement in the Middle East crisis. The LAT was, for example, the only paper which advocated selling arms to Arabs (once); which did not suggest a formal United States alliance with Israel; and, in one instance, which opposed such an alliance. The LAT was also proportionally more in favor of mending diplomatic relations with the Arabs and of offering more evenhanded treatment. The WP and NYT, on the other hand, evidenced a slightly more pro-Israeli stance in terms of military aid and diplomatic support.

The above-mentioned differences should not, however, hide the overall high level of agreement among the three papers. By far the most frequently reiterated theme was the one suggesting that the United States should be active in seeking a negotiated settlement —through the UN, the Big Four, or through encouraging the parties to negotiate directly (an often-stated NYT position). These withdrawal-negotiate themes were often coupled with stated desires to avoid confrontation with Russia in the area, to stabilize the area, and to promote the peaceful interests of all inhabitants of the Middle East.

The findings of the thematic analysis agree closely with those of a Gallup Poll. While 44 percent of those who indicated an awareness of the Arab-Israeli Conflict were more sympathetic to Israel, 58 percent believed that the United States should stay out of the conflict. Only one percent felt that the United States should commit troops in support of Israel.[18]

Summary and Conclusions

The impact of the disengagement mood became apparent in both American politics and foreign policy. Former President Johnson's decision to refuse a chance for reelection was made at a time when his Vietnam policy was under heavy fire. "The impulse to avoid a future Viet Nam is as powerful today as was the impulse in the 1930s to avoid another World War I or the impulse after 1945 to avoid another Munich." [19]

The Nixon administration's gradual withdrawal from Vietnam and rapprochement with China and the Soviet Union represent a natural conclusion of neo-isolationist logic. Nowhere, however, have United States efforts and arms policy been less successful in creating conditions for a negotiated settlement and reduced American military involvement than in the Middle East. Much of the intractability of the Middle East conflict must, of course, be viewed as a result of the local belligerents' clashing cultural imperatives. On the other hand, despite the Nixon administration's public statements refusing to defend Israeli territorial aggrandizement, it has provided that country with so much military firepower that Israeli leaders can effectively resist outside pressures urging them to trade territory for "peace." During President Nixon's first term in office, military aid to Israel averaged $400 million per year, while during the Johnson administration the highest annual military arms sales to Israel amounted to $100 million. Clearly, present United States arms policy is anything but "even-handed" and consistent with the new mood of disengagement in America.

18. LAT, 19 March 1970, p. 3.

19. Graham Allison et al., "Limits to Intervention," *Foreign Affairs* 48, No. 2 (January 1970), p. 246.

In the present instance, several of the findings of this research have implications for United States Middle East foreign policy in the 1970s. The findings may be summarized as follows. First, while the mood of disengagement is most pronounced regarding Asia, there does seem to be a degree of carry-over vis-à-vis the Middle East. Sympathy for the Israeli position was high, but the idea that the United States should seek an active role in negotiating a settlement was expressed much more often than any other theme. And, although this theme often urged direct negotiations between the parties immediately involved (a well-known Israeli position), it was also usually coupled with a statement urging restraint in arming Israel, providing certain conditions were operative. Second, the findings seem to suggest that newspaper opinion is very responsive to specific situations (usually involving international crises). When Israel appeared to be in imminent danger (as in May 1967), newspaper opinion seemed heavily committed to Israel. After Israel's swift victory, attention and opinion soon shifted toward advocating active United States action in providing a diplomatic settlement. Should Israel again find herself in a vulnerable position, it seems likely that opinion would again become more militant in her defense—particularly, if the Soviet Union becomes heavily involved.

The conclusion of the logic contained in these findings (as long as Israel does not appear to be seriously threatened) suggests that the elite opinion base is such that American political leaders could embark, to a limited extent, on a multipronged diplomatic effort to break the deadlock in the Middle East. It is, of course, beyond the scope of this chapter to seriously consider how this deadlock could or should be broken, but the gravity of the Middle East crisis for client states and great powers is self-evident. During the Six-Day War, for example, the attack on the United States communications ship *Liberty* could easily have escalated into a confrontation of the superpowers through a series of miscalculations.

TABLE 1
Content Analysis Results for New York Times

MC = military commitment
MD = military disengagement
NC = non-military commitment

	EUROPE			MIDDLE EAST			AFRICA		
	MC	MD	NC	MC	MD	NC	MC	MD	NC
1967 May June		4		6	2	9			2
July Aug.	1		1	1		2		1	1
Sept. Oct.					1				
Nov. Dec.		1	3	2		4			
Sub Total	1	5	4	9	3	15		1	1
1968 Jan. Feb.		1			3				1
Mar. Apr.		2			1	5		1	
May June	3	4	3		2				
July Aug.		2		1	1				
Sept. Oct.	2	3	1			1			
Nov. Dec.		1			3	1			2
Sub Total	5	13	4	1	10	7		1	3
1969 Jan. Feb.						4			
Mar. Apr.		9						8	1
May June		1							1
July Aug.		1			2	3			
Sept. Oct.		2			1			1	
Nov. Dec.	2	5	1		3	1			
Sub Total	2	18	1		6	8		9	2
Total	8	36	9	10	19	30		11	8

LATIN AMERICA			ASIA			WORLD			TOTAL		
MC	MD	NC	MC	MD	NC	MC	MD	NC	MC	MD	NC
				13				4	6	19	15
	1	1		10	9		2	2	2	14	16
	1			27				1		29	1
			1	11	6				3	12	13
	2	1	1	61	15		2	7	11	74	45
		2		17				1		21	4
			1	10					1	14	5
	2	1		15			2	5	3	25	9
		1	2	10	1		3	5	3	16	7
				2				3	2	5	5
				11						15	3
	2	4	3	65	1		5	14	9	96	33
		1		2	2		1	6		3	13
	1			12			10			40	1
	1			4						6	1
	1	1		8	1					12	5
		2		14	2					18	4
1		2	3	10	4				6	18	8
1	3	6	3	50	9		11	6	6	97	32
1	7	11	7	176	25		18	27	26	267	110

TABLE 2
Content Analysis Results for Washington Post

MC = military commitment
MD = military disengagement
NC = non-military commitment

	EUROPE			MIDDLE EAST			AFRICA		
	MC	MD	NC	MC	MD	NC	MC	MD	NC
1967 May June		4	3	5	8	5		1	
July Aug.	2	4	1	1	2	2	1	5	
Sept. Oct.	1	2	4	1	2	4			
Nov. Dec.	2	4	2	1	5	4		1	
Sub Total	5	14	10	8	17	15	1	7	
1968 Jan. Feb.	3	5	2	2	1				
Mar. Apr.	1	1	3	1					
May June	3	2	4						1
July Aug.	3	7	2	1	2	1			1
Sept. Oct.	5	4	2		4	1			
Nov. Dec.	4		2					2	2
Sub Total	19	19	15	4	7	2		2	4
1969 Jan. Feb.	3	8	1	2	5	1	3	4	1
Mar. Apr.	3	15	1	3	3	1		1	
May June	1	6						1	
July Aug.		2	2	1	2				2
Sept. Oct.	1	4		1	2	1			2
Nov. Dec.	1	2	1	1	3				1
Sub Total	9	37	5	8	15	3	3	6	6
Total	33	70	30	20	39	20	4	15	10

LATIN AMERICA			ASIA			WORLD			TOTAL		
MC	MD	NC	MC	MD	NC	MC	MD	NC	MC	MD	NC
	3	1	4	7		1	1	2	10	24	11
	4	2	6	9	3	2	3	5	12	27	13
1	4	3	4	8	5	2	1	6	9	17	22
1		1	3	9	1		1	10	7	20	18
2	11	7	17	33	9	5	6	23	39	88	64
1	1		5	18	2	1	1	11	12	26	15
		1	2	13	2		5	5	4	19	11
1	2	4	2	6			1	7	6	11	16
	3		2	4			2	5	6	18	9
1	3			4		1	6	3	7	21	6
2		2		12				2	6	14	8
5	9	7	11	57	4	2	15	33	41	109	65
1	3	1	4	12			4	2	13	36	6
	1	2	1	13			4	6	7	37	10
	3	6		1	9		1	1	2	12	16
	4		1	10	2		8	2	2	26	8
1	2			11			6	1	2	25	4
1		3	3	10	1		5	4	6	20	10
3	13	12	9	57	12		28	16	32	156	54
10	33	26	37	147	25	7	49	72	112	353	183

TABLE 3
Content Analysis Results for Los Angeles Times

MC = military commitment
MD = military disengagement
NC = non-military commitment

	EUROPE			MIDDLE EAST			AFRICA		
	MC	MD	NC	MC	MD	NC	MC	MD	NC
1967 May June	1		1	6					
July Aug.				1	1	2		1	
Sept. Oct.			2	2	2				
Nov. Dec.	1	1	4		1	1			
Sub Total	2	1	7	9	4	3		1	
1968 Jan. Feb.		1	1	2	2	2			
Mar. Apr.		2	1	1					
May June		3							
July Aug.	4	4	1						1
Sept. Oct.	1		1		1	2			
Nov. Dec.					2	2			
Sub Total	5	10	4	3	5	6			1
1969 Jan. Feb.	1	1	3	3	4	4			
Mar. Apr.	1		1			1			
May June	1	1							
July Aug.			3			1			
Sept. Oct.			2						
Nov. Dec.					2	2			
Sub Total	3	2	9	3	6	8			
Total	10	13	20	15	15	17		1	1

LATIN AMERICA			ASIA			WORLD			TOTAL		
MC	MD	NC	MC	MD	NC	MC	MD	NC	MC	MD	NC
			4						11		1
	1	1	2	4	2				3	7	5
		4	13		2	1		1	16	2	9
	1	1	3	3	2			3	4	6	11
	2	6	22	7	6	1		4	34	15	26
2		3	7	3	4	3			14	6	10
		1	1	6					2	8	2
				4			1			8	
		1	1	4	1				5	8	4
	1			3	2				1	5	5
			3	3				5	3	5	7
2	1	5	12	23	7	3	1	5	25	40	28
		1	2	1	2	1			7	7	11
	1			2	1				1	3	3
		2		5	1	2		2	3	6	5
	2			4	5	1			1	6	9
	6		6	8		2	2	2	8	16	4
1	2		1	9	1		1		2	12	3
1	11	3	9	29	10	6	3	4	22	50	35
3	14	14	43	59	23	10	4	13	81	105	89

TABLE 4
Normalized Aggregate Content Analysis Results for NYT, WP, *and* LAT

MC = military commitment
MD = military disengagement
NC = non-military commitment

	EUROPE			MIDDLE EAST			AFRICA			LATIN AMERICA		
	MC	MD	NC	MC	MD	NC	MC	MD	NC	MC	MD	NC
NYT	31	13	8	38	7	26	0	4	7	4	3	10
WP	30	20	16	18	11	11	4	4	5	9	9	14
LAT	12	13	23	19	15	19	0	1	1	4	14	16

* The first three rows of figures represent percentage dis
region and by newspaper. The entry in the upper left co
ample, that 31% of all NYT's editorials for the total ti
† These figures show what percentage of all a particul

ASIA			WORLD			TOTAL		
MC	MD	NC	MC	MD	NC	MC	MD	NC
26	66	23	0	7	25	100	100	100 *
33	40	14	6	15	40	100	100	100
53	57	26	12	4	15	100	100	100

NYT	7	66	27 †
WP	17	55	28
LAT	29	38	33

tributions of MC, MD, and NC editorials by region and by rner of the table (MC, Europe for the NYT) means for ex- me period were concerned with Europe.
ar newspaper's editorials were devoted to MC, MD, or NC.

TABLE 5
Commitment vs. Disengagement Theme Frequencies on Middle East Crisis for LAT, WP, *and* NYT

	LAT	WP	NYT
United States should give economic/technical aid or trade to Israel	6	9	6
United States should give economic/technical aid or trade to Arab (s)	9	12	5
United States should give, sell, etc. military material to Israel	7	11	8
United States should give, sell, etc. military material to Arab (s)	1		
United States should make formal military alliance with Israel		1	3
United States should restrain, warn or threaten an Arab state or USSR	3	10	5
United States should restrain, warn or threaten Israel	1	1	5
United States should *not* force a negotiated settlement of Mid. East Crisis	5	6	1
United States should mend diplomatic relations with an Arab state	5	1	
United States should give the Arabs more even-handed treatment	2	5	
United States should seek a negotiated settlement of the Mid. East Crisis	11	28	38
United States should *not* give economic/technical aid or trade to Israel			
United States should *not* give economic/technical aid or trade to Arab (s)			3
United States should *not* give, sell, etc. military material to Israel	1	15	8
United States should *not* give, sell, etc. military material to Arab (s)		7	3
United States should *not* make formal military alliance with Israel	1		

FIGURE 1. *Commitment vs. Disengagement: Middle East*

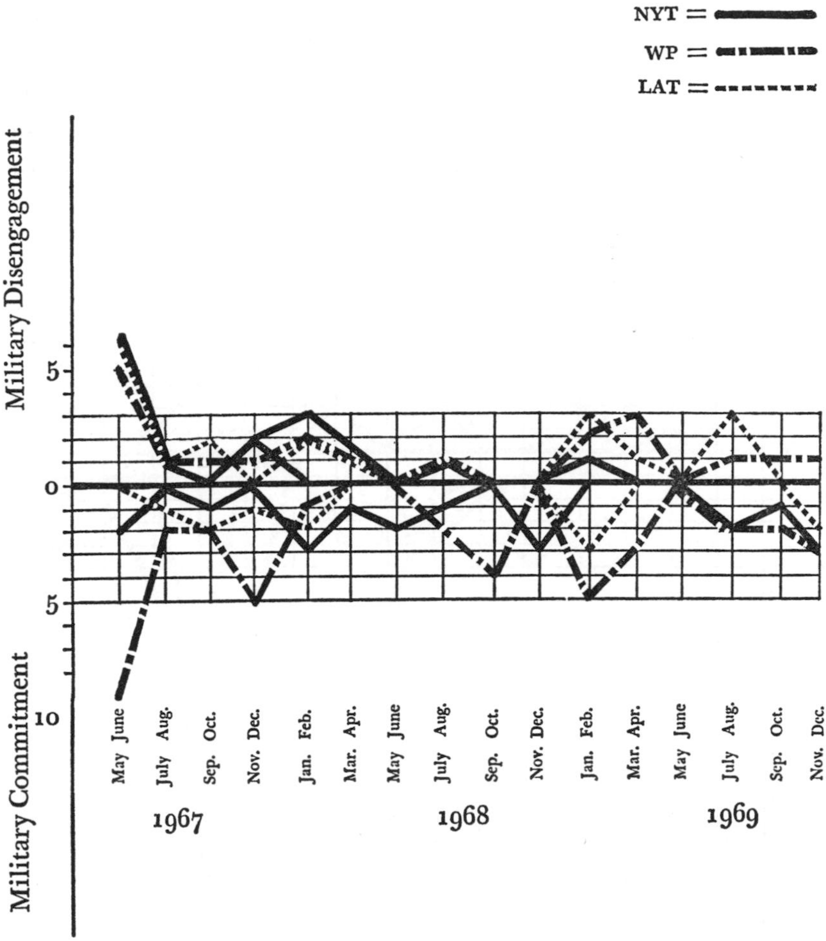

FIGURE 2. *Commitment vs. Disengagement: East and West Europe*

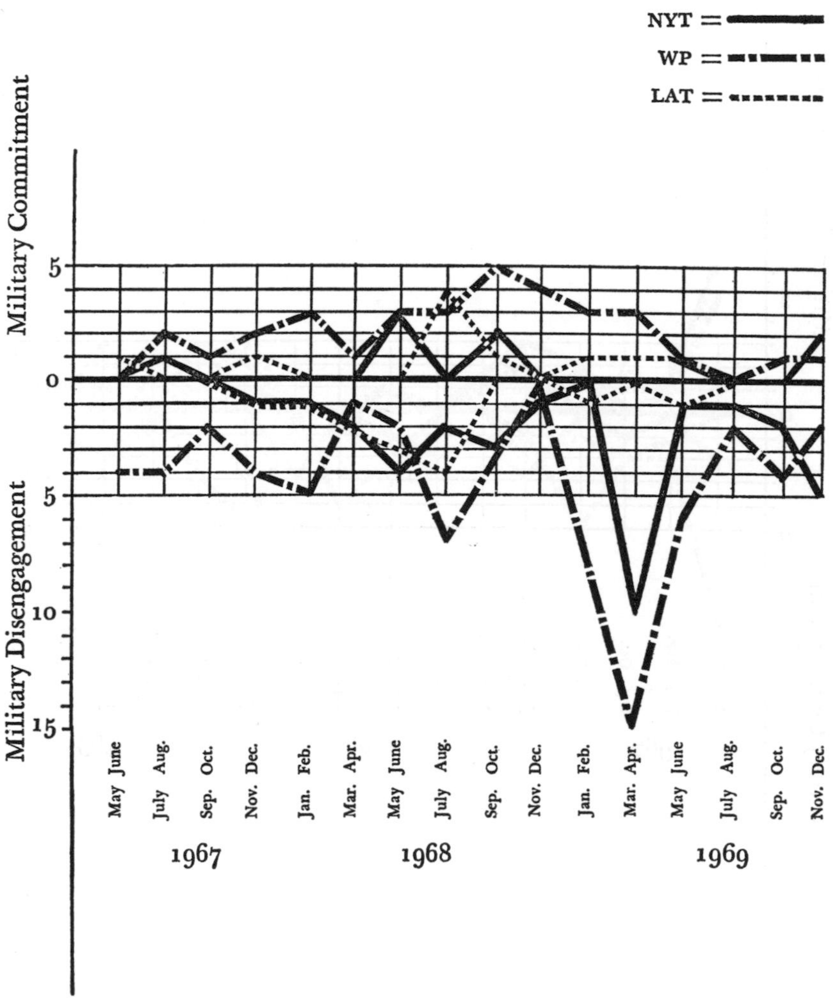

FIGURE 3. *Commitment vs. Disengagement: Asia*

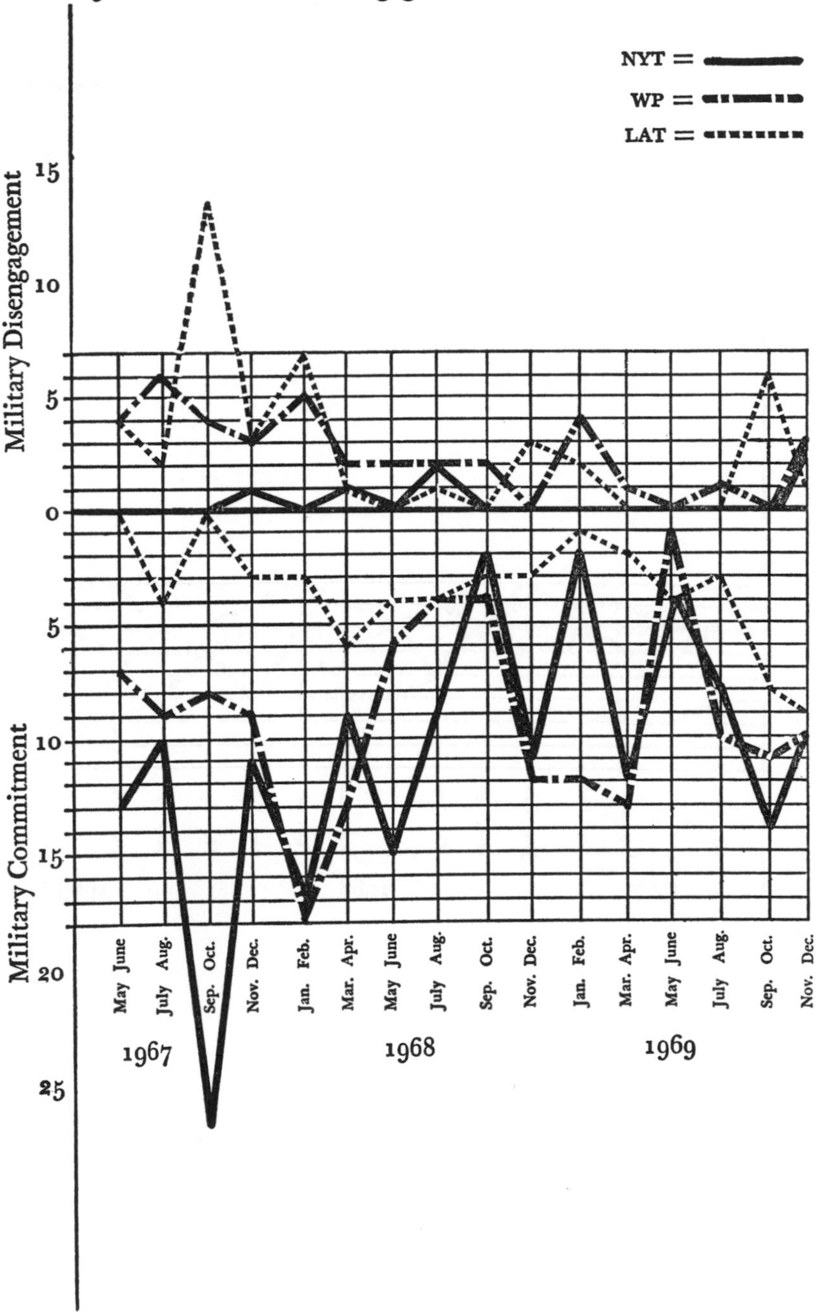

FIGURE 4. *Commitment vs. Disengagement: Latin America*

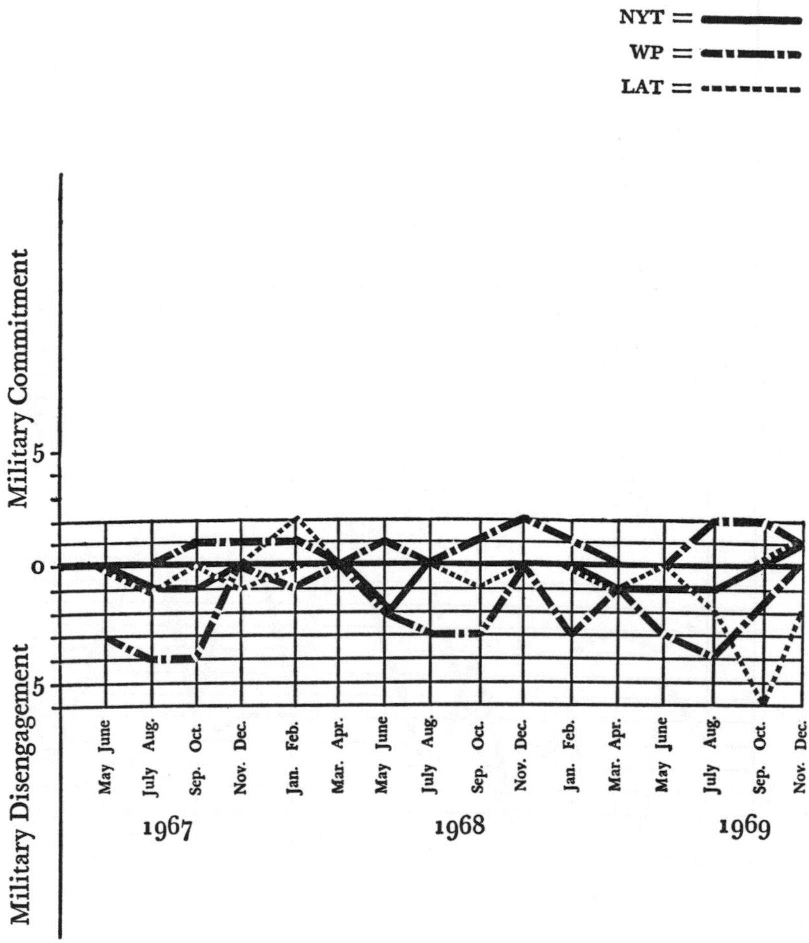

FIGURE 5. *Commitment vs. Disengagement: Africa*

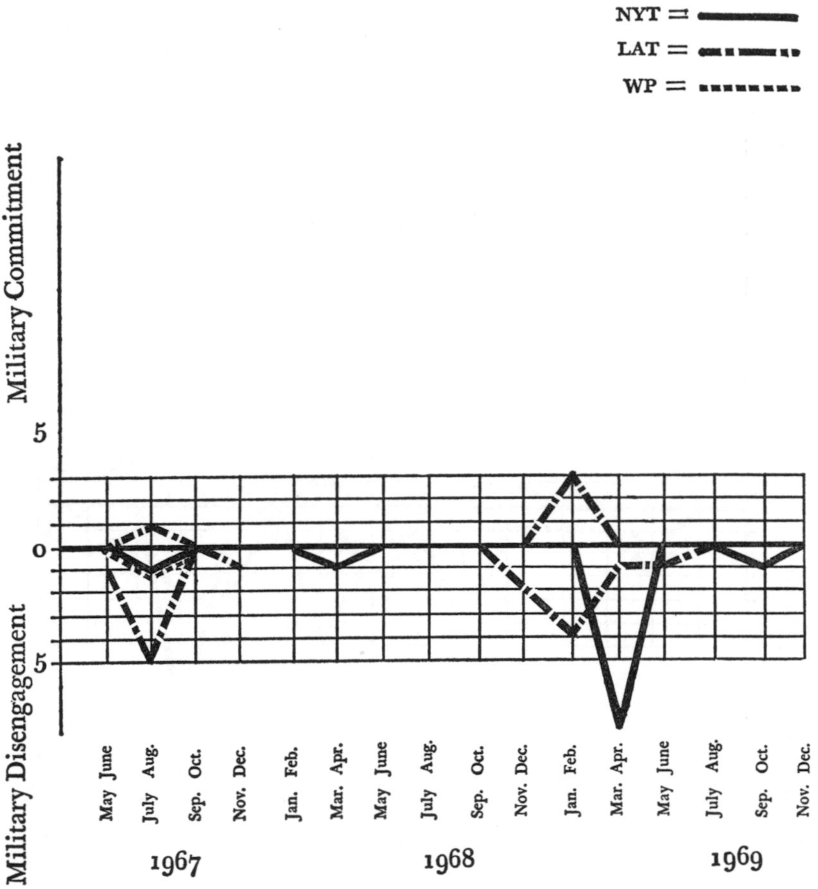

FIGURE 6. *Commitment vs. Disengagement: World*

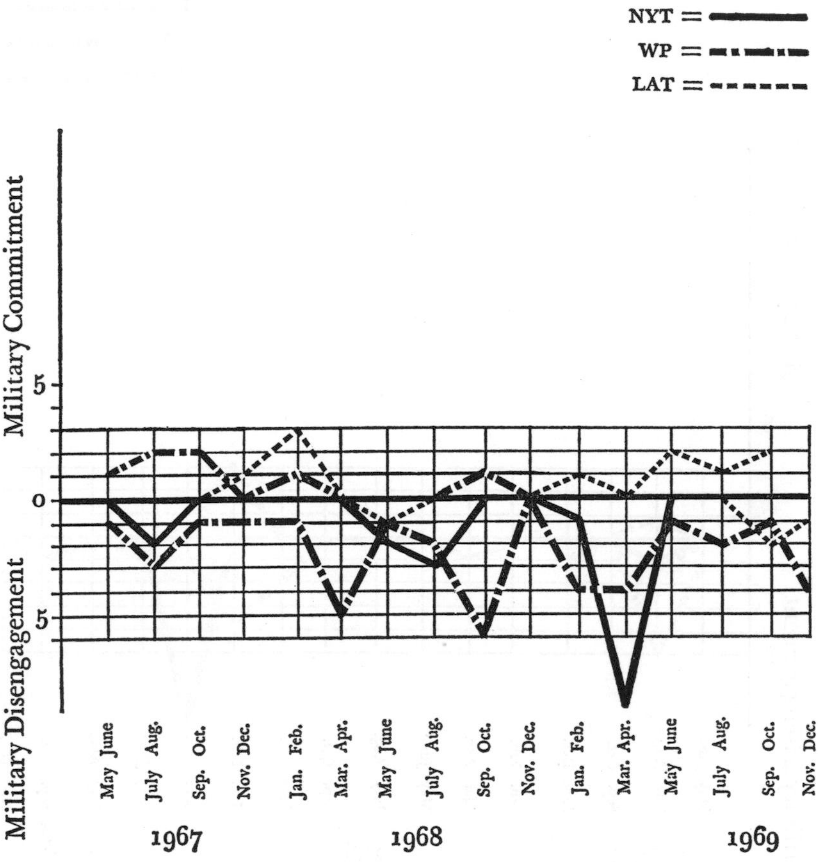

CHAPTER 14

Theological Perspectives on the Arab-Israeli Conflict

JOHN B. ORR

The author rejects the exclusiveness of the realists in international politics, arguing that theologians indeed have their appointed mission to speak to political matters. To claim that they have no business here, he adds, is to argue the inadequacy of Christian perspectives in handling particulars. The author of this chapter, therefore, deals boldly with the Arab-Israeli conflict within his own discipline, theology.

What position has the American Christian community taken on the Arab-Israeli conflict? Is there consensus? Treating these questions first, he then turns to Christian social criticism regarding the Arab-Israeli conflict. Why has the Church treated the Middle Eastern crisis differently than the Vietnamese conflict, on which Christian critics have been both aggressive and articulate?

Any attempt to develop a theological analysis of the Arab-Israeli conflict must proceed on admittedly awkward grounds. In recent years, realists in political criticism have nurtured a healthy revulsion against moralism in politics, a revulsion made understandable by the propensity of American spokesmen to veil national interests in self-righteous idealism, and by the equally disturbing practice of many theologians in making simplistic pronouncements where clarity seems premature.

Still, in this chapter I want to speak both as a thologian and as one who thinks that it is important for religious communities to work out perspectives on international affairs. The Arab-Israeli conflict will be accepted here as a problem for American religious communities, particularly in the Christian tradition, and in my analysis, I do not want to move outside the bounds appropriate to Christian theological reflection.

The Theologian and International Relations

Because I realize the difficulty of communicating across disciplinary lines, at least some broad assumptions ought to be made explicit. I will assume, for example, that international relations, by definition, constitute *moral* relations, that these are properly viewed in terms of value conflict, and that they may be evaluated appropriately in terms of their contribution to some notion of the general welfare. The affairs of nations, and of persons struggling to constitute or destroy nations, can be viewed from many disciplinary perspectives, one of which is that of the theologian-ethicist, who cannot believe that any facet of human relatedness is amoral (that is, exempt from praise or blame) and who views international conflict as an occasion for considering models of normative international order. When critics resist moralism in politics they sometimes also want to deny the possibility of relating politics to morality, but in so doing they commit a mistake. Politics is a dimension of morality. The resistance to moralism serves better purposes when it ceases to attack the integrity of political ethics and focuses its criticism on the suspect notion that politics can become a rational mechanism, systematically implementing moral ideals. The helpful argument about moralism in politics, in other words, concerns the categories in which political-ethical analysis ought to proceed, not whether the enterprise itself is valid.

I will also assume that theologians speak responsibly when they direct their criticism to the behavior of political agents, even when they lend or withhold support for particular policy positions or acts. Churches are associations within which particular perspectives, or ways of organizing interpretations and feelings, are encouraged. They are associations within which meaningful communication proceeds, because churches, like other communities, are constituted in shared symbols, shared institutional memories, shared values, and shared authorities. Disagreements obviously exist among the ethical positions of individual Christians and among the biases of various kinds of ecclesiastical organization, but there are also significant grounds on which argument can proceed.

Churches do not stray from their appointed missions when representatives speak from faith perspectives concerning political matters. Indeed, one mark of an adequate interpretive perspective is its ability to deal with concrete experiences or issues. To claim that Christian councils or critics normally have no business dealing with international affairs is to argue the inadequacy of Christian perspectives in handling particulars. Not that these perspectives contain guidelines, which determine in a peculiarly Christian fashion the exact lines of social policy positions. But perspectives do contain grounds to determine whether social policies "match" or are consistent with Christian styles of reasoning. Theological warrants do not function as the axiomatic foundation for policy conclusions, but as good reasons, compelling reasons, to legitimate certain positions or to create relative satisfaction with a policy-making direction.

Of course, there is always the danger of baptizing biases, confusing Christian perspectives with socialist slants, or forgetting that Adam Smith is not a late, but welcome intruder in the divine Trinity. Such dangers cannot be avoided. We all belong to many perspective-engendering communities; and these can never be differentiated clearly in the experience of looking at politics. But that difficulty is not basic, as if one should aspire to an intellectual singularity that is apparently not possible in the human situation.

In speaking about particular political policies, neither the churches nor theological interpreters pretend to rise above the conflict of a pluralistic society to address political agencies from above the ambiguities. The churches are part of the conflict, and their power is that of a significant confessional community, speaking with whatever level of authority a particular group or person grants to a statement. (If the wider community cannot understand the subtleties of various levels of authority, so much the worse for it.)

It is very possible for churches and theologians to deal with the same data as the State Department, although they are excluded from certain pieces of privileged information. Actually the governmental bureaucracy experiences precisely the same dilemma as do theologians in dealing with "the facts." The facts about any one policy situation are infinite in number, and there never is a time when one has enough facts for a completely confident decision. Likewise, facts are always embedded in perspectives that are bound to conflicting sets of metaphysical assumptions. In his use of expert analysis, the theologian or church spokesman must do what the state does (a procedure which I confess sounds naive): set alternative diagnoses and policy alternatives beside each other, examine these as best one can as to their credentials, and see which "fits" one's own political perspectives.

Lastly, I am assuming that the task of the theologian who deals with international issues is pragmatically limited. It is not the case that there necessarily is a Christian position or positions on every facet of international relations, and at every level of specificity, from abstract generalizations about national goals to specific policy directives. But the limitation is not rigidly principled, as if, for example, the theologian should speak only at the most abstract level about the common good and should leave the matter of strategy to political operators, who are more skilled in the art of chicanery. What the theologian addresses are problems that his perspective suggests are significant. That is, for pragmatic reasons the theologian selects and defines issues which strike his sensitivities. These may range all the way from the specifics of a policy on reparations for refugees to doctrines of man which appear to be implicit within international affairs, from opposition to a strategy of expansionism to concern about the legitimacy of a state.

The Lack of Christian Consensus on the Arab-Israeli Conflict

It is impossible to identify anything like a consensus concerning the Arab-Israeli conflict within the American Chirstian community. The traditional organs of Christian political comment—*Christianity and Crisis, Christian Century, Journal of Ecumenical Studies, Commonweal,* and *Christianity Today*—publish articles on the conflict, and occasionally develop editorial policies. But these articles and editorial policies do not reflect agreement. They range from the blatant espousal of Zionist aspirations by A. Roy and Alice Eckardt [1] to the suggestions by Yale Divinity School's Willard Oxtoby that Christian conscience requires outright rejection of Israeli expansionist policies.[2]

The single extended scholarly expression of a Christian theological position is Millar Burrows' *Palestine Is Our Business,* published by the Westminster Press in 1949. Burrows was partisan in his opposition to the Zionist movement. He dramatized injuries inflicted on the Arabs of Palestine, traced the establishment of Israel in the context of international power struggles, countered Zionist attempts to secure legitimacy in Biblical prophecy, and detailed a political program which he believed Christians should support. This included proposals to resettle refugees, to extend financial compensation for expropriated lands and means of liveli-

1. A. Roy and Alice L. Eckardt, "Again, Silence in the Churches," *Christian Century* 84, No. 30 (26 July 1967): 970–73; 84, No. 31 (2 August 1967): 992–95.

2. Willard G. Oxtoby, "Christians and the Mideast Crisis," *Christian Century* 84, No. 30 (26 July 1967): 961–65.

hood, to restrain Israeli expansionism, to provide international supervision of holy places, and to support the principle of self-determination by plebiscite in the Middle East.

Burrows' general position, particularly his desire to focus attention on particular viable solutions, has been fairly adequately represented in *Christian Century* since 1950, although this journal has never sustained a dogmatic position in the conflict, nor has it limited its selection of articles to those supporting neutralist or pro-Arab positions. In fact, no widely distributed, popular Christian periodical has assumed the role of interpreting consistently and favorably the Arab position to American clergymen and educated laymen. *Christianity and Crisis,* published in New York City by the spiritual successors of Reinhold Niebuhr's Fellowship of Socialist Christians, has moved in the past few years from a pro-Zionist editorial policy to one that can be interpreted as issue-oriented, pragmatic, and neutralist—a movement paralleled by the editorial policies of the liberal Catholic periodical, *Commonweal.* In contrast, the *Journal of Ecumenical Studies* maintains an impressively consistent pro-Zionist position—a fact that undergirds John Bennett's offhand comment in September, 1967, that Christian ecumenical leaders usually assume a pro-Zionist view (presumably because of their deep involvement in efforts to promote Jewish-Christian dialogue) while ecclesiastical bureaucrats usually assume a neutralist or pro-Arab view.[3]

The absence of a stable Christian approach to Middle East conflict was particularly evident in the editorial policy of *Christianity and Crisis* with regard to the June War in 1967. The initial and almost overwhelming response of *Christianity and Crisis,* as of most other Christian journals, was a passionate concern for the continued existence of Israel—a fact not later acknowledged by Zionists, who bitterly resented Christian hesitancy in supporting Israel in this crisis. This immediate pro-Israel response, however, was typified by Reinhold Niebuhr's editorial "David and Goliath." "David, of course, is little Israel," he wrote.

"The Arabs and Communist representatives accused Israel of firing the first shots. [But] obviously, a nation that knows that it is in danger of strangulation will use its fists." [4] Interestingly, Niebuhr was joined in this fear of genocide by editorialists for the *Christian*

3. John Bennett, "A Response to Rabbi Brickner," *Christianity and Crisis* 27, No. 15 (18 September 1967): 204–5.

4. Reinhold Niebuhr, "David and Goliath," *Christianity and Crisis* 27, No. 11 (26 June 1967): 141–42.

Century and *Commonweal,* who expressed also a continuing guilt for gentile crimes against the Jewish people, and a concern that the crisis not be allowed to shatter Christian-Jewish dialogue.[5]

The initial response to the June War, in *Christianity and Crisis,* however, did not prove stable, and its position was qualified by the fall of 1967, with an editorial expression of embarrassment concerning the incongruity of the periodical's hawkishness in the Middle East and its dovish stance with regard to Vietnam.[6] In September, John Bennett, Niebuhr's colleague, who had even signed the pro-Zionist *New York Times* advertisement, "The Moral Responsibility of Christians in the Middle East," had come full circle. Enraged at the expansionist policies of Israel, Bennett wrote,

> Even if Jewish self-understanding does require as a goal the occupation of Jerusalem as a whole, this theological premise should not be allowed to override issues of justice between Israel as a nation and her neighbors. We cannot proceed as though Israel as a modern nation has a Biblical deed to Jerusalem as so much territory. Nothing that was true in an earlier century in regard to the relation of Israel to Jerusalem can sanctify the right of conquest in the twentieth century.[7]

One can hazard a guess that another factor was present in John Bennett's dramatic reversal, which, incidentally, marked the end of *Christianity and Crisis*' comment on the Middle East conflict, with the exception of a single essay in September 1969. Implicit in John Bennett's opinion was widely experienced disillusionment with the Christian-Jewish dialogues in the summer and fall of 1967—a disillusionment made explicit from the Jewish perspective in a July 1967 essay by David Polish, "Why American Jews Are Disillusioned." He wrote:

> In light of the most recent [failure of Christians in the support of Israel] . . . the much-touted Christian-Jewish dialogue is revealed as fragile and superficial. If dialogue is effective only under serene conditions, under critical circumstances, it will prove not only disappointing but even dangerous. ". . . Jews will have to stop instigating dialogue; they must wait for a

5. The interrelation of the Jewish-Christian dialogues and consideration of issues in the Arab-Israeli War of 1967 requires further inquiry. It is clear that rhetorically the two are closely related, but we need reflections from participants concerning the pressures they experienced in this situation.

6. Bennett, "A Response to Rabbi Brickner," p. 205.

7. Ibid.

> true initiative to come from the other side. On the religious level, this means that the Christian world cannot be healed of its ailments by outside agencies. It must heal itself. But how? Can it yet, before it is too late, summon up the courage to speak unambiguously to the world about Israel's unconditional claim—a claim whose justice is symbolized by its own unchallenged sovereignty in Jerusalem, paradigm of Jewish renewal, refutation of the doctrine that we are a God-expelled people? . . ." [8]

The other side of Zionist disillusionment with the Christian-Jewish dialogue, of course, was the increasing conviction in Christian circles that the dialogue was being used as a device to ensure Christian agreement with Zionist policies. Bennett's reversal in the fall of 1967 was announced, in fact, in the context of an editorial response to Rabbi Balfour Brickner, who in early September had placed the matter of Christian support for Israel on the Christian-Jewish dialogue agenda.

Christian Social Criticism and the Arab-Israeli Crisis

In looking at this rather unimpressive record of response by Christian theologians to the Arab-Israeli conflict and at the context in which it has developed, it seems clear that the Christian community has an important in-house task to accomplish. There is little virtue in despairing over the absence of consensus, but there is much vice in the floundering and silence that express intimidation, insensitivity, or the absence of clarity. In the case of Christian reflection on the Arab-Israeli crisis, one cannot avoid wondering about what has happened to Christian social criticism. In the face of the Vietnam conflict, critics have been both aggressive and articulate, and in a host of national issues they have provided an extremely useful expression of conscience. Social criticism has flowered in this post-Social Gospel period, where, under the tutelage of Reinhold Niebuhr, pragmatism and political realism have almost too uncritically been theologized. But the lackluster performance related to the Middle East cannot be overlooked. Why? What has happened to the political realists?

The fact of the matter is that on this issue, Christian theologians

8. David Polish, "Why American Jews are Disillusioned," *Christian Century* 84, No. 30 (26 July 1967): 965–67.

work under pressures that counter the pragmatic, realistic biases that normally would be controlling. They are largely intellectual, having to do with the way in which the issues have historically evolved, and even with the character of the issues themselves. Rather than attempting to develop positions related to the present Middle East situation in the remainder of this paper, I want to address myself to the need within the Christian community to free itself to utilize Niebuhrian categories of analysis and to minister in piecemeal fashion within occasions where power balances are upset and people exploited.

The impressive characteristic of Christian theological reflection on the Arab-Israeli conflict is the degree to which the fundamental legitimacy of the State of Israel continues to be posed or imposed as the watershed issue. As late as September 1969, over twenty years after Israel's establishment, Roger Shinn, professor of Christian Ethics at Union Seminary, still introduces the so-called Arab and Israeli "cases" in terms of their irreconcilable convictions concerning the right of Israel to exist as the legitimate heir of western Palestine.[9] And Shinn's style is not atypical. While most critics, at this point, acknowledge Israel as a fact and urge efforts to find solutions for the concrete tragedies of the conflict, there is still a certain finality or holism presently associated with one's decision about Israeli legitimacy.

It seems to me, however, that the legitimacy issue should largely be viewed as a pragmatic one, its significance resting on the fact that decisions about legitimacy have been represented to American citizens as binding them to the support of a gestalt of diplomatic and military strategies. If we accept the philosopher Immanuel Kant's suggestion that the axiom, "I ought, therefore I can," is necessary to moral reflection, the legitimacy issue has in every sense ceased to be a consideration of viable political alternatives. This is not to say that the critic can simply ignore past injustices, as if the fact of pastness cancels all guilts and makes them irrelevant to one's current stance. But in the case of the Arab-Israeli conflict, there is much danger in being pressed by contenders to the point where it appears that secondary positions are determined in principle, on the basis of decisions concerning the gross legitimacy issue. There is need to resist Zionist intimations that solutions not based on the affirmation of Zionist claims are, by definition, anti-Semitic. And there is equal need to resist pressures, as reported recently by

9. Roger L. Shinn, "The Tragic Middle East," *Christianity and Crisis* 29, No. 15 (15 September 1969): 233–36.

Richard W. Fox[10], which suggest that support of Arab positions must assume commitments to eradicate the Jewish state of Israel.

The Christian community, in this situation, has a role to play in encouraging a climate of American opinion wherein polarization in such broad terms is repudiated as politically unfruitful and theologically naive. On the one hand, the Christian community cannot finally stand with Arab absolutism in representing the State of Israel as a clear-cut case of injustice. Except in John Locke's idyllic state of nature, there is not an inexhaustible supply of territory, and the boundaries of existing states are not guaranteed in the heavens. Since at least St. Augustine's *City of God,* an important stream of Christian thought has represented political justice as tenuous, sustained by shifting balances of power, where coercion is necessary for the tasks at hand. Political jurisdictions are always born in coercive contexts, and hardly any state can represent its origins as having avoided the sacrifice of other interests. Christian theologians, thus, live with political compromise, and at best they are unwilling to view even territorial expansionism as a crime-in-principle. Each circumstance becomes an occasion for inquiring about the requirements of justice. There is little to be served by slipping into an absolutist moralism about the use of force, but much to be served by standing free to the issues and devoting one's energies to compensating for the exploitation of political weakness.

On the other hand, the Christian community ought to reject firmly the slightest notion that Jews have a vested divine right to Palestine, established either Biblically or in the perennial suffering of the Jewish people. Old Testament prophecy, for example, in which is located the promise of the land to Abraham and his heirs, is not best understood either as prediction or as the guarantee of privilege. Prophecy is rather a form of literature within which social-political circumstances are described from the perspective of Yahweh and within which Israel is called to a collective repentance. The gift of prophecy is the gift of interpretation, in which events are invested with moral and theological meaning. Thus, Old Testament prophecy is perverted when it is directed to the present territorial aspirations of a state. Prophecy was never intended for such use.

Indeed, Old Testament prophecy, consistent with New Testament insight, makes justice, not ever the territorial claims of a privileged people, to be the ethical measure of political affairs. Biblical

10. Richard W. Fox, "Protracted 'Jihad' in Palestine," *Christian Century* 86, No. 46 (12 November 1969): 1450–53.

promises, when taken out of this larger concern for justice, assume an ideological function, and they are correctly to be regarded as weapons in the arsenal used for the assertion of collective self-interest. The Biblical tradition is flagrantly pragmatic in the service of justice, raising the problem of discerning right order in changing situations, and never investing any cause—even that of the Chosen People—with permanent claims to divine favor.

The same pragmatism ought to be applied to dealing with pressures that would suggest support of Israeli claims on the basis of a continuing guilt for crimes against the Jewish people. A. Roy Eckardt's desire to deal flexibly with Arab claims to Palestine, while confessing an essential guilt of the Christian community for its "dominant silence amid the Nazi slaughter of the Jewish people,"[11] at best seems incongruous and at worst appears naively apologetic for an unexamined Israeli interest. In fact, a fundamental postulate of the Zionist movement since its inception has been the commitment to a *very* pragmatic utilization of Christian guilt, based on the questionable observation that anti-Semitism is ineradicable. According to Arthur Hertzberg, a proponent of Zionism in the United States,

> the assumption that anti-Semitism "makes sense" and that it can be put to constructive uses—this is at once the sublest, most daring, and most optimistic conception to be found in political Zionism. . . . What is new in Herzl is that, assuming, as the heir of assimilation, that anti-Semitism is rational, he boldly turned this idea outward into the international arena.[12]

Christian theology, of course, makes much of corporate guilt, and extends this guilt across the generations. Yet, granted the fallenness of man, the human race must confess a host of guilts, and the problem of which guilts require the most immediate expiation is always new. The international situation, consistent with man's moral experience in general, requires that we choose among competitive loyalties and that we be willing to sacrifice values which we would prefer to maximize. Unfortunately, one cannot involve him-

11. Eckardt and Eckardt, "Again, Silence in the Churches," p. 971.

12. Arthur Hertzberg, ed., *The Zionist Idea: A Historical Analysis and Reader*, p. 49, cited by W. T. Mallison, Jr., in "The Legal Problems Concerning the Juridical Status and Political Activities of the Zionist Organization Jewish Agency: A Study in International and United States Law," *William and Mary Law Review* 9 (Spring 1968): p. 560. Hertzberg is referring here to Dr. Theodore H. Herzl, the first president of the Zionist Oganization.

self in significant moral action apart from guilt, and we cannot afford, in the name of political effectiveness, to let any one guilt be the controller of our choices.

The pressure of corporate guilt, experienced widely in the Christian community, makes it extremely difficult for social critics to render anti-Zionist judgments without being accused of anti-Semitism. But it is extremely important that critics help American Christians to understand that there is a difference between anti-Zionism and anti-Semitism. At stake is the right of Christian critics freely to contribute their estimates of what is happening in a major area of political confrontation, and to appeal for political strategies that may at times run counter to Israeli interests. At stake, also, is the important advantage of maintaining an atmosphere which does not drive critics to dramatic, brave, holistic pronouncements and flamboyant behavior simply because these are required by the emotion of the circumstance.

While there is a hint of Christian presumption in arbitrarily distinguishing between Israel and the Jewish people, from the Christian perspective, it is a perfectly defensible practice. Judgments concerning the behavior of sovereign states and of guerrilla forces that attempt to establish new jurisdictions ought not to be equated with judgments concerning the character or moral integrity of participants. To do so is to commit a simple categorical error. A people can be granted the right to their own self-understanding—even to conjoin religious and national identities—but that right does not mean that others must accept the unusual (and potentially dangerous) conjunction of identities as a matter of courtesy.

While in the Christian's view (and in that of many Israelis and anti-Zionist Jews), the State of Israel tends to be merely a political reality, for many Zionists, Israel functions as the tangible expression of Jewish identity—as a guard against the inroads of systematic persecution and against the more subtle devastation of cultural assimilation. As Willard Oxtoby comments, "Israel is the answer to European Jewy's need for a haven for everyday life, but it is also an answer to American Jewry's need for a haven *from* the secular embrace of everyday life. That is to say, what is secular nationalism in Israel is piety in America." [13]

Many American Christians are embarrassed by these attempts to identify the cause of a religion with that of a state. Like Roger Shinn, many wonder whether any nation is capable of assuming

13. Oxtoby, "Christians and the Mid-East Crises," p. 964.

"a messianic or near-messianic vocation." [14] Of course, the seventeenth- and eighteenth-century Puritan settlements along the Eastern seaboard and in Europe flirted for a while with something like messianic nationalism, and their experiments produced similar justifications to those generated by Zionists: they, also, made their respective deserts bloom. But, except for the continuance of this messiance social model in Protestant sectarianism and in a religiously inspired radical politics, messianic nationalism is rejected in Christian churches as an abortive attempt to coerce virtue and as a misunderstanding of the legitimate uses of political power. Thus, the stereotype of legalistic Puritan colonies generates analogous suspicion concerning the intentions of a messianic Israel.

There are other immediate problems associated with the identification of Judaism with Israel that should not be avoided, even at the risk of violating the self-identity of a significant portion of the Jewish population. American Christians, for example, need to be aware that fellow United States citizens are being subjected to pressures associated with a Zionist doctrine of dual citizenship, expressed cautiously but effectively by such spokesmen as Bert Lockyer, chairman of the Zionist Executive:

> The State of Israel lays no claim to the political loyalty of Jews resident in other countries. Jews are good citizens in all countries of their domicile and especially in countries in which they enjoy equal rights. *But Jews as a community do possess a collective loyalty to the State of Israel, as Israel is the national home of the entire Jewish people.* (Lockyer's italics) [15]

This doctrine of dual citizenship, strongly voiced by Lockyer's use of italics, plays an important role in the recruitment of Jewish immigrants, the channeling of charitable funds to Israel, the achievement of other Zionist political objectives, and—according to W. T. Mallison—the assertion of jurisdictional authority for the Jewish people in international law.[16] Each of these issues requires the most serious attention by American citizens, because values obviously deep in the American tradition are involved. Frankly, I have not myself come to conclusions, but I think we should at least know the questions.

The identification of anti-Zionism with anti-Semitism also indirectly affects the activity of Christian relief efforts in dealing with

14. Shinn, "The Tragic Middle East," p. 234.
15. Cited in Mallison, "Legal Problems," p. 563.
16. Ibid., p. 562.

Arab refugees. The condition of the refugee population becomes increasingly tragic, not only because of the 1967 war, but because the American political situation makes appropriate relief difficult. It is at least my strong impression that churches tend not to dramatize the need of Arab refugees, partially in fear of the expected charges of anti-Semitism, and partially because of broadly circulated stories that portray the unwillingness of Arab states to initiate massive resettlement efforts. Responsible consideration of relief strategies, however, is a barely minimal obligation. The obligation is humanitarian, involving need that is immediate, and to a significant degree, not even partisan.

Finally, the identification of anti-Semitism with anti-Zionism places Christians in an untenable position with regard to Christian-Jewish dialogues. These have already proved themselves invaluable and have led to major readjustments in American missionary strategies. But Christians cannot afford to be led, without their knowing it, into political commitments as the price of continuing conversations. Too much is at stake: the integrity of Christian social criticism, respect for the self-identities and the interpretive perspectives of all participants, not simply the Zionists. But most important, the ability of Christian theologians to cultivate similar dialogue with Muslim scholars is placed in jeopardy. Christians and Jews have strong theological and historical ties with the Muslim people, but only initial and sporadic efforts have been made to sustain communication. As Christianity finds itself in a global intellectual and religious community, open channels assume much importance. Again, pragmatism! Yet political courtesies apart from convictions within Christian-Jewish dialogues ought not to sacrifice these other values unwittingly. Here, as at every other point, Christian theologians have a larger commitment to their law of love, made evident in their search for just political relations. A whole range of values and interests depends on Christian firmness in standing uncommitted to holistic positions—in other words, in standing committed to ministries that are open to the changing requirements of changing political situations.